FRANCE
TravelBook™

Published by the American Automobile
Association, 1000 AAA Drive, Heathrow,
Florida, FL 32746-5063

This book has been prepared by AA
Publishing, Basingstoke, England exclusively
for the American Automobile Association

Printed and bound G Canale & C, Turin, Italy

Color separation by Daylight Colour Art PTE
Ltd, Singapore. Typesetting by Anton
Graphics

Front cover:
Top left, Port Grimaud, Provence
Top right, Arc de Triomphe, Paris
Bottom left, Versailles, Paris
Bottom right, Le Mont St.-Michel, Normandy

CONTENTS

SYMBOLS

How to use the star rating

★★★ do not miss

★★ highly recommended

★ worth seeing

Map references

20B4 – the number refers to the map page, and the following letter and number to the grid square on the map

4

THE COUNTRY

Covering 543,965 square kilometers (209,970 sq. mi.), France has a largely hexagonal shape and shares borders with six countries (Germany, Belgium, Luxembourg, Switzerland, Italy and Spain).

The country is divided into 22 administrative regions.

There are numerous islands around the coastline, of which the largest off-shore territory is Corsica, 193km (120 mi.) from Nice, the third largest island in the Mediterranean.

After Paris, which covers some 1,200 square kilometers (460 sq. mi.), the largest cities are Lyon and Marseille.

The tallest mountain is Mont Blanc that at 4,807 meters (15,771 ft.) is also the highest in Europe.

The longest rivers are the Loire, Seine, Garonne and Rhone ■

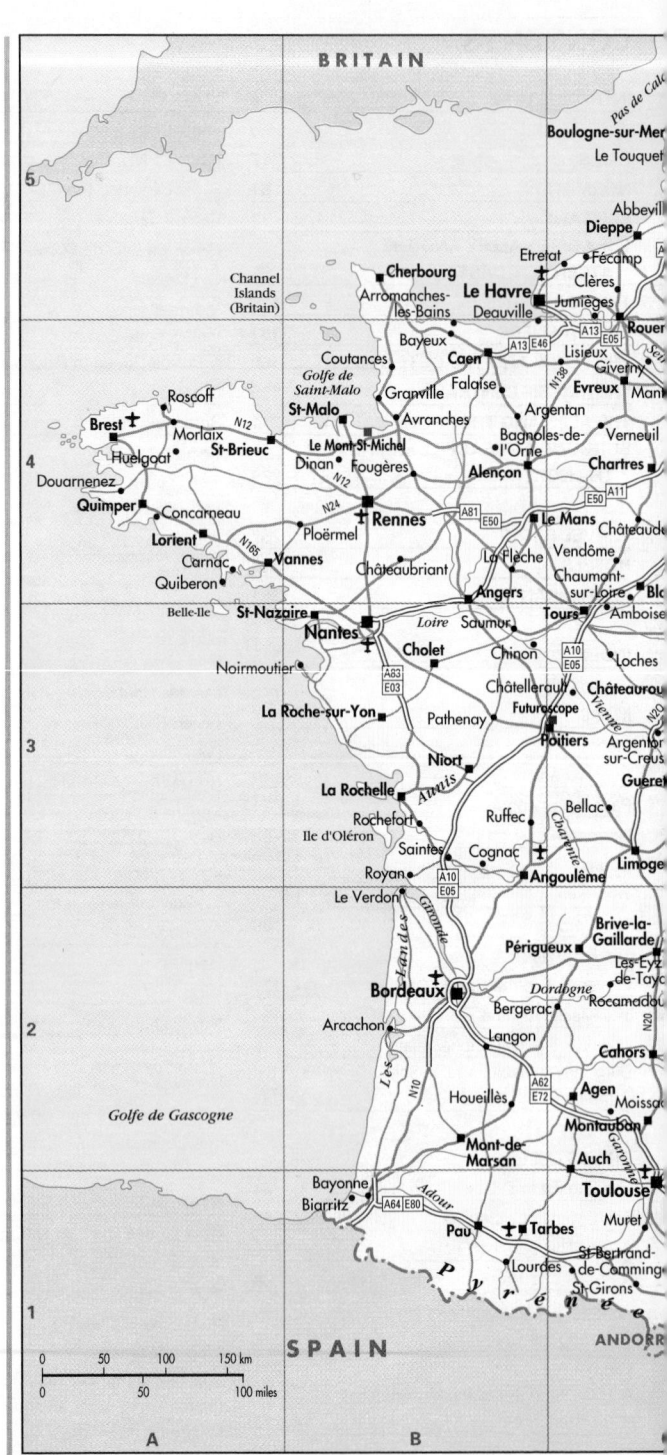

Although France is geographically at the heart of Europe and a dozen other countries are within easy reach, the French are reluctant travelers. With a Gallic shrug, most would dismiss the idea of a vacation anywhere else but in *la douce France*. And who can blame them, when it would take a lifetime of vacations to sample all that this vast country – one of the largest in Europe – has to offer.

Watching the world go by outside a café is a national pastime

Indeed, it is this regional diversity that is one of France's greatest strengths. From the soaring peaks of the Alps to the flat expanses of the Camargue or the lush valleys of the Dordogne, the range of physical landscapes is enormous. This diversity is also reflected in the richness of French regional identities; each *pays* (region) has its own distinct flavor, its own wines and regional cuisine, its own characteristic architecture, and often its own dialect.

Each region also has its share of the country's cultural and artistic legacy, which provides a wealth of attractions from the châteaux of the Loire to the Roman monuments of Provence or the cave paintings of Lascaux. Then there is Paris itself, a vibrant city of great art, leafy boulevards, grand architecture, chic boutiques, and much more besides.

But if there's one thing that unites the French whatever region they're from it's the belief that life should be enjoyed through the taste buds. Despite the advancement of fast-food outlets in many urban areas, the pleasures of the table are still given a high priority: a long, unhurried meal featuring good food, wine and conversation continues to convey the essence of French civilization.

Although sophistication is apparent in the glitzy Riviera resorts or the more elegant *arrondissements* of Paris, life goes on at a more relaxed pace in the countryside – France is still predominantly a rural nation. And it is here that the simple pleasures of touring the country are to be found: lingering over a *café au lait* in a pretty village square, following your nose to find fresh-baked *baguettes* down a narrow back street, picnicking on a scenic riverbank, or bargaining at a local market stall.

Above all, France is a country that should be savored and enjoyed with all the senses.

CULTURE AND CUISINE

In France the two-hour lunch is still very much a thing of the present, and a businessperson is unlikely to be seen eating at their office desk.

It is a country of people's culture rather than intellectual culture, which explains why a man like Bernard Tapie, former owner of the Olympic Marseille soccer team, remained widely loved even when dragged through the law courts.

The French remain vaguely anarchic, on a personal rather than political level, and guard their hard-won freedoms jealously. For instance, there is the universal reasoning that if something is not specifically against the law (which is, after all, codified), then it must be legal. So, if there's no law forbidding you to dump your old automobile in the middle of your field, then that's where it may well end up. In the cities this attitude leads to the spectacularly bad parking you'll see everywhere. Yet at the same time you'll find (if you are brave) that all French drivers will let you merge in with the traffic.

Culture plays a central role in French life. Most French people are more aware of what is happening in theater, film, literature, art, architecture and politics than you'd perhaps expect them to be. A serious conversation is more likely to be about the latest art-house film than the latest ball game. This is a nation of great talkers, almost to a

fault, and you'll find French television full of people discussing culture – for many years the most popular weekly program by far was Bernard Pivot's "Apostrophes," shown at prime time on a Friday night.

Much of France's animated conversation takes place round the table. The French take time to eat, and in spite of the increasing popularity of fast-food among the young this is still a nation of thoughtful eaters, who use meal times as an opportunity to chew over life while they're savoring their meal. Social functions revolve around the table, and the length of time spent over meals is matched by an astonishingly high general knowledge of food and drink. It's simply in the blood. If you are invited to Sunday lunch, don't expect to spend less than 3 hours from the first *apéritif* to the final *digestif* and coffee.

Even so, French cuisine has lightened up. A century ago people had to wade their way through up to two dozen heavy courses at Christmas and weddings; these days you'll rarely be expected to eat more than six or seven.

Radical changes occurred in the 1970s with the introduction of *cuisine minceur* that focused on smaller servings, stronger flavors and lighter sauces. This in turn was refined into nouvelle cuisine, which was fashionable for a while until too many chefs tried to get away with serving small

portions. Now there is the best of both worlds with lighter dishes being developed from traditional recipes, satisfying aesthetes and appetites alike.

Two historical events improved beyond measure the quality and variety of French food: the advent of the automobile, and the long French annual vacation required by law since 1936; the French suddenly took to other parts of their country and developed an interest in their own regional cuisine. It's these local dishes you'll find tastiest and most interesting, and you needn't be overly anxious about the effect on your health; amazingly, a diet rich in butter and cream sauces, fatty liver and red meat, combined with a generous intake of heavy red wines, leaves the French with one of the lowest incidences of heart disease in the world. Indeed the healthiest are in the southwest where the cuisine is heaviest.

Part of the art of good eating in France is in knowing how to choose your restaurant. Find a menu that appeals to you (don't trust a place that doesn't display its menu outside) and see if the people inside are enjoying themselves. Take your time, and ask locals where they go to eat. If you're on a budget, keep an eye out for the *plat du jour* (dish of the day) and the *prix-fixe* menus (offering three or four courses for a set price) that are always much better value than à la carte (see p.301 for a list of recommended restaurants).

WINE

While there's a lot of argument about wine, few would deny that France makes the greatest of the world's wines. It's also probably the best wine country to visit, though with so many different types produced in so many different areas it can be hard to know where to start. What's certain is that on your trip you're likely to try a number of French wines and a little homework before you arrive will pay great dividends.

France has had vineyards since before Roman times, but it was the Romans who established viticulture in a fashion that is still recognizable both in the way the wine is produced and in the location of the vineyards. Apart from Alsace, which was developed much later, most of the major wine regions were cultivated in Roman times, and it's likely that Alsace would have been too were it not that the Rhine flows north instead of south, thus hindering its potential export to Italy.

France has the ideal climate for wine production. The summers are hot enough and the fall is cool enough. This is the reason why you won't find any fine wines in Brittany and Normandy – they're too close to the cold, wet weather that occurs along the English Channel.

Starting from north to south, the following is a brief journey through the main wine regions in France. Almost every one has its specialities, and it's very satisfying to try a wine whose vineyards you've just driven or walked past

The vineyards of the Rhône Valley produce the world-famous Beaujolais nouveau in November each year

Champagne:
Finest – and certainly most renowned – of all the world's sparkling white wines, champagne is best sampled in Reims or Épernay where the biggest and best champagne houses will let you taste their wares. The Champagne region is about as far north in Europe as wine can be grown, and the grapes are barely harvested before the frosts set in.

Alsace:
Wines from Alsace are essentially white, and both refreshing to drink and refreshingly simple in their nomenclature. Most of the wine is simply bottled by the name of the grape from which it was made: Riesling (strong, distinct and dry);

and come from vines grown from the outpost of Chablis in the north to almost as far south as Mâcon. The most famous of all come from the Côte d'Or, a long narrow ridge running from Dijon to Nuits-St.-Georges. Beaune, nearby to the south, is an ideal place to stay, where meals and wine tastings are not to be hurried. Drop in at one of the hundreds of vineyard properties where you can try older and younger variants of each wine to see how they improve with age.

Jura:
Base yourself in Arbois if you want to try the unusual wines from the Jura. These vary from the old, unusually flavored Vin Jaune, which keeps longer than any other French wine, to the delicate rosé that almost all palates find agreeable.

Beaujolais:
Most famous on the third Thursday of November for the worldwide release of the famous Beaujolais nouveau (or Beaujolais Primeur to be accurate). The Beaujolais wine region, just south of Mâcon, is home to ten excellent *crus*: St Amour, Juliénas, Chénas, Moulin à Vent, Fleurie, Chiroubles, Morgon, Regnié, Brouilly and Côte de Brouilly.

Savoie:
All the vineyards of this region, which boasts more wines than you'd expect, touch the mountains of the Alps. While the red wines are a little

Gewürztraminer (faintly spicy and heavier); Tokay d'Alsace (slightly smoky and nutty, properly known as Pinot Gris); and Sylvaner (fresh and simple).

Loire:
The valley of France's longest river is host to nearly a hundred different wines, ranging from the lovely Sancerre and Pouilly Fumé at one end to Muscadet and Gros Plant at the other. The vast majority of the wines are white, though Anjou's rosé is underrated and the red Gamay de Touraine is complex enough to fool even the most sophisticated palates. The sparkling wine from Saumur is an excellent – and also economical – alternative to champagne.

Bourgogne:
Burgundy wines can be red or white

Vineyards all over France are lovingly cared for by their owners, who have had generations of experience in producing the famous wines

thin, the whites are fresh and lovely. Try the excellent Roussette de Seyssel, the Crépy or Ripailles (from the shores of Lake Geneva), or the Apremont (from south of Chambéry).

Cognac:

Few of the grapes from this area end up as wine. The vast majority are used in cognac though some do find their way into Pineau des Charentes, a cool apéritif. By law, only brandies made in this area can be called cognac, and their manufacture is surrounded by strict and complex regulations relating to strength, age and maturing conditions.

Bordeaux:

Locals and aficianados continue to argue about whether Bordeaux or Bourgogne makes the better wine, and whether St.-Emilion or Beaune is the more archetypal wine town. Whichever you believe, a trip to the Bordelais reveals the essence of what making, tasting and buying wine are all about. From the lofty heights of the grand châteaux of Margaux, St.-Estèphe, St.-Julien and Pauillac in Médoc, to the softer, friendlier villages of St.-Emilion, Fronsac and Pomerol, the area is a wine-drinker's paradise. East of Bordeaux, in the Dordogne, are the lighter, less expensive wines of Bergerac and Pécharmant. For a white variety, the famous Sauternes are recommended.

Rhône:

As the Loire is mostly home to white wines, the Rhône is largely home to reds. From St.-Joseph and Côtes du Rhône in the north to Châteauneuf du Pape and Côtes de Ventoux in the south, the river landscape has an abundance of strong wines and superb Mediterranean scenery.

Armagnac:

France's second great spirit, Armagnac, is produced farther south than Cognac in a wonderful unspoiled area little known to tourists. Try the dark, heavy Madiran wine that comes from the same region, but needs many years to mature.

Languedoc-Roussillon:

Nearly a third of all French wine is produced in the hot, fertile plains of Languedoc-Roussillon. Once quantity was more important than quality, but in the last 20 years the focus has changed, and wines like Corbières and Minervois are a great deal more drinkable than they were.

Provence:

Famous primarily for the lusty rosés of the Côtes de Provence, the region's wines are gradually improving and there are now some respectable reds. It will be some time, though, before they can compete with Bordeaux.

FASHION

France lives fashion. In boutiques, restaurants and cafés, on every street, and in every newspaper, magazine and journal you'll see how much effort the French put into looking good and staying chic. The French spend more time and money on their clothes, looks and accessories than any other nation except the Italians. Despite determined competition from London, Milan, New York and Tokyo, Paris remains the world capital of the fashion industry. On many city streets around the globe you can see people wearing styles that have filtered down from the top Paris fashion houses, via the sweatshops of the Far East (and Paris itself, typically) and the department stores of the West.

The show
The whole – glamorous, bitchy, outrageous, backbiting – process starts with the famous fashion shows held twice a year by the elite (fewer than two dozen) *grands* couturiers. Their self-imposed rules make them put on fabulously extravagant shows in January, for the spring and summer collections, and July, for the fall and winter collections, with each fashion house using at least 75 models to present their new creations to the world's press. If you're ever invited to one of the shows, drop everything to attend. But if you want to

buy one of the costumes on show, expect to pay for it!

To avoid clashing with the biggest names, the younger crowd (the *prêt-à-porter* designers) have their shows in March and October, and it's here that the business of replicating the latest designs really starts. The *prêt-à-porter* (literally, ready-to-wear) designers, who went it alone during the 1960s, finally joined the Fédération des Couturiers in the mid-1970s and are now almost as much a part of the establishment as the *grands* couturiers themselves.

Some fashion history
Although it's a solid and venerable tradition now, Paris fashion in the present sense of the term is only as recent as this century. Paul Poiret (1879–1944) deserves the credit for being the first of the modern couturiers, since it was he who shocked society by dispensing with the corset. Poiret was a great admirer of the dancer Isadora Duncan, and in the years before World War I he had the considerable advantage of being able to use her to show off his finest creations. Duncan and Poiret's lives both ended tragically: she being strangled in 1927 by her scarf as it caught in a wheel of her automobile on Nice's Promenade des Anglais, and he suffering financial ruin.

... in the early 20th century
After World War I it was Gabrielle "Coco" Chanel (1883–1971) who pioneered

the concept of democratic fashion. Her huge fame was founded on a straight, simple, uncorseted line, the introduction of jersey dresses, shorter skirts, bell-bottom trousers, trench coats, the Chanel suit, and the archetypal "little black dress" during the 1920s. In that decade there probably wasn't a more famous woman in Paris. Whatever she herself wore was soon seen everywhere, creating a fashion for short hair and costume jewelry that persists to this day as the Chanel look. Chanel was also the first fashion house to branch out, launching the famous Chanel No. 5 perfume in the 1930s.

... and later
After World War II it was the turn of Christian Dior (1905–57), whose New Look of spring 1947 gave everyone an excuse to throw off the drab constraints of the war years and the *Occupation*. More than anyone else, Christian Dior put glamorous hats back on heads, and throughout the 1950s his influence was dominant.

Since then the biggest name has been Yves St. Laurent, who truly popularized trousers for women. During the 1970s he was the first of the great designers to bring in a "retro" look.

Paris today is a lively mixture of the great fashion houses, the *prêt-à-porter* crowd, and the wave of foreign designers – Gaultier, Lagerfeld, Yamomoto and others – who have found their spiritual home here.

ART AND ARCHITECTURE

As a country, France is extraordinarily rich in art and architecture, with a cultural heritage going back over 20,000 years. At Lascaux in the southwest you can see world-famous prehistoric cave paintings – and unless someone told you, you wouldn't know they were reproductions (the originals had to be closed off as the only way of preserving them). In Brittany you can visit the standing stones and megalithic tombs that date from around 4000 BC.

The Romans built a theater in Orange – one reason to visit

Roman ruins

All across the south of France are many impressive Roman ruins, including the amphitheaters of Nîmes and Arles, the theaters of Arles and Orange, and the wonderful Pont du Gard, one of the finest Roman aqueducts anywhere (it's justifiably busy with

visitors). There are also Roman ruins that are visited less often – check out Paris, Reims, Toulouse and Bordeaux.

Romanesque style

After the Merovingian and Carolingian periods, the building of Romanesque churches and monasteries from the 10th to the 12th centuries confirmed the re-emergence of civilization. They are found all over, but it is in Burgundy that the style reached its apotheosis. Of the great reformed Benedictine monasteries, Paray le Monial is perhaps the best surviving example, though Tournus has some exceptional Romanesque churches.

Gothic and Renaissance

The next great movement was Gothic, which spread from the north of France. The cathedrals of Laon, Chartres, Amiens, Bourges, Strasbourg, Reims and Paris are just some of the magnificent Gothic edifices.
With the return of François I from Italy came the Renaissance. This style largely affected palaces and many of the best examples can still be seen along the banks of the Loire; Azay le Rideau, Blois, Chambord, Chaumont and Chenonceaux all owe a debt to François I.
As the Renaissance developed into baroque across much of Europe, in France it became neoclassicism, best seen at Versailles (see p.50).

Chenonceau's château is supremely elegant, with fine formal gardens and a park

Royal relics

Until the 19th century the majority of art was related to religion or royalty (or both, in the case of Louis XIV and Napoléon). You'll see the best of this in churches and châteaux, though much has found its way into museums. The Louvre in Paris is the most famous but there are also museums of fine art in many other towns.

The art collections

Most of the best modern collections are in Paris, since this is not only where artists such as Delacroix, Rodin, Picasso, Giacometti, Modigliani, Soutine and dozens of others lived and worked, but also where the business side of the art world took place. For comprehensive collections there is little to beat the Musée d'Orsay (see p.38) or

associated with furniture than buildings (the Arc de Triomphe and the Madeleine, both in Paris, are exceptions). Art nouveau flourished briefly at the end of the 19th century and left its mark on the Métro. But it is the 20th century, with the invention of new building materials and techniques, that has seen the biggest changes in architecture, particularly on the Paris skyline. New landmarks abound – the Bastille Opéra, the controversial pyramid at the Louvre, designed by I.M. Pei and completed in 1988, La Grande Arche de la Défense, and the Pompidou Center (Beaubourg) completed in 1977.

Elsewhere in France you can see the famous work of Le Corbusier, most successfully at Notre-Dame du Haut de Ronchamp (see p.249); his influence lives on in a willingness to experiment architectually.

the Musée National d'Art Moderne (in the Beaubourg – see p.38), though for individual artists there is often an alternative – notably, in Paris, the Musée Rodin (see p.39), the Musée Picasso (see p.38), and the Musée Marmottan (see p.38; one of the best complete Monet collections).

Sometimes you'll find exceptional collections outside the capital, so keep an eye out for local museums. Toulouse-Lautrec's work, for example, is far better seen in his home town of Albi (see p.132) than in Paris, while Chagall and Matisse both have museums in Nice (see p.187).

In spite of more or less continuous warfare in various parts of France (the last 50 years have been the most peaceful in the country's turbulent history) much of the nation's architectural heritage has been preserved, and wherever you go you'll be able to see fine buildings from

cathedrals to palaces. Since World War II the French have been unusually strong on public building projects, so you'll also notice the best – and worst – of late 20th-century architecture.

... into the 20th century

As France struggled from the 18th to the 19th century Empire was the style of the day, though it is more often

The outside of the Pompidou Center still amazes

HISTORY

Modern humans have been living in France for at least the past 35,000 years. The paintings at Combe d'Arc, in the Ardèche, date back to 18000 BC, but little is documented until the founding of Marseille by Greeks around 600 BC. The Romans expanded their empire into Gaul, securing the south in 121 BC and the north over the next 75 years; although Roman remains can still be seen in Paris, the greatest treasures are found in the southeast.

The Roman occupation ended in the 5th century with a period of migrations by Germanic tribes from northern Europe. These

A statue of Jeanne d'Arc at the place du Martroi in Orléans, which was delivered under her leadership from the English in 1429

various barbarians are epitomized by Clovis, who trounced the Romans at Soissons in 486 and established the kingdom of the Franks. Charlemagne later tried to unify the kingdom and in 800 was crowned Emperor of the West in Rome. However, the core of modern France was only established in 843 with the partition of this empire. A new dynasty began with the accession to the throne of Hugues Capet in 987. The Capetians began centralizing power in Paris from the early 11th century onwards, and this process continued throughout the Middle Ages despite many political vicissitudes.

15th–18th century
Parts of France were at times under English rule in the late Middle Ages, benifiting from the Burgundy–Armagnac civil war in 1407. The English

burned Jeanne d' Arc at the stake in Rouen in 1431, yet by the end of the Hundred Years War (1337–1453) all they possessed was Calais.

The reigns of the Capetian and Valois kings saw Paris become the intellectual and cultural center of western Europe, and for over 400 years educated classes conversed in French. During the early 16th century, in the reign of François I, the royal fashion for keeping the court out of Paris led to the building of the Loire châteaux. This period culminated in the rise of the Sun King, Louis XIV, who built the palace at Versailles and took political power into his own hands. Strong on personality but weak on economics, Louis' death in 1715 left France impoverished. Nevertheless, by 1768 funds were found to buy Corsica from Genoa.

Failed economic reforms, careless and greedy rulers, and political awakening meant that by 1789 the

scene was ripe for revolution. Louis XVI lost his head in January 1793 and his wife Marie-Antoinette soon met a similar fate. For over a year the Terror reigned with nobody safe from the whims of Robespierre (whose close friend Danton even got the chop), until a brave few plucked up the courage to send Robespierre himself to the guillotine in 1794.

Enter Napoléon

Two years later a young Corsican named Napoléon was fighting and winning major battles as a general in the French army. Seizing control of the country in 1800, he went on to dominate most of Europe, but was finally brought down by two catastrophes: losing most of his 600,000 soldiers during the retreat from Moscow; and defeat by the Duke of Wellington at the Battle of Waterloo in 1815. A great civil organizer, Napoléon left France with a new legal system, a network of roads, and a simple street-numbering scheme still in use today.

The rest of the 19th century saw France's empire expand under both republican control and dictatorship, as the capital's population grew to over a million. Many starved in the Siege of Paris during the Franco-Prussian War of 1870–1, while those who survived ate anything they could, from sewer rats to the creatures at the zoo.

Art and war

The year 1870 also marked the debut of impressionism,
followed by the *belle époque* (1885–1914) and the style of art nouveau. This era came to a grisly end with World War I, which left 1.4 million French dead and another million disabled.

Between the world wars Paris became a glamorous city where dollar-rich Americans lived: Miller, Hemingway, Fitzgerald and many others sojourned here until the money ran out. Surrealism appeared at the same time under the ruthless leadership of André Breton, with art deco providing a sane, if less imaginative, alternative.

World War II to the 1980s

World War II saw Paris fall without a fight and the country split in two by the German Occupation. 200,000 Jews were sent to Nazi death camps, and from 1943 onwards spontaneous resistance movements were co-ordinated by the Comité National de la Résistance, leading to the liberation of Paris in August 1944. De Gaulle was there, but he resigned in 1946 and watched France lose all her colonies from 1949 to 1962. He returned in 1958 to create the Fifth Republic and was President of France until 1969. Pompidou succeeded him until 1974, and Giscard d'Estaing took over until Mitterrand came to power in 1981.

... and to present day

With Mitterrand's election things changed rapidly. Power was devolved to the regions for the first time in centuries. In spite of being a socialist president leading a
conservative Assembly for 4 of his 14 years, he was nonetheless one of the most popular presidents France has ever had. In 1995 Jacques Chirac was elected as his successor.

The French president is directly elected for a 7-year term. Far from being just a figurehead he also deals with foreign affairs and appoints the prime minister. Parliament consists of two

The Marseillaise frieze on the Arc de Triomphe symbolizes military victory and power

houses, the National Assembly and the Senate. Both houses make policy, but whereas the Senate can only block votes, the National Assembly can overturn them.

The president is answerable to the Conseil Constitutionnel, an independent elected body, but the prime minister is answerable to the National Assembly. Hence there is the potential difficulty, as in 1986, of having a socialist president and a right-wing prime minister.

CROSSROADS OF EUROPE

France lies at the heart of western Europe and is forever being visited, crossed over, traveled through and used as a stopping place on the way someplace else. Fortunately it has an excellent system of roads, a superb high-speed train network, and good links by sea, air and tunnel with the rest of the world.

The high-speed train (*Train à Grande Vitesse*, TGV) came into service in 1981 and now achieves speeds of over 300 kph (186 mph) on certain sections of track. This has reduced traveling time enormously. For those traveling from England, by the year 2000 it seems likely that the journey from London to the Riviera will take only 7 hours (it took over 18 hours as recently as 1993, before the opening of the Channel Tunnel).

The smooth TGV trains (Train à Grande Vitesse) provide an excellent service across France, and are also stylish to look at!

Freeway (*autoroute*) construction continues and makes many drives safer and quicker than they used to be, but be warned that the tolls are fairly high. The extensive road-building program is planned to continue into the next century. Congestion is a problem around Paris and the bigger towns at certain times, but that's true just about anywhere where there are people and automobiles.

Take the quiet route

For more interesting driving there is little to beat the spectacular mountain roads and passes in the Alps and the Pyrénées, but there are also thousands of miles of peaceful country roads all across France. A leisurely drive along these can often be more rewarding (and less expensive!) than hurtling down an *autoroute* without seeing anything other than traffic.

It takes all sorts

As you travel through France you will discover that it is a crossroads of people as well as geography. Regional differences are affected by the proximity of Spain, Italy, Switzerland, Germany, Holland, Luxembourg and Belgium. Don't expect someone from Nice, which was Sardinian until 1860, to be anything like someone from Metz, which was German between 1870 and 1918. In the south there are whole communities that have been nearly half-Italian since the Mussolini-prompted exodus of the 1930s, and throughout the foothills of the Pyrénées you'll find a strong Basque and Catalán influence from across the border.

When in Rome ...

It's not just the natives of France who are cosmopolitan. There are over a million foreign residents and many more visit every year. Tourism is as important as the automobile industry, and there is a strong local push to promote a cheerful welcome to visitors.

You'll also find France a crossroads of ideas and language. The latest ideas and theories from America, the East and the rest of Europe are all given fair consideration, and often adopted. Although the French have historically spoken only French, you'll discover that many young people learn English and will be eager to practise it. That said, there's no substitute for knowing a few words of French; the people will more than appreciate your efforts. (See p.276 for some useful expressions in French.)

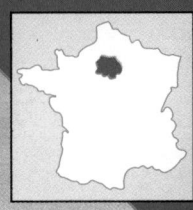

PARIS

"Paris is the heart of France ... Let's put all our efforts into embellishing this big city. Let us open new roads ... and may charitable light penetrate everywhere in our walls" NAPOLÉON III

CALENDAR OF EVENTS

LATE JANUARY – Vincennes racetrack holds the **America Stakes**.

FEBRUARY TO EARLY MARCH – Parc des Expositions, Porte de Versailles, offers an **Agricultural Show**.

LATE MARCH – Parc des Expositions, Porte de Versailles, has the **World Trade Fair on Tourism and Travel**.

APRIL – See the competitors in the **Paris Marathon** race through the city.

EARLY MAY – The **Paris Fair** takes place at the Parc des Expositions, Porte de Versailles.

EARLY JUNE – The Roland Garros courts play host to the exciting **French Open Tennis Championships**.

JUNE – Starting at the Champs-Élysées is the **Waiter and Waitresses Race**, with the finish at La Bastille.

JUNE 21 – A **Music Festival** is celebrated all over the city ∎

PARIS

Paris remains – in spite of all the hackneyed clichés and millions of tourist feet that have trampled across it – one of the most inspiring and rewarding cities in the world. You may perhaps feel frustrated by the slow and arbitrary way that things happen here, but you'll be impressed with what that slow and arbitrary lifestyle has produced over the last two thousand years or so. Who could fail to be captivated by the Eiffel Tower, Notre-Dame,

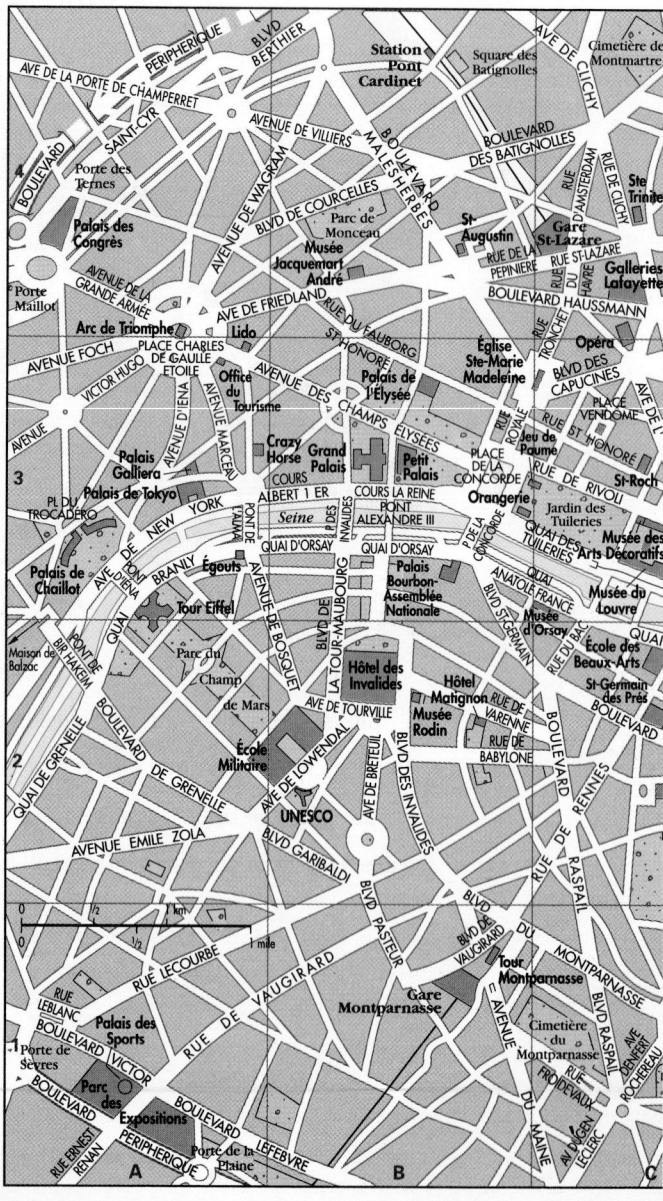

Sacré-Cœur, the Latin Quarter and the Arc de Triomphe? Paris is packed with cultural monuments, old and new, and takes nothing for granted – one look at the ambitious projects planned for the next decade is proof that Paris isn't resting on its laurels yet. And even when you've tired of the city's magnificent sights, you'll find an unlimited supply of culture, art, nightlife, eateries and chic shopping experiences to delay your departure.

Any city is only the sum of its people, and Parisians are writ

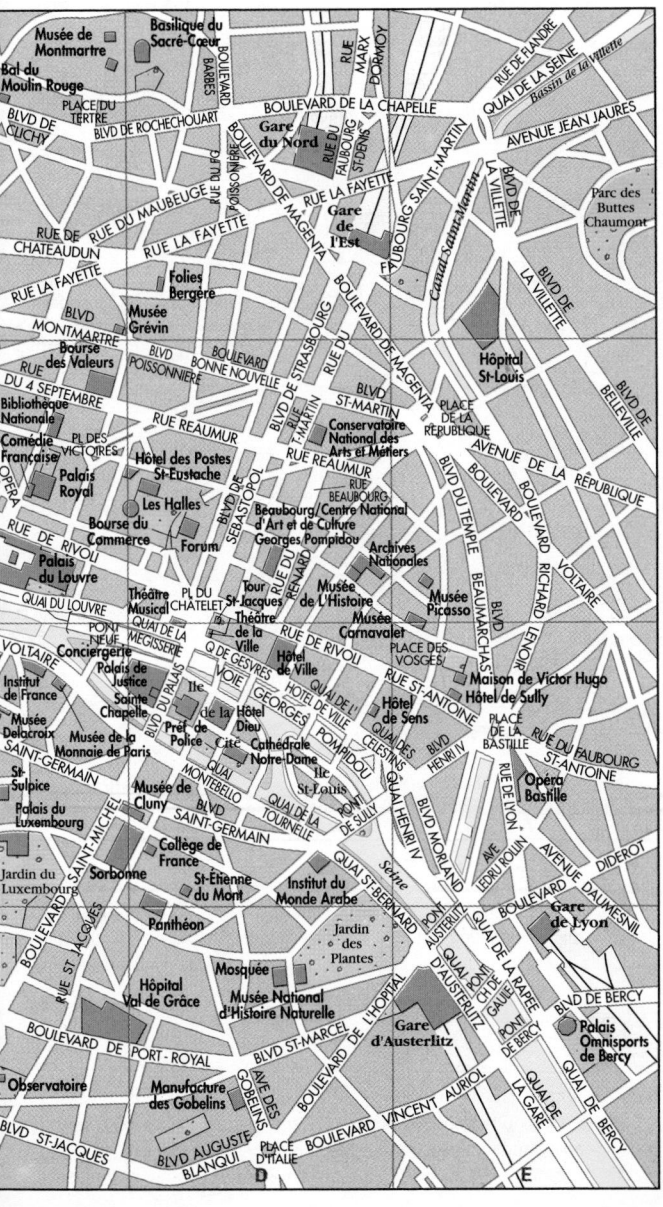

CALENDAR OF EVENTS

JULY 14 – Commemorating the **Storming of La Bastille**, fireworks and open-air celebrations on the Champs-Élysées add to the military march past.

SEPTEMBER – Vincennes racetrack hosts the **Summer Grand Prix**.

LATE SEPTEMBER – at selected sights throughout the city there is reduced or free admission as part of **National Heritage Days**. This includes some sights not normally open to the public.

OCTOBER – Montmartre plays host to a **Wine Harvest Festival**. On the Seine, starting at the Eiffel Tower, is the **Six-Hour Power Boat Race**. L'Espace Eiffel Branly plays host to the **International Contemporary Art Fair**.

NOVEMBER 11 – A **Military Parade for Remembrance Sunday** is held at the Arc de Triomphe ■

CALENDAR OF EVENTS

FEBRUARY TO MARCH – Parc des Princes Stadium hosts the **Five Nations Rugby Tournament**.

MARCH – Parc des Expositions, Porte de Versailles, offers a **Book Fair**.

APRIL – On a Sunday during the first two weeks of April, Auteuil race-track puts on the **President of the République Stakes**. Bagatelle (Bois des Boulogne) shows azaleas, while the Floral Gardens at Vincennes shows tulips.

LATE APRIL TO EARLY JUNE – Vincennes Floral Gardens shows its rhododendrons.

JUNE – At the Parc des Princes Stadium the **Soccer Cup Final** takes place. Auteuil racetrack sees the **Grand Steeplechase of Paris** ■

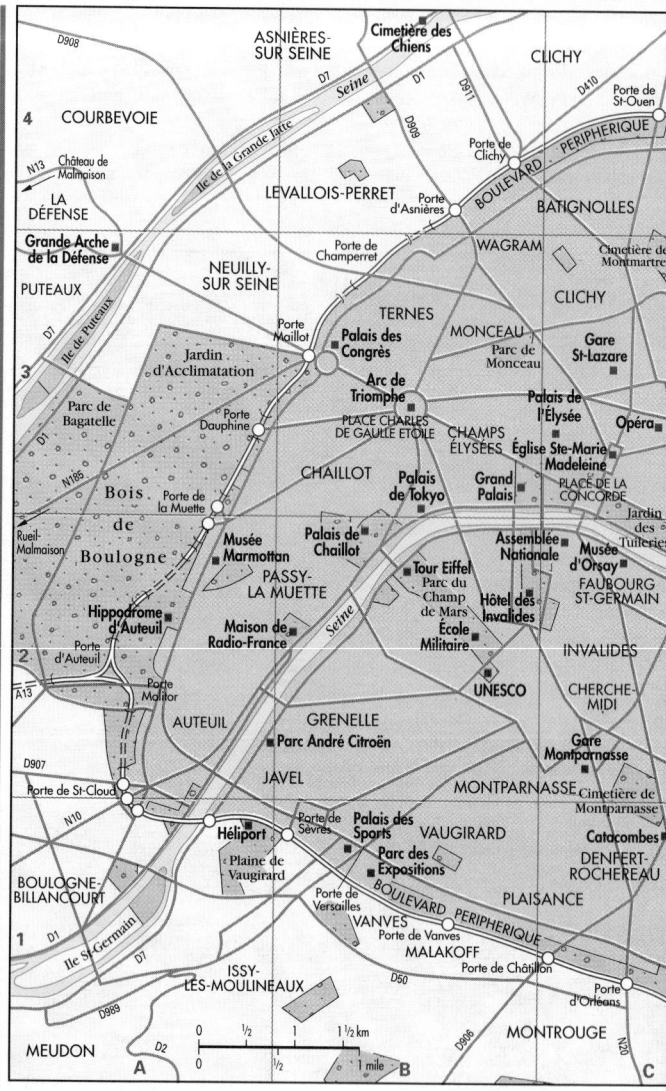

large across Paris. From the sheer elegance of the way people dress, to the painstaking detail evident even in the purchase of fruit or vegetables, you can see that, above all else, Parisians care about quality. You may find yourself at the rough end of a busy waiter's or shopkeeper's tongue, but it's nothing personal; these people simply care about what's happening. Watch the

arguments developing in the Left Bank bars between the closest of friends and you could be excused for thinking they're arranging a duel for the next morning!

Paris is irrevocably divided between the Left and Right banks of the Seine. The **Right** (north) **Bank** is the focus of most of the power and business of the city, and is very much part of the government, though nonetheless

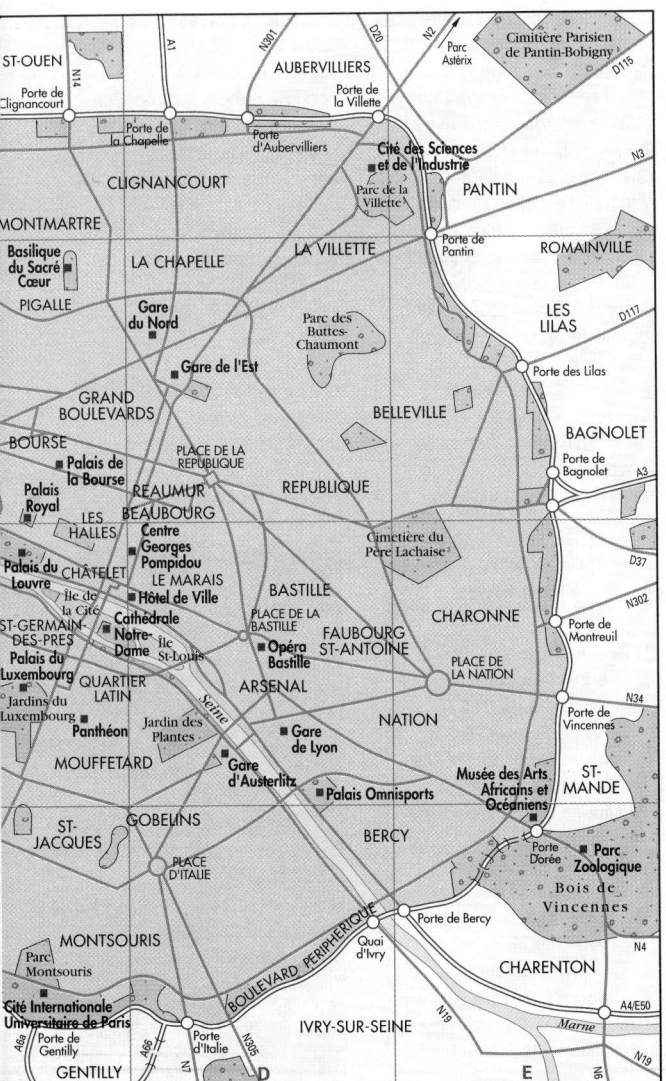

loosely defined as such. The **Left** (south) **Bank** is where the students and intellectuals are grouped, where historically the challenges have come from. In the middle are two islands, dominated by **Notre-Dame** and government buildings. To the north lies **Montmartre**, hotbed of artistic fervor a century ago (and now simply a hotbed), while to the south lies the former Bohemian area of **Montparnasse**, not easily categorized today, but which played such a crucial role in the development of the city, both intellectually and artistically, prior to World War II.

All of this (and over 2 million residents) is contained within a surprisingly small, dense city – at under 10 kilometers (6 mi.) across, the whole of Paris is walkable if the mood takes you.

HAUSSMANN'S PARIS

The street plan of Paris today, with its geometrical grid of magnificent, tree-lined boulevards and avenues, is largely the work of one man, Baron Georges-Eugène Haussmann (1809-1901).

Appointed Prefect of the Seine by Napoléon III in 1852, he set about transforming the city over the next 17 years.

The city was divided up into 20 *arrondissements*; narrow, medieval streets were demolished; beautiful parks (such as the bois des Boulogne and Vincennes) were created; and water supply and sewerage services were improved.

One of Haussman's key schemes was the creation of the Place de l'Etoile at the western end of the Champs-Élysées, with 12 broad avenues radiating from the Arc de Triomphe ■

Even if your feet should tire, you're never far from a Métro station. Historically it has always been fashionable to live right in town rather than in the more spacious suburbs, and this is what has kept the center so alive, with its local cafés, markets, and stores in every district. Compare this with the famous Square Mile of the City of London, for example, which has a working population of half a million but fewer than 5,000 residents, or with the business district of any large American city.

It all started in what is still the geographical center of town, and from which all distances in France

★★★ HIGHLIGHTS

are still measured. The Ile de la Cité is a strategic location and well protected, and was the first part of Paris to be inhabited. Colonized by the aptly named Parisii, the city fell (like so much of Europe) to the Romans in 52 BC. The Romans left to us the roads and ruins that can still be seen today, but they themselves succumbed to the relentless

pressure of waves of barbarians, and it was only in the Middle Ages that Paris started to become the city we recognize today. By 1250 it was the biggest city in Europe, and the continent's intellectual and cultural center. In spite of internecine royal feuds, bloody wars, political intrigues, harsh occupations, and even a revolution or two, Paris has never looked back.

Paris is as much a city for tasting as for sightseeing. Every street has its own cafés, brasseries and restaurants, and you'll find the rich diversity of France's regional cuisines

represented right across the city. Food from every nation, race, and culture around the world can be found here, too, as is only right and proper in a capital city. Look out for the *prix-fixe* lunchtime menus that still epitomize some of Europe's best-value gourmet dining.

Whatever you eat, you won't leave Paris empty handed. From the great department stores to the tiniest *boulangerie* on the street corner, Paris is one shopping experience after another. And getting from store to store is particularly easy, with the excellent **Métro** and **RER** systems running both underground and overground. Opened in 1900, the Paris Métro has 366 stations, never more than a few hundred yards apart, and the government subsidies make it one of the cheapest and easiest forms of transportation in the world. If you want to stay above ground, then there is also a good, if complicated, bus network; only if you're very adventurous would you want to drive through Paris, even if you could find parking anywhere near where you wanted to go.

Paris is, then, a city to be savored slowly. Don't try to see everything in one visit.

At the Jardin du Luxembourg, the usual frantic pace of Parisian life slows down. At the eastern end of the Quartier Latin, these gardens offer peace and quiet with occasional bands playing on the old-fashioned bandstands

One of the most famous landmarks in Paris, the Arc de Triomphe was commissioned by Napoléon to commemorate the victories of his French fighting forces. From the top there are superb views over the city and the twelve elegant avenues radiating from the Arc

★ **ACADÉMIE FRANÇAISE** *19C2*
Institut de France, 23 quai de Conti, 75006
Métro: Odéon, Pont-Neuf
Famous for its tenacious grip on the French language (a 1994 edict outlawed the use of such useful non-French words as *meeting*, *sandwich*, *snack* and *weekend*), the Académie Française is a 40-strong body of academics that has met weekly since 1635 to bemoan declining standards and to deliberate the very language itself. Although the meetings are private, the distinctive 1663 facade of the Institut de France, which overlooks the Pont des Arts, is worth inspection.

★★★ **ARC DE TRIOMPHE** *18A4*
Métro: Charles de Gaulle-Étoile
Competing only with the Eiffel Tower for the title of Paris' most distinctive monument, the Arc de Triomphe was intended to be Napoléon's tribute to his army.

By the time of Napoléon's coronation in 1804, however, the landmark had reached less than 1.5 meters (5 ft.) tall, so a wood and canvas model had to be hastily erected in time for the grand parades. The Arc was completed in 1836 and has been a tourist attraction ever since. Underneath lies the Tomb of the Unknown Soldier from World War I, with the eternal flame above, and around the Arc flows an endless circle of traffic. The climb up its spiral staircases inside (much quicker than waiting for the elevator) gives superb views from the 50-meter (164-ft.) roof right across Haussmann's redesigned Paris.

★★ **AQUARIUM/MUSÉE** *21E1*
DES ARTS AFRICAINS ET OCÉANIENS
293 avenue Daumesnil, 75012
Métro: Porte Dorée
The aquarium in the basement of this museum is one of the best in France. Beautiful shoals of brightly colored tropical fish vie for attention with sluggish turtles, rapacious sharks, patiently sinister moray eels and torpid crustaceans. Children will be delighted with a visit here.

On the other three floors are stunning collections from Africa, the Maghreb, Australasia and Polynesia, all set in splendid art-deco surroundings. The building itself dates from the 1931 Exposition Coloniale. The Paris Zoo, France's largest, is a pleasant 15-minute walk away across the Bois de Vincennes.

ART GALLERIES

New York has dominated the world art market since the 1950s, but from the late 1980s Paris has been reasserting itself. For up-and-coming artists the Left Bank is still very much the place to buy and sell (though check out the latest gallery invasion around La Bastille – see below); for sheer variety you can't beat the area between, roughly, rue Mazarine to the east and rue Bonaparte to the west (map 18C2). Top-quality antiques can be found a little farther west between rue des Saints Pères and rue du Bac. For known names and works (and correspondingly high prices) cross the Seine and wander into the famous galleries between avenue Matignon and boulevard Haussmann north of the Champs-Élysées.

★★ BASTILLE, LA   19E2
Métro: Bastille

As late as the mid-1980s La Bastille was still a strong working-class area of Paris, but since the completion of the glass and steel Opéra in 1989 the area has been rapidly gentrified, to the regret of many. There are still some anachronisms to be found in a few of the back streets, but you're more likely to see smart art galleries and neat little furniture shops than the small factories and craftsmen's *ateliers* that once crowded the area. Although the place itself is best known for being at the heart of the Revolution in

1789 (the Marquis de Sade was among the prisoners released during the storming of the Bastille), the Colonne de Juillet in actual fact commemorates the uprising of 1830, during which Charles X was deposed in favor of his relative Louis-Philippe, and the many hundreds of victims who are buried underneath the square. The figure on top of the column represents the Genius of Liberty, and also appears on the 10F coin.

★★ BEAUBOURG   21D2
(CENTRE GEORGES
POMPIDOU)
Métro: Châtelet-Les Halles, Rambuteau

Now more commonly known as the Beaubourg, the Pompidou Center was opened in 1977 and has attracted floods of visitors ever since. Waiting in line is the norm rather than the exception, with most people trying to get to the Musée National d'Art Moderne (MNAM, see p.38). The Center also has a record and reference library, restaurant and snack bar, bookshop, contemporary music center, and children's workshop. Outside the building there's a constant crowd of talented (and less-talented) buskers and street performers willing to entertain you for small change. The square is a natural focus for tourists and locals alike.

★★ BELLEVILLE   21E3
Métro: Belleville

Although not traditionally a tourist area, Belleville's colorful social mix and cheerful restaurants and cafés make the *quartier* an interesting detour if you're in the northeast of Paris. It also offers great panoramic views across the city. If you head back into Paris on foot, the newly restored Canal Saint-Martin makes a pleasant place to stroll along the waterside and the new marina.

On the eastern side of Paris, the Bois de Vincennes is a popular area for recreational pursuits. There are waymarked paths for walkers, a zoo, and a tropical garden, as well as sporting facilities. In the 12th century the wood was used as a royal hunting ground, while in the 17th century the forest became a fashionable area in which to stroll

★ BERCY 21D1
Métro: Bercy

Once famous for its wine warehouses, Bercy, like much of central Paris, has fallen prey to office development and apartment buildings. Notable exceptions in the area are the Parc de Bercy where some of the wine warehouses and the ground plans of others have been preserved, and the Palais Omnisports de Bercy, a huge multifunctional hall that hosts everything from sumo wrestling to rock concerts. The Bibliothèque Nationale de France was transferred to its new site at Bercy and opened to the public at the end of 1996.

★ BIBLIOTHÈQUE 19C3
NATIONALE DE FRANCE
58 rue de Richelieu, 75002
Métro: Bourse

The main attraction of France's national library is not so much the fact that you can read any book ever published in France (nearly 13 million so far), but that you can see the colossal glass-domed reading room and the magnificent Galerie Mazarine designed by François Mansart. Only the very brave, or foolish, would dare to try out the famous echoes in these hushed chambers. Also interesting is a visit to the Cabinet des Médailles et des Antiques with its extensive collection of coins and antiques, mostly built up from royal collections.

BOIS DE BOULOGNE 20A2
BOIS DE VINCENNES 21E1
Métro: Porte Maillot/Porte Dorée

Baron Haussmann may be more famous for his grand avenues, but another of his great gifts to Paris was the green spaces of the Bois de Boulogne and the Bois de Vincennes, on the west and east sides of the city. Both parks boast huge areas of woodland, lakes, open country, and the occasional château and racetrack, and provide refreshing breathing spaces for the 2 million inhabitants of the city. By day they provide walkers, joggers,

the street is a good place to photograph one of the remaining original art-nouveau métro signs.

BOURSE, LA 21C3
place de la Bourse, 75002
Métro: Bourse
If watching brokers and bond dealers doing their thing interests you, then the neoclassical Paris Bourse is as good a place as any to see it happen. Guided tours take you through to the visitor's gallery that overlooks the sumptuous circular exchange. The overspill of all this financial activity can be seen in the surrounding streets where cafés and restaurants cater for those in the money trade.

★ CATACOMBES 20C1
★ SEWERS 18A3
1 place Denfert-Rochereau, 75014/Pont de l'Alma, quai d'Orsay
Métro/RER: Denfert-Rochereau, Pont de l'Alma, Alma-Marceau
Some of the most unusual attractions in Paris are found deep underground. The Catacombes are the result of Voltaire's efforts to persuade the 18th-century authorities to dig up the disease-infested cemeteries and stack the bones along 65 kilometers (40 mi.) of underground corridors; another 100 kilometers (62 mi.) of corridors exist, but without the bones). Visitors are checked in and out through turnstiles – it's all too easy to wander away from the better-lit tunnels and down the dark paths among the bones of over 6 million dead. Take warm clothing and a flashlight.

The sewers are also a surprisingly popular attraction. Guided tours demonstrate yet again Haussmann's genius for town planning, and take you along part of the 2,100-kilometre (1,305-mi.) network of tunnels.

rowers and racegoers with a focus for their activities; by night, however, both parks are frequented by prostitutes and transvestites. The Parc de Bagatelle in the Bois de Boulogne is particularly beautiful and has one of the finest rose gardens in France. The tropical garden and Parc Floral in the Bois de Vincennes are also delightful.

★ BOULEVARD 19C2
ST.-MICHEL
Métro: St.-Michel
The boulevard St.-Michel ("boul' Mich" to the locals) achieved fame in May 1968 as the center of the student riots. Now it's just another busy street, though the side roads running from it still have the best of the bookshops and student hangouts, and the university population from the Sorbonne gives a young feel to the area. The main attractions today are the late-night shopping and the excellent movie theaters showing new releases. The St.-Michel métro at the north end of

SEASONS
There are things to do in Paris all year round, but if you can choose your dates think about coming in late spring or early fall when the air is at its clearest.

In August Paris can be alarming if you are not aware that half the inhabitants have gone away for the whole month. Many shops and galleries will have the blinds drawn and the shutters closed, displaying the ubiquitous *Fermeture Annuelle* sign. But that also makes Paris easier to visit because it is less crowded. If you're driving, August is the safest and easiest time of the year to be in the city – street parking is free for the whole month in most streets, though it is advisable to check at the ticket dispensers before you park ■

CAFÉS

Paris is, to some extent, epitomized by its numerous cafés.

There were once as many as 12,000, but their number is constantly decreasing in spite of the fact that they represent the opposite of fast-food. You'll be served quickly enough, but then you can take time to enjoy a quiet pause or the chance to be with friends.

The most-famous cafés are usually full of tourists, but the ghosts of Sartre and others still haunt the Café de Flore and Les Deux Magots, and Henry Miller's distinctive Brooklyn accent echoes down the decades at the Dôme and La Coupole in Montparnasse.

Remember the rule of thumb: the farther you are from the bar, the more expensive it gets – standing up is cheapest, sitting outside on the sidewalk is most expensive ■

★★ CHAMPS-ÉLYSÉES 18B3
avenue des, 75016
Métro: Champs-Élysées Clémenceau
Certainly the most famous street in France, the Champs-Élysées (Elysian Fields) runs from the place de la Concorde to the Arc de Triomphe. The best day to be here is on the third Sunday in July, when the Champs is closed to motor traffic so that cyclists in the Tour de France can make their bid for glory as they go up and down the avenue.

The week before, on Bastille Day (July 14), you can see most of the French army march by accompanied by low-flying jets.

For the rest of the year the Champs makes a busy living from its fast-food establishments, movie theaters, airline offices and shopping arcades, though at the end nearest the place de la Concorde, below the Grand and Petit Palais, commercial activity is restricted to a few select restaurants.

★ CHAMP DE MARS 18A2
75007
Métro: Champ de Mars
Originally a genuine battlefield (historic Roman victories and Viking defeats took place here), the Champ de Mars was later used as a military training base before becoming public grounds. Dominated by the Eiffel Tower at one end and the École Militaire at the other, the Champ is a favorite strolling ground for the chic inhabitants of the 7th and 15th *arrondissements*. Don't miss the popular puppet shows (*guignols*) held here on weekends and Wednesday afternoons.

★ CHINATOWN 21D1
Métro: Place d'Italie
A significant part of Paris' South-East Asian community is in the 13th *arrondissement*, south of place d'Italie. Here you'll find restaurants and shops that focus not only on China itself, but also on Cambodia, Vietnam, Laos, Thailand and Hong Kong, presenting a less homogeneous picture than other Chinatowns around the world, but all the richer for that reason.

★ COMÉDIE FRANÇAISE 19C3
2 place Colette, 75001
Métro: Palais Royal
Founded in 1680 by Louis XIV with members of Molière's theater company, the Comédie Française has been resident since 1812 at the Théâtre Français, mostly performing French classics by Molière, Racine, Corneille and Marivaux. In the foyer look out for the armchair that cushioned Molière's dying fall in his own production of "Le Malade Imaginaire" in 1673. Guided tours of the theater are occasionally provided, though you're more likely to see the interior by seeing a performance.

★ CONCIERGERIE, LA 19C2
1 quai de l'Horloge, 75001
Métro: Cité; RER: St.-Michel
A grim reminder of the city's more violent past, the Conciergerie was for over 500 years the most infamous prison in Paris. Situated right at the heart of Paris on the Île de la Cité, the Conciergerie even now has the somber look of a medieval prison. During the Terror this was the last stop for thousands of prisoners, including Danton and Robespierre, before being taken to the guillotine across the river at the place de la Révolution (now the place de la Concorde). Marie-Antoinette's cell has been reconstructed to show how she spent her last hours here; despite her appalling arrogance and foolishness, you can still feel sorry for her kept in this place.

COUPOLE, LA *18C1*

102 boulevard du Montparnasse, 75014

Métro: Vavin

Despite tourists comprising the majority of customers at La Coupole these days, it's easy to imagine Hemingway, Man Ray and Henry Miller here in the 1920s and 1930s. Quite apart from the historic significance of this brasserie, it's also one of the foremost monuments to grandiose art deco you'll see in Paris or anywhere else. Across the street is the equally famous Dôme brasserie.

★★ LA DÉFENSE *20A3*

RER line A: Grande Arche de la Défense

Dominated by the immense white marble hollow cube known as La Grande Arche (designed by Danish architect Johan Otto von Spreckelsen and completed in 1989 for the bicentennial celebrations of the French Revolution), this area was first developed massively in the 1960s under Général de Gaulle. Controversy has always reigned over the architecture and planning, but now – at last – la Défense seems to have settled down as a business and residential center. It makes an interesting visit from the older, more traditional center of town.

On the Parvis de la Défense is the Musée de l'Automobile, which uses imaginative displays to tell the story of the automobile.

LES DEUX MAGOTS *18C2*

170 boulevard St.-Germain, 75006

Métro: St.-Germain des Prés

Patronized and popularized by writers André Gide and Jean-Paul Sartre, Les Deux Magots is named after the two Chinamen sitting on moneyboxes inside (*magot* is French slang for "a stash"). It has a famous, and famously expensive, whiskey list, but you can get away without going bankrupt if you opt for the excellent hot chocolate or espresso. Next door is the Café de Flore, the local haunt of Picasso, Camus and Simone de Beauvoir, which has a lovely 19th-century wood-paneled interior.

Les Deux Magots on boulevard St.-Germain is alive with literary associations. Once frequented by Jean-Paul Sartre and André Gide, the café is still a favored meeting place for the city's intellectuals. The terrace affords good local views

restored Chapelle des Petits-Augustins (1608). Occasional exhibitions by the students are open to the public in the halls opening onto the *quai.*

ÉCOLE MILITAIRE *18B2*
Champ de Mars, 75007
Métro: École Militaire
Louis XV and his mistress Madame de Pompadour commissioned Gabriel to design and build the École Militaire as a military academy in 1751 following the successful completion of the major new works at Versailles, and the building was finally finished in 1775. Given its natural dominance of the Champ de Mars, it's interesting to wonder what anyone at the time would have thought of the Eiffel Tower's complete dominance, just over a century later, of not only the Champ de Mars but the whole of the Paris skyline.

★★★ EIFFEL TOWER *18A3*
Métro: Bir-Hakeim; RER: Champ de Mars
Most distinctive of all the Paris landmarks and symbols, the Eiffel Tower shouldn't really be standing at all since it was intended for demolition in 1909, 20 years after it had been built for the 1889 Universal Exhibition. Pragmatism won the day, however, and the broadcasting antennae at the 300-meter (984-ft.) top tipped the balance in favor of the tower's survival. Built from pig iron, the tower was constructed by Gustave Eiffel in less than two years, and until his death in 1923 he maintained an office on the top platform (with the unforgettable address: M. Gustave Eiffel, Tour Eiffel, Paris).

One consequence of being the tallest building in the world (until New York's Chrysler Building outstripped it) was its fatal attraction as a leaping point for

Emblem of the French capital, the Eiffel Tower was constructed for the Universal Exhibition of 1889 in just under two years. At over 320 meters (1,050 ft.), the tower offers splendid panoramic views

ÉCOLE DES BEAUX-ARTS *18C2*
17 quai Malaquais, 75006
Métro: Odéon
The stately 19th-century facade of this school masks its dusty interior where the brightest hopes of hundreds of art students are nurtured. From the courtyard (use the entrance on rue Bonaparte) you can wander into the run-down central hall and galleries, and into the newly

suicides. Some 370 deaths occurred before the rather ugly protective shields were installed in 1971. A trip to the 276-meter (906-ft.) third platform is a must for all visitors to Paris; there's a long wait for the elevators (upwards of 4 million people make the trip annually), but the views from the top more than repay your patience – on a clear day you can see 67 kilometers (42 mi.). Also try to make sure that you see the tower at night, when it's illuminated.

FAUBOURGS

Literally meaning "false borough," the Faubourgs were originally names for streets that carried over into another city boundary. As a result, people brought up in the Faubourgs were thought to be lower class. With time, though, some of the streets have become the most chic and fashionable of all Paris streets (notably Faubourg St.-Honoré and Faubourg St.-Germain). More interesting by far, however, are the Faubourg Poissonnière, which runs its narrow course all the way up from the 2nd *arrondissement* to the border of the 18th, and the Faubourg St.-Denis, which runs northwards through the 10th *arrondissement*, providing shelter to modest schools, tiny *ateliers*, hidden workshops, minute factories and small-fronted stores along their length.

FOLIES BERGÈRE   19D4
32 rue Richer, 75009
Métro: Cadet, Rue Montmartre
In spite of its somewhat diminished reputation, the Folies Bergère remains one of the oldest and most traditional of Paris cabarets (the impressionists loved it). Even if the routines look familiar, the club still draws the crowds. More importantly it's a relatively inexpensive night out.

GALERIES LAFAYETTE   18C4
40 boulevard Haussmann, 75009
Métro: Chaussée d'Antin
This spectacular, glass-domed department store is worth a visit as much for the architecture as for anything you might buy here. But if you want to see what's current from the top designers it's worth noting that many of them have boutiques here, displaying the very latest designs on two floors.

Printemps, just up the street, has a wonderful tea room and self-service restaurant with great views and a beautiful stained-glass roof.

La Samaritaine, on rue de la Monnaie, is the nearest French equivalent to Macy's in New York, housing almost anything you could possibly want in one of its several buildings, and possessing one of the best out-door roof cafés in Paris on the 10th floor (open only in summer), with lovely views up and down the Seine and across Pont Neuf.

★★ GRAND PALAIS   18B3
avenue du Général Eisenhower, 75008
Métro: Champs-Élysées Clémenceau
Built for the Universal Exhibition in 1900 (along with the Petit Palais), the Grand Palais has an extraordinary iron and glass roof that is visible from far along the river – one of the best views is at night from the Pont Alexandre III, when it is illuminated. The west wing of the Grand Palais houses the Palais de la Découverte, a fine science museum with an excellent planetarium. Temporary art exhibitions are held in the rest of the Grand Palais, while the Petit Palais is home to the Musée des Beaux-Arts de la Ville de Paris, which contains among other exhibits a rich collection of Renaissance furnishings.

MARKETS

Every *arrondisse-ment* has its own market, supplemented by itinerant markets that set up at a different site each day. Visit at least one local market for the sheer vitality of it all.

More colorful is any one of the city's exuberant *marchés aux puces* (flea markets) ∎

A view of the Ile de la Cité, home of Notre-Dame and the Sainte-Chapelle. This is the historic heart of Paris, an area of great cultural and architectural interest

★★ LES HALLES   19D3
75002
Métro: Châtelet Les Halles
There was a huge food market on the site of Les Halles from the early 12th century until 1969, when, with soaring rents and increasing problems of distribution, the old market was pulled down and moved to the outskirts. A decade later the modern shopping center was opened and has become a vital hub of Parisian life, with shops like FNAC in the underground Forum offering a focus for all. The surrounding streets provide the infrastructure of cafés and restaurants so essential to any modish part of Paris.

HÔTEL DES INVALIDES   18B2
avenue de Tourville, 75007
Métro/RER: Invalides
Primarily known (and visited) for housing Napoléon's wildly extravagant six-layered coffin, Les Invalides at one time was home to as many as 6,000 pensioner soldiers, though now the number is down to a mere hundred.

If you go to see Napoléon's tomb don't neglect the other military tombs, including the poignant memorial to Maréchal Foch, the Allied commander at the end of World War I. Also hidden behind the 17th-century facade is the Musée de l'Armée, containing many things Napoleonic; of particular interest are the collections from world wars I and II.

★★★ THE ISLANDS   19D2
Métro: Cité, Pont Marie
Right at the very heart of Paris, and where Paris actually began, are the city's two islands, the Ile de la Cité and the Ile St.-Louis. The Ile de la Cité is the busier of the two, containing Notre-Dame, the Palais de Justice, Sainte-Chapelle and the Conciergerie.

The *quais* bordering the Seine are at their most beautiful here, with weeping willows dropping into the water at the western end of the island. At the eastern end, behind Notre-Dame, is a rarely discovered and rather sobering monument to the deportees sent to the concentration camps during World War II. The Ile St.-Louis is the quieter and more elegant of the two islands, containing one or two lovely little hotels and a surprisingly large number of upmarket restaurants.

JARDIN DU   19C2
LUXEMBOURG
boulevard St.-Michel, 75006
RER line B: Luxembourg
Saved from the urbanizing Haussmann only by a 12,000-signature petition, the Jardin du Luxembourg remains the quintessential and most idyllic of Paris' gardens. Originally created for Marie de Medici in 1613, the garden's statues, fountains, chess players and newspaper readers have appeared in so many films and books that the surroundings are instantly familiar, even on your first visit. There's something venerable, too, about the measured pace of those out walking, and the quiet way the pigeons wait for the

same old men to feed them every day. If you're here with children on a Wednesday afternoon or on the weekend be sure not to miss the *guignols* (puppet shows).

★ **JARDIN DES PLANTES** *19D1*
quai St.-Bernard, 75005
Métro: Gare d'Austerlitz
Created originally to cultivate medicinal plants for the king in the 17th century, the Jardin des Plantes is even now a series of neatly laid-out horticultural experiments presided over by the huge Musée National d'Histoire Naturelle (Natural History Museum). A rather sad zoo takes up one side of the gardens – you'd be much better off going to the zoo in the Bois de Vincennes.

★★★ **JEU DE PAUME** *18C3*
place de la Concorde, 75001
Métro: Concorde
Once used as a tennis court, and famous from 1945 to 1986 as being the best place in the world to see impressionist paintings, the Jeu de Paume was closed in 1986 after its collection was moved across the river to the newly opened Musée d'Orsay (see p.38). It was refurbished over the next five years and reopened in 1991: its light, airy galleries are now used to house

temporary exhibitions of international contemporary art.

LIDO, LE *18A3*
116 bis Champs-Élysées, 75008
Métro: George V
If you want to see the Bluebell Girls dance, then go to Le Lido. Despite the special effects, you'll notice few French people in the audience – this is a show for the tourists. The same applies to the **Crazy Horse**, 12 avenue George V, 75008, where the show is, if anything, even more professional.

WALK

CITY ISLANDS
From Pont Neuf cross to place Dauphine, then right into the quai des Orfèvres that once served as the gold and silversmiths' quay.

Follow the walls and impressive turrets of the sprawling Palais de Justice (an old royal palace that now houses the law courts) around to the left, passing the masterpiece of Sainte-Chapelle, and then turn right into rue de Lutèce. Visit the colorful flower market **and turn right and then left to reach Notre-Dame.**

Cross the Pont St.-Louis and follow the quai de Bourbon around the tip of the island to the quai d'Anjou, lined with splendid hotels, including one of the most famous, the 17th-century Hôtel Lambert. Turn right into rue St.-Louis-en-l'Ile, the island's main street, with its chic bistros, boutiques and cafés.

Cross back to the *Rive Droite* via the Pont Louis Philippe ■

★★★ LOUVRE, PALAIS DU
19C3

rue de Rivoli, 75001
Métro: Palais Royal
Converted from a fortress to a palace in the 14th century, the Louvre has undergone frequent

In the Cour Napoléon, the glass pyramid designed by I.M. Pei allows light to filter through the Louvre's main entrance. The Louvre, with over 30,000 exhibits, is the world's largest museum

transformation ever since. One of the more radical changes was by the American architect I.M. Pei, whose transparent pyramid was added in 1988 as the new main entrance to the museum.

After the court moved with Louis XIV to Versailles, the Louvre was used more like an alternative arts center than a museum. Only at the end of the 19th century did anything like

the museum you see today come into existence.

Within the Louvre boundary is one of the best perspective views in Paris. Standing in the place du Carrousel, you can look through the Arc de Triomphe du Carrousel to the obelisk on the place de la Concorde; this is lined up with the Arc de Triomphe at the far end of the Champs-Élysées, and behind that is the massive Grande Arche de la Défense.

Don't try to take the Louvre by storm in a single visit. It's simply far too big, and several short visits will repay the effort far better than the complete sensory overload you can expect from one long visit. Try to decide what you want to see in advance and plan your visit carefully. There's a lot more than just the "Mona Lisa" here, and you'll never have time to see all 30,000 exhibits. Up-to-date plans in all languages can be found at the entrance.

The collections in the Louvre range from Egyptian and classical antiquities to the Renaissance, and 19th-century paintings and sculpture, making this the largest museum in the world – it covers a staggering 240,000 square meters (2,583,734 sq. ft.).

★ MADELEINE, LA (STE. MARIE)/FAUCHON
18C3

place de la Madeleine, 75008
Métro: Madeleine
Designed to look like a Greek temple, and owing more than a little to the Maison Carrée in Nîmes, la Madeleine is a church that looks better from the outside than the inside – which fact reflects the many doubts that have been expressed over its function (it was nearly converted into a train station). The best view of la Madeleine is from the place de la Concorde, with the building nicely complemented by the Hotel Crillon on the left.

Walking up to la Madeleine along the rue Royale, look out for **Fauchon** on the right side of the place de la Madeleine, possibly France's best grocery store and certainly its most expensive. Window-shopping is the recommended option.

MAISON DE BALZAC 18A2

47 rue Raynouard, 75016
Métro: Passy, La Muette
This underrated museum shows the house where Balzac lived 1840–7 under a pseudonym while being pursued by debt collectors. It is also a good example of the genteel houses found in the 16th *arrondissement*. If you have time, walk down to the river and across Pont de Bir-Hakeim either onto the man-made island or across into the 15th *arrondissement* for lovely views back to the 16th.

★★ MAISON DE 19E2
VICTOR HUGO

6 place des Vosges, 75004
Métro: Bastille, St.-Paul
As well as presenting an exceptionally clear look at the writer's life and works, this lovely residence affords an unrivaled opportunity to see what many of the other apartments on the place des Vosges are like inside. By re-creating rooms from Victor Hugo's other residences (notably a *salon chinois* from the house where he lived with Juliette Drouet on Guernsey), augmented by drawings, photographs, letters and books, the museum achieves a charming homogeneity and sense of completeness.

★ MANUFACTURE 21D1
DES GOBELINS

42 avenue des Gobelins, 75013
Métro: Gobelins
Since the 17th century the Manufacture des Gobelins has been turning out some of the choicest and most valuable

tapestries in the world. If you go to Versailles, much of what you see will have been woven here. The ancient looms used then are amazingly still in service today, operated by weavers apprenticed from the age of 16.

WALK

LE MARAIS

Turn right from St.-Paul métro and walk along rue St.-Antoine as far as No. 62, Hôtel de Sully, a magnificent 17th-century mansion built for a notorious gambler and now superbly restored to its original appearance.

Cut through rue de Biragua to the place des Vosges, a symmetrical square built in 1609 and lined with aristocratic residences including the Maison de Victor Hugo, considered one of the finest in the city.

Follow the rue des Francs Bourgeois, which is flanked by several museums including the Musée Carnavalet (dedicated to the history of Paris) and the Musée Cognacq-Jay (18th-century art and furniture).

Turn left on rue des Hospitaliers St.-Gervais and left again onto rue des Rosiers; this colorful street in the heart of the Jewish area is lined with bakeries, synagogues and restaurants.

Turn right on rue Pavée to return to St.-Paul ∎

★★ LE MARAIS 21D2

Métro: St.-Paul, Chemin Vert
Centered on an area west of the place des Vosges (famous not just for Victor Hugo's apartment at No. 6, but also for other luminaries who passed through), the Marais has only recently recovered its fame having lain ignored for nearly two centuries following the Revolution.

The word *marais* means marsh, and a successful scheme to drain the area for development was not proposed until the 16th century. A walk along the rue des Francs Bourgeois, and up and down the streets that run off it, offers tempting glimpses of some of the many beautiful courtyards as well as the architectural masterpieces that are the finest of Paris' town houses.

Montmartre has long attracted artists of every level of talent. The place du Tertre in the shadow of Sacré-Cœur is alive with pavement artists, licensed at two easels per square meter

MARCHÉS AUX PUCES

Paris' flea markets are all situated shrewdly outside the Périphérique. They exert an irresistible attraction for locals and tourists alike, though there are a lot more overpriced or shoddy goods than real bargains to be had. All the same, a trip to one of the flea markets is a treat not to be missed – you never know what you're going to find. The Porte de Clignancourt market is by turns the biggest, the best and the worst, with real finds possible in spite of its reputation as a tourist trap. The Porte de Vanves market is much more fashionable with Parisians, but rarely turns up anything exotic as at Clignancourt. The Marché de Montreuil is good for clothes, less so for bric-a-brac.

★★ MARCHÉ MOUFFETARD   *19D1*

rue Mouffetard
Métro: Place Monge
Most famous of the Paris street markets, the Marché Mouffetard holds few surprises now, though the quality of the fresh fruit and vegetables, not to mention the cheese stalls and succulent shellfish, is excellent. Look out, too, for exotic North African spices, Greek olives, and dried mushrooms. If you can, visit one of the other many street markets in the city: every *arrondissement* has its own, usually daily.

★★★ MONTMARTRE   *21C4*

75018
Métro: Abbesses
High above the rest of Paris, Montmartre has long been the focus of revolutionaries as well as artists. Even today, in the sham that is the place du Tertre, you can't help being affected by the vaguely artistic aura of the whole place, with its charming little bars and restaurants. Expect to be asked whether you would like to be caricatured, drawn or painted by one of the (mostly) talented artists here (for a fee of course).

With the white marble magnificence of **Sacré-Cœur** (see p.46) and the superb panoramas visible from all over the area, Montmartre is irresistible to all but the most coldhearted, in spite of high prices and all the tourists.

★ MONTPARNASSE   20C2
75014
Métro: Montparnasse-Bienvenue
Montparnasse started out as a grass-covered mound of debris from ancient Roman quarries, and the area became a favored haunt for student poets, who gave it the nickname "Mount Parnassus" after the mountain of Apollo.

Montparnasse still manages to draw the crowds in spite of having lost almost everything that was bright and noteworthy about it to property developers and speculators. Nonetheless, the Dôme and La Coupole (see p.29) provide a focus for the area and it's still possible to find small streets and houses with the old *Gaz à tous les étages* signs as you head east towards Denfert.

The **Tour Montparnasse**, for all its fundamental ugliness, impresses by its sheer size, and a fast elevator to its 210-meter (689-ft.) top floor gives tremendous views over the city, particularly of the Eiffel Tower.

MOULIN ROUGE   19C4
82 boulevard de Clichy, 75018
Métro: Blanche
Although it's arguably the most spectacular of all the shows, with 1,000 costumes worn by 100 girls, singers, acrobats and actors, in fact all you get here is the top end of the standard Paris tourist cabaret – though, of course, with the added cachet of Toulouse-Lautrec's endorsement. Opened in 1885, the Moulin Rouge was once one of over 30 working mills in Montmartre, but is now the last such building in the city.

MUSÉE D'ART MODERNE   18A3
DE LA VILLE DE PARIS
Palais de Tokyo, 75016
Métro: Iéna
Often ignored in the rush to see the Louvre and the Beaubourg, the Musée d'Art Moderne is housed in the Palais de Tokyo, a superb example of pre-war architecture standing above the Seine and created for the 1937 Universal Exhibition. Main attractions include Raoul Dufy's magnificent 60-meter (197-ft.) by 10-meter (33-ft.) mural "La Fée Electricité," which was also created for the 1937 exhibition, and Matisse's "La Danse," but there is also a permanent collection running the gamut from the postimpressionists through to the expressionists, fauves and cubists, and leading through to abstractionism and *nouveau réalisme*. Don't miss the excellent collection of art-deco furniture, probably the best of its kind. The museum also presents first-class temporary exhibitions by 20th-century greats.

★★ MUSÉE DES   18C3
ARTS DÉCORATIFS
107 rue de Rivoli, 75001
Métro: Palais Royal
The best of all possible museums for lovers of art nouveau and art deco, this collection is housed on four floors of an obscure wing of the Louvre. Make sure you have a floor plan (available on arrival).

★★ MUSÉE DE CLUNY   19D2
6 place Paul-Painlevé, 75005
Métro: Cluny La Sorbonne
The Hôtel de Cluny, a Benedictine resting house dating from 1500, stands on and beside the oldest Roman ruins in Paris. Today it shelters a superb medieval collection as well as being home to a perfectly preserved set of 2nd-century Roman baths, the Thermes de Cluny. Don't miss the many fragments of church architecture, and the jewels and crowns collected by art buff Alexandre de Sommerand who bought the house in 1833. Also on display are six 15th-century tapestries woven near Aubusson.

ATELIERS
Although famous artists often seem to have managed in the unheated darkness of basements and garrets – Giacometti, Modigliani, Marc Chagall and Chaim Soutine, to name but a few – their preferred habitat is without doubt an *atelier*, or studio, with an abundance of north-facing windows.

Artists have perennially flocked to Paris, so the demand for *ateliers* has always been high. Most of the best are still inhabited (though some, like Delacroix's, have been converted into museums).

At the excellent Villa Seurat, near Montparnasse, you can see from the outside where the writers Henry Miller and Anaïs Nin, and the painters André Derain, Georges Braque and Salvador Dalí worked at their respective arts ■

HÔTELS PARTICULIERS

Throughout the 17th century, and to some extent during the 18th, competition was rife among the very wealthy to come up with the finest courtyard or most elegant interior, and the *hôtels particuliers* (private houses, often used later as embassies) reached heights never since matched.

Most were sold off and left to decay after the Revolution, but since the mid-1970s many have been restored.

Among those of particular note in the Marais area are: the Musée Carnavalet, at 23 rue de Sévigné; Hôtel de Sully, 62 rue St. Antoine; Hôtel de Sens, 1 rue du Figuier; Hôtel Guénégaud, a Mansart masterpiece; and Hôtel Salé, home to the Musée Picasso ∎

★★ MUSÉE DELACROIX   18C2
6 place de Furstemberg, 75006
Métro: Mabillon, St.-Germain-des-Prés
When visiting Delacroix's apartment and studio, be prepared to see where and how the painter lived and worked rather than his works, which are mostly in the Louvre across the river. That said, the museum is full of interesting artifacts and memorabilia, and a visit here is sure to be a pleasant one. The place de Furstemberg, with its beautiful magnolias and old-fashioned street lighting, is best seen in April and May when the square is in full flower.

★★ MUSÉE MARMOTTAN   20A2
2 rue Louis Boilly, 75016
Métro: La Muette
The Marmottan contains probably the best Monet collection anywhere, comprising 65 later works donated by his son and beautifully hung in the basement galleries. Other works include paintings by Renoir, Gauguin, Corot and Sisley, and memorabilia from Monet house. Upstairs there's a rarely visited Empire hoard (the actual Marmottan collection), which looks quite at home in this 19th-century town house.

MUSÉE NATIONAL D'ART MODERNE (MNAM)   21D2
Centre Georges Pompidou, 75004
Métro: Châtelet Les Halles, Rambuteau
Housed on the third and fourth floors of the Beaubourg (Pompidou Center – see p.25), the MNAM is the principal reason most people come here. A superbly presented chronological collection charts the progress of 20th-century art, from the fauves through cubism, Dada, surrealism, abstractionism, pop art and minimalism to conceptual art. The collection is one of the most complete for 20th-century art and rivals those in the museums of modern art in Washington and New York.

★★★ MUSÉE D'ORSAY   18C3
1 rue de Bellechasse, 75007
Métro: Solférino; RER: Musée d'Orsay
Built for the Universal Exhibition of 1900, the Musée d'Orsay was originally a hotel and railway station, and still has a fantastic *belle-époque* restaurant and ballroom, not to mention a tea room up by the old station clock that allows you to see right through its face. Converted in the mid-1980s into a museum to take some of the pressure off the overcrowded Jeu de Paume, it now contains arguably the best impressionist collection in the world, and includes many of the most famous pictures of all – there's almost a surfeit of works here by Monet, Manet, Cézanne, Renoir, van Gogh, Sisley and Degas. The collection also includes sculptures by Rodin, Camille Claudel and Maillol, and a wealth of other art, all related to the period 1848–1914.

★★ MUSÉE PICASSO   19E3
Hôtel Salé, 5 rue de Thorigny, 75003
Métro: Chemin Vert
Perhaps the best single Picasso collection anywhere, this museum contains a quarter of his own collection and embraces over 200 paintings, 150 sculptures and 1,500 drawings by the great artist. More than anything it reveals just how talented Picasso was at whatever he turned his hand to, and how interested he was in exploring the frontiers of contemporary art. After seeing his very earliest works here nobody could ever again say that Picasso couldn't

paint properly. The works are arranged chronologically and are displayed to good effect in this lovingly renovated *hôtel particulier*. It's impossible to take everything in during a single visit, so try to make time for more than one trip.

★★★ MUSÉE RODIN 18B2
Hôtel Biron, 77 rue de Varenne, 75007
Métro: Varenne

For just the magnificent gardens alone, the Musée Rodin is one of the foremost attractions of Paris. Used by the sculptor from 1908, the house was home to other notable contemporaries (Matisse, Cocteau and Isadora Duncan were also residents) before being turned into a museum following Rodin's death in 1917, by which time he was already a national hero. The exhibits are shown chronologically in large, airy rooms; you can see how the artist matured then lingered, and ponder on the awful tragedies of Camille Claudel's life as you see her works displayed alongside his. In the grounds you should take time to enjoy the wonderful rose gardens and see some of Rodin's largest and most important works.

Inside the Musée d'Orsay. The iron and glass rail terminus that was built on the site of the ruined Orsay Palace in the late 19th century now houses one of the finest collections of impressionist art in the world. You'll need at least a day to see all the exhibits

In a beautiful setting on the Ile de la Cité, the cathedral of Notre-Dame is one of the world's most harmonious religious edifices. Construction was begun in the mid-12th century under the reign of Louis VII on the site of a former Roman temple. The view across Paris from its towers amply repays the effort of the climb

★★★ NOTRE-DAME   19D2
Ile de la Cité
Métro: Cité; RER: St.-Michel, Notre-Dame

The undisputed importance of this magnificent cathedral, which has occupied a sacred site going back to Roman times, is shown by the fact that it is used as the point for measuring distances from Paris. Built gradually between 1163 and 1330, this Gothic masterpiece is 130 meters (426 ft.) long, with towers soaring to a height of 69 meters (226 ft.). It is far more imposing when it's completely hushed inside, so if you have the opportunity of being here at unusual hours, when it's empty or just nearly so, then do seize the moment. Also well worth the effort is the steep climb up the towers, which give you the closest possible view of 19th-century restorer Viollet-le-Duc's fantastic gargoyles, and a great panorama across the river and over the whole of Paris. The three famous rose windows, with their opulent stained glass, are another essential sight, though much of the glass is newer than it looks, as the windows had to be remade after World War II.

★★★ L'OPÉRA DE   20C3
PARIS GARNIER
place de l'Opéra, 75009
Métro: Opéra; RER: Auber

Once the largest theater in the world, the Opéra Garnier now focuses mainly on dance since the opening of the glass and steel Opéra Bastille at La Bastille. If possible, try to come for a performance if only to look at the Second Empire decoration and the stunning Chagall ceiling.

The **Opéra Bastille** (Métro: Bastille) was completed in 1989. It is now Paris's main venue for opera, with 3,000 seats.

★★★ L'ORANGERIE   18B3
place de la Concorde, 75001
Métro: Concorde
Paired elegantly with the Jeu de Paume on the other side of the Tuileries (see p.33), the Orangerie is now home to the Walter-Guillaume collection, covering the period from the impressionists to about 1920. There are some lovely Modigliani paintings, but nothing catches the eye as much as the spectacular series of eight "Water Lilies" by Monet.

★ PALAIS BOURBON   18B3
33 quai d'Orsay, 75007
Métro: Assemblée Nationale
The superb 18th-century facade of the Palais Bourbon hides the parliament of France, the Assemblée Nationale, where 577 elected deputies perform the daily business of government. The Palais is open to the public on Saturdays, except when the Assemblée is in session. There is a good view of it from the place de la Concorde across the river.

★★ PALAIS DE CHAILLOT   18A3
place du Trocadéro, 75016
Métro: Trocadéro
Housing four museums (Musée de la Marine, with model ships and navigational instruments, Musée de l'Homme, an amazing anthropological collection, Musée des Monuments Français, and Musée du Cinéma), as well as the Théâtre National Populaire and the Cinémathèque Française (best venue for old movies), the Palais de Chaillot was built, like the nearby Palais de Tokyo, for the 1937 Universal Exhibition. The space between its giant curved wings is one of the best places from which to see and then approach the Eiffel Tower. Indeed, the Palais and the Eiffel Tower are so complementary it's as if they were built together.

PALAIS DE L'ÉLYSÉE   18B3
55–57 rue du Faubourg St.-Honoré, 75008
Métro: Miromesnil
Home to the President of France since 1873 (Mitterrand spent 14 years here from 1981 to 1995 when the present incumbent Jacques Chirac took up office), the Palais de l'Élysée was originally built in 1718. It became the chic residence of Madame de Pompadour, Louis XV's mistress, in 1753. The Palais boasts the largest private garden in Paris. (Not open to the public.)

★ PALAIS DE JUSTICE   19D2
2 boulevard du Palais, 75001
Métro: Cité; RER: St.-Michel
One of the more unusual forms of entertainment in Paris is a trip to the central law courts (you know you're in the right place with *Liberté, Égalité, Fraternité* written everywhere). It's possible to see the way the building itself has been modified from its earliest function in Roman times, through its use as the dreaded Tribunal during the Revolution, to today's center of justice. The Première Chambre Civile, with its extravagant blue and gold decoration, is the room where hundreds of citizens were condemned to the guillotine.

★ PALAIS DU LUXEMBOURG   19C2
15 rue de Vaugirard, 75006
Métro: Odéon; RER: Luxembourg
Completed in 1631 and always of political importance, the Palais du Luxembourg has been used as a political prison, palace, and a headquarters of the Luftwaffe during World War II. Now it is home to the Senate and can only be visited by special arrangement on the first Sunday of the month. If you do get in, make sure you see Delacroix's extravagant paintings on the library ceiling.

Low reliefs and sculptures adorn the steps to the gardens of the Palais de Chaillot, from where there is a stunning view across the Seine towards the Eiffel Tower and the Champ de Mars

★★ PALAIS ROYAL 19C3

place du Palais Royal, 75001
Métro: Palais Royal
Not proving large enough for the mighty ego of Louis XIV, the Palais Royal was eventually taken over by the foppish Philippe d'Orléans, who had not only married Louis XIV's great-granddaughter but was also one of the people who voted during the Revolution to have his cousin King Louis XVI guillotined. Under Philippe in the late 18th century

---

WALK

EXPLORING THE RIVE DROITE

From place de la Concorde head east down the rue de Rivoli to the courtyard of the Palais Royal – now enlivened with modern sculpture – via a discreet archway.

Walk the length of the garden, bordered by stores and restaurants (including le Grand Véfour, a famous restaurant with period decor once frequented by Victor Hugo and Napoléon Bonaparte, among others), and

exit to the rue des Petits Champs.

Turn left, turning right eventually into avenue de l'Opéra, an elegant street lined with prestigious stores.

At place de l'Opéra turn left into rue de la Paix, more upmarket stores, to reach place Vendôme, a perfectly proportioned 17th-century square whose graceful buildings house jewelers, perfumiers, banks, and the Ritz hotel.

Return via rue de Castiglione to the rue de Rivoli ∎

---

the palace and its surroundings became the place to be seen in – and, being off-limits to the police, a hotbed of revolutionary ideas. Now home to the Ministry of Culture, the Palais Royal has a formal garden that is public, shaded, and a popular place in the summer.

★ PANTHÉON 19D1

place du Panthéon, 75005
RER line B: Luxembourg
Built in the form of a Greek cross, the 18th-century Panthéon

houses the remains of illustrious men and women from all walks of life, such as Voltaire, Rousseau, Victor Hugo, Jean Jaurès and Marie Curie. Lying at the heart of the university district, the building's austerity is partly counterbalanced by the atmosphere of frivolous youth to be seen on the square and in the neighboring streets.

PARC ASTÉRIX 5C4

RER line B3: Roissy
A lively summer outing for kids – obviously much more so if they are familiar with the Goscinny and Uderzo cartoon characters of Astérix and Obélix. The theme park, with the five "worlds" that make it up, is a popular attraction, situated 38 kilometers (24 mi.) northeast of Paris and easily accessible by shuttle bus from Roissy station on RER line B3.

★★ PARC DE LA VILLETTE 21D4

30 avenue Corentin-Cariou, 75019
Métro: Porte de la Villette, Porte de Pantin
All but one of the major slaughterhouses on this site were torn down in 1979 to make way for one of the most ambitious cultural projects in Paris, covering some 55 hectares (135 acres). The Parc de la Villette's main attractions today are the Cité des Sciences et de l'Industrie, with its spectacular interactive displays of science and technology, and the neighboring Géode, the famous spherical movie theater with its 1000-square meter (10,764-sq. ft.) cinema screen.

★★★ PÈRE LACHAISE 21E2

Métro: Philippe-Auguste
Cemeteries may not normally attract you but a visit to the Cimetière du Père Lachaise could prove an exception. Apart from the wealth of famous people interred

CINEMA
Cinema was invented here in 1895, and over a century later Paris is still the world capital of movies.

Many of those on release come from Hollywood ("VO" means the movie is in the original language with French sub-titles), but Paris also specializes in art-house movies, French movies, European classics, new movies from around the world, and forgotten Hollywood black-and-white masterpieces.

It's estimated that at any time of the day or night there's a choice of 300 different movies on show some-where in the city – look out for the latest posters in café windows ∎

here (Edith Piaf, Jim Morrison, Simone Signoret, Max Ernst and Amadeo Modigliani, to name a few), there's an extraordinary luxury of revealing detail. Purchase the absolutely essential plan at whichever entrance you use and wander the slopes and paths of this most extraordinary of burial grounds. Fantastic sculpture, decrepit sepulchers, and fresh flowers on the same graves every day make the place more poignant than bleak.

★★ PIGALLE   *21C3*
Métro: Pigalle
Heart of Montmartre nightlife and the Paris sex trade, the Pigalle district was popularized by Renoir and Toulouse-Lautrec, who came here scouting for models at the end of the 19th century. Don't let this reputation dissuade you from a visit: the area also offers some of the best theaters, bars and nightclubs in Paris.

PLACE DU CHÂTELET   *19D3*
75001
Métro: Châtelet
Famous primarily for its two massive, identical, rival theaters, the place du Châtelet is now a little soulless, perhaps because of its size and the relentless stream of traffic across the square. On the west side is the Théâtre Musical, which puts on opera and classical music, while the Théâtre de la Ville across the way preserves Sarah Bernhardt's dressing room and specializes in contemporary French dance and new theater.

★★ PLACE DE LA CONCORDE   *18B3*
75008
Métro: Concorde
Metamorphosing from the place Louis XV to the place de la Révolution in 1793, the place de la Concorde was once again renamed after the Terror ended in 1795. Famous for being the scene where over a thousand heads rolled, including those of Louis XVI, his hapless spouse Marie-Antoinette, and their enemy Danton, the square is now a mass of traffic zooming around the exotic Egyptian Obélisque, Paris' most ancient monument, carved in 1250 BC and given to France in 1829.

BRIDGES

It won't be long after you arrive in Paris that you'll find yourself walking across the Seine on one of the city's 36 bridges (the newest one, the Pont Charles de Gaulle, was completed in 1994).

Always popular with lovers is the romantic planked footbridge, the Pont des Arts, not least because of the views it offers upriver to the Ile de la Cité.

The Pont Neuf, Paris's oldest bridge, is well liked, and the Pont Alexandre III, typifying the *belle époque*, has many fans too.

Farther down-river the Pont de Bir-Hakeim, connecting the 15th and 16th *arrondissements*, has a lower level for pedestrians and vehicles, and an upper level, supported by art-nouveau pillars that carries the Métro across the Seine ∎

★ PLACE VENDÔME   *18C3*
75001
Métro: Opéra, Tuileries
The height of Parisian chic, and home to jewelry shops and the Ritz hotel, the place Vendôme has been a fashionable place to live since it was completed at the end of the 17th century. Franz Mesmer practiced his successful new technique of mesmerism at No. 16 in the 18th century, and Chopin died at No. 12 in 1849, then being laid to rest at the Cimetière du Père Lachaise (see p.42). If you can afford to stay in the *place* you'll find it a well-located square in a beautiful area.

PONT ALEXANDRE III   *18B3*
Métro: Invalides
Built for the Universal Exhibition of 1900, the Pont Alexandre III sports gilt and bronze cupids and typifies everything that is meant by the *belle époque*. The bridge was symbolic of an alliance between Russia and France, and has always been popular with Parisians and visitors. Try to see it from the Left Bank at night when it's fully lit, providing a tremendous foreground for the glowing roof of the Grand Palais across the river.

★★★ PONT NEUF   *19C2*
Métro: Pont Neuf
Connecting the Ile de la Cité with both banks of the Seine, Paris's oldest and most-famous bridge, the Pont Neuf, was opened in 1607 by Henri IV who galloped across it on his best horse (this event is commemorated by an equestrian statue of him in the middle of the bridge). At the time, the bridge was considered controversial for not having houses built along it. Equally controversial was the wrapping of the bridge in gauze by Bulgarian artist Christo in 1985; look out for postcards of just how strange the bridge really looked at the time.

★★ QUARTIER LATIN, LE   *21C2*
Métro: St.-Michel
Known as the Latin Quarter since the founding of the Sorbonne in 1253, when students and masters alike spoke only Latin, the area is still lively, relaxed and unbusinesslike as ever. At the heart of the Quarter, which extends north to the St.-Séverin and Maubert areas and south to the rue Mouffetard, is the boulevard St.-Michel, bustling with café terraces, shops and ethnic eateries. Boasting more bookshops, art galleries and schools than the rest of Paris put together, the Latin Quarter remains the one area where people really do sit in cafés all day putting the world to rights. Try not to spend too much time among the over-popular streets and wealth of Greek fast-food restaurants around the rue de la Huchette; instead, drift further east into the smaller side streets with their specialist shops and old-fashioned atmosphere.

★ RUE DU BAC *18C2*
75006
Métro: rue du Bac
Heavily laden with celebrated connections, the rue du Bac was once the road to the ferry across to the Louvre (*bac* is French for ferry) before the Pont Royal was built. Running south from the river and across boulevard St.-Germain, the road ends at the spectacular Au Bon Marché department store. Note the Galerie Maeght at No. 46. Maeght launched many an impoverished artist on the road to fortune, and made a small fortune himself by having unlimited access to Alberto Giacometti's output right up to his own death in 1963. For smart (but expensive) shopping go south of boulevard St.-Germain.

★ RUE DE RIVOLI *18C3*
75001
Métro: Louvre Rivoli
Built to celebrate yet another Napoleonic victory, the rue de Rivoli now takes advantage of its prime location opposite the Louvre, the Musée des Arts Décoratifs, the Musée des Arts de la Mode, and the Tuileries garden to shelter tourist shops and a small clutch of hotels. Smith's, the English bookshop, is here, with a fine tearoom at the back, but doesn't rival the great Galignani bookstore at No. 224, which has an excellent selection of English and American books.

★ RUE ST.-HONORÉ *18C3*
75001
Métro: Palais Royal
The rue St.-Honoré, lined with smart stores, has an unmistakable air of class. It is very old: Jeanne d'Arc was wounded here, Molière was born here, and the condemned Marie-Antoinette rode along here on her way to the guillotine. For top-quality (but expensive) antiques go to the Louvre des Antiquaires. Farther along, where the street becomes du Faubourg, you'll find one of the greatest concentrations of stores selling luxurious clothes.

One of the city's most romantic bridges is Pont Alexandre III, a gift from the tsar of Russia in 1900. The roof of the Grand Palais can be seen in the background

RUE ST.-JACQUES   19C1
Métro: St.-Jacques
The rue St.-Jacques is proud of its status as Paris' first street, once the starting point for pilgrims heading south to the popular shrine of St.-Jacques de Compostelle (Santiago de Compostela). The pilgrims wore the saint's symbol, a scallop shell, which is why the French for scallop is *coquille St.-Jacques.*

★★★ SACRÉ-CŒUR,   19D4
BASILIQUE DU
Montmartre, 75018
Métro: Anvers, then funicular
Built by subscription over a 35-year period to atone for the 58,000 dead in the Franco-Prussian War (1870–71), this marble Byzantine basilica was completed in the early years of the 20th century. (Ironically, the two monuments that most people name first to symbolize Paris – the Eiffel Tower and Sacré-Cœur – are barely a hundred years old.)

After the steep climb from the streets of Montmartre to Sacré-Cœur you may not feel like tackling the extra 90 meters (295 ft.) up to the dome; but the panorama from the top is well worth it, and the interior of the church can be seen as you come back down. The steps outside the building provide the city's finest views of the setting sun.

★★ ST.-GERMAIN-   20C2
DES-PRÉS
75006
Métro: St.-Germain-des-Prés
Heart of the literary intelligentsia, St.-Germain-des-Prés is centered on its *boulevard*, with narrower streets and a more eclectic way of life towards the north and wider, smarter streets south of it. Little has changed: properties have been maintained instead of being allowed to decay before being restored, as has happened so often in the Marais.

★★ SAINTE-CHAPELLE   19D2
boulevard du Palais, 75004
Métro: Cité; RER: St.-Michel
Completed in 1248, the Sainte-Chapelle used revolutionary engineering ideas to build a tall spire unsupported by flying buttresses. The royal chapel of Saint Louis (Louis IX) still stands, and the simply astonishing stained-glass windows are what draw the crowds today, given its discreet location hidden behind the Palais de Justice. Difficult to take in on even a prolonged visit, there are over a thousand biblical scenes depicted here, created using some of the finest stained glass you'll ever see. The best views are from the upper chapel reached by a steep staircase.

SEINE, LA/   18A3
BATEAUX-MOUCHES
Métro: Alma Marceau, Bir-Hakeim, Trocadéro, Cité
As you explore the sights of Paris you'll keep greeting the Seine. Stroll along some of the *quais* as

---

WALK

EXPLORING THE RIVE GAUCHE
Start at the 12th-century church of St.-Germain-des-Prés, Paris' oldest church, with several notable tombs. On the corner with rue de l'Abbaye is a Picasso sculpture, "Homage to Apollinaire," a tribute to his friend the poet Guillaume Apollinaire, who held court in the nearby Café de Flore. Head east towards the 16th-century Palais Abbatial and turn left into rue de Furstemberg: **this tiny square with its old-fashioned lamps and shady trees was built in 1699 and is often used as a movie set. Follow the rue Cardinale and cross the boulevard Saint-Germain to the Marché Saint-Germain, which dates from 1818 and is one of the few covered markets left in the city. On the other side of the market walk through to St. Sulpice, a classical 17th-century church. From place St.-Sulpice head north to rejoin boulevard St.-Germain-des-Prés ∎**

well as getting onto the river itself. *Bateaux-mouches* – sightseeing boats – can be boarded at the Pont de l'Alma; in spite of their touristy feel, they give a completely different view of the city (which almost looks its best from the water). Aboard a *bateau-mouche* you can have a meal and learn something about the city from the multilingual commentary. Smaller craft set off from the Ile de la Cité.

★ SORBONNE, LA 19C2
45–47 rue des Écoles, 75005
Métro: Cluny la Sorbonne
Founded in 1253 for 16 poor theology students by Robert de Sorbon, confessor to Saint Louis, the Sorbonne was the epitome of free academia in the sense that the state had no right to intervene in university affairs, and indeed did not until the student riots of 1968. The Sorbonne continues to show a healthy disrespect for the establishment that many of its students go on to join.

Although reconstructed under the chancellorship of Cardinal Richelieu in the 17th century, most of the Sorbonne buildings used today date from the 19th century. However, the traditional spirit still pervades the university and its surroundings, centering on boulevard St.-Michel.

The gleaming white basilica of Sacré-Cœur was constructed as an act of repentance after the Franco-Prussian War. Designed in late 19th-century taste by Paul Abadie, work was finally completed in 1910

With its fountains and carp pond, the Renaissance château of Fontainebleau is one of the most delightful in France. It became a favorite retreat of Napoléon, who in 1814 signed his abdication here

TATI 19D4
boulevard de Rochechouart, 75010
Métro: Barbès-Rochechouart
Based on profoundly unbusinesslike principles (no credit, cash on delivery to its suppliers, zero debt and near-zero margins), Tati is one of the great Paris success stories. Loathed intensely by the high-fashion industry and small department stores alike, Tati provides up-to-the-minute fashion at the cheapest possible cost and aims to give the best quality for the best price. When you see people leaving the outlet on rue de Rennes with full Yves St. Laurent bags it makes you wonder who's fooling who.

There has to be a disadvantage at these prices and it's mainly the crowds, the negligible service (they assume you know what you want), and the surfeit of choice in a too-small area. But you can be sure at Tati of finding today's fashion at a tenth of the price

charged anywhere else – just avoid the place on Saturday.

★★ TROCADÉRO 18A3
75016
Métro: Trocadéro
Although the Palais de Chaillot grabs most of the tourist attention, the place du Trocadéro is interesting in its own right, not least because of the view across the fountain and through the wings of the Chaillot to the Eiffel Tower. The Trocadéro forms the hub of a whole network of popular, smart cafés and restaurants, so don't be put off by the somber Cimetière de Passy on the west side of the *place*.

★★★ TUILERIES, 18C3
JARDIN DES
Métro: Tuileries
Famous for decades as one of the best places in Paris to be seen taking a stroll, the garden has fallen into neglect since World War II. It is now undergoing major restoration of

(Compare this to Milan, whose cathedral is still not complete after 700 years.) The flying buttresses support the widest nave in France, and the 176 stained-glass windows (covering nearly an acre) are among the finest in the world; they all date from the 13th century or earlier. Visit by automobile, by train from Montparnasse, or by bus tour from Paris.

★ DISNEYLAND PARIS 5C4
77777 Marne la Vallée
Getting there: By automobile: take the A4, E50. By train: RER line A4 to Marne-la-Vallée/Chessy
Some 32 kilometers (20 mi.) east of Paris lies one of the most ambitious projects ever undertaken in France, eventually planned to be nearly a fifth the size of Paris and to include golf courses, film studios, and the giant theme park itself.

All of the traditional Disney features can be found here: the Magic Kingdom, with its cast of Disney characters; Fantasyland, where Disney dreams come true; Adventureland, with Aladdin's Cave and the Temple of Doom; and Discoveryland, the one concession to French culture, where Jules Verne's visions of the future are shown in 360° circle-vision. On-site accommodations are provided by a number of Disney hotels, each designed in an American regional style, plus a self-catering "ranch" of mobile homes and campgrounds.

★★ FONTAINEBLEAU, 7C4
CHÂTEAU DE
77300 Fontainebleau
Getting there: By automobile: take the N7 from Porte d'Italie. By train: from the Gare de Lyon
Some 65 kilometers (40 mi.) southeast of Paris lies the small town, magnificent château (second only to Versailles) and

such a nature that it will be the best part of 30 years before the newly planted trees have their intended effect. Together with the renovation of the Louvre in the 1990s, certain improvements, from the quality of the landscaping to a general cleanup of the whole area, are becoming visible. Despite this, the Jardin remains lovely with statues by Maillol and Rodin, and the pleasing octagonal basin.

★★ CHARTRES 4C4
Getting there: By train: from Gare Montparnasse to Chartres
The medieval city of Chartres is 85 kilometers (53 mi.) southwest of Paris, and is dominated by its stunning cathedral. Built originally to house the Virgin Mary's tunic (a relic given to Chartres in the 9th century), the original church burned down spectacularly in 1194 while leaving the precious tunic miraculously untouched. A new cathedral was completed on the same site in just 25 years.

INSPIRING VERSAILLES

Louis XIV's grand plan to transform Versailles from a modest hunting lodge into the largest palace in Europe was inadvertently inspired by his finance minister Nicholas Fouquet who built a magnificent château for himself at Vaux-le-Vicomte, southeast of Paris.

Fouquet had challenged the royal architect Louis Le Vau and the decorator Charles Le Brun to create the most sumptuous palace possible – which they duly did, aided by the famous landscape gardener Andre Le Nôtre. But Fouquet's delight with his new palace was short-lived, since the king was so enraged by this blatant piece of one-upmanship that Fouquet was arrested and jailed for life on embezzlement charges.

Louis XIV then recruited the same team to build him something similar – only a hundred times bigger ■

vast forest of Fontainebleau. The château was originally built as a hunting lodge before being converted into a royal residence by François I in the 16th century. It is full of marvelous Renaissance details, many of which were only discovered in the 19th century behind other paintings. Don't miss the fabulous Salle de Bal (ballroom) or Napoléon's private apartments. The forest provides great cycling, rock climbing (easily the closest to Paris) and walking.

★★ MALMAISON, CHÂTEAU DE

avenue du Château de Malmaison, 92500 Rueil-Malmaison
Getting there: By automobile: take the N13 from la Défense. By train: RER line A to la Défense. By bus: 158A
This is the château made famous by Joséphine, Napoléon's young bride. Behind its rather modest exterior lies one of the best-preserved and luxurious Empire houses. Although more her house than his (exclusively so after their divorce in 1809), there are many signs of Napoléon's sense of grandeur, including the silk-striped walls and ceilings, and his famous desk with its array of secret drawers. Joséphine's own apartments are also magnificent and in their own right merit the excursion out to Rueil-Malmaison.

★★★ VERSAILLES/   5C4 GRAND ET PETIT TRIANONS

Getting there: By train: RER line C5 to Versailles-Rive Gauche
A château with a town attached to it rather than the other way around, Versailles exists through the will of one man, Louis XIV. The "Sun King's" massive ego created a seat of power that even now overawes visitors with its sheer scale and grandeur.

The garden frontage of the palace is 570 meters (1,870 ft.) long, easily the largest in Europe, and provides a fitting focus to the perfection of the 100-hectare (247-acre) gardens. Don't miss the opportunity of seeing the fabulous royal apartments (expect to wait in line), including the most-famous room of all, the Hall of Mirrors. Today it's hard to appreciate the wonder that these 17 great mirrors once inspired, but even so the room itself is so impressive that most visitors have their breath taken away.

So big was the estate that there was even room for two weekend retreats, the Grand and Petit Trianons, to be built within the grounds. The Grand Trianon was the refuge of the Sun King himself, who would disappear here for a bit of peace and quiet with a favored mistress. The Petit Trianon, designed and built for Madame du Barry, the mistress of Louis XV, found far greater fame when it was taken over by Marie-Antoinette, who treated the whole area as her private hamlet and returned to the so-called "simple life" here.

★ VINCENNES,   21E1 CHÂTEAU DE

Métro: Porte Dorée, Château de Vincennes
It's difficult now to imagine the one-legged General Daumesnil refusing to surrender the château by uttering the immortal words: "I'll give you back the castle when you return my leg!" (lost five years earlier in the Battle of Wagram). The medieval château stands on the north side of the Bois de Vincennes. Its chapel and dungeons are particularly interesting, and the whole place provides a rarely visited contrast to the infinitely more extravagant Versailles on the other side of the city. Spare a thought for Mata Hari, executed here in 1917.

NORMANDY

Idyllic rural scenes of orchards and placid meadows contrast poignantly with reminders of war in the townscapes of Normandy

CALENDAR OF EVENTS

APRIL 30 TO MAY 1 – Rouen: **International Motor Boat Race** takes place over 24 hours around the Ilê Lacroix.

MAY – Le Mont-St.-Michel: **Spring Festival of Saint Michael.**

WHIT SUNDAY/ MONDAY – Honfleur: **Seamen's Festival** with a blessing of the sea and the seamen's pilgrimage.

MAY 30 – Rouen: Sunday nearest to May 30 is the **Jeanne d'Arc Festival.**

JUNE 6 – Ste.-Mere-Église and Ste.-Marie-du-Mont: **commemoration of June 5 and 6, 1944. D-Day June 6, 1944** commemoration at Utah Beach.

MID-JULY – Château de Balleroy: **International Hot-Air Balloon Meeting.**

JULY – Le Havre: **International Regatta.**

JULY AND AUGUST – Sées: *son et lumière* (sound-and-light show) in the cathedral ■

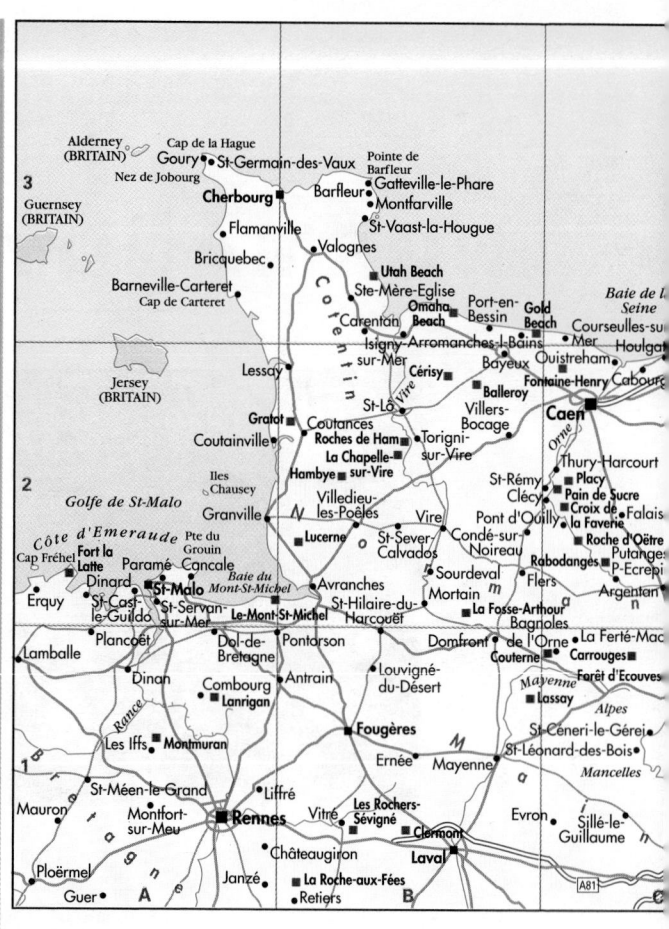

NORMANDY

Normandy is no stranger to the sound of battle. Its natives descend from the fierce Vikings – Norsemen (Normans) – who invaded via the Seine during the 9th century and established an authoritarian but civilized culture in this prosperous fertile region. Within two centuries the vigorous Normans had extended their rule throughout England under William the Conqueror, exporting their administrative and architectural knowledge (abbeys, churches, manors and castles proliferated), and entwining English and French destinies for many years. In 1944

Normandy witnessed another great conflict as the Allies landed on D-Day. Veterans revisit the battlefields, while war museums capture the imagination of younger generations.

Happily, Normandy has more to offer than history lessons. Its cuisine is rich with cream, apples, cheese and shellfish; its timber-framed, slate-roofed buildings are set amid lush woodland; and its breezy coastline beckons with long beaches and bright chalk. Art lovers will quickly recognize the landscapes that inspired the **impressionists**, especially Bonnard at Honfleur and Monet in Giverny; fine collections can be

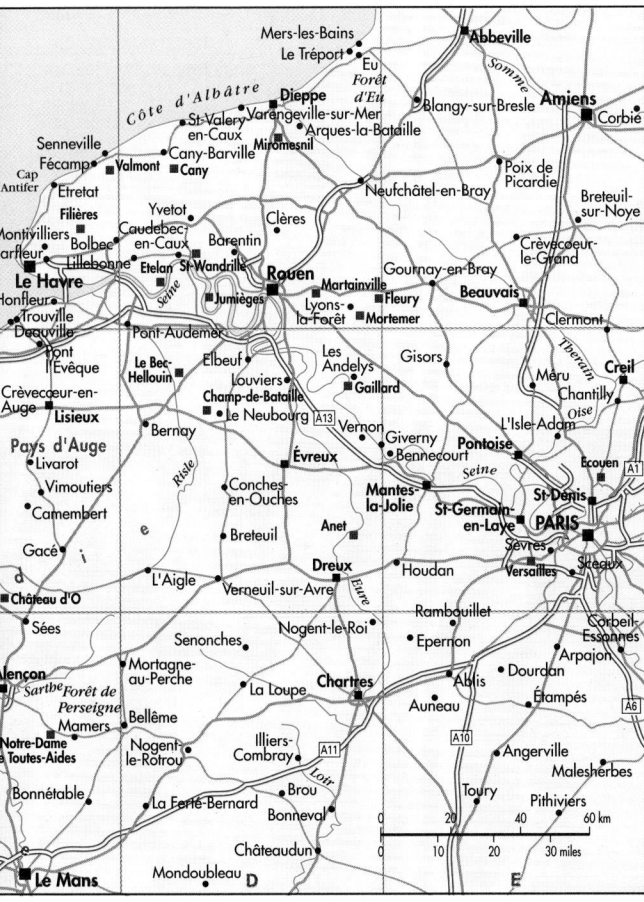

SUNDAY NEAREST JULY 15 – Lisieux: consecration of the Basilica.

LAST WEEKEND IN AUGUST – Cabourg: historical "William the Conqueror" procession.

LAST SUNDAY IN AUGUST – Deauville: **Grand Prix; polo championship; horse racing.**

EARLY SEPTEMBER – Deauville: **American Film Festival.**

LAST SUNDAY IN SEPTEMBER – Lisieux – **Sainte Thérèse Festival;** procession with shrine of Sainte Thérèse. Caudebec-en-Caux: **Cider Festival** (biennial – even years). Le Mont-St.-Michel: **Feast of Saint Michael.**

LAST SUNDAY IN NOVEMBER – Essay: **White Pudding (Boudin Blanc) Fair.**

MID-DECEMBER – Sées: **Turkey Fair** ■

seen in Rouen, Le Havre and Caen. Equine culture thrives at the national stud farms of St.-Lô and Haras du Pin, with annual bloodstock sales and race meetings. The seaside bears the formal stamp of the 19th century: Napoléon III was a great devotee of the Norman riviera. Older coastal towns like **Dieppe** and **Honfleur** generally have a more relaxing air than smart, self-conscious resorts like **Deauville** or **Cabourg.** Attracted by its cliffs and beaches, Parisians flood into Normandy, their nearest region of coast, all summer long, and for off-season weekend breaks too.

***
★★★ HIGHLIGHTS

Les Andelys and Château Gaillard (➤55)
Bayeux Tapestry (➤57)
Caen (➤58)
Coutances cathedral (➤60)
D-Day beaches (➤60)
Etretat and the Côte d'Albâtre (➤61, 59)
Giverny, Monet's house (➤62)
Jumièges (➤63)
Le Mont-St.-Michel (➤68)
Pays d'Auge (➤69)
Rouen (➤69)

The site of Les Andelys is an impressive one, commanding the Seine Valley and the old highway between Paris and Rouen. The ruins of the medieval stronghold of Château Gaillard, built by Richard the Lionheart, make a pleasant place to explore

Normandy is large and very diverse. **Haute** (upper, or eastern) **Normandy**, where most of the region's heavy industry is based, is bordered by the Seine river. Traditional crafts such as metal-working and lace making survive in the older towns. **Basse** (lower) **Normandy** is less wealthy and more rural, to some extent resembling the landscape of Brittany to the west.

Normandy's two main towns are **Caen** and **Rouen**, with ports at Cherbourg, Le Havre and Dieppe. Tourist interest is liberally scattered the length and breadth of Normandy; the area is ideal for exploring by automobile or bicycle. Most of the coast attracts visitors: the white cliffs of the **Côte d'Albâtre**, the D-Day beaches, the craggy headlands of the **Cotentin**, and the marsh and mud flats around Le Mont-St.-Michel. Inland, there's the seductive **Pays d'Auge**, with its farmland and manor houses, the **Suisse Normande**, perfect for activity breaks, the serpentine

valley of the Seine, and the rolling forests of the Perche.

★ ALENÇON 53C1

Now occupied with light industry, agricultural produce and Percheron horses, Alençon was once renowned for lace making. From the mid-17th century the town's needlework was much in demand at court, and the tradition still continues at the lace school. Fine samples can be seen in the Musée de la Dentelle and the Musée des Beaux-Arts et de la Dentelle. In 1944 the French 2nd Division took the town in the final fortnight of the Battle of Normandy; a new museum has displays commemorating the struggle. Alençon's Flamboyant church of Notre-Dame merits a visit; other noteworthy buildings include the 15th-century Maison d'Ozé (now the tourist office) and the glass-domed grain market. The medieval château seen from place Foch, once utilized by the Gestapo, now serves as a prison.

★★★ ANDELYS, LES 53D2

The ruins of Château Gaillard overshadow the adjacent Seine towns of Petit and Grand Andely. Grand Andely, once the site of a 6th-century monastery, is both older and larger. Petit Andely provides mooring places for pleasure craft. The château upstream attracts most attention, though. Rapidly built by Richard the Lionheart in 1196–7 ("See my fine yearling," he boasted on its completion), it created a humiliating obstacle to the French king's advance along the river to Rouen. Yet in 1204 it was stormed, and later mostly demolished. Today the remains can be explored.

★★ ANET, CHÂTEAU D' 53D2

Less than half the original lordly château is still standing, but Anet remains a tour de force. For many years it was the home of Diane de Poitiers, mistress of Henri II, who exerted great influence at court and held her sovereign in thrall throughout his life, though 20 years his senior. When Henri died and his widow evicted her from the Château de Chenonceau (see p.105), Diane returned to Anet, where representations of the goddess Diana flattered its *patronne*. Her funerary chapel reveals her quasi-royal status.

ARGENTAN 52C2

Like Alençon, Argentan was once a lace town (it even has exclusive rights to a stitch known as *point d'Argentan*). Similarly, it was badly damaged in the Battle of Normandy. Its main interest for visitors is its association with Thomas à Becket, whose assassins originated from here. King Henry II of England heard of the dread deed in the local fortress (now the law courts). Argentan's principal church, St.-Germain, has a few fine Flamboyant features that survived the fighting of 1944.

ARQUES-LA-BATAILLE 53D3

A ruined fortress on a spur above the confluence of the Béthune and Varenne valleys is the dominant feature of this town. The defenses date from the 11th century and were once besieged by William the Conqueror. The battle referred to in the name recalls the Wars of Religion. In 1589 some 7,000 Protestant soldiers led by the future Henri IV made a ferocious stand within the château against 30,000 Catholic Leaguers, who retreated in disarray. A chapel in Notre-Dame church commemorates the famous battle.

LACE MAKING

The lace made in Alençon is known as needlepoint lace, a complex and laborious art that takes 8 years to master.

Alençon's lace industry was promoted by Louis XIV's finance minister in 1665 in an attempt to stem the importation of Venetian lace and add revenue to the French coffers.

In the 18th century a quicker technique using flower, leaf or fruit designs replaced the original point style.

At the École Dentellière in Alençon you can watch artisans demonstrating their lace-making skills ■

NORMANDY

CAP DE CARTERET

The dunes north of the Cap de Carteret are reached by a breezy walk along the *sentier des douaniers* (the old customs-officers' path) north of Carteret beach. Take care around the headland, where the path narrows past lichen-covered cliffs and the site of an 18th-century gun battery.

Once around the rocky promontory you will eventually reach Carteret's second beach, the Plage de la Vieille Église (unsupervised, and with dangerous offshore currents), which is backed by dunes.

Naturalists will be in their element here: this part of the Cotentin peninsula is famous for a profusion of coastal plants, birds and insects ∎

ARROMANCHES-LES-BAINS   52B3

Arromanches is a low-key seaside resort with an unexceptional beach. But it had a crucial role in the daring wartime operation to install two artificial "Mulberry" harbors on the exposed Norman coastline to shelter the Allied landing fleets. Molded concrete barges, hidden in England beneath the River Thames, were towed across the Channel and sunk in the seabed in a protective semicircle around the beach. Floating steel pontoons and piers were added to allow shore access in any tide. Requiring a huge input of resources and manpower, the project was kept secret from the Germans right up until D-Day, as they expected an attack on a major port rather than these peaceful beaches. Soon after construction began a violent storm damaged the Mulberries at Arromanches and Omaha Beach; Omaha's Mulberry was abandoned but the one at Arromanches was repaired. You can still see some of the wave-worn caissons, which appear as islets just offshore. The Musée du Débarquement on the waterfront shows models, photographs and memorabilia of the landing operations.

AVRANCHES   52B2

This little town has a grandstand view of the famous abbey across the tidal mud flats of the bay of Le Mont-St.-Michel. It is best seen from the attractive botanic gardens, once the site of a monastery, or from the *plate-forme* in place Daniel-Huet, where King Henry II of England did public penance for the murder of Thomas à Becket. The local museum in the former bishop's palace recounts some of the town's considerable history, and has a splendid collection of

illuminated manuscripts from Le Mont-St.-Michel. In the Middle Ages Avranches was a great religious center and place of learning. Aubert, its 8th-century bishop, at first doubted Saint Michael's visionary commands to found an chapel on the rock in the bay, but the archangel reappeared and made his point by jabbing a finger into Aubert's head; you can see the doubting bishop's skull, complete with hole, in the church of St.-Gervais. In 1944 Avranches, like many Norman towns, saw fierce fighting. Southeast of the town a monument commemorates General Patton's decisive American offensive staged from here, the break-out towards neighboring Brittany.

BAGNOLES DE L'ORNE   52C1

One of France's biggest spas, Bagnoles has a leisurely if somewhat elderly atmosphere. Its entertainment scene mostly revolves around the casino, the lakefront gardens, concerts, and other cultural events. The surrounding Forêt des Andaines offers attractive walks and drives, the Château de Couterne, and a medieval watchtower called the Tour de Bonvouloir.

★ BALLEROY, CHÂTEAU DE   52B2

The austere facade of this 17th-century building belies an ornate and eccentric interior, with portraits of Wellington and Napoléon, silk hangings, and the signs of the zodiac on the drawing-room ceiling. The château was owned by the de Choisy family until it passed into the hands of a flamboyant American publishing tycoon, Malcolm Forbes, whose passion for hot-air ballooning is apparent in a fascinating museum housed in the stable. The 11th-century abbey of Cérisy-la-Forêt lies to the west.

The cathedral of Notre-Dame at Bayeux is a harmonious blend of styles. Its flying buttresses date from the 13th century, and the interior is well worth exploring

THE BAYEUX TAPESTRY

Housed in an 18th-century seminary in rue de Nesmond, the amazing, historic "Tapisserie de la Reine Mathilde" measures over 70 meters (230 ft.) long, but is only half a meter (19 in.) high.

The tapestry, worked in wool on linen, is believed to be Saxon work commissioned in England soon after the Norman Conquest. It depicts not only the battle of 1066, but also the clothes, armor and lifestyle of the period.

Before seeing the real thing, take advantage of the audiovisuals and look at the reproduction. The audiotape commentary (in English) explains the historical background ■

BARFLEUR   *52B3*

Now a pleasant, workaday fishing village, Barfleur was an important port in William the Conqueror's time. In 1120 Henry I's son was shipwrecked nearby and drowned with 300 Norman nobles, and in 1194 Richard the Lionheart sailed to England from here for his coronation. The lighthouse is one of the tallest in France, with a panoramic view from the top.

BARNEVILLE-CARTERET   *52A3*

This is a popular resort, its port sheltered on an inlet. Nearby on the main beach of Barneville-Plage families sunbathe among dunes or against the sea wall, but Carteret's beaches can have treacherous currents. The coastal path makes a good walk (see p.56). Catamarans make regular excursions to the Channel Isles from the port. Barneville's church has interesting carvings.

BAYEUX   *52B2*

Even without its great treasure – the famous **tapestry** ★★★ – Bayeux is a town worth seeing. Many of its old stone or timber-framed houses have been restored. The elegant cathedral has flying buttresses, soaring spires, and an interior full of interest; the chapter house is especially fine. Bayeux's Musée Mémorial de la Bataille de Normandie is one of the most comprehensive of all Normandy's war museums.

BOCAGE, LE   *52B2*

The word *bocage* denotes a type of lightly wooded, managed farmland found in western France, but most typically around St.-Lô south of the Bessin. Villages, orchards and cattle pastures typify the landscape, and fields are divided by a dense network of ancient hedgerows on the top of earth banks.

NORMANDY

GUILLAUME LE CONQUÉRANT and 1066

Making sense of the most-famous battle in English history involves wading through much historical propaganda, both Norman and English.

When William became duke of Normandy, his illegitimate birth raised objections. Impressing the English king, Edward the Confessor (who was largely Norman in background and sympathy), he was declared his successor.

On Edward's death, however, Earl Harold of Wessex assumed the throne. In Norman eyes this made him a usurper and perjurer, since he had sworn loyalty to William ∎

Today a busy port, Cherbourg was the terminal for an undersea fuel supply pipeline from England in World War II, and much heavy equipment was landed here during the Battle of Normandy

CABOURG   *52C2*

This large, elegant resort centers on the Grand Hôtel, an Italianate building where Marcel Proust stayed while writing his novel "A l'Ombre des Jeunes Filles en Fleurs" ("Within a Budding Grove"). In season, the beach area is pleasantly busy.

★★★ CAEN   *52C2*

Heavily bombarded during the Battle of Normandy, William the Conqueror's capital was reduced to rubble after two months of fighting. Caen steadily repaired its damage and today is a lively town with good shops, a university and various industrial interests. Major sights include the remnants of William's castle, a pair of abbeys, the church of St.-Pierre, and an ambitious war memorial and museum dedicated to peace, le Mémorial. The town church, badly bombed but restored, has fascinating capitals and some original Renaissance vaulting in the side chapels. The churches of Abbaye aux Hommes and Abbaye aux Dames were founded by the Conqueror and his wife Mathilda to atone for marrying without papal consent. William's remains were interred in the former, Mathilda's in the latter in the east of the town.

CANY, CHÂTEAU DE   *53D3*

Cany, in the Durdent Valley, dates from the reign of Louis XIII. The main building is approached through a large courtyard with side pavilions and a splendid double staircase. The apartments are furnished in 17th- and 18th-century styles.

CAUDEBEC-EN-CAUX   *53D3*

Spreading up the confluence of two valleys, Caudebec has a natural amphitheater setting that once provided a ringside view of the tidal bore that, before embankment, once swept up the Seine. You can watch old films

recording the event in the Musée de la Marine de Seine. Just outside the town lies the abbey of St.-Wandrille (see p.70).

CHERBOURG 52A3

From the 17th century onwards its deep-water harbor made Cherbourg a major Atlantic port. The military engineer Vauban first began the building of a massive breakwater, but work on it continued until the 19th century. Now it is used by the navy, transatlantic liners, and lesser craft bound for Britain, Ireland and the Channel Isles. As a strategic target in wartime the port was devastated. Today the rebuilt town has a good museum in the hilltop Fort du Roule commemorating the Liberation, and a good art museum with a collection of Millet portraits.

CLÉCY 52C2

This attractive stone village has assumed the role of tourist base for a region dubbed La Suisse Normande. Though scarcely alpine in scale or landscape, the cliffs above the Orne river provide a scenic backdrop for leisure facilities such as fishing, climbing and canoeing. Clécy is an excellent excursion center for local beauty spots. The hill known as Sugar Loaf (Le Pain de Sucre) beckons via a marked trail to the north (see opposite), and the Croix de la Faverie (southwards) offers outstanding views of the surrounding countryside.

CLÈRES 53D3

The town's large and popular zoo, set in the grounds of a onetime fortress, boasts diverse fauna roaming in comparative liberty. A few ruins of the original defenses remain, and parts of a neo-Gothic edifice now inhabited by rare birds. Clères also has a good veteran vehicle museum with many wartime exhibits.

CLERMONT ABBEY 52B1

Volunteers have been restoring this Cistercian abbey, first founded in 1152; its original abbot was Saint Bernard. A half-hour tour gives some idea of its pre-Revolution appearance. Mansard dormers crown the 17th-century monks' building, and rounded arches adorn the church.

★★★ CÔTE D'ALBÂTRE 53D3

The Alabaster Coast, stretching from Le Tréport to Le Havre, is named for its striking chalk cliffs, broken by coves formed by small rivers. The cliffs are being eroded by as much as several meters per year, leaving the side valleys stranded in mid-air. Isolated sea stacks show where the cliffs once stood, but these too will disappear. Numerous harbor resorts nestle in the coves, among them Dieppe (see p.60), Fécamp (see p.62) and Étretat (see p.61), which have some life all year round. The beaches are mostly banks of pebbles guarded by sea walls. The twisting coast road makes a rewarding drive, especially in the morning. One of the best sections of the Côte lies between Senneville and Fécamp.

★ COTENTIN PENINSULA 52B3

Jutting into the Channel is a large rugged area of granite encompassing flat marshlands, cattle pastures, and the hedged landscape of the *bocage* (see p.57). The west side has some of Normandy's most enticing beaches, dune backed and still unspoiled. Many travelers head for Utah Beach where American forces landed in 1944.

To the east lie the attractive fishing towns of St.-Vaast-la-Hougue and Barfleur. Dramatic scenery lies around Cap de la Hague. Inland, Bricquebec is worth a visit, especially for its Saturday market.

WALK

CLÉCY: LE PAIN DE SUCRE

The "Sugar Loaf" makes a good half-day's walk, with glorious views over the looping Orne river and the cliffs of the Suisse Normande.

Despite some climbing, this isn't a difficult walk. Starting from Clécy church, head downhill towards the Manoir de Placy (you can visit en route). Join the marked Circuit du Pain de Sucre. Cross the bridge and rail-road tracks at the village of Le Vey.

From the chapel the long-distance footpath GR36 goes past the Rochers de la Houle (a hang-gliding ramp) and around Le Pain de Sucre to La Serverie.

Return to Clécy on the D135 ■

NORMANDY

WALK

OLD DIEPPE

Start on the quai Henri IV, where tall dark houses fringe the harbor, with its wonderful fish restaurants and the old fish market.

Head into the old town to the church of St.-Jacques, where the illustrious privateer Jehan Ango (see Varengeville-sur-Mer on p.72) is buried.

Meander the workaday streets by the port for an authentic French experience, especially on market day. The pedestrianized Grande Rue has excellent stores.

Next make your way towards the seafront and see the witch-hat turrets of Les Tourelles, remains of Dieppe's 14th-century defenses.

Finally, ascend to the cliff-top château and enjoy the views, followed by a visit to its museum ■

COUTANCES   *52B2*

The stunningly proportioned twin-spired **cathedral ★★★**, dating mainly from the 13th century, is a superb example of Norman Gothic style. Its most admired features are the gallery above the facade, and the magnificent vertical thrust of the nave. Some venerable 13th- and 14th-century glass survives in the transepts. The revered 14th-century statue of Our Lady of Coutances, in the central chapel of the apse, survived war-time bombing. Nearby, the picturesque ruined Château de Gratot is worth a visit.

DEAUVILLE   *53C3*

Normandy's answer to the Riviera attracts a crowd of celebrities in season; in July and August beautiful people flock here from Paris in search of seaside diversions. This ultra-chic sea spa offers a huge range of sports facilities and entertainment, particularly sailing, horse racing and a vast swimming pool. The August Grand Prix is one of Deauville's annual equestrian highlights. The town's hotels and apartments are an elegant pastiche: turreted *faux châteaux* and rambling farmhouses occupy the grid-like streets behind the famed Promenade des Planches, a boardwalk running the length of the beach.

★★★ D-DAY BEACHES   *52B3*

These melancholy stretches of sand, on the Calvados and Cotentin coasts, witnessed the extraordinary events of June 6, 1944 when a huge Allied invasion force broke through Hitler's Atlantic Wall to liberate France. First to attack on D-Day were minesweepers and airborne troops, followed by over 4,000 landing craft carrying tanks and infantry divisions. Gold, Juno and Sword beaches were the British

and Commonwealth landing sites, while the Americans landed at Omaha and Utah. Utah was the easiest of all the landings, with under 200 casualties. Omaha presented a sharp contrast. Greeted by shellfire, the 1st Division suffered over 2,000 losses within a few hours in the bloodiest of all the D-Day battles. Many museums, monuments and graveyards commemorate the epic struggle that altogether cost over 100,000 lives. The main American cemeteries are located at St.-Laurent-sur-Mer and La Madeleine.

★ DIEPPE   *53D3*

This historic seaside resort dates back to Roman times and later became a significant port, though it developed mainly in the 19th century. It also saw the disastrous Operation Jubilee raid of 1942 when some 7,000 Canadian commandos fell. Today Dieppe is an interesting and attractive port, famed for its fishing fleet (the local specialty is a delicious fish casserole, *marmite Dieppoise*). Old stone buildings surround the harbor area. Apart from exploring

Dieppe's charming older quarter, don't miss the museum in the 15th-century cliff-top castle, with 17th-century carved ivory artifacts. In the lower town, St.-Jacques church has some good Gothic features.

DOMFRONT   52B1
Dramatically set above the Varenne, this fortified town has a fine view of the pear-growing heart of the *bocage*. The ramparts and ruins of the medieval stronghold remain, fringed with public gardens. A neo-Byzantine church (St.-Julien) is the focus of a well-restored old quarter. The ancient church of Notre-Dame-sur-l'Eau (Our Lady on the Water), with 12th-century frescoes, is a damaged Romanesque masterpiece where Thomas à Becket celebrated Christmas Mass in 1166.

ETELAN, CHÂTEAU D'   53D3
This Flamboyant building, sometimes used for exhibitions and concerts, is built on the site of a former stronghold. The interesting chapel contains 16th-century frescoes and accomplished wood carving.

★★★ ETRETAT   53C3
Etretat presents a memorable coastline of natural arches and fast-eroding chalk cliffs. One cliff, the Falaise d'Aval, linked to a solitary sea stack, is the subject of countless postcards and paintings from impressionism onwards. The cliff-top walk gives marvelous views. Attractive seafood restaurants, old houses, and a covered market add to the appeal of this agreeable resort.

EU   53D3
Eu clusters around the collegiate church of Notre-Dame-et-St.-Laurent O'Toole, named in honor of a venerated 12th-century Irish primate whose statue can be seen in the crypt. The 16th-century Château d'Eu stands in a park of giant beeches. Its interior, with portraits and tapestries, owes much to the bourgeois-style reign of Louis-Philippe (1830–48), and to the controversial architect Viollet-le-Duc. Don't miss the marble monuments to the duke of Guise and his wife in the chapel. William the Conqueror married his cousin Mathilda in the original fortress that stood here.

Set in the chalk country of the Caux region, Etretat was a tiny fishing village in the 19th century. The magnificent Falaise d'Aval, with its solitary stack and arch, was a favorite subject of the impressionists

NORMANDY

MONET IN NORMANDY

Giverny is the place most closely associated with Monet, who lived there contentedly from 1883 until his death in 1926.

But other places along the Seine will also appeal to his admirers. Just upstream is Bennecourt where Monet spent the summer of 1868, painting his mistress Camille.

During the 1860s he spent time in Honfleur; there he met Boudin, and painted both harbor and fishing scenes. His family home was at Ste.-Adresse, a suburb of Le Havre.

His 1872 painting "Impression: Soleil levant," of the Pointe de la Hève, gave its name to the style that dominated French painting for the rest of the century ■

★ ÉVREUX   53D2

This agricultural center on the Iton river is now the peaceful domain of ducks and municipal flowerbeds, but it has a history of martial mayhem from its 5th-century sacking by Vandals to air raids in 1944. After each trauma the citizens of Évreux patiently rebuilt the town. The cathedral, whose lead spire melted during the last conflagration, has many fine features inside and out, such as the stained glass, and wooden and ironwork screens.

★ FALAISE   52C2

William the Bastard, as he is still known in Normandy, was born in Falaise in about 1027, son of the 17-year-old Duke Robert II and a local tanner's daughter. Tradition claims the future conqueror was born in the impressive fortress, though the present ruins are no older than the 12th century. Falaise took the brunt of the Germans' final struggle in the Battle of Normandy; the town was almost completely destroyed, but has since been attractively rebuilt.

FÉCAMP   53C3

This port on the Côte d'Albâtre is perhaps best known for Bénédictine, the liqueur produced by the monks who shelter a relic of the Precious Blood, which tradition says arrived here in the 1st century via a nephew of Joseph of Arimathea. The church of La Trinité, rebuilt several times, is a simple structure of chalk stone. Near the Lady Chapel stands the tabernacle containing the alleged phial of Christ's blood, venerated by thousands of pilgrims on the Feast of the Trinity. At the Palais Bénédictine, you can see where the liqueur was once distilled. The 27 ingredients are displayed in large tubs in the *salle des plantes*.

FILIÈRES, CHÂTEAU DE   53C3

This 16th- to 18th-century moated grange of gleaming Caen stone stands in parkland designed by Le Nôtre (of Versailles fame); its most celebrated feature is a magnificent beech avenue. It contains fine Oriental porcelain, Fragonard prints, wall hangings, hand-painted wallpaper, and other period furnishings.

GISORS   53E2

Capital of the Vexin region, a chalk plateau devoted mostly to sugar beet and cereal crops, Gisors' strategic hilltop location led to fortification in the early 12th century by the Conqueror's son. The stronghold remains a fine example of Norman military architecture and the grounds are now laid out as attractive public gardens. The church of St.-Gervase and St.-Protase is almost as old as the fortress, though it has many later additions.

★★★ GIVERNY   53E2

Monet's house near Vernon is one of the best-loved sights in France, visited by impressionist fans from April to October. The green-shuttered house contains much Monet memorabilia, including his prized Japanese engravings. But it is the gardens that steal the show. In 1895, after buying the beloved house he had previously only rented, he began landscaping the gardens and creating the water-lily pool with its graceful, inspiring bridge. Planted with many old varieties of species that Monet would have recognized, the gardens are at their best in early summer. Disappointingly, there are no original works here, only reproductions of the famous "Nymphéas" canvases. The new American Museum, just down the road, contains works by U.S. artists of the same period.

GRANVILLE 52A2

The Cotentin peninsula's prettiest town vies with St.-Malo in a number of ways, not least in its views towards Le Mont-St.-Michel. Granville, too, is a fortified town and was a pirates' lair in privateering days. Today it's a stylish resort with a casino, marina and sea-water therapy center. Main sights in the walled upper town are the austere church of Notre-Dame and the Musée du Vieux Granville. Boats ply regularly to the Iles Chausey (which supplied the granite building blocks for Le Mont-St.-Michel) and the Channel Isles.

LE HAVRE 53C3

Le Havre's superb port facilities made it a strategic target during World War II. Over 4,000 civilians died in air raids as the Allies tried to dislodge the Germans before they destroyed the harbor installations. Inevitably, today's town is modern and somewhat bleak (its principal architect championed reinforced concrete). It is one of France's most important seaports for freight and ferry traffic. To see what the pre-war town looked like (when Jean-Paul Sartre taught here), head for the Musée de l'Ancien Havre. There's also the well-designed Musée des Beaux-Arts.

HONFLEUR 53C3

This fine old port at the mouth of the Seine is as attractive today as it was to the 19th-century impressionists. The harbor scene is a charming and lively assembly of tall slate-roofed houses, cafés, restaurants and pleasure craft. The heart of the old city has a Saturday market and the lovely church of St.-Catherine.

HOULGATE 52C2

This somewhat sedate resort, with its steep-roofed, turretted villas, has a fine beach, sandy and shell-strewn, though much of it vanishes at high tide. The Vaches Noires cliff to the northeast is the main scenic attraction, an eroded fossil-rich wall of clay and marl. The *vaches noires* ("black cows") are pieces of debris that have broken away from the main block and lie covered with seaweed on the beach.

★★★ JUMIÈGES 53D3

This splendid ruin on the lower Seine is one of Normandy's most striking sights. The first monastery, founded in the 7th century, was destroyed by Vikings. The refounded abbey rose from those ashes to become a great center of religious scholarship; William the Conqueror was present at its consecration.

Monet's garden at Giverny was the inspiration for many of his works, especially the "Nymphéas" series

ARTISTS IN HONFLEUR

One of the forerunners of impressionism, Eugene Boudin was born in Honfleur in 1824.

The son of a ferryman, he influenced the impressionists both in his techniques (such as painting outside) and subject matter: bright and breezy Normandy seascapes with simple figures.

He was also tutor to the 15-year-old Monet.

Other artists who visited Honfleur included Sisley, Cézanne, Courbet, Pissarro and Renoir ■

DRIVE

THE LEGACY OF D-DAY

456 kilometers/283 miles (3 days)

The Allied invasion of June 1944 on the shores of Normandy eventually liberated Europe. Many towns and villages were obliterated, some restored in their original style, and others hastily rebuilt. Few places are as evocative of those events as the beaches along the Channel coast west of Caen.

1 Pegasus Bridge

Pegasus Bridge is the most easterly of the Allied landing sites, and the first target captured by the Allies on D-Day. Three gliders crash-landed here just after midnight on the morning of June 6, 1944. The bridge on the Caen–Ouistreham canal was a vital strategic link, the only way supplies and troops could cross the waterway to confront the German defenses, and it had to remain intact. Within a few minutes of fierce fighting, it was safely in the hands of British troops, who held it until reinforcements arrived from Sword Beach. Three monumental columns southeast of the bridge mark the glider landings. Alongside the the bridge, the Café Pegasus was the first house in France to be liberated; a museum in the grounds exhibits invasion memorabilia.

A Liberty Way marker at Utah Beach stands as a lasting testimony to the courage of those who fought to liberate France from German occupation. There are many such memorials along this coast

Take the D35 to Douvres, then follow "Bayeux" signs. Go right on the D79 to Courseulles, then right on the D12 and follow signs to Arromanches.

2 Arromanches-les-Bains

Heading west along the coast from Pegasus Bridge you will pass the eastern landing beaches in the following order: Sword, Juno and Gold (British/Canadian). At Arromanches, you can see the remains of the "Mulberry" harbor, towed across the Channel in prefabricated sections to be reassembled here so that supplies and armaments could be safely landed to equip the invasion forces. The Musée du Débarquement on the seafront explains many aspects of this extraordinary feat of engineering.

Leave Arromanches for Bayeux on the D516.

3 Bayeux

Bayeux, famed for its tapestry illustrating the Norman Conquest, miraculously avoided much wartime damage, but its Musée Mémorial de la Bataille de Normandie has one of the most comprehensive accounts of the events following D-Day, including a remarkable collection of contemporary photographs, uniforms and military vehicles. The war cemetery on the outskirts of town recalls the human cost of Operation Overlord in nearly 4,000 British and Commonwealth graves.

Leave Bayeux on the D6 to Port-en-Bessin. Go left on the D514 for Omaha Beach.

4 Omaha Beach

Continuing via the D6 to Port-en-Bessin, don't miss the Musée des Épaves Sous-Marines du Débarquement, a fascinating assembly of war relics salvaged from the seabed. The shore west of Port-en-Bessin is Omaha Beach, the main American landing site. Many monuments there commemorate the western

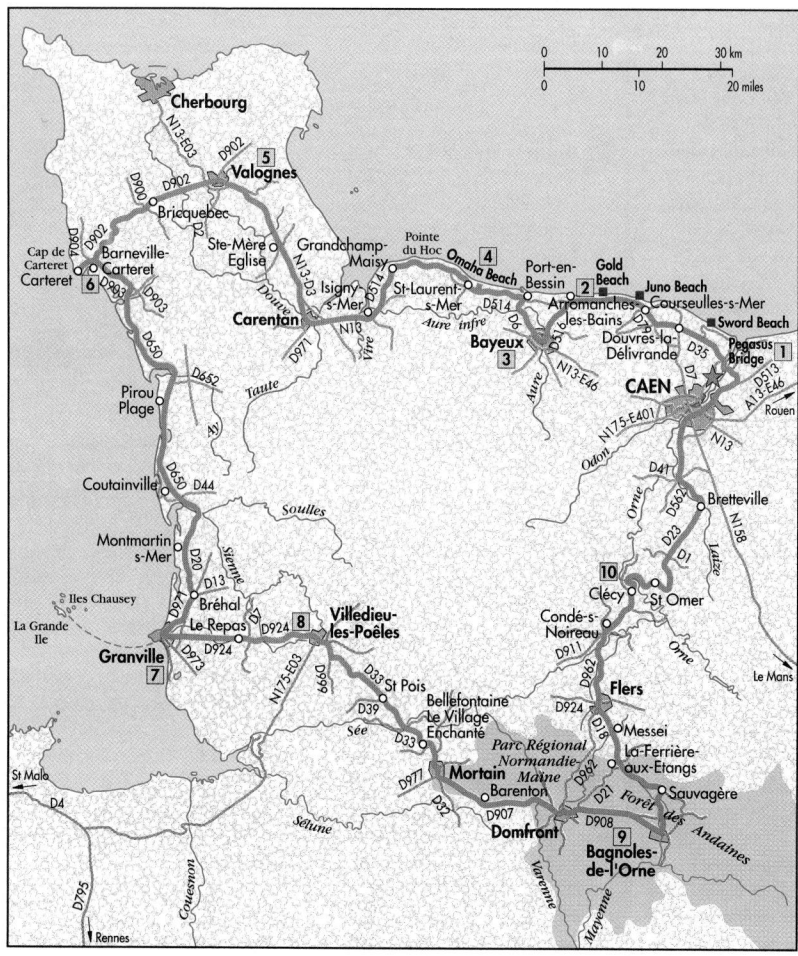

sector of D-Day activity, which was intense and bloody with a huge loss of life. The American military cemetery nearby is a place to contemplate this, a site covering 70 hectares (173 acres). The orientation table above the beach shows how German defenses were able to inflict such damage. At the western end of Omaha Beach are the cliffs of Pointe du Hoc, which American Rangers bravely scaled under heavy fire to dislodge a German battery. Shell craters and gun pits are still visible. The film "The Longest Day" retells the events.

Continue on the D514 then go right on the N13 for Cherbourg and continue to Valognes.

5 Valognes

Valognes was once called the "Versailles of Normandy," but its aristocratic lifestyle came to an abrupt halt in 1944. Several elegant mansions miraculously survived, notably the 18th-century Hôtel de Beaumont. There are various museums to visit, including a cider museum in a medieval dye house, as well as a public garden and a town square.

THE FINAL PUSH

"Mulberry" harbors at Arromanches and Omaha were instrumental in landing over 2 million Allied troops, but it was not until August 22, 1944 that Normandy was liberated as the last Germans were defeated at the Battle of Falaise Pocket ■

FLAMBOYANT GOTHIC

Throughout Normandy many churches and cathedrals were built in the ornate late Gothic style known as Flamboyant.

This style developed after the end of the Hundred Years War when a period of peace and prosperity led to the development of new architectural ideas. The great cathedrals had already been built, so the exuberant new style was used for projects such as tombs, chantry chapels and other embellishments to existing buildings.

The term Flamboyant refers to the flame-like tracery of the windows, a characteristic that is also found on portals, porches and vaults ∎

Leave Valognes and head along the D902 through Bricquebec to Barneville-Carteret.

6 Barneville-Carteret

Barneville-Carteret is a twin resort with lovely sands. The lighthouse on Cap de Carteret is an excellent vantage point for the Channel Isles. Just to the north, the dunes form an important nature reserve.

Leave Barneville for La Haye-du-Puits on the D903, then keep right on the D650. Go straight on along the D20 to Bréhal, then right on the D971 and into Granville.

7 Granville

Granville is one of the most appealing of Normandy's resorts. At the end of July, a Pardon of the Sea is a colorful spectacle.

Leave Granville for Villedieu on the D924.

8 Villedieu-les-Poêles

Villedieu-les-Poêles is one of the most delightful towns in Normandy, with a distinguished history as a property of the Knights of Malta. "God's Town of the Frying Pans" is also a famous center of metalworking.

Leave Villedieu on the N175 east for St.-Hilaire. Go right on the D999, then left on the D33 and continue through Mortain. Turn left on the D907, go through Domfront center then follow "Bagnoles-de-l'Orne" signs along the D908 and right on the D335.

9 Bagnoles-de-l'Orne

Continuing southeastward from Villedieu on the D33 you pass through some appealing Norman countryside, a gentle ride through wooded valleys and ridges. **Le Village Enchanté**, a woodland theme park of fairy-tale scenes and pet animals, makes a good stop for children.

Following the D-Day history inland, **Mortain** was the scene of the only serious German counterattack during the Battle of Normandy. It petered out within a week. Today Mortain's claim to fame is an ancient reliquary known as the Chrismale that is popularly supposed to have been the original of the Holy Grail, kept in the Église St.-Evroult.

Barenton's Maison de la Pomme et de la Poire will tell you all you could likely need to know about cider making. You are now passing through the Parc Régional of Normandie-Maine.

Leave Bagnoles for St.-Michel-des-Andaines on the D386. Go left and right on the D53 and continue to Flers on the D18. Go right for Caen along the D962, then take the D562 to Clécy and turn off for Clécy center.

10 Clécy

The final leg of this roughly rectangular tour takes you through the wooded, rocky escarpments of the Suisse Normande. Above Clécy, the scenic Route des Crêtes takes in some of its best views.

Leave Clécy on the D133c, then go left for St.-Rémy. Just over the brow of the hill, go sharp right and follow Routes des Crêtes to St.-Omer. Avoid St.-Rémy itself. In St.-Omer turn right as for Pont d'Ouilly. Ignore the "La Suisse Normande" turning. Go left at a stop sign to Bretteville. Turn left on the D132, left at a give way sign, then return to Caen.

LAVAL *52B1*

Laval, once famous for linen, carries on its textile-making traditions with cotton and synthetics. The old quarter, around the cathedral and fortress (note the keep's timbered roof), retains traces of ramparts and gateways, and there are several churches worth visiting. The terraces of the Jardin de la Perrine and the quays along the Mayenne river offer fine views of the town. Notice the 13th-century bridge, and the public washing stages (used until 1960) moored along quai Paul-Boudet. Henri Rousseau was born in a tower of the Beucheresse gate (his tinsmith father's workshop) in 1844; an art museum in the château commemorates the naive style he pioneered.

LISIEUX *53C2*

Set on the hills above the Touques river, Lisieux is renowned for its association with Sainte Thérèse. Thérèse Martin was born in Alençon in 1873, but spent the latter part of her brief life here (she died of TB at 24). From the age of nine she desired to become a nun, and at 15 she got a papal dispensation to join the Carmelites. Cheerful, energetic, yet intensely pious, she described her spiritual quest in her extraordinary little book "The Story of a Soul" and was canonized in 1925. Her statue appears in almost every church in France. Pilgrims flock to see the house where she lived, the Carmelite chapel where she is entombed, and the basilica erected in her memory. A tourist train takes visitors around the town in summer. Lisieux contains some charming houses, and also the 12th-century cathedral of St.-Pierre, where England's Henry II married Eleanor of Aquitaine. St.-Pierre houses the bones of Pierre Cauchon, betrayer of Jeanne

d'Arc. The lush surrounding countryside is full of interest.

★ LYONS-LA-FORÊT *53D3*

This picturesque village has a covered market with a fine roof, timbered houses, a historic church (St.-Denis) containing huge statues, and has starred as the setting for a film of Flaubert's "Madame Bovary." The surrounding beech forest, where the dukes of Normandy once hunted, is lovely for walks, drives and picnics. Several trees have grown to a colossal size, notably the Bunodière beech (signposted from the N31). Country churches, the ruined abbey of Mortemer, and the château of Fleury also make good touring destinations.

MARTAINVILLE *53D3*

One of the villages near the Forêt de Lyons has an imposing 15th-century château whose main adornments are huge brick chimneys and an old dovecote. Inside, a folk museum gives a fascinating insight into traditional rural life, with furniture, glassware and ceramics.

MIROMESNIL, CHÂTEAU DE *53D3*

Guy de Maupassant's alleged birthplace near Dieppe is a 16th-17th-century building in extensive gardens and parkland. The celebrated novelist was actually born in humbler circumstances near Fécamp, but his mother determined that his birth should be registered somewhere more exalted. Open in summer, it displays documents and furnishings of former owners including the Maupassants. The building has two markedly different facades, one grand, the other older and simpler. The 16th-century chapel has fine carvings.

CAMEMBERT

Camembert cheese, imitated all over the world, should be firm, creamy, mild, and made from unpasteurized milk.

The genuine Norman article is now protected, like wine, by an *appellation d'origine controlée* stamp. It is traditionally eaten either by itself or with bread, but no butter.

The Musée du Camembert at Vimoutiers describes the cheese-making process in detail, while in the town is a statue of Marie Harel (1761–1812), the first commercial producer of the cheese, who was given the recipe by a priest she had sheltered in the Revolution.

Other Norman cheeses include Livarot and Pont l'Evêque ■

★★★ MONT-ST.-MICHEL, LE *52A2*

Across the mudflats and salt marshes of the Couesnon estuary, flooded by quick tides, the pinnacles of this splendid abbey on its granite islet form an unforgettable silhouette.

The history of Le Mont-St.-Michel stretches back to the 8th century. Then, a vision of the Archangel Michael instructed the bishop of Avaranches to build a chapel on the rock in the bay. From modest beginnings the structure grew to its present splendor, as Carolingian, Romanesque and Gothic buildings were superimposed on the precipitous crags.

Pilgrims have long journeyed from far and wide, filing up the steep streets to the airy summit, where Saint Michael brandishes his sword from the highest spire. The views are breathtaking, with the tide speeding across the sands to the causeway. Despite the crowded and commercialized Grande Rue, Le Mont-St.-Michel is essential viewing. If you can, explore the abbey in peace at dawn or dusk.

O, CHÂTEAU D' *53C2*

This delicious 15th-century confection stands mirrored in its moat amid velvety lawns, a Gothic fantasy of witch-hat turrets and towers. Its builder, Robert d'O, overspent so catastrophically that his creditors stripped the château of its contents as he lay dying within it. After a checkered history, this lovely building has been restored to its former glory. The long gallery, Salon des Muses, and the old kitchens are worth seeing.

OUISTREHAM *52C2*

This popular sailing center and ferry port caters for transient passengers with its supermarkets, hotels and restaurants, but also has a good stretch of sand and a casino. The main sight is the elaborate church of St.-Samson. At Riva-Bella, where German defences wilted at the hands of the 4th Anglo-French Commando on D-Day, the Musée du Débarquement commemorates the actions of the only French troops involved in the main Allied landing operation.

★★★ PAYS D'AUGE 52–53C2

Inland from the Côte Fleurie, this tapestry of pastureland, manor houses, timbered farms and wooded slopes is an area of cider and cheese production. Two tourist routes (Route du Fromage and Route du Cidre) are marked through attractive countryside, where opportunities abound for tasting and buying local products; tourist offices have a list of farms open to visitors. The Manoir de Crèvecœur-en-Auge is one of the few manors you can go inside. Restoration work was carried out by the American Schlumberger Foundation, and a museum of oil prospecting is housed inside.

PERSEIGNE, FORÊT DE 53C1

Alençon makes a good base for exploring this expanse of mixed woodland ideal for walking, fishing or riding. Of its several picturesque valleys the Vallée d'Enfer is one of the prettiest, with a belvedere at the highest point of the Sarthe from which marked paths lead.

★★★ ROUEN 53D3

Rouen was badly damaged during World War II, and the gracelessly rebuilt Seine riverfront comprises France's fifth largest port, the nearest a container ship can get to Paris. But, past the congested outskirts, Rouen's center has been restored to something like its traditional appearance. (Driving here can be a problem, so it's best to park at the edge.)

Rouen's historic associations alone make it a place of pilgrimage. Jeanne d'Arc, France's patron saint, was tried, falsely convicted, and burned alive in the place du Vieux-Marché in 1431. Today, restaurants overlook Jeanne's execution site, while little streets full of lovely old houses and smart shops spread all around. To the east lies the Palais de Justice, a veritable forest of fretted Gothic stonework, while the rue du Gros-Horloge takes you towards the cathedral of Notre-Dame, Rouen's pride and the highest in France, its west front painted by Monet and its interior skylit by amazing stained glass. Bombs seriously damaged the structure, and restoration work continues. Inside, the tombs of Richard the Lionheart, the cardinals of Amboise, and Louis de Brézé, the forebearing husband of Diane de Poitiers (Henri II's lifelong mistress), can be seen on a guided tour. Other churches of interest are St.-Maclou and its *aitre* (plague cemetery), with a grim frieze of bones around its ossuary; St.-Ouen, a Gothic abbey church; and the modern Église Ste.-Jeanne-d'Arc.

Among Rouen's excellent museums are its art gallery, the Musée des Beaux-Arts; the Musée Flaubert, which includes a fascinating collection of antique surgical instruments (Flaubert's father was a surgeon); and the Musée le Secq des Tournelles, an exhibition of wrought ironwork. Other places of interest include the Musée de la Céramique (ceramics) and the Musée des Antiquités de la Seine Maritime. The latter museum, housed in a 17th-century convent, contains gold and silver plate, enamels and glassware.

ST.-LÔ 52B2

The town was devastated during the war and virtually no prewar buildings survived. The bombed Notre-Dame, left as it was after 1944 while a new church was erected behind, shows the ferocity of the conflict. During the Battle of Normandy St.-Lô was a vital link in the struggle that resulted in the American advance to the Cotentin peninsula.

SAINTE JEANNE D'ARC

After her capture at Compiègne, Jeanne was betrayed to the English for 10,000 gold ducats.

Accused of heresy and sorcery by the devious Bishop Pierre Cauchon, her defense amazed the court, but by this time her death had become politically expedient.

Recanting at the scaffold, she was resentenced to life imprisonment. Jeanne's reprieve required her to forswear her habitual male clothing, but one day her guards removed her female garb. In desperation, she put on the only (male) clothes she had in order to relieve herself outside. It was what her enemies were waiting for: Jeanne was burned alive in Rouen on May 30, 1431 ∎

WHERE THE CIDER APPLES GROW

Normandy is one of the few French regions that have no vineyards, but it does possess orchards in abundance, providing the apples for some of the region's characteristic drinks.

Local cider varies from light to fairly strong and goes very well with lunchtime _crêpes,_ though locals consider it the perfect companion for any food. One variety, _poire,_ made from pears, is common in the _bocage_ region – _cidre bouché_ has a champagne-style cork.

For a more potent drink, try calvados (apple brandy). Its traditional role is as the _trou Normand_ ("Norman hole") when a shot is knocked back during a long meal to help digestion and "bore a hole" for the next dish. Most now drink it as an after-dinner liqueur.

Pommeau is a mixture of calvados and apple juice and is best drunk iced as an aperitif ∎

STE.-MÈRE-ÉGLISE *52B3*

Ste.-Mère-Église, the first village in France to be liberated as dawn broke on D-Day, is an unremarkable place, but still welcomes visiting war veterans. A military museum is devoted to the heroic 82nd and 101st American divisions. The eye-catching model parachutist dangling from a buttress of the church commemorates John Steele's bizarre wartime landing on its roof; he played possum for several hours, watching the battle rage below. The Musée de la Ferme du Cotentin, in a 16th-century farmhouse, displays agricultural bygones. A milestone at the town hall symbolizes the first marker along "Liberty Way," the trail blazed through France by American troops.

ST.-SEVER-CALVADOS *52B2*

The abbey church, from the 13th and 14th centuries, is the focal point of this market town. Its lantern tower and rood beam are noteworthy, along with some early glass; the belfry is 17th century. In the Forêt de St.-Sever you can enjoy a picnic among wild boar, deer and goats in the Parc Animalier, or inspect a dolmen called La Pierre Coupée.

ST.-WANDRILLE *53D3*

The abbey complex, now partly in ruins, was founded in the 7th century by a count who chose his wedding day to renounce all earthly pleasures. He became a hermit, while his like-minded wife joined a convent. A Benedictine community still sings Gregorian chant here daily. The present church is a 13th-century tithe barn, transported piecemeal from another village and reassembled by the monks in 1967. A shrine by the door contains the head of Saint Wandrille, the ascetic count who founded the abbey.

★ SÉES *53C1*

An unexpected, magnificent cathedral and imposing bishop's palace attract visitors to this pleasant but otherwise ordinary riverside town (once a Roman settlement). The cathedral, buttressed in the 16th century against subsidence, has a Gothic interior with remarkable 13th-century stained glass, a beautiful choir, and pierced triforium. Our Lady of Sées, a sweet-faced statue in the south transept, is 13th century.

★ SUISSE NORMANDE *52C2*

This popular tourist region lies along the Orne Valley south of Caen, roughly between Thury-Harcourt and Putanges. Despite the name, don't expect much alpine drama: there are no lakes or mountains, though the crags, cliffs and escarpments provide plenty of scenic interest along the river's winding course. Undulating wooded countryside contrasts sharply with the flat cereal fields closer to the coast. It's a well-known leisure-activity area, drawing rock climbers, canoeists, kayakers and hang gliding. Many explore the region on horseback or bicycle, go camping or fishing, or take a pedal boat along the quieter reaches of the Orne. Generally the region is more suited to driving than exploring on foot. Marked tourist routes lead along minor roads bright with broom in spring and a golden blaze in the fall. Several places along the river make attractive starting points.

Thury-Harcourt, at the north of the Suisse Normande, has been restored since its wartime blitzing – though not the 18th-century château. Its extensive parkland stretches along a riverside ridge, offering walks amid lovely gardens. From the old station, an excursion train (*Train Touristique*) runs upstream to Clécy (see p.59) or coastwards to Caen. South of Thury-Harcourt is the small chapel of Bonne Nouvelle, perched on a hilltop. St.-Rémy was once an important iron-mining town; the old installations can still be seen. Beyond Clécy, leave the river valley for a look at the pilgrimage chapel in St.-Roch, scene of a colorful August *pardon* in local costume. Pont d'Ouilly makes another excellent stopping place.

The Rouvrou Bend (Méandre de Rouvrou) is an impressive stretch of the Rouvre tributary, best seen from a lookout a short walk from the war memorial. Not far away is the Oëtre Rock (Roche d'Oëtre); a convenient café offers another breathtaking view overlooking the Rouvre Gorges, perhaps the most Swiss-like part of France. Farther south is the Gorges de St.-Aubert (good walks), La Jalousie Mill, popular for fishing, and the Rabodanges Dam with its long lake (there's a good campground here with play areas and water sports). On a nearby hill is the château of Rabodanges , now used as a stud farm. Putanges-Pont-Écrepin – a small town on both banks of the river – is the last settlement along the Suisse Normande section of the Orne Valley.

LE TRÉPORT *53D3*

The Romans established this seaport northeast of Dieppe. It's popular with Parisians in summer (and served daily by five trains) although the beach is of shingle, and blighted by an ugly casino. But there are plenty of cafés and fish restaurants by the quai François I. There's a cable-car ride up the chalk cliffs behind the beach, or you can climb all 378 steps from the town hall; a calvary and a magnificent view reward you at the top. The 16th-century church of St.-Jacques, farther down the hill, has a Renaissance doorway and a number of memorable keystones. Mers-les-Bains, north of the Bresle river, is quieter than Le Tréport, with its own beach.

TROUVILLE *53C3*

Across the Touques estuary from Deauville, Trouville has rival resort facilities and just as much charm, but a rather different atmosphere: respectably upmarket but less obviously glamorous and exclusive. As such it is more relaxed and, some would say, enjoyable (and less pricey). Up until the 1830s it was simply a fishing village; then the artist Charles Mozin publicized its attractions, and the beau monde

Brightly colored beach tents are lined up along the white sands of Trouville. This former fishing village has been a popular resort since Napoléon III started bringing his court here for the summer

NORMANDY

NORMANDY CUISINE

Norman cuisine makes good use of the products of its fertile *paysage* and is characteristically rich in cream, cheeses and butter.

Although low-calorie products (such as yogurt, skimmed milk and *crème fraîche*) are also made here, nouvelle cuisine (or even vegetarianism) have not really found a niche in the traditional restaurants.

Veal cooked in cream and butter, *canard rouennais* (Rouen duck), *tripe a la mode de Caen* (stewed tripe), or *boudin noir* (black pudding) are popular traditional dishes, but not for the faint-hearted!

Normandy also has excellent fish (including brill, turbot, mackerel and sole) as well as superb shellfish – particularly *moules* (mussels), crab, oysters, lobster, crayfish and pink and grey *crevettes* (prawns and shrimps) ∎

began flocking in. For a glimpse of Trouville's heyday, look at the pictures in the Villa Montebello (a fine brick and stone villa open in the summer). The beach is slightly smaller than Deauville's, but a similar boardwalk runs along. Unlike many Norman seaside resorts, Trouville retains some sense of life even out of season. A sizeable resident population of fishermen and others keeps it humming throughout the year. The route de la Corniche above the town gives a fine view over of Trouville's beach, with Deauville and the whole Côte Fleurie beyond.

VALMONT   53C3

The remains of a Benedictine abbey vie for attention with a hilltop château in this little place. Valmont has a patrician history: the Estouteville family, which owned the château, may be traced back to Viking times. A later seigneur of Valmont, Nicholas, founded the abbey in 1169 as a thanksgiving after a terrifying ordeal in battle. Though much altered, the ruins make a charming picture amid their grassy lawns, and the Renaissance chapel is intact. The present château retains an 11th-century keep, but the rest dates from the reigns of Louis XI and François I. The keep and the Louis XI wing can be visited.

VARENGEVILLE-SUR-MER   53D3

The wooded coastline adds to the appeal of Varengeville, whose rural charms and traditional architecture have long attracted artists. Its Renaissance Manoir d'Ango was the home of a 15th-century shipowner. Built by Italian craftsmen, the delightful ensemble forms a huge courtyard approached by a sculpted loggia, while a fine dovecote graces the

outbuildings. Equally worth seeking out is the Parc des Moutiers, a house and garden full of rare shrubs and trees, designed by the English architect Edwin Lutyens and the great landscape gardener Gertrude Jekyll. The cubist painter Georges Braque is buried in Varengeville's church, in its glorious seaview setting; window glass in the nave is the work of Braque.

VILLEDIEU-LES-POÊLES   52B2

Pots and pans have been a staple manufacturing industry in this intriguing town since the 12th century (*poêle* means frying pan). Despite these humdrum concerns, however, Villedieu has a noble history. With its quaint medieval courtyards and stepped alleyways huddled within a loop of the Sienne, it was once the headquarters of the Knights of Malta, first known as the Knights of St. John of Jerusalem. William the Conqueror's son, who became King Henry I of England, established the first commandery here in the 12th century. The Knights established a famous bell foundry here, which still exports worldwide. Guided tours show the molds and methods of bell-testing. The Atelier du Cuivre gives a chance to see some of France's famous copper cooking utensils being made.

VIRE, VALLÉE DE LA   52B2

The most scenic stretch of the Vire river, as it flows through the *bocage* country, lies just south of St.-Lô (see p.69). At Torigni-sur-Vire a restored 19th-century wing of the Château des Matignon is open to the public; it contains impressive tapestries and period furniture. The park is ideal for a stroll. La Chapelle-sur-Vire is an ancient place of pilgrimage: the revered statue of Our Lady of Vire stands near the chancel arch.

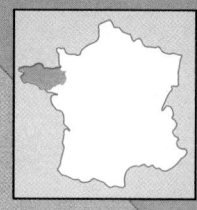

BRITTANY

**Brittany's Celtic heritage and
geographical remoteness set it apart
from the rest of France – vacations
here are tantalizingly different**

CALENDAR OF EVENTS

MAY – Brest: **French Olympic Sailing Championships**.

JULY – Vanne: **"Fêtes Historiques"** (Historic Festival).

2ND WEEK JULY – Nantes: **International Summer Festival** with music, singing and dancing.

JULY – Brest: the start of the **Figaro-Relais et Châteaux Solo Sailing Race**.

AUGUST – Guingamp: **festivals of Breton Dance and St.-Loup**. Lorien: **Inter-Celtic Festival**.

LATE AUGUST – Crozon Peninsula: **Celtic Watersports Festival**, various venues. Moncontour: **Medieval Festival**.

SEPTEMBER – Dinan: **Festival of the Ramparts** (every 2 years). Dol-de-Bretagne: **The Buckwheat Festival** ■

BRITTANY

For millennia the Bretons have been strongly influenced by the battering Atlantic waves. One of the Celtic names for Brittany, *Armor*, means "the land by the sea." In the days of sailing ships and new-found lands, many Bretons became merchant adventurers, explorers or privateers. Others joined the navy or built ships. Fishing is still a vital source of revenue for many families, though the seas are now farmed as much as hunted.

Today, however, Brittany's economy depends more upon the land than the sea. Its great natural forests have gradually dwindled into plotted farmland, and its acidic, rocky soils have been coaxed into intensive production zones for vast quantities of vegetables, especially artichokes, onions and cauliflowers.

Although visitors make occasional forays into the interior, they stay mostly by the sea, taking advantage of the region's superb clean, sandy beaches and picturesque rock formations. The **Breton coastline** varies greatly: gorse- and heath-covered cliffs on the Emerald Coast (Côte d'Emeraude), bizarrely eroded rock sculptures of rose-tinted granite, promontories jutting into snarling waters, calm estuaries, islet-strewn gulfs, a mosaic of

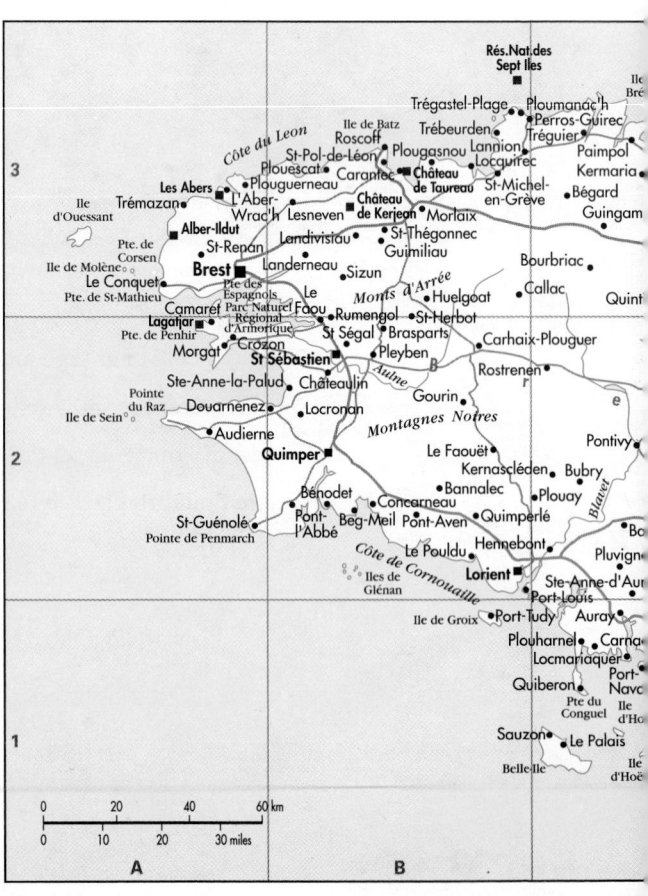

Fishing boats at Erquy, on the Emerald Coast, are a typical sight in this area, conjuring up everyday Breton charm. Fishing is a major part of life here

SOCIAL GAMES

As elsewhere in France, the locals tend to gather in quiet town squares in the evenings to play a game which looks like *boules* **or** *pétanque.*

In Brittany, however, they use flat disks (similar to quoits) to throw at the target instead of a ball. This Breton game is known as *palet* ■

THE SALT MARSHES OF GUÉRANDE

The marshes on Brittany's south-east coast (*marais salants*) were once an important source of salt.

Today production is limited, but Breton salt is still highly prized for its purity and sold by the roadside in small bags.

The salt marshes of the Guérande peninsula are a weird scene of lagoons, ponds and a complex web of drainage channels. At high tide, seawater floods in, trickling gradually into smaller, shallower pits from which the salt eventually evaporates into large white flakes. The museums at Batz-sur-Mer, Guérande and Saillé explain this fascinating process.

Unusual birds (egrets and purple herons) and salt-tolerant plants inhabit the marshes ∎

★★★ HIGHLIGHTS

Belle-Ile (▶77)
Carnac (▶79)
Crozon Peninsula (▶80)
Dinan (▶81)
Dinard and The Emerald Coast (▶85)
Morbihan, Golfe du (▶88)
Parish closes (▶90)
Perros-Guirec and the Pink Granite Coast (▶90)
Quimper (▶91)
St.-Malo (▶93)

---

salt marshes. The southern coast, milder and more sheltered, is generally less dramatic than the north or far west. Several of the larger islands make enticing excursion destinations.

The culture and traditions of Brittany are distinctive, too. It is a region of deep religious faith, imbued with many myths and legends. It even has its own language: a Gaelic tongue, heard mostly in western Brittany, which is a blend of related languages from both sides of the Channel. During the summer, festivals both secular and religious are held in many centers, at which local costume is worn. Look out for the lace headdress (*coiffes*) worn by the women, which vary from one area to another and are sometimes seen on the older women at Sunday Mass. Except on feast days and festivals, you're unlikely to see the full traditional costume except in museums.

Many towns are appealing in themselves, apart from any museums and heritage centers. Countless towns and villages have beautiful examples of domestic architecture, including timbered, stone or thatched buildings, and interesting churches, while ornate parish

closes reveal a unique form of Breton art. Another Breton curiosity is its wealth of prehistoric **megaliths**, predating even the ancient Celts. The most famous survive near Carnac in Morbihan, an amazing series of rows of stones whose purpose remains a mystery.

ABERS, LES   74A3

The northwest coast of Finistère frays into a series of shallow drowned valleys known as *abers*, created when sea levels rose and flooded former estuaries. At high tide they mirror a landscape of low-lying moorland pierced by lighthouses, fortresses and church bell towers. At sunset this west-facing coast makes an appealing drive, keeping close to the sea on minor roads.

The *abers* lie between Plouguerneau (the site of France's tallest lighthouse, the Phare de l'Ile Vierge) and the attractive fishing town of Le Conquet. En route you can explore the wild dunes of Ste.-Marguerite, where seaweed is dried for fertilizer, and the reef-strewn coastline around Trémazan. The Aber Wrac'h estuary is one of the largest and most attractive. The Pointe de Corsen, where the Atlantic meets the English Channel, is France's most westerly promontory.

★★ LA BAULE   75C1

The chief attraction of this glamorous resort is its sweeping vista of soft sand that shelves gently into the waves. Until the mid-19th century La Baule was an insignificant fishing village called Escoublac. When pine trees were planted to stabilize the dunes and reduce the winds, La Baule began to boom. The entire seafront is now developed, with a variety of imposing *belle-époque* hotels, modern apartment blocks and decorous villas in luxuriant gardens. Leisure facilities include thalassotherapy (a popular Breton hydrotherapy treatment using sea water), sailing, golf, tennis, bridge, boat excursions, a continual round of summer events and a casino. Inland is a fascinating maze of salt marshes.

★★★ BELLE-ILE   74C1

Brittany's largest offshore island is easily reached from Quiberon, a 45-minute crossing. If you only have a day, join one of the bus tours that go to most parts of the island. Le Palais, where the boats land, is the main town. Looming over the harbor is a star-shaped fortress, built in the 16th century and enlarged by Louis XIV's military architect Vauban. The little museum there explains much of the island's considerable history: Belle-Ile was much prized and repeatedly attacked by foreign fleets.

The interior is undulating farmland and sheltered valleys. The coast, though, is, more spectacular: a mix of fine beaches (safer on the eastern side), dramatic rock formations and sea-worn headlands. Monet painted the Aiguilles de Port-Coton, a spiky cluster of sea stacks, nearly 40 times. Sauzon is a pretty, sheltered fishing village with a lighthouse. The actress Sarah Bernhardt once had a large house on the island, now surrounded by a golf course.

BREST   74A3

Brest is an important naval base, built on a magnificent deep-water harbor. During World War II the Germans used it as a submarine base from which to attack transatlantic convoys. Thus, as a target for Allied bombing raids, the port was devastated by 1944. Since the war Brest has been rebuilt in a functional modern style, but its historic fortress remains unscathed and now contains a maritime museum. The docks and harbor area bustle with activity; watch what's going on from the ramparts, or the Pont de Récouvrance (Europe's largest swing bridge). A harbor cruise is one of the best ways to see the city. The municipal art gallery features the Pont-Aven School of Painters (see p.91). East of the port is Brittany's best aquarium, the crab-shaped Océanopolis.

Offloading the crab catch at Aber Wrac'h. The coast along northwest Finistère is characterized by its estuaries, known as abers, which are especially attractive at high tide or at sunset

The alignments at Kermario, Carnac. Over 3,000 stones are to be found in the Carnac region alone. They were probably erected between about 5000 and 2500 BC, though little is known of their real significance

BRETON PARDONS

A distinctive aspect of Breton cultural life is the *pardon*, originally a community ritual to seek anything from the forgiveness of sins to a bumper harvest.

Nowadays, the religious aspects are invariably followed by a feast or festival, a chance to wear traditional costumes, and have some fun ■

★ BRIÈRE, PARC RÉGIONAL DE *75C1*

This unusual region north of St.-Nazaire, renowned for its diverse wildfowl and fish, covers an area of about 40,000 hectares (99,000 acres). The marsh was formed after the last Ice Age, when rising sea levels flooded a low-lying wooded basin, turning its trees and vegetation into peat bog and reed marsh. When the sea retreated, the marshes drained sufficiently to allow habitation.

For centuries the Brièrons jealously guarded their ancient rights and traditional economy, based on hunting wildfowl and fishing for eels. They thatched their houses with locally gathered reeds and punted around the canals in flat-bottomed barges. For a few days a year they were permitted to cut peat, a vital source of fuel and revenue. Inevitably, the prospect of higher wages in the dockyards and factories of St.-Nazaire and Nantes lured many people away.

The Grande Brière's unique ecosystem and way of life are now protected to some extent by the advent of tourism and its regional park status. A boat trip through the reed beds is a good introduction to its strange, watery landscape (an excellent place for birdwatching), while several small museums in the main villages focus on Brièron life and custom.

★ CANCALE *75D3*

Millions of oysters are raised here from year-old spats in shallow concrete beds that cover most of the muddy beach. You can wander around and see them slowly maturing in their packs of plastic mesh, then buy and eat them at dozens of seafront stalls and restaurants. In the early 20th century, disease virtually wiped out the wild oysters that once thrived along the coast. Today the molluscs are raised in captivity, like any other crop. The spat, or seed oysters, are brought from southern Brittany, particularly Auray and the Bélon estuary. A museum in an oyster farm just outside the town offers tours and tastings. The Pointe du Grouin, some 4 kilometers (2 mi.) to the north and accessible on foot or by automobile, is a rocky promontory full of wild flowers and sea birds. In the summer a restored oyster boat – *La Cancalaise* – offers trips around the bay.

CARANTEC *74B3*

Sheltered by the Roscoff promontory, Carantec is lush and mild, with popular clean beaches in an attractive setting on Morlaix Bay, yet it remains low-key and uncommercialized. Cliff paths make excellent local walks; some lead to secluded coves or afford lookouts over the bay to the Château du Taureau, built to repel

English invaders. A tidal causeway leads to the Ile Callot and the Chapel of Notre-Dame, site of an August *pardon* (Breton religious procession) and a Blessing of the Sea ceremony. The estuary road from Morlaix is a lovely drive through artichoke fields and fishing villages.

★★★ CARNAC   74C1

Visitors seek out the attractive town of Carnac for the **megalithic monuments** on its northern outskirts. An excellent museum in the old village center explains facts and theories about these extraordinary and mysterious rows of standing stones. Nearby is the parish church dedicated to Pope Saint Cornelius, persecuted by the Romans in the 3rd century, and now the patron saint of horned beasts. Carnac-Plage is a more recent development along a long, gently shelving beach of fine sand. Accommodations in Carnac abound, although in summer many places are fully booked. The nearby low-lying coast and brackish lagoons provide anchorages for sailboats.

CHÂTEAULIN   74B2

The winding Aulne river flows through Châteaulin on its way to the Rade de Brest, providing a placid waterfront scene of wooded cliffs and lush meadows. In spring, salmon and trout leap the lock weirs to reach the spawning grounds upstream. There are several good walks along the towpaths.

★★ CONCARNEAU   74B2

Concarneau is still one of the country's foremost fishing ports. If you get up early enough, you can visit the fish auction (*criée*) by the harbor, where the night's catch is unloaded and sold.

The Ville Close is an ancient walled quarter on an island linked to the rest of the town by a fortified bridge and gateway. Its history dates back to the Middle Ages, though it was extensively remodeled, like many of Brittany's citadels, by Vauban. The excellent fishing museum (Musée de la Pêche), in the former arsenal, has lively displays of nets and fishing gear. From the ramparts there are good views over the inner port and marina.

★★ CORNICHE   74B3
DE L'ARMORIQUE

This stretch of Channel coast between Lannion and Morlaix is exceptionally scenic. It straddles two regions, Côtes d'Armor and Finistère, encompassing a range of lovely sandy beaches, rocky headlands and estuaries. There is no obvious route and you may get lost among some of the lanes. Try to stick close to the sea.

Lieu de Grève is one of Brittany's best beaches, with St.-Michel-en-Grève a small village at the eastern end. Locquirec has more lovely beaches and a headland setting. High viewing points along the coastal road offer panoramic coastal vistas and make good spots for picnics.

St.-Jean-du-Doigt's parish close (see p.90) contains a splendid Renaissance fountain depicting the baptism of Christ. The parish is named for its celebrated relic, the alleged index finger of John the Baptist, brought to Brittany in the 15th century. The finger is said to be able to cure eye diseases.

Westwards lies a series of pretty fishing ports such as Le Diben and Térénez. If you enjoy megaliths, visit the Barnenez tumulus on the Morlaix estuary, a huge mount of granite containing about a dozen burial chambers and erected in about 4600 BC. There's an entrance fee, but the guided tour is very informative.

MEGALITHS

The impressive alignments of standing stones, or menhirs, at Carnac have puzzled archeologists for many years, but they are presumed to have some ritual or religious significance.

Many of the stones were erected between about 4000 and 1800 BC. Some of the main groups of alignments are now fenced off to reduce erosion, but you can get a good view of them from raised viewing platforms.

Around Carnac are tumuli and dolmens, earth mounds or megalithic structures made of large slabs, both once used as burial chambers. A flashlight can be useful for exploring.

Some of the larger monuments have an entrance charge ■

CRÊPES

While visiting Brittany, don't miss out on one of its gastronomic specialties.

Pancake houses (*crêperies*) can be found in virtually every town or village, offering a range of fillings, sweet and savory, from ice cream to seafood. Two or three *crêpes* make a complete meal.

Sweet *crêpes* tend to be made of wheat flour, while the traditional Breton *galette*, once a staple food in poorer homes, is made of coarser buckwheat flour.

Making *crêpes* is quite an art. Temperature and consistency of the batter are vitally important. Watch the cook deftly oil a hot griddle and smooth out the batter, flipping it over at just the right moment ■

★★ CORNICHE BRETONNE   74C3/B3

This drive takes in some of Brittany's most dramatic scenery, which has given its name to the region: the Pink Granite Coast (Côte de Granit Rose).

It starts near Paimpol and runs around a series of ragged headlands to the resort of Trébeurden. The most striking section of all lies near Perros-Guirec, Ploumanac'h and Trégastel, with extraordinary boulders of pinkish granite, worn by wind and waves into strange, almost organic shapes. Many of these have been given fanciful names such as the Tortoise, the Rabbit, the Devil's Castle or the Pile of Pancakes. Sometimes the rocks are smooth and rounded, balancing on each other as delicately as ballerinas. Other formations are jagged and splintered, depending on how the mineral layers of feldspar and mica have leached out. A coastal footpath leads around this headland (see p.91).

★★★ CROZON PENINSULA   74A2/B2

A drive around this hammerhead promontory shows you some of Brittany's most exciting cliffs; the best are at the western capes. There are also some lovely quiet beaches, though not all are safe for swimming. Inland, the scenery is agricultural land scattered with vacation homes. Sightseeing is fairly limited, with only a few small museums. But there are plenty of opportunities for breezy walks, enjoying the beaches, or even a short boat trip. Wear sensible footwear, as some of the rocky paths can be slippery. The northern route gives good views of the Rade de Brest through wooded inlets.

Le Faou makes a pleasant starting point, with good hotel-restaurants and shops for buying picnic provisions. The Térénez Corniche is a fine approach to Crozon via the modern suspension bridge over the Aulne. Detour to Landévennec to see the evocative ruins of the abbey in its lush, watery setting. Argol, south of the main Crozon road, has an interesting parish close (see p.90) and a cider museum. Trégarvan's Musée de l'École Rurale, on the south bank of the Aulne, is housed in the former local school.

Crozon, the peninsula's main town, has little of interest except its church, which has an unusual altarpiece. The lobster port of Camaret makes a good place to stop for lunch, with excellent fish restaurants scattered around its sheltered harbor. A natural spit of pebbles protects the port. On it stand a tiny pilgrim chapel, Notre-Dame-de-Rocamadour, and a small red-brick fortress erected by Vauban in 1689.

The lookouts jutting into the Atlantic are the highlights of the trip, especially at the Pointe de Penhir and the Pointe de Dinan, where a natural rock arch leads to a formation called the Château de Dinan. The headland juts northwards ending at the Pointe des Espagnols, with a splendid view of the Brest roadstead. This promontory was once held by Spanish forces, hence its name. The church at Roscanvel has striking modern glass.

Heading south again, **Morgat** is one of Crozon's principal resorts, a good sailing and water sports center with a sheltered beach. Excursion boats go to local caves (*grottes*), remarkable for their mineral colorations. The southerly headland is a wild expanse of exposed rock and heath. Drop in at the Maison des Minéraux en route, a well-displayed collection of local rocks, some eerily lit by ultraviolet light.

On the southerly return road, detour to the beautiful beaches of Trez-Bellec or Pentrez-Plage, popular for parascending and hang-gliding. Ménez-Hom is one of Brittany's best lookouts; at 330 meters (1,083 ft.) it commands a view of the entire peninsula.

South of Crozon, the little town of **Locronan** makes a delightful base for a night, and a good place to look for souvenirs. It is one of the best-preserved of all Breton towns. The finest of its granite mansions stand around the cobbled main square, where the 15th-century church of St.-Ronan and Le Pénity chapel make a striking assembly in a style known as Ogival Flamboyant.

★★★ DINAN   75D3

Don't miss Dinan, a medieval town standing high over the Rance estuary looking downstream towards St.-Malo. Its half-timbered old quarter is best explored on foot. The castle was built from the 13th century on; the keep houses the town

museum. From here, you can follow the ramparts all the way around town. The section called the Promenade de la Duchesse Anne leads past splendid views of the Rance Valley to the neat Jardin Anglais and the Romanesque to Gothic church of St.-Sauveur. Inside it lies the heart of the famous Breton hero, Bertrand du Guesclin. His statue stands in the main square, the scene of his duel with Thomas of Canterbury in 1357.

Dinan's narrow streets are lined with corbeled buildings and shady arcades. The pretty Hôtel Kératry houses the tourist office. The steep rue du Jerzual leads down to the river past 15th- and 16th-century houses, now art studios and craft shops. At the quayside cafés and restaurants you can enjoy the port scene before climbing back to the old town (a little tourist train operates in summer). Regular boat trips ply down the Rance towards Dinard and St.-Malo; you can make the return journey by bus or train.

One of the best ways to arrive in Dinan is by boat along the Rance from either St.-Malo or Dinard. With its medieval ramparts almost completely intact, this picturesque town is the most visited of France's citadel towns

DRIVE

THE EMERALD COUNTRY

392 kilometers/244 miles (allow 3 days)

Brittany's scenic drama lies mostly on the coast, and nowhere more so than in the northeast where a series of jagged headlands separated by sandy bays lunges into the Channel. Highlights of this tour include the abbey of Le Mont St.-Michel, the oyster beds of Cancale, the historic port of St.-Malo, and the capes of Fréhel and Grouin. Inland, the towns are full of interest, featuring castles, museums and picturesque buildings.

Rennes makes a good starting point for this tour. Though many visitors overlook the Breton capital, the center of Rennes is well worth half a day's exploration for its excellent museums.

THE NAMING OF CANADA

One of St. Malo's famous explorers was Jacques Cartier (see also p.94).

He first reached Newfoundland in 1534. Two years later he sailed up the St. Lawrence River and asked the native Indians where he was. Their reply was "Canada," the name of their home village, and thus the name of this huge new country was established ∎

Leave Rennes for Fougères on the N12. Go right on the D528 to Liffré and in the town center turn right toward Vitré via La Bouëxière. Enter Vitré on the D857.

1 Vitré

Vitré has a charmingly preserved section of medieval streets around its formidable fortress perched high over the Vilaine river. Views from its ramparts are perhaps more dramatic than views of the stronghold itself, best seen from the northeast, a hilly belvedere called Tertres Noirs. The old houses in rue Baudrairie are worth a look, as is the suburb of Rachapt below the fortress.

Take the D178 due north towards Fougères.

2 Fougères

This is another massively fortified border town that once guarded the independent Breton dukedom from the unwelcome incursions of French kings. Fougères' castle is one of the most impressive in France, virtually moated by the Nançon river, but – unusually – set below rather than above the town. See it from the public gardens behind the church of St.-Léonard, and don't miss the charming Marchix quarter around the church of St.-Sulpice.

Leave Fougères as for St.-Hilaire on the D177. Immediately after leaving the town, bear right via the route forestière to the north, and pick your way through Poilley, Coglès and Antrain, via the D15, before heading north on the N175 to Le Mont-St.-Michel.

3 Le Mont-St.-Michel

As you approach the coast, the unmistakable pyramid of Le Mont-St.-Michel rises like a mirage across the flat, sheep-grazed polders behind the bay.

The Couesnon river, which marks the Normandy border, has shifted its course through the centuries and now runs west of the abbey, thus placing it in Normandy (see p.68). You can drive to the base of the abbey on a causeway road, a safer approach than former pilgrims enjoyed through perilous quicksands and racing tides. A small village huddles around the lower slopes of the rock, which inevitably resound with the ring of cash tills as thousands of visitors pour in. Persevere through the commercialized religiosity of the Grande Rue to the ethereal heights above, where France's most glorious assembly of Gothic and Romaneque buildings awaits.

Return to Beauvoir. Go west to take the D797 through St.-Brolade, and then the D155 toward the village of Mont Dol.

4 Mont Dol

After paying homage at Le Mont-St.-Michel, head for the historic bishopric of Dol-de-Bretagne, where the austere cathedral of St.-Samson dominates the town atop a rocky escarpment.

Even more striking views of the Dutch-like landscape around Le Mont-St.-Michel can be seen from the granite outcrop of Mont Dol, legendary site of the epic struggle between the Archangel Michael and the Devil. A surface road goes all the way round the mound, and there's a panoramic view from the top. The coastal village of Le Vivier-sur-Mer specializes in mussel cultivation. If you have time, take a trip on the curious amphibious vehicle *Sirène de la Baie* to see the *bouchots*, a forest of dark wooden posts on which the mussels are farmed.

Leave Mont Dol on the D123. Take the D155 and follow signs towards Cancale on the D76. Go through Cancale and leave following "St.-Malo par la Côte" and "Pointe du Grouin" signs along the D201. Take the D76 to Pointe du Grouin and then return to the D201 for St.-Malo.

5 St.-Malo

Follow the coast road down to St.-Malo, the prettiest of all the Channel ports. It may come as a surprise to realize the old town is, to put it unkindly, a fake. It was almost entirely rebuilt after World War II in its original style using granite from the nearby Îles Chausey. St.-Malo boasts a proud maritime tradition, and has launched boatloads of privateers, explorers and fishermen on the waves from its granite walls. The area to focus on is the old town

CELTIC BRITTANY

Although the Breton language is largely in decline, Celtic culture thrives through folk music.

The Celtic traditions of singing and storytelling, passed down through generations, are on show at concerts and festivals through the summer.

Look for Breton instruments such as the *bombarde* (oboe), *biniou* (bagpipes) and *vielle* (hurdy-gurdy) ∎

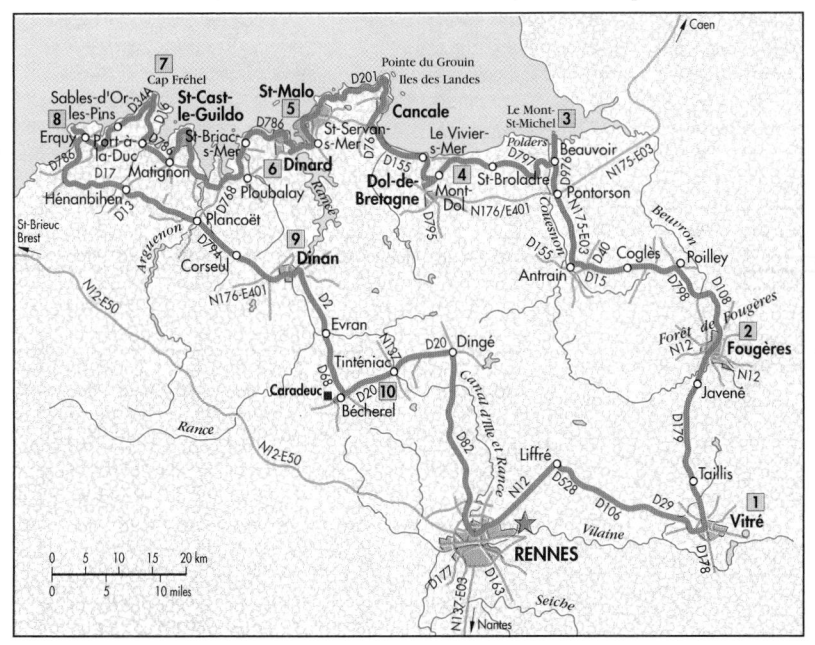

DINAN'S MEDIEVAL WARRIOR

Bertrand du Guesclin was born in Dinan in 1320. The eldest of 10 children, he was disowned by his parents and became the leader of a lawless peasant gang.

He seized the chance of military adventure during the War of Succession, and such was his prowess on the battlefield that he was ransomed for a massive 100,000 crowns when he was later captured.

He became Constable of France in 1370, but died whilst on active duty in the Massif Central in 1380.

He had wanted to be buried near his native Dinan, but due to the summer heat parts of his body had to be disposed of en route, and only his heart made it the whole way home ∎

within the ramparts, known as *intra-muros*. The resort suburb of St.-Servan-sur-Mer is also worth a look. See the 14th-century Tour Solidor, now housing a museum devoted to Cape Horn sailors, and walk around the Aleth Corniche for a grand view of St.-Malo and the Rance estuary.

Leave St.-Malo following signs for Dinard. Take the D114 and then the D266 to Dinard.

6 Dinard

As you cross the road bridge leading to Dinard, pause for a look at one of Brittany's most ambitious engineering projects, the tidal dam (*usine marémotrice*) across the Rance which generates about 8 percent of the province's electricity entirely from the ebb and flow of the river. A free walk-through exhibition shows you how it works.

Dinard, on the other side of the Rance, offers every facility for the fashionable vacationer. Whether or not you need casinos and thalassotherapy, the resort's lovely setting on a series of bays and rocky promontories can hardly fail to please. Take a stroll along the Promenade du Clair de Lune to prove it.

Take the D786 through St.-Briac and continue to St.-Brieuc. After Port-à-la-Duc turn right to Cap Fréhel on the D16.

7 Cap Fréhel

Cap Fréhel is the most spectacular natural sight on this tour. A lighthouse (completed in 1948) guards the cape, which gives amazing views of the entire coast. Try a walk around these wave-gnarled, heath-covered cliffs of schist and red porphyry where sea birds crowd on every

rocky foothold. Fort la Latte, a medieval castle, guards another headland a mile or two east.

Turn right from Cap Fréhel onto the D34a for St.-Brieuc. Rejoin the D786 for Erquy.

8 Erquy

Erquy is an attractive little scallop-fishing port with more fine beaches and exhilarating headlands. You can windsurf and rent canoes here as well. At Cap d'Erquy you can climb to the headland for spectacular views over offshore reefs, or head for the east-facing beach.

Leave Erquy on the D786 for St.-Brieuc, then take the N176 for Dinan.

9 Dinan

Though some way inland, Dinan was once an important port, the lowest bridging point on the Rance until recent times. Its splendid, rampart-girt medieval center is a delight to explore. More views can be had from the Promenade de la Duchesse Anne and the Jardin Anglais behind St.-Sauveur church, where the heart of Dinan's hero, Bertrand du Guesclin, lies buried.

Leave Dinan and turn right through Evran on the D2. In Bécherel take the D20 to Tinténiac.

10 Tinténiac

Meander back to Rennes via the pleasant rural countryside around Caradeuc, site of a fine château, and Tinténiac on the Canal d'Ille-et-Rance. The church at Tinténiac is a 20th-century rebuilding on an old ecclesiastical site.

Continue on the D20 to Dingé. Then return to Rennes via the D82.

★★★ DINARD and THE EMERALD COAST   75D3

From a simple fishing village, Dinard expanded into a fashionable watering hole in the 19th century, when an American tycoon built a palatial villa on the cliffs. The resort's setting is a series of sandy beaches scooped between wooded cliffs and rugged headlands, with a mild climate supporting subtropical vegetation. Exceptional tidal variations make it a sailing mecca. In summer, lines of chic striped beach tents face the sea and French families occupy every available space, playing volleyball and *pétanque* (a form of the popular French game of *boules*). The walk along the garden-fringed promenade to the Plage du Prieuré gives one of the best overviews of Dinard. Summer sees a continuous round of activities, including regattas, concerts and its celebrated *spectacles d'ambiance* (light shows). From this excellent, if pricey, base you can easily explore the whole of the Emerald Coast. Take a boat trip if you have a fine day to spare: parts of the coast, and the Rance Valley, are best seen from the water.

From Dinard it's an easy hop across the bridge to St.-Malo (see p.93). On the way, look in at the tidal dam (*usine marémotrice*) across the Rance, which generates some of Brittany's electricity. There's a free exhibition and audiovisual show.

In the deeply indented coastline west of Dinard lie a host of smaller, lower-profile resorts, all in fine settings with excellent beaches, especially Sables-d'Or-les-Pins and Le Val-André. The highlight, however, is Cap Fréhel, where cliffs of sandstone and porphyry soar 70 meters (230 ft.) above the sea; park by the lighthouse (which you can visit).

DOL-DE-BRETAGNE   75D3

Once a bishopric of one of the seven founding saints of Brittany, Dol's hilltop site protected it from the tidal wave of 709. When the sea retreated, brackish salt marshes were left behind, which have since been drained. The salty reclaimed fields are now pasture for Brittany's famous *pré-salé* lambs.

Dol's austere granite cathedral still stands sentinel over the surrounding countryside. The nearby history museum contains strange collections of local antiquities. Around it thread narrow streets full of ancient houses. The Promenade des Douves, along the line of the old ramparts, gives a fine view over the marshes. Another good lookout is Mont-Dol, a flat-topped outcrop just north of town, occupied since prehistory.

White sand, blue sea and striped parasols give the coastal resort of Dinard a distinctly Mediterranean air. The resort was "discovered" by an American in the 1850s; since then, it has lost none of its appeal

DOUARNENEZ 74B2

Douarnenez's raison d'être is fish. Canning factories surround the quays, and a fish auction is held most days. Douarnenez has a deep-water harbor and modern facilities; sardines and lobster are its specialties. Parts of the town are very ancient, though lacking obvious old-world charm. Around the quayside are good-value fish restaurants, and on the Port-Rhu river is a splendid maritime museum, with a living collection of sailing and fishing craft of all kinds, some moored on the banks, others in its Musée du Bateau, housed in an old cannery. The best beaches are at Tréboul, across the Port-Rhu. Boat trips are available in summer.

FORÊT DE HUELGOAT 74B3

Huelgoat is one of the last remaining great forests of Brittany. Sadly, not much is left since the hurricane-force winds of 1987. The lakeside town of Huelgoat offers plenty of summer activities and walking. Marked paths through the woods lead through a mossy tumble of boulders and streams. The canals were dug during the 19th century, when lead and silver mines were worked. One hilly site is even older: the Camp d'Artus was used by both Celtic and Roman settlers.

FORÊT DE PAIMPONT 75D2

Although no longer a great woodland cloaking central Brittany, Paimpont (the ancient Brocéliande) is still full of legend and strongly linked with Arthurian myth. Merlin's grave is reputedly hidden here, as well as the enchanted spring where the sorceress Viviane imprisoned him in a circle of air. Sprinkling water on the slab near the Barenton fountain, it is said, will bring a great storm. At the Val sans Retour, Morgan le Fay ensnared faithless lovers after being jilted by a knight. The little church at Tréhorenteuc has a stained-glass window with Arthurian scenes.

The village of Paimpont is the main base for exploring this forest. Its summer tourist office can provide you with some ideas and maps for forest walks.

The fortress at Fougères remains a fine example of medieval military architecture. Built on a promontory overlooking the Nançon river, the immense walls and formidable appearance did not prevent it from being frequently taken by assailants

★ **FOUGÈRES**   *75E2*

Fougères' location in the swampy marches between Brittany and the rest of France determined its purpose as a defensive site. Built on a promontory above a tight loop in the Nançon, Fougères seems an impregnable fortress. For all that, its massive medieval castle – built, unusually, below the town – was frequently captured. Rocky spurs soar above it, supporting its mostly 18th-century buildings. The Marchix quarter near the castle is an assembly of pretty half-timbered houses, mills and tanneries (Fougères is now a centre for shoe manufacture). It's best seen from the upper town, by the gardens in the church of St.-Léonard. The castle walls and towers are virtually intact, but the rest stands mostly in ruins.

ILES D'OUESSANT and MOLÈNE   *74A3*

The waters around these reef-strewn islands are among Europe's most treacherous. Despite this, regular ferries ply swiftly from the mainland through a maze of marker buoys, docking briefly at Molène before heading for Ouessant. The islands are a last remnant of a maritime community and lifestyle that's almost disappeared on the mainland, and are now part of a nature reserve, the Parc Naturel Régional d'Armorique (see p.89). If you have enough time, you can see both islands; with only a day to spare, the larger Ouessant has more to offer. Visitors arrive at the Baie du Stiff, where a lighthouse stands. The best way to explore the island is to rent a bicycle from the harbor. Minibus tours are also offered. Lampaul is the main village, with a few cafés and simple hotels. You can wander over most of the island on sheep tracks. Best places to visit are the lighthouse museum at the Creac'h lighthouse, on the west side of Ouessant, and the *écomusée* at Niou Uhella, made from two tiny cottages furnished in their original style.

JOSSELIN   *75C2*

Founded in about 1000, Josselin is most memorable for its castle, rising sheer from the Oust river. The forbidding exterior disguises a charmingly domesticated Renaissance wing. The castle suffered various humiliations at the hands of Cardinal Richelieu and during the Revolution, but was restored in the 19th century. An appealing doll collection is housed in part of the castle. Also worth seeing is Josselin's fine 12th-century church, Notre-Dame-du-Roncier (Our Lady of the Brambles); half-timbered houses stand nearby.

KERJEAN, CHÂTEAU DE   *74B3*

Most of Finistère's many fine mansions are private or in ruins. Kerjean is neither, and easy to find between Plouescat and Landivisiau. Dating from the 16th century, it was damaged by fire and revolutionaries in the 18th century. Now it is run by the state as a museum and cultural center. The château is set in a large park, walled and moated in medieval fashion. Inside, the building is mostly Renaissance, with displays of Breton furniture.

LANNION   *74B3*

This attractive old town on the Léguer estuary is a good base for inland and coastal excursions. A busy market is held here on Thursdays. Its main sights are old houses decorated with carved figures. Brélévenez church stands at the top of a long flight of steps. Its unusual interior is full of interest, while the terrace has a good view of the town.

WALK

MONTS D'ARRÉE

Two lookouts, Roc Trévezel (accessible on foot) and Montagne St.-Michel (road access), give splendid views of the Monts d'Arrée, Brittany's highest hills.

   For a lonely but unusual walk, head for the Marais du Yeun Elez (Mouth of Hell), a swampy area around the Réservoir St.-Michel.

   Paths lead all around the reservoir, a conservation area with interesting wildlife, including otters, bog plants and over 90 species of bird.

   The looming structure on the eastern shore is a nuclear power station. Keep strictly to the paths (marked with orange signs) or you may end up in a bog ∎

LORIENT *74B2*

Extensive docklands, heavy industry and a German U-boat base meant Lorient was all but destroyed by Allied bombs (the U-boats' concrete pens are used today by nuclear submarines). But the town still has a thriving fishing industry and a bustling

commercial harbor. Visitors' interest is focused near the port and the nearby Maison de la Mer in the tourist office building. In summer, a popular international Celtic music festival attracts visitors from far and wide.

Morlaix has some attractive half-timbered houses. The most striking is the house in which Anne of Brittany is said to have stayed on a visit here in 1505. The old town is an enjoyable place to explore on foot

★★★ MORBIHAN, GOLFE DU *75C1*

This large landlocked bay is the most striking feature of Brittany's southern coast. It lacks good beaches, but offers a host of water-sports facilities, boat trips and natural interest, particularly for birdwatchers. A huge number of sea birds congregate in the varied habitats of the gulf – salt marsh, estuary, reedbed, dune, pinewood and heath. Over 300 islands sprinkle the waterline, some mere grassy hummocks, others larger and inhabited. Many are privately owned. Boat excursions visit three, the Ile aux Moines (the largest and most varied), the Ile d'Arz (which has a good restaurant) and the Ile de Gavrinis, which has one of Brittany's best megalithic sites, an ornately carved burial chamber beneath a grass-topped cairn. The Gavrinis ferry operates from Larmor-Baden. Other boat trips or boat rental can be arranged from Vannes, Locmariaquer, Port-Navalo and Auray. Oysters are a specialty in some parts of the gulf, and lush Mediterranean vegetation flourishes in its sheltered climate. Currents can make swimming dangerous; the tide rips through the narrow neck at Locmariaquer with great force.

MORLAIX *74B3*

This attractive town was once one of Brittany's leading ports. During the heady trading days of the 16th to 18th centuries it prospered from fishing, linen, paper, shipbuilding, tobacco – and privateering. Morlaix's old town is a very enjoyable place to explore for half a day. A giant railroad viaduct dominates the port area, and the compact old town spreads out at its feet, climbing the steep-sided valley in flights of steps or quaint lanes called *venelles*. The lower level of the viaduct is accessible on foot and provides good views.

Morlaix has lots of charming old buildings, an interesting church or two, and a good local museum exhibiting archeological artifacts unearthed in the area. Its most striking house is the Maison de la Reine Anne, a three-storied 16th-century timbered building known as a "skylight" house. It contains a fascinating spiral staircase. The handsome old tobacco factory still stands by the port (occasional tours offered).

★★ NANTES   75D1

Technically, Nantes is now capital of the Pays de Loire region, but historically and spiritually it still belongs in Brittany. Its modern industrial outskirts are ugly and confusing, but the older central quarters are well worth exploring, and Nantes makes an interesting base for a short break. The surrounding area offers river trips and vineyards (all the châteaux of the Loire lie at Nantes's feet).

The cathedral and the castle are the most important sights. The cathedral of St.-Peter and St.-Paul is quite different from most Breton churches, for it is constructed of airy white tufa instead of solid granite. The soaring nave gives an astonishing impression of light and space. Look for the 16th-century marble tomb of François II and his wife (the Duchess Anne's parents), a masterpiece by the Breton sculptor Michel Colombe. The ducal castle dates back to the 15th century, the historic seat of the dukes of Brittany who enjoyed a glorious, almost royal court in the days before unification with France. The Edict of Nantes, granting tolerance to Protestants, was signed here by Henri IV in 1598. A number of museums are housed within the castle (closed Tuesday). The Musée des Beaux-Arts, in a 19th-century building nearby, contains a solid repertoire of French and European art. There are several other museums in town: two of the best are the Palais Dobrée

complex, the former home of the wealthy Nantes shipowner Thomas Dobrée (three museums in one, including a remarkable archeological collection), and an idiosyncratic natural history museum housed in the former Mint. Equally enjoyable, though, is an unscheduled wander around the various districts of the old town, particularly Ste.-Croix, with its stately 15th- and 16th-century houses, the Ile Feydeau, a rich shipbuilders' quarter, and the two 19th-century squares, place Royale and place Graslin. If you feel like a rest, make for the delightful art-nouveau brasserie called La Cigale on place Graslin, with its flamboyant interior of mirrors, mosaics and plasterwork. The seafood is pretty good too.

PARC NATUREL   74A2
RÉGIONAL D'ARMORIQUE

This regional nature reserve of 112,000 hectares (278,000 acres), first set up in 1969, is one of 26 similar conservation areas in France. It represents a great variety of typical Breton land- and seascapes and much of its flora and fauna, stretching far inland to Brittany's highest hills (the Monts d'Arrée) and way out to sea to include the islands of Ouessant and Molène (see p.87). It also encompasses the Aulne estuary and the Crozon Peninsula.

The aims of the park are to foster traditional rural ways of life and Breton culture, to protect the environment, and to preserve the peninsula's ancient megalithic sites. There is plenty to interest keen walkers, birdwatchers or fishing enthusiasts, and a cluster of little museums, tracing various aspects of the regional lifestyle, have been set up in traditional dwellings. Some of the finest examples of Brittany's parish closes (see p.90) lie within or very close to the Armorique reserve.

GAUGUIN
(1848–1903)

Paul Gauguin conformed to the Bohemian stereotype – the artist who abandoned everything (his safe but boring office job in Paris, his wife and children) for a nomadic and often poverty-stricken lifestyle.

His later works were mostly inspired by his travels in Tahiti and the South Seas, but while in Brittany he was undoubtedly the most talented of the "Pont-Aven school of painters" (see p.91).

Paul Gauguin found Brittany a great source of inspiration: "When my clogs strike the granite underfoot, I hear the dull, powerful tone I'm searching for in my painting."

Sadly, little of his work remains in Brittany ■

Built in 1555, the magnificent stone calvary at Pleyben is set inside one of the most impressive of all the parish closes. The figures are carved with acute observation to detail, and many are dressed in contemporary Breton costume

★★★ PARISH CLOSES   74B3

Brittany's enclosed churchyards are unique, and one of its highest forms of artistic expression. Some of the best lie clustered in the Élorn Valley near Landivisiau, but others can be found scattered throughout Finistère. They are all highly individual, but many display one or more typical features.

Generally, the hallowed ground around a church is surrounded by a low wall pierced with stiles to keep animals out. The main entrance, through which funeral processions pass, may have an imposing gateway, sometimes a classical triumphal arch. Inside the close, there is usually a chapel-like ossuary, where bones were once stored, and a calvary.

Breton calvaries are more than mere crucifixes: they are extremely elaborate and highly wrought works of art. The central theme is invariably the Passion, but other scenes (biblical or secular) are carved in granite around the base of the cross. In an age when many parishioners were illiterate, these carvings graphically reinforced the Gospel message. Over time, some have been badly weathered by the elements or deliberately defaced.

The best of the parish closes date back to the 16th and 17th centuries, when Finistère grew rich on sea-borne trade. Rival parishes spent most of their resources on their churches, and these closes became both a local status symbol and a showroom for the most skillful masons and artisans of the age. Much of their art can be seen inside the churches too, especially in fine woodcarving and decorated beams. Famous parish closes include Guimiliau, St.-Thégonnec, Sizun and Pleyben. If you get hooked, there are dozens to visit.

★★★ PERROS-GUIREC   74C3

This is one of the main resorts on the **Pink Granite Coast**, ideal for family holidays. Though extensive, it never feels too commercialized or crowded. A coastal road winds around scenic headlands connecting its various sandy beaches with the pleasure port. There is a casino and a thalassotherapy center on the seafront at Trestraou, and many boat trips are advertised, several to the Sept-Iles (a bird sanctuary) in summer. In town, the unusual church of St.-Jacques is worth a look; just outside, track down the pretty pink-granite chapel of Notre-Dame-de-la-Clarté, used as a landmark for shipping and full of model boats. One of the most enjoyable excursions is a walk up the customs-officers' path to Ploumanac'h (see opposite).

PONT-AVEN 74B2

This attractive town is mainly associated with a group of painters who colonized the area from the mid-19th century onwards. The most famous of these was Paul Gauguin (see p.89). Even today, the town makes the most of its artistic connections, with an excellent municipal art gallery containing a cross-section of the Pont-Aven school's work, and many modern commercial galleries. Sketchers and watercolorists were mesmerized by the prettiness of the watermills and wooded river scenery that composed so many of their paintings, and by the availability of local models and cheap lodgings. Today many of the original mills have gone, but the Aven river, rushing over granite boulders, still offers a delightful picture (take a drive or boat trip downstream), and trails lead through the woods behind. It's a good place to look for souvenirs (cookies are a local specialty). Two local chapels, Trémalo and Nizon, contain primitive but strangely powerful crucifixes that inspired Gauguin's "Christ Jaune" and "Christ Vert."

★ QUIBERON PENINSULA 74C1

A narrow causeway of sand and silt attaches this odd excrescence of land to the Morbihan coast. The west side, exposed to the Atlantic, is windswept and wave-torn, with dramatic cliff and rock scenery but treacherous under-tows. The sheltered eastern side offers safe, gentle beaches and calm sailing waters. Quiberon,

the main town and port at the far end of the spinal road, is one of Morbihan's liveliest resorts, often crowded in high season as travelers converge for the Belle-Ile ferry. Several hotels and a large thalassotherapy center take advantage of the fine beach.

★★★ QUIMPER 74B2

This large town was once the capital of the Celtic duchy of Cornouaille, whose influence once stretched well beyond southern Finistère. Apocryphal tales tell of its association with King Gradlon, who brought his court here after the legendary city of Ys sank, Atlantis-style, beneath the waters of Douarnenez Bay. He and his bishop, Saint Corentin, founded the great cathedral, built between the 13th and 15th centuries, whose twin spires dominate the city.

Quimper has a small airport and good shops. The old town is delightful, with quaint, flower-decked houses lining its narrow streets and an extensive river frontage. Sights include good regional folk and art museums near the cathedral, plus a ceramics museum and pottery workshops (open for tours) a short walk downstream in the suburb of Locmaria. In July the city hosts a Celtic folk festival.

REDON 75D1

Waterways, roads, railroads and regional boundaries intersect at Redon, which once functioned as an inland port. Today the leisure industry supplements its small factories. All summer long, houseboats, pleasure cruisers, canoes, fishing and sailing craft converge at Redon on various arms of the Oust, Vilaine, and the Nantes–Brest Canal. Sights include the church of St.-Sauveur, a waterways museum and old houses along the quaysides.

WALK

PINK GRANITE COAST: PERROS-GUIREC TO PLOUMANAC'H

This headland walk takes in one of the most dramatic stretches of the Pink Granite Coast. It is particularly enjoyable towards sunset at high tide, when the rocks take on a fierce orange glow.

Follow the *sentier des douaniers* (customs-officers' path) from Perros-Guirec by the Plage de Tres-traou, which hugs the shore beneath the cliffs.

At Pors Rolland you enter a chaos of weirdly shaped rocks eroded into fantastic, almost lifelike shapes.

You can follow the path around through a park (where the rocks are neatly labeled with a variety of fanciful names) as far as the Plage St.-Guirec ■

CORSAIRS

Many fine buildings in Brittany, particularly in and around St.-Malo, were built on the lucrative profits of piracy.

Breton corsairs were licensed privateers with "letters of marque" signed by the king of France. These empowered them to board and seize enemy ships (merchant or naval). The captured booty was then shared out between the king, the shipowner and the corsairs in a strict percentage ratio.

Foreign governments often retaliated by sending troops to storm Breton ports (usually without success).

Two of the most famous corsairs were the 18th-century René Duguay-Trouin and Robert Surcouf, whose monuments you will see on the ramparts of St.-Malo ∎

★★ RENNES   75D2

The present capital of Brittany has all the unattractive aspects of a sizeable modern city: confusing traffic, parking problems and dull outskirts. But the historic quarters merit at least a good half-day's sightseeing. In 1720 a huge conflagration destroyed much of medieval Rennes, whereupon it was rebuilt in a severe neoclassical style along Parisian lines. But a few older sectors survive, along with some striking timbered buildings.

The Palais de Justice (temporarily closed for repairs) also predates the fire and contains some spectacularly ornate public assembly rooms. The excellent Musée de Bretagne and Musée des Beaux-Arts (in the same building on the south bank of the canalized Vilaine) explain Brittany's culture and history, from prehistoric through Gallo-Roman and medieval times to life under the *ancien régime*. Just outside the town, the Ecomusée du Pays de Rennes (at Bintinais Farm) presents the rural history of the province from the 16th century to the present day.

ROCHEFORT-EN-TERRE   75C1

Set on a rocky spur over the Arz Valley, Rochefort overlooks a wooded landscape of great charm, and is itself conspicuously pretty. Old mansions sporting carved woodwork and stone figures line the cobbled streets, several converted into shops or restaurants. Notre-Dame-de-la-Tronchaye is a lovely old church with a gabled facade and a three-tiered calvary. The castle at the top of the town was destroyed during the Revolution, but was imaginatively restored at the turn of the 20th century by two American artist brothers. It is now open to the public, with a small museum inside.

★ ROSCOFF and ILE DE BATZ   74B3

The ferry port of Roscoff is often regarded as a place to get into or out of as quickly as possible, but you won't regret giving it more of your time. The old town clustered around the fishing port is small but pretty, and its church, Notre-Dame-de-Kroaz-Batz, has one of the finest belfries in Finistère. The exterior is decorated with model galleons, showing its patronage by well-to-do seafaring communities (some of whom were corsairs).

Just offshore, accessible via a 15-minute boat ride, the Île de Batz makes a pleasant half-day's excursion. Its mild climate makes the tiny island a centre for market gardening. This was once the hermitage of one of Finistère's founding saints, Pol the Aurelian, who, it is said, tethered a fierce dragon with his stole and cast it into a pit back in the 6th century.

ST.-BRIEUC, BAIE DE *75C3*

St.-Brieuc itself is a sprawling, confusing place spreadeagled across two deep river valleys. Apart from its weighty cathedral and a smallish old town, there is little to see. However, the rest of this wide V-shaped bay has much to recommend it. On the east side are the gorgeous beaches of the Emerald Coast (especially Le Val-André). Touring westwards through a series of coastal resorts (Binic, St.-Quay-Portrieux), you reach a scenic stretch known as the Circuit des Falaises between Plouha and Paimpol. These coves, hidden beneath brooding cliffs, were the scene of many daring rescue operations during World War II, when Allied airmen and prisoners of war were spirited out of occupied Brittany by the Resistance and the British Navy under the noses of the German patrols. Ruined Beauport Abbey is one of this coast's main sights.

Paimpol, farther north, is a pleasant town with a strong maritime tradition. Its former deep-sea fleets were among Brittany's most adventurous, trawling for cod off Iceland. A maritime museum on rue de la Benne charts their history. Today the boats are still busy with fish and trippers, but confine their activities much closer inshore. The place du Martray is the center of the old town, with fine 16th-century houses. Trips to the lush and automobile-free Ile de Bréhat make a popular excursion from the Pointe de l'Arcouest, strewn with a bracelet of reefs at low tide.

★★★ ST.-MALO *75D3*

Though badly damaged during World War II, St.-Malo was imaginatively reconstructed in its original style. At high tide be sure to take a walk along the encircling ramparts for a fine overview of

A walk along the Aleth Corniche footpath at St.-Servan yields exhilarating views over the Tour Solidor. St.-Servan was the Roman and early medieval predecessor of St.-Malo, nearby to the north

BRITTANY

WALK

OLD VANNES

Enter via Porte St.-Vincent or place de la République. Place des Lices was once the site of medieval jousting tournaments. Close by is the Maison de Vannes, with two jovial wooden carvings known as "Vannes and His Wife." The archeology museum contains prehistoric finds.

Head next for place Henri IV, surrounded by 16th-century gabled houses. On one side is La Cohue, the former covered market (now a museum) and the cathedral where Saint Vincent Ferrier once preached.

Now head for the 15th-century Porte Prison and stroll along the ramparts, beside formal gardens. Near the Porte Poterne are the photogenic old washhouses ■

the town and its 18th-century-style houses. Some of the original versions were built by St.-Malo's corsairs (privateers), including Robert Surcouf. On the seaward side lie several little fortified islands, the marina and modern port, and the Emerald Coast stretching into the distance.

St.-Malo's castle contains a couple of history museums, and its cathedral includes the tomb of Jacques Cartier, discoverer of Canada (his birthplace can be visited a few miles east of St.-Malo, at Rothéneuf). On Grand Bé, one of the islets accessible at low tide, lies another of Brittany's celebrities, the romantic author François-René de Chateaubriand, buried beneath a granite slab topped by a cross. There are plenty of restaurants, cafés, bars and hotels in St.-Malo, which is always lively. After exploring the old town within the walls (*intra-muros*), have a look at the outlying suburb of St.-Servan, a separate resort. Its Tour Solidor by the harbor contains a maritime museum, and the Aleth Corniche footpath around the headland makes a fine evening walk. Paramé to the east has long stretches of sand.

★ ST.-POL-DE-LÉON   74B3

St.-Pol, founded by Saint Pol the Aurelian, was a great religious center in the Middle Ages. It remains a sizeable town and a bustling agricultural center for Brittany's fertile Ceinture Dorée (Golden Belt), where many of its prized vegetables are grown. Many people visit St.-Pol's fine cathedral of Norman limestone, and the even more impressive Kreisker Chapel bell tower, which dominates the flattish landscape for miles around, its enormous steeple pierced with daisy-shapes to reduce wind resistance. You can climb the tower for extensive

views. The building is now used as a college chapel. There are a number of old houses on the main street (rue General Leclerc) and around the cathedral; the Maison Prébendale is one of the most interesting, a 16th-century canon's residence.

★★ VANNES   75C1

Vannes is an appealing place with a well-preserved old quarter enclosed by sturdy ramparts. Park somewhere near the walls and walk around. Best views are from the Promenade de la Garenne, which passes the best bit of the fortifications, now mellowed by pretty gardens. Notice the picturesque washhouses (*lavoirs*) near the Porte Poterne. Close to the cathedral (which spans six centuries of architectural style) stands La Cohue, a former covered marketplace that now houses a museum. Just off place des Lices, look for an old house with two comical carved wooden statues known as Vannes and His Wife. The nearby Musée Archéologique is worth a visit. Vannes is a great center for water sports and boat excursions to the Morbihan Gulf (see p.88).

★★ VITRÉ   75E2

From a distance Vitré looks very inviting, its ramparts bristling on a ridge above the Vilaine. Close up it loses none of its appeal: the old town is a delightful assembly of timber-framed, slate-hung houses on cobbled streets. Vitré's principal landmark is its massive castle, much targeted during the Hundred Years War (until the local inhabitants paid them a ransom to go away, English forces camped for years in the sector to the northwest). Inside are several small museums. Not far southeast lies the Château des Rochers-Sévigné, Madame de Sévigné's former home.

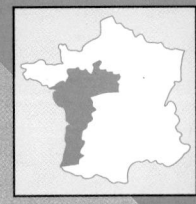

THE LOIRE VALLEY AND THE ATLANTIC COAST

France's lovely "Valley of the Kings" is
unrivaled in its architectural sights,
and well endowed with handsome
towns and villages

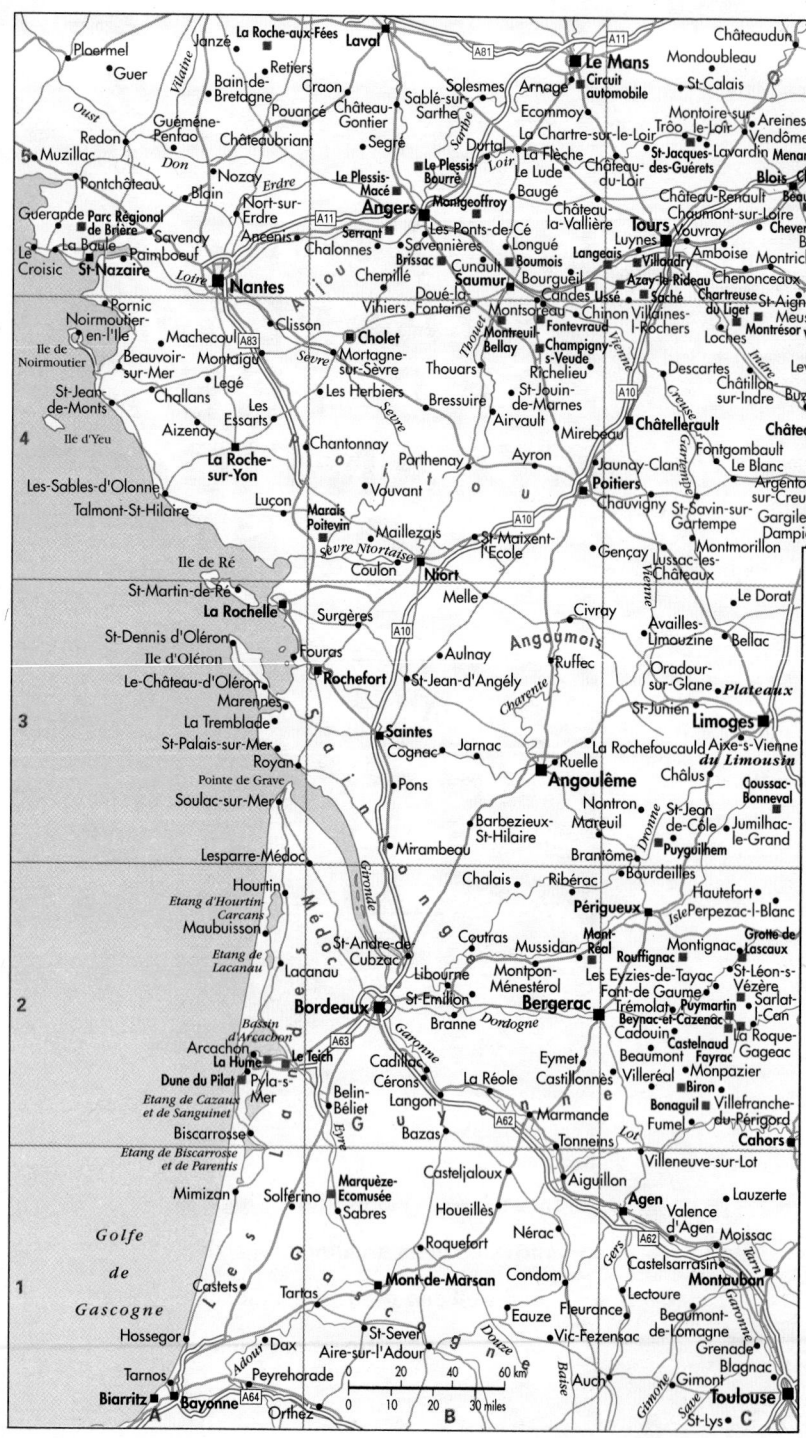

THE LOIRE VALLEY AND THE ATLANTIC COAST

The Loire is the longest river in France. For the most part it is wide and shallow, no longer the great navigable thoroughfare of historic times, when every height along its course was crowned with a medieval fortress and every bridge was strongly defended. Now wide highways follow its length, past nuclear power stations and busy cities. Yet its great history survives, adorning village, town and countryside. For the Loire Valley is incomparably rich in splendid **Renaissance châteaux** and manor houses, built of the local tufa stone and roofed and turreted with shiny gray slate.

The Val de Loire is the historic heart of France. As the capital of the English Plantagenet kings' empire, which at one point stretched from northern England to the Pyrénées, it was the focus of almost three centuries of war between the French and English. The successful campaigns of

Jeanne d'Arc, which culminated in the expulsion of the English, heralded a return of French pride that in turn led to a period of vigorous royal building programs. As the court settled in the Loire, palaces, country houses and hunting lodges were built, and the crafts and trades associated with all this activity flourished too.

One of the Loire region's attractions is its **mild climate**, responsible for its epithet "the garden of France." The region still provides the capital with early fruit and vegetables, particularly asparagus. Greenhouses, nurseries and flower gardens proliferate, as do vines, which provide good-value wines of almost every type.

Here, too, you will find an abundance of tourist facilities: charming hotels and restaurants in both town and country, plentiful opportunities to taste (and buy) wine, and châteaux open to visitors. Much of the interest of the great castles lies in their architecture and history,

---

★★★ HIGHLIGHTS

Angers (►98)
Azay-le-Rideau, Château de (►100)
Blois (►102)
Bordeaux (►103)
Chambord, Château de (►104)
Chenonceau, Château de (►105)
Cheverny, Château de (►106)
Langeais, Château de (►108)
La Rochelle (►119)
St.-Benoît-sur-Loire (►120)
St.-Savin (►121)

OYSTERS

The oyster beds of Arcachon are renowned, and relatively cheap oysters can be bought from stalls all around Arcachon's bay. Another major center on the Atlantic coast is Marennes, on the mainland by the Ile d'Oléron.

There are two main types. The *huître plate*, a native since Gallo-Roman times, has a fairly smooth, flat, often round shell. The variety called *vertes de Marennes*, which is naturally green from algae, is said to be the finest. Oysters from Arcachon are called *gravettes*.

The *huître creuse* is a more commonly found oyster with a longer, thicker and rougher shell. The cultivated oysters are called *huîtres de parc*; and the fattest are the *spéciales* ■

which is often explained in guided tours – in French. Smaller, more intimate châteaux, furnished and perhaps inhabited, will better acquaint you with the atmosphere of château life through the ages.

The Atlantic coast from Nantes to the foothills of the Pyrénées runs straight and sandy, buffeted by strong winds and seas, with a hinterland of dunes or marsh, oyster beds or the flat pine forests of the Landes. With some notable exceptions such as La Rochelle, there are few scenic resorts or charming fishing ports. Bordeaux, however, is one of France's most elegant cities, a great port in former times, founded on its trade in fine wines. The region's vineyards are world famous, their great châteaux sought out by wine connoisseurs and tourists alike.

★★ AMBOISE   96C5

One of the earliest Loire Valley settlements, this attractive and bustling small town is still dominated by the substantial remains of its magnificent château, which overlooks the town and river from a low promontory. The building of this, one of the greatest of the royal châteaux, heralded a new era in palace architecture – influenced by the exuberance of the Italian Renaissance and in marked contrast to the spartan fortress strongholds of previous royal dwellings. Highlights of a guided tour include the king's apartments, furnished with heavy Gothic furniture and Aubusson tapestries, and the remarkable Tour des Minimes, 21 meters (69 ft.) in diameter with a spiral ramp able to accommodate horses and carts. On the ramparts is the former oratory of the queen, the richly sculpted chapel of St.-Hubert.

Another sight that is well worth visiting is the manor of Le Clos-Lucé, the home of Leonardo da Vinci, who died here in 1519.

There are displays and working models constructed from his drawings, including a parachute, helicopter and tank.

★★★ ANGERS   96B5

A large and busy town, with ancient houses in the old quarter and wide boulevards marking the line of its former ramparts, Angers is renowned for its superb collections of tapestries. Most are housed in the medieval château, a striking pentagonal fortress of dark-gray shale ringed with white stone, with 17 truncated drum towers encircled by a moat (now filled with formal gardens).

Inside the defenses, a special gallery was built in 1952 to house Angers' great treasure, the extraordinary series of tapestries illustrating – in superb and often grisly detail – the Apocalypse of Saint John the Evangelist. The huge works, measuring around 100 meters (328 ft.) in length and 5 meters (16 ft.) in height, were commissioned during the 14th century from Nicolas Bataille, the greatest weaver of the age, from cartoons by the Flemish painter Hennequin of Bruges. The story of their survival is little short of miraculous, following fragmentation and haphazard storage, and finally disposal during the Revolution. In 1843 the prescient bishop of Angers set about buying and restoring all the fragments he could find.

On the opposite side of the river, the Ancien Hôpital de St.-Jean houses a very fine series of contemporary tapestries by the painter and designer Jean Lurçat.

★ ANGOULÊME   96B3

The capital of the *département* of Charente is a big town of little charm, bypassed efficiently by a network of encircling roads with numerous hypermarkets. Yet its hilltop center, with an interesting domed 12th-century cathedral, offers more attractive small-scale shopping opportunities, and a maze of quiet old cobbled streets.

★ ARCACHON and   96A2
THE CÔTE D'ARGENT

The arrow-straight and aptly named Silver Coast stretches from the Gironde river to the foothills of the Pyrénées, buffeted by fierce Atlantic waves. Its constantly shifting sands have created Europe's largest dunes, and were responsible for the burying of many coastal

The massive feudal fortress of Angers now has some lovely formal gardens in its former moat. Inside, the world's largest set of tapestries, from the 14th century, is on display

THE LOIRE: FRANCE'S LONGEST RIVER

The longest river in the country, the Loire surfaces in the Massif Central and meanders for over 1,000 kilometers (620 mi.) on its journey to the Atlantic coast.

France's most historic water-way, for centuries it was a major transport route for goods and people, with timber, fruit and wine loaded on to flat-bottomed *gabarres* and *cha-lands*, boats that could easily slide on and off the river's notorious sand banks and shoals.

The broad, flat Loire may appear a docile river, but it is prone to flooding; quick-sands and whirlpools are also a hazard for river users ∎

settlements until the dunes were finally stabilized in the 19th century by the planting of vast pine forests. Behind, the trapped river waters formed lakes, which are now the focus of recreational facilities. Pine-shaded lakeside campsites now offer ample accommodations, and the gentler waters of the lakes are popular with families.

Among a string of undistinguished coastal resorts, Arcachon in its sheltered, muddy bay reigns supreme, and has catered for the Bordeaux bourgeoisie long enough to give it an air of sophistication. There's a neat white casino, a promenade, and ornate "seaside Gothic" villas with turrets, pointed roofs, and large balconies. At night Arcachon's restaurants and cafés are lively. There are better beaches, however, at the resorts to the south. The bay, popular for yachting, is emptied almost completely twice a day by the tide. It provides ideal conditions for oyster-farming, and all around are roadside stalls selling cheap oysters. In the east is a bird reserve, Le Teich.

Just south of Arcachon, the resorts of Pyla-sur-Mer and Pilat-Plage provide a wide selection of accommodations and all the ingredients of a classic beach vacation. Pilat-Plage enjoys an extraordinary feature, being dwarfed by the 114-meter (374-ft.) bulk of its dune, which can be climbed with or without benefit of the stairway.

AUBIGNY-SUR-NÈRE   97D5
Set in the peaceful, wooded marshland of the Sologne between Orléans and Bourges, Aubigny is an attractive and venerable small town. It has several old gabled and timbered houses dating mainly from the 16th century, and the pattern of

its old streets testifies that it was once a circular walled town with ramparts. Taken into the royal domain in the 12th century, its ownership passed to the Scottish Stuart clan in 1423 as a gift of Charles VII. This association lasted for several hundred years, extending to other Scottish families whose members came to work in the glass factory and cloth mills that ensured Aubigny's prosperity over the years. The Stuart arms can be seen on the entrance of the town hall, the former castle of Robert Stuart, and in the church. In the Maison du Bailli, formerly owned by Charles VII, the initials of Berold and Anne Stuart can be seen carved in a recess.

Southeast of Aubigny is the pretty little 15th-century Château de la Verrerie, another Stuart possession. It has an elegant Renaissance gallery and 16th-century frescoes in the chapel.

★ AULNAY   96B3
Isolated among cypress trees at the edge of a village between Poitiers and Saintes, this fine Romanesque pilgrimage church boasts a beautiful doorway, with richly decorated arches in the typical Poitevin style.

★★★ AZAY-LE-RIDEAU,   96C5
CHÂTEAU D'
The unremarkable village of Azay-le-Rideau seems to exist entirely to service the tourists who visit its small, graceful château, whose image tempts photographers from between the trees. Azay-le-Rideau was built in a relatively short period of time – from 1518 to 1529 – and, unlike so many of the region's châteaux, has not been added to in later years. It was designed in its entirety by a single architect, Bastien François, and used the river foundations of a previous building.

THE DUNE DU PILAT

To the south of Arcachon there are several resorts, all with sandy beaches.

At Pilat-Plage, which is to the south of Pyla-sur-Mer, the beaches are backed by huge dunes, dominated by the extraordinary Dune du Pilat, at 114 meters (375 ft.) the highest in Europe.

Follow the ascending boulevard de la Corniche from Pilat-Plage, then take a right turn to a parking lot. From there you can walk up the dune, or take the rather easier 190 steps to the top, from where there are fine views over ocean and forest – especially recommended at sunset ■

Moated by the waters of the Indre river, Azay's turrets, machicolations and sentry path, like so many similar fortress features of the region's mansions and pleasure palaces, are merely symbolic and have ornamental decoration. There are wide-arched and dormer windows, corbels and tall conical roofs on the towers. Sculpted over the main entrance is a salamander, the emblem of François I.

Inside, the most notable feature is the innovative and richly decorated grand staircase, built with straight flights (as opposed to the more usual spiral). Renaissance furniture and tapestries, though fine, fail to evoke the original atmosphere.

BAUGÉ   *96B5*

This small market town surrounds its castle, founded on one of the many early fortresses built by the indomitable Foulques Nerra in the 11th century. Baugé is known for its possession of a piece of the True Cross (one of numerous such relics). This particular double-armed cross is distinguished by its great size and by the fact that it became known as the Cross of Lorraine, which was adopted as the emblem of the Free French Forces in 1940. The cross is housed in the chapel of a former hospice, the Chapelle des Filles de Coeur de Marie, on the rue de la Girouardière.

In the dispensary of another hospice, the Hôpital St.-Joseph, there is an especially good collection of colorful faience pots dating from the 16th and 17th centuries.

★ BEAUGENCY   *96C5*

The small town of Beaugency served as an important bridgehead in medieval times, and its strategic location led to frequent attack.

During the Hundred Years War, Beaugency passed into the hands of the English before its final delivery to the French by Jeanne d'Arc in 1429.

Beaugency still retains several 16th-century bridge arches

The beautifully carved octagonal spiral staircase at Blois was added by François I in the 16th century. With its rich decoration, it is a fine example of the French flair for early Renaissance ornament

★★ BIARRITZ   96A1

The premier coastal resort of southwest France, enjoying a splendid position high on tamarisk-covered cliffs, Biarritz has styled herself "Queen of the Basque coast."

Her fortunes were created by the patronage of the Empress Eugénie and Napoléon III, whose regular visits were followed by those of British, European and Russian royals and aristocrats. Grand villas (and a Russian Orthodox church) were built to accommodate the elevated clientèle. The Empress' villa exists still, dominating a headland and renovated as a hotel, but some of the others are past their best. The turn of the 20th century was the resort's heyday; now it cannot rival those of the French Riviera on the Mediterranean. Biarritz, however, has in recent years developed a style of its own, meeting the needs of tourists of more modest means, many of whom come for the superb surfing offered at its broad beaches, whose treacherous rollers need to be treated with respect.

(others were rebuilt after 1940 to the original design) and is dominated by the ruins of an 11th-century keep. There is a Renaissance town hall and a small regional museum housed in the 15th-century castle.

★ BEAUREGARD, CHÂTEAU DE   96C5

Despite having served as one of François I's hunting lodges, this is one of the area's smaller and lesser-known châteaux.

It is relatively unfrequented, but is well worth visiting for, among other things, its beautiful Delft tile floor and a fascinating 17th-century portrait gallery of some 363 of France's most notable men.

★★★ BLOIS   96C5

Another of the Loire's important medieval bridgeheads, Blois came under royal control under Louis XII, who carried out many important changes to the medieval fortress and established his court here. This was to be the start of a golden age for the city, as it enlarged to accommodate the courtiers, merchants and traders who accompanied and serviced the royal household. Still a busy and lively town, clustered on and around a hilly center, Blois serves as the tourist capital of the Loire Valley, offering a variety of bus excursions for those without an automobile, and attractive pedestrian-only shopping streets well provided with cafés.

Blois also boasts one of the finest of the royal châteaux, high on a cliff. It gives a unique insight into the development of secular French architecture, from feudalism to classicism, for it encompasses a fascinating variety of architectural styles. Most notable are the wings labeled Louis XII, with Italianate arabesque decoration, and François I, which is even more sumptuous, with asymmetrical windows and a magnificent spiral staircase with balconies added to the facade. This is considered the Renaissance masterpiece of the Loire area. Inside the François I wing, Catherine de Médicis' apartments have an extraordinary series of secret cupboards behind the 237 carved wood panels.

The history of the château is well explained in a popular *son-et-lumière* show (with performances in English), which covers such moments as the bloody murder of the Duc de Guise by Henri III.

★★★ BORDEAUX 96B2
The great port of Bordeaux lies at the first bridging point on the Garonne river, 100 kilometers (62 mi.) from the ocean. It is the most elegant and formal of France's provincial cities, whose prosperity was founded on the wine trade – a trade that has existed for several centuries and that continued undeterred by the Hundred Years War in the 14th and 15th centuries.

In the 18th century, in order to accommodate the prosperous *bourgeoisie*, wide boulevards and imposing buildings were created, the grandest flanking the *quais* along the Garonne and in the remarkable place de la Bourse (commercial exchange). These contrast with the quaint alleys and closely clustered houses of the charming old town (roughly between the place de la Bourse and the cathedral), beautifully restored and lively at all hours of the day and night. The finest building is the colonnaded Grand Théâtre – another 18th-century splendor – whose grand domed staircase was copied in the Paris Opéra a century later.

Other sights include the large Gothic cathedral of St.-André, which has beautiful carving on its doorways, a well-endowed fine arts museum and several smaller museums. Pedestrian shopping areas and an appropriately large choice of wine shops add to the visitor's possible pastimes.

Bus tours go to the vineyards of the Médoc, which produces the red wine known as claret. The top vineyards are named after the château on their estate. Some of these buildings are worth visiting in their own right, in particular Château Mouton-Rothschild, Château Batailley and Château Loudenne. The areas east and southeast of Bordeaux, towards St.-Émilion and along the Garonne Valley, with hillier countryside and more picturesque villages, produce a wide variety of wines – red, white and sweet dessert wines – at all price levels.

★★ BOUMOIS, CHÂTEAU DE 96B5
It's worth making a short detour northwest of Saumur to visit this château. Its fierce fortress exterior, complete with solid towers and machicolations, belies the delicate Renaissance courtyard facade and interior, and a fine Flamboyant chapel.

★★ BOURGES 97D4
This large industrial town boasts one of France's great Gothic cathedrals, an enormous edifice, mainly 12th- and 13th-century. It is renowned for its magnificent stained glass (especially that in

THE LOIRE VALLEY AND THE ATLANTIC COAST

WALK

BORDEAUX

Start at the esplanade des Quinconces, said to be the largest square in Europe, that leads to the river.

Follow the river bank along the quai Louis XVIII to the elegant place de la Bourse, flanked by stately 18th-century buildings, and take rue Phillipart to the place du Parlement, a harmonious square of typical Bordelais mansions. Walk through to the pedestrianized rue Ste.-Catherine, the city's main shopping street, and turn right into place de la Comédie, which is faced by the lofty, classical facade – crowned by 12 muses – of the Grand Théâtre.

Crossing over to the cours du 30 Juillet, on your left is the Maison du Vin (with information on Bordeaux wines).

At place des Quinconce you will find the richly decorated Monument aux Girondins, which commemorates the Girondists guillotined by Robespierre in the 1790s ∎

and between the choir chapels, which dates from the 13th century), wonderfully sculpted portals and a majestic double-aisled interior. Bourges also has one of the finest examples of a secular Gothic building, the palace of the very wealthy 15th-century trader Jacques Coeur.

★★ BRISSAC, CHÂTEAU DE   96B5

Brissac's château lies to the south east of Brissac-Quincé, just off the main D748. It features the familiar mixture of styles: 11th-century cellars, 15th-century round towers and a sumptuous 17th-century wing with fine tapestries and carved ceilings.

★ CANDES   96B5

Situated at the wide confluence of the Loire and Vienne rivers, Candes has an interesting fortified church. Built in the 12th and 13th centuries on the site of the death of Saint Martin of Tours, the church was endowed in the 15th century with crenellated towers, which provide a strong contrast to the lightness of the soaring vaults. From the steep path behind the church there are attractive river views.

★★★ CHAMBORD, CHÂTEAU DE   96C5

This wonderfully extravagant château, a mere hunting lodge for François I, epitomizes the Renaissance Loire Valley pleasure palace. One of the area's most promoted images, the reality still manages to confound the senses, whether confronted at close quarters or glimpsed in the distance through the dense growth of the surrounding hunting reserve.

Chambord was the passion of François I, who even failed to ransom his two sons, held captive in Spain, because of the

enormous amount spent on the palace. Built in an inhospitable part of a huge hunting forest – without benefit of views, roads or water for transportation, and at some distance from the royal palace at Blois – the exact reasons for François' choice of location remain a mystery (perhaps he just wanted to begin from scratch, creating something where nothing had existed before).

Chambord's scale is daunting: 440 rooms, 63 staircases, and a richly sculpted roof terrace comprising 365 chimneys, spires and bell turrets, gables and dormer windows. This provided the venue for court gatherings at the start and return of hunts, and also more intimate corners for intrigues and secret assignations. François's plans for the diversion of the waters of the Loire to provide a moat came to nothing, and those of a smaller river had to suffice.

The interior is sparsely furnished but can be enjoyed at leisure, without a guided tour. Its most fascinating element is an extraordinary double-spiral staircase, sometimes attributed to Leonardo da Vinci, which permitted inhabitants to ascend and descend simultaneously without meeting each other.

The exterior can be best experienced in the magical light of a *son-et-lumière* performance, or in the brief, soft glow of the night illumination that follows it – especially from the bedrooms of the solitary hotel that enjoys an enviable position nearby.

Chambord's huge surrounding forest estate, whose enclosing wall extends to 32 kilometers (20 mi.), is home to deer and wild boar, and there are several observation points; feeding is likely to occur at dawn and dusk.

CHAMPIGNY-SUR-VEUDE   96B4

Champigny's château was demolished on the orders of the jealous Cardinal Richelieu, First Minister of France under Louis XIII, who feared that it would eclipse the grandeur of his own home nearby. But the remaining Gothic chapel (the Sainte Chapelle), ornamented in fine Renaissance style, rejoices in an exceptional series of 16th-century stained-glass windows depicting the life of Saint Louis. Their luminous colors, especially the rich purples, are memorable.

★★ CHAUMONT, CHÂTEAU DE   96C5

Above its small riverside village, and almost obscured from view by tall cedar trees in its fine park, this creamy-white residence is famous for its associations with the scheming Catherine de Médicis, wife of Henri II. A hybrid of fortress appearance and Renaissance decoration, the interior gives an impression of the less than luxurious lifestyle of its royal inhabitants. The terrace, which affords fine views of the Loire, was built for precisely this purpose in the 18th century after the demolition of the north wing.

★★ CHENONCEAU, CHÂTEAU DE   96C5

This is arguably the most beautiful of the great royal châteaux of the Loire Valley, and is undeniably the most popular. Chenonceau, with its 61-meter (200-ft.) gallery arching across the Cher river, is set off by formal gardens. Its unusually graceful lines are attributed to the influence of a succession of powerful women upon its construction and surroundings (notably Diane de Poitiers, mistress of Henri II). As at Azay-le-Rideau (see p.100), Chenonceau features an innovative straight-flighted staircase, better suited to grand receptions than the more common spiral staircase. The château contains some very fine paintings, tapestries and furniture. The interior can be enjoyed without a guided tour, using explanatory leaflets. The park is worth visiting for the fine

A bridge links the main buildings of Chenonceau with the opposite bank of the Cher river. Added by Diane de Poitiers, the bridge was later embellished by Catherine de Médicis in the 16th century

A fortress has stood overlooking the Vienne river at Chinon since the 10th century. The old town that lies beneath the ramparts is now a popular center

CHINON'S CHÂTEAU

Chinon's original fortress was much enlarged during the 12th century by Henry Plantagenet (later Henry II of England), and he himself died here in 1189.

His son, Richard the Lionheart, died outside the castle walls after a battle with the French, but the stronghold was lost to the Plantagenets when Philippe Auguste besieged it 1204–5 ∎

views it affords of the château.

Diane de Poitiers was responsible for many of the fine gardens and for a bridge linking the building and the bank of the Cher. On Henri's death, Diane was forced to give up the château by Queen Catherine de' Médicis, who then set about making her own improvements, adding a two-story gallery to the bridge and laying out a formal park.

★★★ CHEVERNY, 96C5 CHÂTEAU DE

Cheverny is another of the Loire Valley's most popular sights. Its modest size makes the tourist congestion seem even greater, and very exasperating in high season. Yet the waits and crowded conditions of a guided tour are well worth enduring, for this place is quite unlike the other châteaux of the area.

Cheverny is a symmetrical, severely classical building constructed without interruption and unaltered, and sumptuously furnished with its original 17th-century decor. Still privately owned and inhabited, it is one of the few châteaux to evoke the feel of a home.

Cheverny's white-stone and gray-slate exterior is striking, with

square domes on its huge corner pavilions and bull's-eye windows in the roof. Inside there are wonderful fabrics, tapestries, furniture and Cordoban leather. In the "King's" bedroom, kept in permanent readiness for a passing royal visit, there's a magnificent bed covered in 15th-century white Persian silk.

Cheverny has a famous liveried hunt, and the kennels and impressive trophy room in the grounds are also open to the public.

★★ CHINON 96B4

Delightfully located on the leafy Vienne river, the small town of Chinon is dominated by the mighty ruins of the medieval château. The fortress is famous for its association with Jeanne d'Arc: it was here in 1429 the Maid of Orléans persuaded the Dauphin Charles to let her take charge of an army, which was to lead to the expulsion of the English from France.

Now a busy tourist center with ample accommodations and restaurants, and with some very attractive cobbled streets and timbered houses in its restored old town, Chinon is a good base from where to explore the area.

COGNAC   96B3

Once an important river port on the Charente river, Cognac's reputation was founded on her trade in wine. The growing demand for cognac – a product of wine distillation originally carried out here to reduce tax and facilitate storage – resulted in the establishment of the great cognac houses, several of whose names (Hine, Hennessy) testify to longstanding associations with the British Isles. Now the town has little of interest apart from guided visits to cognac houses.

★★ CUNAULT   96B5

This quiet river-bank village rejoices in a simple and elegantly beautiful Romanesque church, part of a former Benedictine monastery. Its cool white interior rises to a great height, which makes it advisable to use binoculars to inspect the 223 superb sculpted capitals. Some fragments of wall paintings remain, and there is also a rare 13th-century wooden shrine.

★ DAX   96A1

On the banks of the Adour river, between the flat Landes forests and the foothills of the Pyrénées, the sedate spa town of Dax is one of the oldest spas in France, its beneficial waters having been discovered in Roman times or even earlier. Dax's famous hot spring, whose waters gush up at a temperature of 64 C (147 F), can be seen in a fountain at the very center of town. Nowadays, Dax provides mud baths, which are believed to be efficacious for rheumatism. The church of St.-Paul-lès-Dax has some interesting 11th-century reliefs on the apse, but there is little else of sightseeing interest for visitors, apart from gentle walks along the banks of the river.

LA FLÈCHE   96B5

A light-industrial and market town on the banks of the Loir river, La Flèche is famous for the large military training school founded by Henri IV in 1604 and run by Jesuits until shortly before the Revolution. Among its pupils was Descartes, the philosopher, mathematician and logician. His "Discourse on Method" ("I think, therefore I am"), written in 1637, was to have profound influence on French thinking, and provided the foundation for analytical geometry. The college buildings are now occupied by a school, but guided tours are available.

★★ FONTEVRAUD   96B4

The great abbey of Fontevraud, founded by an itinerant preacher and named for a spring known as the Fontaine d'Evraud, was established in the 11th century as a community for monks, nuns and lepers. The order was headed by an abbess, no fewer than 14 of whom were princesses, and came to enjoy great social cachet. It thus acquired great wealth.

After much destruction in the Revolution, relatively little remains of the abbey buildings now – and it's remarkable that what does exist survived at all,

WALK

CHINON
This walk passes some of the most interesting old houses in this ancient city.

From the parking lot on the quai Charles VII, take the alley leading up to the rue Haute St.-Maurice and rue Voltaire.

These are edged with fine 14th- to 16th-century houses, with courtyards, turrets, mullioned windows and wooden gables. In between are alleys that offer glimpses up towards the fortress. The beautiful Grand Carroi crossroads is the most scenic part of town.

Continue to the place de l'Hôtel de Ville and take the stairway (behind the statue of Rabelais) up to the rue du Puy-des-Bancs, which will take you to the medieval château ■

COGNAC

Cognac was first produced in the 17th century, and was known by the Dutch as *brandewijn* ("burnt wine"), the origin of the term "brandy."

White wine made from selected grapes – themselves from a legally defined region of about 100,000 hectares (250,000 acres) – is distilled according to strictly defined methods (the casks, for instance, must be Limousin oak).

The top-quality *appellation* is Grande Champagne, a small area just southeast of the town of Cognac; Petite Champagne lies south and southeast of Cognac; and Borderies to the northeast.

Larger *appellation* areas are Fins Bois, Bons Bois and Bois Ordinaires. La Fine Champagne is a mixture of Grande and Petite Champagne ■

having served for many years as a prison. The remaining buildings are well restored and enormously evocative, in particular the soaring Romanesque church, a Gothic refectory, fine cloisters (some with Renaissance vaulting) and a chapter house decorated with 16th-century murals. Most remarkable is an octagonal tower roofed with overlapping stones and topped by 20 chimneys.

Fontevraud is the resting place of the Plantagenet Henry II, his wife Eleanor of Aquitaine, and their son Richard the Lionheart, whose effigy in the abbey church bears the crown of England.

GIEN   *97D5*

The small town of Gien is another important Loire bridgehead – this one lying on the eastern stretch. The terrain and buildings have little in common with the area west of Orléans, looking towards the styles of Burgundy in their use of multicolored brick rather than the white tufa of the royal hunting grounds. Gien was heavily bombed in World War II and suffered serious damage. However, much remains and all was restored, including the dominant red-brick 15th-century castle. Next to it stands a modern church, in harmonious black-patterned pink brick, dedicated to Ste. Jeanne d'Arc; the original 15th-century church was destroyed in 1940, and only its tower remains. Inside, terracotta capitals atop slender pillars tell the story of Jeanne's life.

ILE D'OLÉRON   *96A3*

Joined to the mainland by a toll bridge over 3 kilometers (2 mi.) long, this is France's largest island after Corsica, measuring some 30 kilometers (19 mi.) in length and 6 kilometers (4 mi.) across. Its west coast is well endowed with sandy beaches

backed by pine-covered dunes. Oléron's eastern coast is muddy and full of oyster beds, and the flat interior specializes in growing vegetables and vines. There are few places of any age apart from the 17th-century fortifications of the Château-d'Oléron, which provided protection to a citadel destroyed in 1945.

ILE DE RÉ   *96A3*

Attached to the mainland near La Rochelle since 1988 by a soaring toll bridge, this island is popular for its sandy beaches on the west coast and the lively old ports (now full of modern yachts) on the eastern side. The capital of the island, St.-Martin-de-Ré, is a proud and historic little place. Its citadel was besieged by the English during the Hundred Years War, and the ramparts (restored by Vauban) still bear witness to its importance. The port area is a focus for pleasure boaters, with chic shops, restaurants and cafés.

★★★ LANGEAIS,   *96C5*
CHÂTEAU DE

The small, unexceptional town of Langeais lies on the north bank of the Loire, along which is a busy highway. But at its heart is one of the most impressive of late-medieval fortresses, erected on the orders of Louis XI in 1465 and built in only four years. All the features of a typical fortress are here – forbidding drum towers, drawbridge, battlemented sentry walk – and the inner facade has Renaissance features such as mullioned windows, pointed dormers, turrets and sculptures.

What makes this château remarkable is that it has remained largely unaltered and without additions ever since it was built. An additional bonus is that the last private owner of the château, a wealthy 19th-century banker and shipowner from Le Havre, amassed an exceptional collection of medieval furniture and works of art, so that the interior evokes aristocratic life in the early Renaissance period more than almost any other of the area's châteaux. Fine tapestries, portraits of Anne of Brittany and her husband Charles VIII (look for their monogram, an intertwining K and A), chests, and beds hung with fine drapes, all contribute to the atmosphere.

In the grounds are the ruins of the 10th-century keep, built by Foulques Nerra, one of the counts of Anjou. The keep was built on the site of an even earlier fortress and a Roman camp.

LIGET, CHARTREUSE DU 96C4

Between Montrésor and Loches, in a peaceful stretch of countryside among the leafy tributaries of the Indrois and Indre, lie the ruins of the Carthusian monastery (*chartreuse*) of Le Liget. Henry II founded it in expiation, it is said, of the murder of Thomas à Becket in Canterbury Cathedral. The round chapel of St.-Jean-du-Liget, isolated and overgrown in a field, contains Romanesque frescoes (ask locally for the key). Nearby, on the Montrésor road, La Corroirie is a harmonious group of buildings that formed a monastic annex.

★★ LOCHES 96C4

On the banks of the Indre, the fortified medieval city of Loches dominates the modern town from a rocky hill. This was one of the most important strongholds in medieval France. It has been preserved largely intact; within its walls are castle and keep, church and many elegant private houses. The approach to the old city is best made on foot through a Renaissance quarter of ornately decorated houses. The massive

13th-century gateway, the Porte Royale, leads into the medieval city; a walk along all or part of the surrounding walls is well worth undertaking.

The two main sights of the city are the château and the keep, separate buildings at either end of the city walls. Guided tours provide details of their long history, but there is little to see. The château was the residence of the beautiful Agnès Sorel, favorite mistress of the unfortunate Charles VII; her recumbent alabaster figure can be seen in the Charles VII Room. It was here, too, that Jeanne d'Arc persuaded the same Charles to go to Reims to be crowned.

With its circular towers and old drawbridge, the castle at Langeais has a forbidding feudal aspect. The 15th-century building where Anne of Brittany married Charles VIII of France in 1491 has largely remained intact

TAPESTRIES

Some of the most notable medieval tapestries in existence can be found in the Loire area.

A vital part of medieval furnishing, tapestries prevented drafts in châteaux and more modest dwellings, and served to cover beds, chairs, tables, cushions, and even horses.

Tapestries were woven from initial sketches using wool with silk, gold or silver threads. The style known as *mille fleurs* ("a thousand flowers") has been attributed to Loire Valley workshops; these depict idealized medieval scenes on a background of flora and small animals.

Good examples exist at Saumur and Langeais, as well as those at the Tapestry Museum at Angers ■

The keep has quite different associations, mainly to do with its role as one of France's fearsome prisons. In its dungeons and torture chambers, prisoners are said to have been incarcerated for years in cages little bigger than themselves. One such prisoner was the patron of Leonardo da Vinci, Ludovico Sforza, who covered the walls of his prison with all manner of inscriptions and drawings; on his release after eight years, the sudden sight of natural light was too much for him, and he succumbed to a heart attack. No cages remain today, but some instruments of torture are displayed in the few cells that are open to the public.

★★ LE LOIR   96B5

The Loir river, the confusingly named tributary of the larger Loire, is considered by many to offer scenery which is even more charming and less spoilt than that of its more famous sister. Although the valley doesn't match that of the larger river in architectural significance, there is no lack of sightseeing. The river meanders gently through shivering poplars and willows, past attractive villages, and the surrounding countryside is green and fertile, untroubled by highways or busy through-roads.

One of the Loir's attractions is its numerous tiny Romanesque churches, which were on one of the medieval pilgrimage routes to the shrine of Santiago de Compostela in Spain. Orders of Benedictines, Cistercians and Knights Templar housed and fed the pilgrim travelers, and in Montoire-sur-le-Loir and Trôo hospices and leper hospitals offered comfort to the sick. The churches are distinguished by particularly interesting, brightly colored frescoes, some of which are exceptionally well preserved.

Several can be seen on the pretty stretch of river between La Chartre-sur-le-Loir and Vendôme, at the village of Lavardin (St.-Genest), in the small town of Montoire, and in the church of St.-Jacques-des-Guérets, just across the Loir from the steep hillside village of Trôo.

Trôo is notable for another feature of the Loir Valley – troglodyte dwellings or caves, carved out of the soft tufa stone of the river's steep banks and inhabited, in many cases, since neolithic times. Some even form chic second homes. The constant temperature and humidity of the tufa caves also provide ideal conditions for mushroom cultivation and wine storage.

One of the relatively few major sights of interest along the stretch of Loir west of Château-du-Loir is the château of Le Lude, externally impressive and set in a fine park. The most spectacular *son-et-lumière* show in the Loire region is performed here on some summer evenings. The château is richly furnished, and in the oratory of the François I wing are some notable Italian frescoes.

★ LUYNES   96C5

The village of Luynes is bypassed by the main road following the north bank of the Loire, although it merits a short diversion on account of its age and attractive demeanour. Its severe medieval fortress is not open to the public, but remains of the aqueduct that served the Gallo-Roman camp on the site can still be seen.

★★ LE MANS   96B5

Bypassed by many tourists who know only of Le Mans's automobile-racing reputation, this industrial city deserves a visit. Its medieval center, which is surrounded by the remains of Roman walls, is extremely attractive, and there are further sights in the town and suburbs.

In the heart of the old town, the cathedral of St.-Julien is of great interest. Mainly Gothic, with a low Romanesque nave and beautifully sculpted south doorway, it contains remarkable Renaissance works of art: the tomb of Charles IV of Anjou, sculpted by Francesco Laurana, and that of Guillaume du Bellay, showing him reclining somewhat nonchalantly on one elbow. The 13th-century stained glass in the chancel is strikingly colorful.

Within the old city ramparts are more churches and several fine houses, particularly the Maison de la Reine-Bérengère and the Tessé Mansion, both of which contain museums. Outside the walls, the Église de la Couture is an old abbey church with elegant vaulting and fine, though damaged, sculptures around the west door. The church of Ste.-Jeanne-d'Arc is of interest for its role as a medieval hospital, built by Henry II of England to atone for the murder of Thomas à Becket in Canterbury Cathedral.

South of the city, off the D139, lies the great *circuit automobile*, a 13-kilometer (8-mi.) racing track, part of it on public roads. The famous 24-hour automobile race takes place in June, attracting thousands of spectators. Near the track, a large museum housing a collection of vintage automobiles is open throughout the year.

★ **MARAIS POITEVIN** 96B4
Between Niort and the coast north of La Rochelle, and linked to the Sèvre Niortaise, lies a network of waterways that drain a wide area of reclaimed marshland. Some are the work of medieval monks, whose method of travel by punt is still followed by locals today – even cattle are carried on the large flat-bottomed boats. The moss-covered waters are overhung by trees and surrounded by lush woodland. The strange, silent beauty of this "Green Venice" can best be appreciated from a boat; trips are most easily arranged from the large village of Coulon, west of Niort, where there is also a small museum. The villages are

LE MANS GRAND PRIX D'ENDURANCE

The great Le Mans 24-hour race, held here since 1923, was originally conceived as a test of endurance.

The race circuit lies south of the city between the D139 and N138, with some parts on public roads. You can follow the circuit along the Hunaudières straight, then around the Mulsanne hairpin bend, and take the double S-bend at Arnage corner.

Serious racers can apply at the Circuit Bugatti, used for training racing drivers. Automobiles with sports bodies can enter the race ■

CIRCUIT DES 24 HEURES DU MANS

LES LANDES

The hinterland of the Aquitaine coast is a vast, flat pine forest, planted in the 19th century to stabilize shifting dunes and drain a marshy heath supporting only sheep (shepherds used stilts to get about).

There are few villages, only some timber-and-brick farmhouses set in clearings surrounded by a corn field, a small vegetable patch and a few farm animals.

The open-air Landes Ecomuseum at Marquèze, which is reached by train from Sabres, presents the traditions and ecology of the area before its transformation; original buildings, dating from the 18th and early 19th centuries, include a farm that is set in 18 hectares (45 acres) of land ■

generally simple, the canals lined with plain whitewashed fishermen's houses; some are on little islands (Marans, Chaillé). Eel is a local culinary specialty.

★ MEILLANT,   97D4
CHÂTEAU DE

Lying south of Bourges, off the Loire Valley tourist track, this is one of the finest châteaux of the area, an early Renaissance building that was completed, like Chaumont, by Charles II of Amboise. Like many of the Loire châteaux, it combines fortress and palace, Flamboyant Gothic and decorative Renaissance. It has the added attraction of being beautifully furnished and finely decorated, and is still inhabited.

MENARS, CHÂTEAU DE   96C5

This imposing 18th-century mainly neoclassical building is known primarily for its association with the famous Marquise de Pompadour, born Antoinette Poisson, mistress of Louis XV. The gardens and park overlooking the Loire, which Pompadour embellished, are particularly fine.

MEUSNES   96C4

A quiet and unremarkable village, which may be worth a stop if you have an interest in the former industry of flint-knapping. The Mairie (town hall) has a small and old-fashioned museum devoted to the subject, which delves into the history with displays and old photos. The annual supply of 50 million flints to the army after the Napoleonic wars kept many hundreds of workers employed.

★ MONTGEOFFROY,   96B5
CHÂTEAU DE

East of Angers, it is well worth making a short detour north of the Loire to this very handsome and harmonious 18th-century château, which clearly evokes the

domestic life of a great family at the end of the 18th century. Miraculously surviving the Revolution, the château together with its original decoration have remained intact, and it is still owned by members of the original family. Neither grand nor impressive, the rooms are none the less well furnished.

MONTRÉSOR,   96C4
CHÂTEAU DE

Beside the little Indrois river, in a beautiful rural setting, this is another impressively situated château, one of the many built in the area in the 11th century by the mighty Foulques Nerra, Count of Anjou. Within its extremely well-preserved medieval walls there is an attractive 15th-century château, beautifully restored and furnished by the Polish family that acquired it in 1849, and whose descendants own it still. Below, in the tiny and picturesque village, there is an old timbered market and a well that leads to an underground river. Legend has it, treasure (*trésor*) was found here, so giving the town its name.

★ MONTREUIL-BELLAY,   96B4
CHÂTEAU DE

On the leafy banks of the Thouet river, the towers and huge hulk of the Château de Montreuil-Bellay dominate the attractive small village that lies below its walls. Inside the predominantly 15th-century building there are several interesting things to see, in particular the fine old kitchen, which has a round central chimney inspired by that at Fontevraud. In the section of castle called the Château Neuf (also 15th century), there is a grand spiral staircase up which the Duchess of Longueville once attempted to ride on horseback. Frescoes decorate the walls of the oratory, and there are rich furnishings in the Grand Salon.

★ **MONTRICHARD**   96C5

This is a lively little market town on the banks of the Cher river, clustered at the foot of a square, ragged and ruined keep (another of the many built by Foulques Nerra), which can be viewed from the old bridge across the river. Also of interest are the troglodyte houses in the hillside on the edge of town, wine cellars where you can sample sparkling Vouvray, a swimming pool and bathing area beside the river, and an attractive park. The church was the scene of the marriage of the unfortunate 12-year-old Jeanne-de-France (deformed daughter of Louis XI) and the 14-year-old Louis d'Orléans, who later divorced her.

★ **NOHANT,**   97D4
CHÂTEAU DE

The small hamlet of Nohant lies in the heart of the quiet and rural Berry, due south of Orléans and well out of the way of the Loire Valley. It attracts visitors on account of its association with the writer Amandine-Aurore-Lucile Dudevant (née Dupin de Francueil), better known as George Sand, who lived between 1804 and 1876 and who spent much of her childhood and the later years of her life here. Sand's controversial stance as a defender of women's rights to emotional freedom, together with her affairs with Chopin, Musset and others and her penchant for smoking and dressing in men's clothes, have ensured her fame at least as much as her large literary output. She never tired of the countryside around Nohant,

which she called the Black Valley because of its thick woods.

★ **NOIRLAC, ABBAYE DE**   97D4

South of Bourges, in the Berry, this old abbey on the banks of the Cher river is a typical and well-restored example of the austere style of Cistercian buildings.

Some living quarters have been furnished, giving an idea of monastic life from the 12th century.

The Château de Nohant, built in the 18th century and extended in the 19th century, has largely been left as it was when she lived, and died, there. The table is set for a dinner party for the intellectual and artistic elite of her day – Liszt, Balzac, Delacroix, Flaubert. There's a little theater, designed by Chopin, in which Sand performed her own plays, and her boudoir and study.

OLIVET   97D5

A suburb of Orléans, with market gardens, flower nurseries and pleasant walks along the banks of the Loiret, Olivet has ample accommodations and is popular for boating and fishing. Nearby,

SPECIALTIES OF THE ATLANTIC COAST

Fish and seafood are excellent everywhere, in particular mussels (which are used in _mouclade_, a mussel stew with white wine and cream) and oysters; sardines can be found in the north, tuna in the south.

Inland there's lamb from the salt marshes of the Médoc, and much game, including partridge (_perdreau_), ortolans and wood pigeons (_palombes_) from the Landes.

Bordeaux specializes in _lamproie_ (lamprey eel) and a red wine sauce made from bone marrow, shallots and tarragon (_à la bordelaise_). The creamy _chabichou_ goat's cheese is from Poitou ∎

The area around Nevers was renowned for its pottery in the Middle Ages. The Municipal Museum contains a fine collection of faience, and some delicate Blue Persian pieces

Orléans-la-Source has a fine 35-hectare (86-acre) floral park.

★ ORLÉANS 97D5

Now a large industrial city on both banks of the Loire at its northernmost point, Orléans' fame rests on a relatively brief encounter with Jeanne d'Arc, who delivered the city from the English in 1429 after a siege of eight months. There is much to commemorate "The Maid,"

century. The carved panels that surround the choir are particularly impressive. Other sights in the city include a couple of medieval hotels, which house the fine arts and local history museum.

★ PLESSIS-BOURRÉ, 96B5
CHÂTEAU DU

To the north of Angers, the magnificent late 15th-century Château du Plessis Bourré is a rare example of a château built in

Inside Orléans' cathedral of Ste.-Croix are some exquisitely carved 17th-century choir stalls, with superb detailing on the wooden panels that adorn their high backs

including road, house and school names, a statue, and a museum devoted to her and to the siege. Every May celebrations are held here in her honor.

Orléans today is a rather gray and severe place. Having suffered enormous damage from bombing during World War II, it's not an attractive city, although not without places of interest. Certain parts of the old town remain, notably the cathedral of Ste.-Croix, unusual for the consistently Gothic style of restoration work since it was partially destroyed in the 16th century. The nave and choir are 17th century, the transept a little later, the aisles early 18th century, and the towers and facade late 18th-

a single period, without addition or alteration. It provides an ideal opportunity to study the features that characterized that period marking the transition from feudal fortress to elegant dwelling, when nobles were starting to think about comfort as well as defense. The building has a fine, wide moat crossed by an arched bridge, a tower with pepper-pot roof at each corner, a fortified gateway (it used to have a drawbridge) and a chapel. Inside, the rooms are sumptuously decorated; a highlight is the ceiling of the guardroom, painted with allegorical and comic figures.

Any similarities to the Château de Langeais are not coincidental:

it was built by Jean Bourré for his own personal use after he had built Langeais for King Louis XI.

★ PLESSIS-MACÉ, 96B5 CHÂTEAU DU

Northwest of Angers, this is a charming medieval fortified manor house, inevitably with moat and keep. It was renovated in the 15th century and remains largely as it was at that time. In the central courtyard, notice the decorative elements of a gracious dwelling, especially the decorated balcony and fine windows.

During a long period of neglect, the château was used as a farm. It was put into some sort of order at the end of the 19th century, though its contents were sold. The chapel has excellent medieval, Flamboyant woodwork.

★ POITIERS 96B4

Poitiers is a large industrial and university city, set in rather dull countryside between the historic Loire heartland and the coast at La Rochelle. Its main sights miraculously survived World War II, when much else suffered. Now the city center is being revitalized, with pedestrian sections and continued restoration of its old buildings. One ambitious project is the restoration of its greatest treasure, the Romanesque facade of Notre-Dame-la-Grande church, in the old town on the market square.

This great enterprise involves cleaning and repairing, inch by inch, the richly sculpted but time-blackened facade. The chore has necessitated tall scaffolding and the building of a cover for the facade, but spectators are encouraged to watch the work from viewing platforms arranged on the scaffolding, and can obtain an explanatory leaflet from the site office. The interior of the church is somewhat gloomy, but

there's a beautiful 12th-century fresco in the vault of the choir.

The other main sights of the city are also churches. The earliest is St John's Baptistery. One of the oldest Christian buildings in France, dating partly from the 4th century, it retains some medieval frescoes. St.-Hilaire-le-Grand is another fine Romanesque church – despite the addition of a 19th-century facade – with a row of domes and splendid carved capitals. The mainly Gothic cathedral of St.-Pierre is bright and spacious, with fine 13th-century choir stalls.

By contrast, the Palais de Justice presents a grand 19th-century facade enclosing earlier buildings, including a medieval tower. In its Grande Salle, Jeanne d'Arc was interrogated by an ecclesiastical committee, which finally could find no fault with her.

Just north of Poitiers, in Jaunay-Clan, **Futuroscope** is France's answer to Florida's Epcot Center. It's a park devoted to technology, with a variety of attractions, including several cinemas, a rotating tower and a huge Lego exhibition (see p.273).

★ PORNIC 96A4

West of Nantes, Pornic is a small fishing port on a rocky inlet, with old streets and houses and a new marina, but few of the beaches that characterize some of its neighboring resorts on the stretch of coast known as the Côte de Jade. Ferries go to the island of Noirmoutier in the summer.

The medieval castle in the village has a murky past. It once belonged to the infamous Gilles de Rais, portrayed in one of Perrault's fairy-tales as Bluebeard. After a heroic military career, which included accompanying Jeanne d'Arc at the seige of Orléans, Gilles de Rais turned to satanism and was finally hanged.

WALK

THE CANAL D'ORLÉANS

This 1-hour easy-going and level walk follows the 17th-century Canal d'Orléans, part of a network of waterways connecting Seine and Loire.

Forming part of the long-distance footpath GR3 (marked in red and white), it explores the eastern fringes of the Forêt d'Orléans.

Start at Grignon (near Lorris, northeast of Sully) and walk along the canal towpath parallel to the Châtenoy road, past the Étang du Gué des Cens. At the fork, bear left away from the canal and into the forest, then walk to the Étang de la Noue Mazone. Follow the lakeside path (to the left) through the woods, turn left on the Châtenoy road and return to Grignon ■

DRIVE

A TOUR THROUGH THE CHÂTEAUX

428 kilometers/266 miles (allow 3/4 days)

This route takes in part of the most popular stretch of the Loire Valley, encompassing famous royal Renaissance châteaux, and passing ancient towns and wine villages. The route goes off the beaten track, winding along the tributaries of the Cher and the Sauldre rivers.

The route starts at Tours, which makes a good overnight base. Several sights of interest include a fine cathedral.

Take the D751 to Amboise.

1 Amboise

The scenic part of the route begins, appropriately, at Amboise, famous Loire bridgehead and site of one of the most famous royal châteaux, which towers above the town center. Apart from the château itself, the town has several other sights of interest and is best visited on foot.

Take the D31 from Amboise in the direction of Loches.

The minor road climbs behind the town. After 3 kilometers (2 mi.) a sign indicates the Pagode de Chanteloup, a folly that is the only remaining part of an 18th-century château that was built in imitation of Versailles by the Duc de Choiseul, minister under Louis XV. From the top of the pagoda there is an excellent panorama, which takes in the Loire Valley and the Forest of Amboise.

Continue on the D31 and D40 towards Chenonceaux.

2 Chenonceaux

The château of Chenonceau (strangely without the "x" of its adjacent village) is the most popular of the Loire châteaux. Unusually for this area, the great château is barely visible from the village. However, a stay in the village makes it possible to beat the morning crowds and, later, to take in a *son-et-lumière* show.

Continue on the D40. In Chisseaux, go right on the D80 to Francueil, take the D81 to Céré-la-Ronde, then the C5 and D90 to St.-Aignan. Go left on the D675, right on the D17, right for Valençay on the D33, left on the D37 in Villentrois and right on the D956 into Valençay.

3 Valençay

The village of Valençay has plenty of accommodations, and the magnificent château is well worth

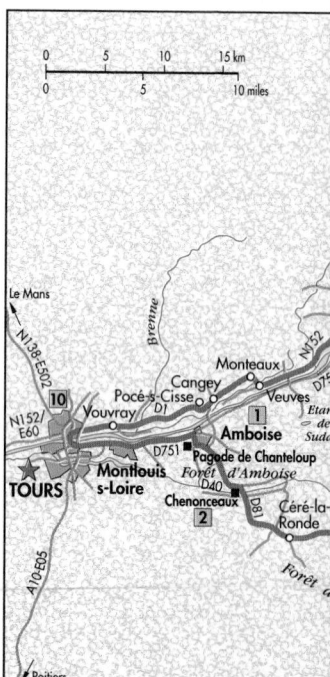

the detour from the main Loire Valley tourist track. The château's park and gardens are also fine.

> *Leave Valençay on the D4 through Chabris, then continue straight ahead on the D128. Cross the N76 and follow the signs towards Romorantin.*

4 Romorantin-Lanthenay

Romorantin-Lanthenay is the main town of the Sologne area, a delightful place on the Sauldre river with several timbered buildings in its center.

> *Leave on the D49, following signs for Marcilly-en-Gault, then St.-Viâtre.*

5 La Sologne

This is the heart of the Sologne countryside, remote and marshy heath and woodland, dotted with red-brick thatched houses.

> *Continue on the D49 from St.-Viâtre, then take the D93 to Nouan-le-Fuzelier. Go left as for Orléans, then right as for Chaon on the D122 and left on the D44. Go right on the D923 as for Aubigny, to Clémont. Turn left at the crossroads on the D7, then follow signs to Étang du Puits. Continue to the D948, turn right for Argent-sur-Sauldre, then left on the D940 to Gien.*

6 Gien

This important bridgehead town offers views over roofs and river from the plateau dominated by castle and church, the latter a modern building in Romanesque style and built of the local brick.

> *Leave Gien for Lorris on the D44. Continue as for Bellegarde. Immediately after the "La Chausée" sign, take*

RENAISSANCE CHÂTEAUX

The great age of châteaux-building in the Loire region followed the campaigns of Jeanne d'Arc and the subsequent expulsion of the English from France in 1453.

As national pride grew in an atmosphere of peace, ambitious royal building programs began and the emphasis shifted to comfort and elegance. Ornamentation became important, inspired by royal admiration for the Italian Renaissance.

Italian architects, artists and even gardeners were brought to the French court, and schools of design were established at Amboise, Tours, Blois and Fontainebleau.

Four of the finest Renaissance châteaux are without doubt Azay-le-Rideau, Blois, Chambord and Chenonceau ■

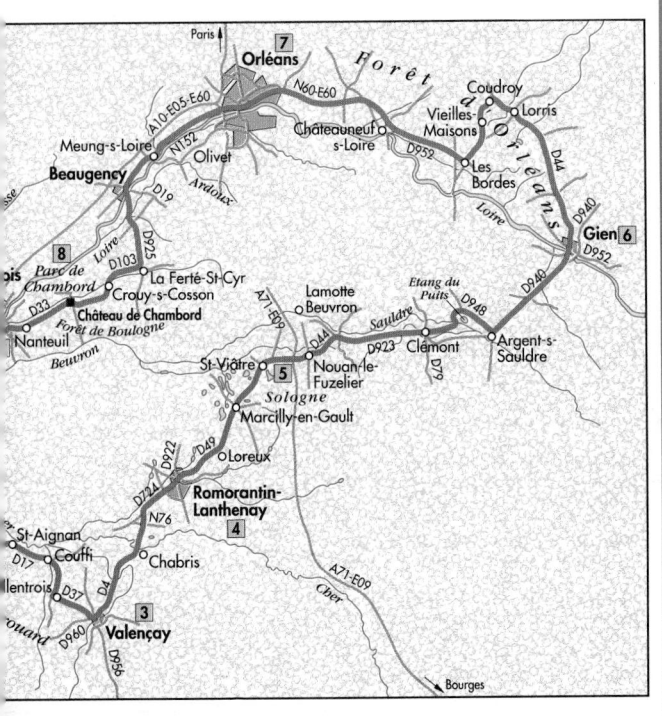

WALK

MONTSOREAU

This 2-hour walk, steep in parts, passes two windmills and offers fine river views, vineyards and tufa caves.

Starting from the main square, go up the Haute Rue, then the steep Ruelle de la Motte. At the top, follow the track to the Moulin de la Tranchée.

Continue through vineyards, then fork right down a cave-dotted hillside. Turn left on the D947, then first right, a minor road marked Fabrique de Savon. Fork right by the Fabrique (a handsome farmhouse), then take the road for Turquant, passing the Moulin de la Herpinière.

Either the road to the right or tracks through the vineyards lead back to Montsoreau ∎

the first left. Go right on the V3 into Coudroy. Turn left at the stop sign, through Vieilles-Maisons and left on the D88. Bend right, then left, and watch for a right turn at the crossroads along a gravel forest road, passing the "3 t" sign. Bear left at a junction of forest roads, left after a 50-meter warning sign indicating "give way ahead," and turn right along the tarred road (the D961). Turn right on the D952 and follow the N60 and the N152 to Orléans.

7 Orléans

Forever linked with Jeanne d'Arc, who broke the English siege of the city in 1429, even the stained-glass windows of Orléans' cathedral tell the Maid's story. Orléans has several museums and an animated town center, but lacks the charm of many of the other Loire towns.

Leave Orléans on the N152 as for Blois, avoiding the autoroute. Continue through Meung-sur-Loire to Beaugency. Go left on the D925 as for Limoges, crossing the river bridge. Continue straight over the D951 and onto La Ferté-St.-Cyr. Turn right on the D103 to Crouy-sur-Cosson, then left on the D33 and continue through the Parc de Chambord towards the Château de Chambord.

8 Château de Chambord

A sight not to be missed on any Loire itinerary, the great Renaissance pleasure palace at Chambord sits in no less than 5,443 hectares (13,450 acres) of estate, circled by one of France's longest walls. Parts of the forested estate are open to visitors. The château itself,

though lacking the intimacy of some of the other great buildings and rather sparsely furnished, has a number of extraordinary features, particularly its double-spiral staircase and an amazing rooftop viewing terrace.

Continue on the D33. After Nanteuil go under the bridge through St.-Gervais-la-Forêt and then turn right on the D956 to Blois.

9 Blois

Blois is a lively tourist center in the Loire Valley, with one of the area's great royal châteaux, site of the court of King Louis XII. The town, arranged on and beneath the castle hill, has some good shops and attractive cafés, and makes a good base. Tours of the Poulain chocolate factory, which was founded in 1848, can be arranged. Bicycles can be rented from the train station.

Leave Blois on the N152 as for Tours. In Veuves, turn right on the D65 to Monteaux. Bear left for Cangey along the D58, which becomes the D1. Continue through Limeray. Keep left in Pocé as for Amboise, then go right following the "Vouvray" sign. Turn left on the D46 and continue to Vouvray.

10 Vouvray

A well-known wine-producing center, Vouvray specializes in still and sparkling white wines and one of the richest and most honey-sweet dessert wines in the world. There are plenty of cellars at which to taste and buy, many of them carved out of the tufa stone – which also contains numerous troglodyte houses.

Leave Vouvray on the N152 and return to Tours.

POUILLY-SUR-LOIRE 97D5

Pouilly is a small commune on the eastern section of the Loire Valley between Gien and Nevers. It is known for its flinty, fragrant Pouilly-Fumé wine (one of the most expensive wines in the Loire area), classically reminiscent of gooseberries. Made from the Sauvignon Blanc grape, it achieves its full potential at about two to three years of age. There are several places at which to buy and taste; the most picturesque is the charming, fairy-tale Château de Tracy.

RICHELIEU 96B4

This fascinating small town gives an insight into the ambitions and personality of one of the great characters in French history. Cardinal Richelieu, Prime Minister of France under Louis XIII, commissioned the architect of the Sorbonne and the Palais Royal in Paris to build him a château and surrounding town whose grandeur would reflect his elevated status. Not content with the splendor of his treasure-packed palace – set amidst 475 hectares (1,174 acres) of parkland crossed by tree-lined avenues and served by a classical-style wall-enclosed town – Richelieu set about destroying several other châteaux in the vicinity in order that none would outshine his creation. Richelieu's own palace was destroyed after the Revolution, and all that remains are a few domed pavilions, the park and the small town – well worth a visit in its own right.

★★★ LA ROCHELLE 96A3

This is one of France's greatest and most historic ports, whose wealth was founded on the export of salt and wine and the import of cloth and wool from Flanders. Trade in spices and coffee resulted in its association later on with Canada and the Antilles. La Rochelle was also a center of Protestantism, a fact that led to a famous 15-month siege by Cardinal Richelieu during which the population of 28,000 was reduced to 5,000 souls.

Few of La Rochelle's former defenses remain, although the old port is still guarded by three medieval towers. The handsome yachts and fishing boats are overlooked by smart quayside cafés, and the lively streets offer stylish shops and attractively decorated arcaded Renaissance houses. Those seeking a beach resort should take the soaring toll bridge from the industrial quarter, La Pallice, to the nearby Ile de Ré, which has sandy beaches and plenty of family facilities.

The old port of La Rochelle is still guarded by its medieval towers. The town was an important trading center, and today remains a thriving resort, with smart shops, lively cafés and a number of worthy museums

LOIRE WINES

The Loire region produces several types of wine, many of which offer exceptional value and make good quaffing wines.

The Pays Nantais in the west is Muscadet country, the best being *"sur lie"* and taking the *appellation* "de Sèvre-et-Maine."

South of Angers lie the excellent sweet-wine vineyards of the Côteaux du Layon, Bonne-zeaux and Quarts de Chaume, while Savennières near-by produces one of the best dry white wines.

Touraine produces red wines from the Cabernet Franc grape and sweet whites from the Chenin Blanc.

Farther east are the well-known Pouilly Fumé and Sancerre. Rivals for Sauvignon Blanc wines include nearby Menetou-Salon ■

SACHÉ   96C5

This small village has had two famous residents. One was the American sculptor Alexander Calder, one of whose mobiles can be seen in the village square. The other was the French novelist Honoré de Balzac; when tired of Paris, he frequented his friends' charming 16th-century manor house in order to savor the tranquillity of the countryside.

The house, now arranged as a Balzac museum, has been kept just as he left it: in his bedroom the quill pen and inkwell are there, the coffee pot awaits. There is a good collection of Balzac memorabilia, too, including some extraordinary proof pages covered in such an abundance of notes that many a printer was driven to despair.

★ ST.-AIGNAN   96C5

A small town on the Cher river, St.-Aignan has a cluster of narrow streets with timbered houses that lead up to a grand Renaissance *château* (access only to the terrace). The Romanesque church has several features of interest, particularly the fine capitals and frescoes in the crypt.

★★★ ST.-BENOÎT SUR-LOIRE   97D5

The great abbey of Fleury, built on an ancient site of Druid worship, was renamed for Saint Benedict after his remains were retrieved from the destroyed monastery of Monte Cassino in Italy and laid to rest in the crypt. In the Middle Ages the abbey became a center of learning and was renowned for its illuminated manuscripts. Its great abbey church, built in the 11th and 12th centuries, is one of the finest Romanesque buildings in France.

During the Wars of Religion between 1562 and 1598, almost all of the abbey's treasures were either destroyed or dispersed, including its extraordinary library and collection of manuscripts; many of these can now be found in major European collections. The abbey was closed in the Revolution, and the monastic buildings were destroyed. Only in the 19th century was the great church declared a national monument, becoming the subject of extensive restoration. The abbey has now been revived as a monastic community, and daily services with Gregorian chant are open to the public.

The basilica is wonderfully tall and light, with beautifully sculpted capitals. The most remarkable feature of the building is the richly decorated vaulted porch supporting the belfry at the west end; one of the capitals bears the inscription: *Umbertus me fecit* (Umberto made me).

ST.-ÉMILION   96B2

One of the most delightful small wine towns of the Bordeaux vineyard area – indeed, one of the very few wine towns or villages that has any degree of charm – St.-Émilion is an interesting old site, worth visiting for its own sake even if one is indifferent to the attraction of its noble wines. St.-Émilion is beautifully situated, confined within well-preserved ramparts on a horseshoe-shaped hill. Its houses are built of warm, honey-colored stone and roofed with red pantiles, while the surrounding land is covered with tight green lines of vines.

The heart of the town is the old market square, from which can be seen the bell tower of St.-Émilion's strange and rare subterranean church. There are several other churches and monastery buildings to visit here: the Couvent des Cordeliers, with a fine 14th-century cloister; the Chapelle de la Trinité, with its catacombs; and another cloister, which can be reached from the tourist office. The dungeon tower of the château, called the Tour du Roi, offers a splendid view of the town and vineyards. St.-Émilion is well provided with good hotels and restaurants, making a short stay here a seductive possibility.

Around the little town are several hamlets and communes that share St.-Émilion's great wine name: Puisseguin, Lussac, Parsac, Montagne and St.-Georges. The last three all have little Romanesque churches, as does Petit-Palais, whose church has a particularly beautiful facade. A short tour around the vineyards can take in villages and wine tasting; St.-Émilion's tourist office has details of vineyards open to the public.

ST.-SAVIN *96C4*

The pleasant little town of St.-Savin, on the Gartempe river, is famous for its abbey, founded in the 9th century. Following the usual destruction that took place during the Hundred Years War and the Wars of Religion, little of the abbey survived, with the exception of the wonderful 11th-century abbey **church ★★★**. This large and graceful edifice rejoices in some of the finest mural paintings in France. All along the high barrel vault are vivid frescoes depicting stories of the Old Testament: the Creation, Abel, Noah, Abraham, Joseph, Moses. They were painted by a single team of painters using only a small range of colors: red and yellow ochre, green, and black and white. In the narthex there are some magnificent frescoes of the Apocalypse; in the crypt, the frescoes have retained their brilliance through less exposure to light. All are being painstakingly restored, a process that is likely to take several years; one section

only is carried out at a time, thus leaving plenty for the visitor to see. For best appreciation of the frescoes, pick up the explanatory leaflets and take binoculars (some may be available for rent on site).

In a picturesque location in Bordeaux, St.-Émilion's pretty houses are roofed with red tiles

★ SAINTES *96B3*

This ancient red-brick town with long tree-lined avenues, on the banks of the Charente river, was once an important stopping-off place on the pilgrimage route to Santiago de Compostela in Spain. Some of its most interesting sights are well outside the old town center: a well-preserved Roman amphitheater (*arènes*); the remains of the great pilgrimage church of St.-Eutrope, with a beautiful Romanesque underground sanctuary; and the Abbaye aux Dames, with its Romanesque church. The Arch of Germanicus, which once stood on the Roman bridge across the river, was moved to the opposite bank when the bridge was demolished in the 19th century.

SANCERRE *97D5*

While not in itself full of historic interest, the village of Sancerre is an attractive little place, well situated on a round hill in the wine country of the Sancerrois. Unlike much of the rest of the Loire Valley, the land here is gently hilly, which ensures some fine, wide views of vineyards and river. Sancerre is topped by a 15th-century round tower, a landmark for miles around, and has a pleasant jumble of red-roofed houses and narrow alleyways. Sancerre is best known for its wine, produced from the Sauvignon Blanc grape.

★ SAUMUR *96B5*

Large and lively, ancient and modern, Saumur has been much renovated and improved to make the most of its small old-town area below the castle, whose pepper-pot towers dominate the countryside for miles around. The site of a major Loire bridgehead (one of only a very few in the days of the great pilgrimages to Santiago de Compostela), Saumur became a center of Protestantism. Much of its population emigrated after the Revocation of the Edict of Nantes in 1685, when Protestants were deprived of their religious and civil liberties.

Saumur's château stands high above the town, its turreted roofs and distinctive towers visible for miles around. There are splendid views over the river valley from the castle ramparts

Saumur was the poorer for their loss, but revived somewhat following the establishment of the cavalry regiment here in 1763. It now is the headquarters of the Cavalry Academy and National Riding School, including the famous crack squad the Cadre Noir; they put on a splendid display every July, and their practice sessions at other times can sometimes be watched. There are no less than three equestrian museums in Saumur: the Museum of the Horse (housed in the château), the Cavalry Museum and the Armored Cavalry Museum.

The fame of the château rests largely on its depiction in the medieval illuminated book of hours "Les Très Riches Heures du Duc de Berry" by the brothers Limbourg (now housed in the Château de Chantilly north of Paris). Despite the picture's idealized rural surroundings, the castle is still recognizable, built of the region's luminous white tufa and topped with fine gray slate. Inside are three museums – one devoted to equine matters, one for toys and the third a decorative arts museum, with fine enamel work and porcelain. All of these are included in a lengthy guided tour of the building. The nearby church of Notre-Dame-de-Nantilly has a very fine collection of 15th- to 17th-century tapestries.

Saumur is a renowned wine center, specializing in a sparkling white wine made according to the champagne method. This is stored in the many miles of tufa caves surrounding the town and its wine suburb of St.-Hilaire-St.-Florent, where most of the wine houses have their headquarters – and where you can taste and buy. The tufa also provides the ideal conditions for the cultivation of mushrooms (Saumur produces over half of France's edible fungi).

SELLES-SUR-CHER 96C5

Selles is a small town on the banks of the Cher river, whose waters reflect the towers of its château – a not very harmonious combination of graceful 17th-century buildings and medieval fortress behind a small park. The part-Romanesque, part-Gothic church of St.-Eusice is almost all that remains of a former abbey, yet another of those destroyed in the Wars of Religion.

SERRANT, 96B5
CHÂTEAU DE

This very imposing château was built over a period of 300 years, but manages to convey a sense of harmony. Moated and domed in Renaissance style, it was built with an unusual combination of brown-gray schist and white tufa. A guided tour includes beautifully furnished apartments, a splendid staircase and tapestries, and a library well stocked with works about Napoléon, for whom a bedroom was specially designed (although it was never to be used by him). In the chapel is the Baroque tomb of the Marquis de Vaubrun by Coysevox.

SOLESMES, ABBAYE DE 96B5

The village of Solesmes, north of Sablé-sur-Sarthe, is dominated by the riverside buildings of this Benedictine abbey, built in a Romanesque-Gothic style at the end of the 19th century. The buildings in themselves are not terribly distinguished, but the reputation of the abbey's choral singing most definitely is – for Solesmes has become associated with the revival of Gregorian plainchant, enjoying a resurgence of popular interest. Here you can listen to fine singing at daily Mass or evening Vespers services, conducted in Latin. In the abbey church are some beautiful 15th- and 16th-century sculptures.

WALKS

WALKS NEAR ROYAN

The forest of La Coubre near La Tremblade, just to the northwest of Royan, offers well-maintained and easy-going shady woodland footpaths. Less sheltered is the corniche coastal footpath, which is accessible from the little resort of St.-Palais-sur-Mer situated about 5 kilometers (3 mi.) to the north-west of Royan.

At the far end of the resort's beach, to the right, take the rue de l'Océan, at the end of which the coastal path starts. The path winds through oak woods to the savagely battered coast, where the rocks have become eroded into strange shapes ∎

RABELAIS

Born in the late 15th century in Chinon, François Rabelais was a humanist writer, renowned for his *joie de vivre* and his satirical masterpieces "Gargantua" and "Pantagruel."

It was Rabelais who first called this region "the garden of France," and his spirit is annually commemorated with grandiose banquets in the caverns under Chinon castle.

His childhood home, the manor house of La Devinière, is now a Rabelais museum, with fine views over the countryside about which he wrote.

The beautiful Château du Coudray-Montpensier, mentioned in his writings, can be seen (but not visited) just off the D24 southeast of the village of Lerné ■

★ SOLOGNE   97D5

A mysterious, secretive and silent area of low marshland, ponds and woods, the Sologne has long been cut off from mainstream French life by its inhospitable, infertile countryside and the consequent lack of population. During periods of improvement, the Sologne economy was given a boost and her few inhabitants enjoyed brief periods of relative prosperity – such as when 10th-century monks made clearings in the forest and attempted to channel water into lakes and streams, or when the 16th-century French court became established at nearby Blois and courtiers built châteaux in the area. At other times, though, its history is that of neglect, poverty and disease, with lakes reverting to stagnant marsh and malaria a constant threat.

The high water table, which hindered the construction of foundations, resulted in many low one-story houses, built typically of timber and cob or with diagonal patterns of red brick, and often with thatched roofs. Another characteristic Sologne feature can be seen in some of the tile-roofed village churches, which have a wooden gallery used for the discussion of parish affairs. A particularly fine example can be found at Souvigny-en-Sologne.

Nowadays, the Sologne is in a phase of relative prosperity. Since the region was taken in hand by Napoléon III – when canals were dug, pools were dredged and drained, and trees were planted – the Sologne has become popular for hunting and fishing. Visitors appreciate the well-stocked lakes, bright with water lilies, and the fine fall colors of silver birch and ancient oak. There are bluebells, heather, gorse and bracken, and the area is rich in mushrooms. It is also important for asparagus cultivation. Pesticides are prohibited

locally, and an ecological reserve has been set up. One of the lakes – the Étang du Puits, in a woodland setting 25 kilometers (16 mi.) southwest of Gien – has tourist facilities, including boats and children's areas.

While much of the interest of the Sologne is natural, there are several man-made sights worth visiting. Some are the result of the period of château building that began after the construction of the Château de Chambord nearby: the 17th-century brick and stone Château de la Ferté-St.-Aubin, whose interior illustrates château life in the 18th and 19th centuries; the miniature Château du Moulin, picture-book pretty and furnished in Renaissance style; and the equally charming

Château de Villesavin, near Bracieux, which has a particularly interesting 16th-century dovecote with space for 3,000 birds.

Picturesque villages typical of the area include Bracieux with its attractive, old, covered market; Chaumont-sur-Tharonne, with a 15th-century church; and Brinon-sur-Sauldre, which has a church with wooden gallery. It's worth visiting the main town, Romor-antin-Lanthenay; the brick-and-timber houses in the old center have detailed carving on their pillars and beams, and the Musée de Sologne is devoted to local life down the ages. The area is also lovingly evoked in Alain-Fournier's novel "Le Grand Meaulnes," written in the early 20th century.

★ **SULLY, CHÂTEAU DE** *97D5*
On the eastern stretch of the Loire, between Orléans and Gien, this magnificent medieval fortress, surrounded by a moat, boasts one of the finest timber roofs in France. This remarkable vault, which spans the enormous upper hall, was fashioned by ship carpenters out of chestnut and resembles an inverted boat hull, arching upwards for more than 9 meters (30 ft.). The trees, as saplings, had their tops tied together so as to grow to the required shape; they were then seasoned for several years, both in and out of water, and required no restoration for over 600 years.

The château has a number of historical associations, including Jeanne d'Arc and Voltaire.

The moated feudal fortress of Sully is renowned for its remarkable 14th-century timber roof, still in an excellent state of repair. Voltaire staged two of his plays in the castle, and Jeanne d'Arc met Charles VII here

Elegant flying buttresses on the north transept of Tours' cathedral of St.-Gatien. The building is a harmonious blend of styles, from late Gothic on

★ TOURS *96C5*

The administrative capital of the Indre-et-Loire *département*, Tours is an industrial and university city, with swelling outskirts of high-rise blocks and highway sprawl. Heavily bombed in 1944, when 12 hectares (30 acres) of central Tours were razed to the ground and many thousands of people were killed, the heart of the city became little more than a slum, parts of which were left without sanitation or running water. The middle classes deserted the remaining buildings, and fine old town houses were sold off piecemeal – a staircase here, wood paneling there. In the 1960s the center of Tours was finally declared a conservation area, and redevelopment and restoration began. The project has become a model of its kind; its success has been amazing, and has resulted in total urban regeneration. Beautiful houses were restored and new buildings created to blend with the old, or indeed built in the original style using traditional materials. Vieux (Old) Tours became a fashionable area in which to live, and cafés, restaurants, craft workshops and stylish boutiques consequently abound. In the 1970s the city council decided to site the new university in the heart of the old town, which has contributed much to the lively atmosphere.

The center of the compact old town is the attractive place Plumereau, overlooked by several 15th-century timber-framed houses. Streets worth wandering down include rue Briçonnet, which has several fine Gothic and Renaissance houses; rue Paul-Louis Courier, with a 17th-century mansion; rue du Change, with a slate-hung timber-framed house; place de Châteauneuf, faced by the mansion of the Dukes of Touraine; and the small, charming place des Carmes. At the southern end of this area, two isolated towers – the Tour Charlemagne and the Tour de l'Horloge – are almost all that remain of an enormous Romanesque pilgrimage basilica. Slightly further afield lies the cathedral of St.-Gatien, which was rebuilt from 1235 onwards after an earlier structure burned down. Its remarkably ornate late Gothic facade is crowned by twin Renaissance lanterns. The interior represents earlier Gothic styles.

Tours has several museums. The Hotel Gouin, the remains of a gracious Renaissance mansion,

houses archeological finds (Tours was a prosperous city in Roman times) and medieval art; the Musée du Gemmail is devoted to modern stained glass. There's a fine arts museum (Musée des Beaux-Arts) in the Archbishop's Palace, and two small museums devoted to craft guilds and wine-making, the latter housed in old wine cellars off the cloisters of the church of St.-Julien.

Tours makes a good place to stay for those without an automobile, offering opportunities for bus tours to the surrounding countryside and châteaux.

TROUSSAY, CHÂTEAU DE   96C5

This small manor house was refurbished in the late 19th century by a historian with a passion for collecting items from demolished buildings, including doors, wood carvings and floor tiles. The outbuildings house a collection of old agricultural tools.

★ USSÉ, CHÂTEAU DE   96C5

This has become known as the ultimate romantic château since its use by the fairy-tale writer Charles Perrault as the model for his setting of "Sleeping Beauty." Ussé's exterior of turrets and tall chimneys, set against a dark background of forest, certainly provides the classic fairy-tale ingredients, and its terraces offer good views of the Loire. It also has fine gardens and a park.

Inside, Ussé is less interesting, with the sole exception of its Renaissance chapel. Only a small part is open to the public.

★ VALENÇAY   96C4

In the Berry region south of the Cher, and quite a drive from the main Loire Valley tourist area, Valençay is the setting for a stunning château – an excellent example of classical Renaissance

TROGLODYTES

The Loire region is covered with a deposit known as tufa, a yellowy-white porous rock that has been a traditional source of building material (Loire châteaux are nearly all built of it).

Tufa caves abound, making ideal places for the cultivation of mushrooms and for wine storage. In addition, the caves have served as workshops, schools, chapels, prisons – and even homes.

Whole troglodyte villages can be found along the Loir, from Vendôme to Trôo; at Rochecorbon and Vouvray, east of Tours, on the Loire; and at Doué-la-Fontaine, southwest of Saumur, where they form part of a network of underground quarries and galleries. Many are increasingly sought after as second homes ■

SPECIALTIES OF THE LOIRE REGION

River fish are plentiful and fresh, particularly _brochet_ (pike), _carpe_ (carp), _alose_ (shad) and _saumon_ (salmon).

Fish is often served _à la beurre blanc_ (with a sauce of butter, vinegar and shallots) or _à l'oseille_ (with a sorrel sauce).

Game is popular, notably in the Sologne. _Rillons_ and _rillettes_ (cold, potted pork) is a specialty of Tours.

Goat's milk cheeses are a regional specialty, especially the salty _crottin de Chavignol_. _Crémets_ (fresh cream cheeses) are eaten with sugar and cream.

Fruit tarts and confectionery featuring prunes are popular, as is _tarte Tatin_ (a delicious caramelized upside-down apple tart) ■

style. Vast and domed, its great round towers decorated with classical pilasters, Valençay is extremely grand. Its grandiosity undoubtedly appealed to the famous 19th-century financier, diplomat and political survivor Charles Maurice de Talleyrand, who acquired it in 1803 and used it to entertain ambassadors and foreign dignitaries in regal style.

The château is sumptuously and appropriately furnished in Louis XV, Louis XVI and Empire styles, and there are many beautiful objets d'art to be seen inside. In the surrounding park and gardens there are cranes, black swans, sheep, llamas, flamingoes, deer and peacocks.

VENDÔME 96C5

On the leafy Loir river, Vendôme is a fascinating town built on islands, with waterside mills, weirs and gardens. The waters contributed to a flourishing tanning industry in Renaissance times; gloves are still made here.

On a wooded mound (rather grandly called La Montagne) lie the remains of an old castle. In the center of town, reached by a fine bridge and the massive 14th-century gateway of St.-Georges, there is a busy market square overlooked by an elegant Renaissance bell and clock tower, all that remains of an earlier church. The former abbey of La Trinité was once an important place of pilgrimage; its Gothic abbey church has a simple interior, which contrasts with a very elaborate west front in the late-Gothic Flamboyant style.

VILLAINES-LES-ROCHERS 96C5

This small village is the site of one of France's first agricultural cooperatives; founded in the middle of the 19th century, it still employs many of its inhabitants. This is the center of the local basket-weaving industry. In the traditional way, willow rushes are grown beside the Indre, cut in winter and steeped in water until May, when they are woven into a variety of products. Basket-makers can be seen at work in individual workshops or at the cooperative in the village center.

★★ VILLANDRY, CHÂTEAU DE 96C5

A splendid Renaissance building, which was added to an original fortress keep, Villandry's great fame rests on the magnificence of its formal gardens. Although the château hasn't much of additional interest for visitors who may already be sated on the architectural treasures of the Loire Valley, the guided tour does explain the significance of the formal layout and provides views over the gardens, which can also be enjoyed from the terraces.

The present gardens owe their existence to the purchase of the château by a 19th-century historian, Dr. Carvallo, who was also the founder of the French Historic Houses Association. He painstakingly converted the landscaped English-style gardens back to the formal terraces of the 16th century, which were faithfully reconstructed from old drawings according to a complex symbolic design. The result is a very fine and almost unique example of this style: water garden, ornamental and kitchen gardens on separate terraces, all bordered by yew or box, with canals, fountains and pergolas adding decorative details. The kitchen garden contains over 85,000 plants, chosen for their color as much as culinary value. Delightful aromas waft from the herb garden, while trellised bowers provide seats from which to regard the enchanting scene.

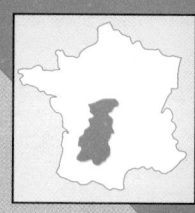

THE DORDOGNE

With its châteaux, picturesque
villages, vineyards and one of the
country's best-loved rivers, the
Dordogne is the essence of France

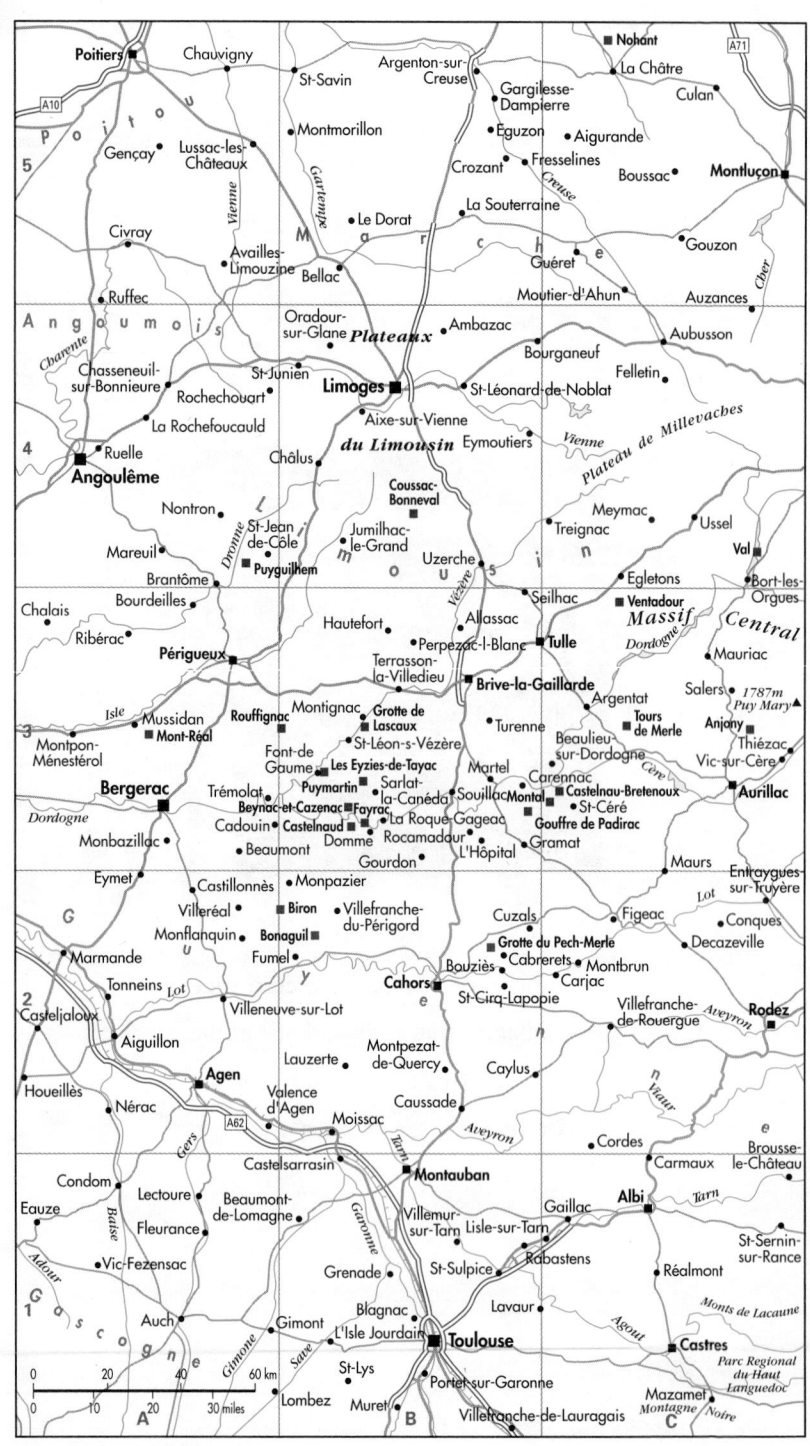

THE DORDOGNE

Rising in the Massif Central and flowing through varied countryside to meet the Garonne north of Bordeaux, the Dordogne is a river of exceptional beauty. The provinces of Périgord and Quercy (roughly overlapping the *départements* of Dordogne and Lot), which make up the Dordogne region, are renowned for their food and wine, their fortresses and for their cave paintings by prehistoric man.

Périgord, covering a high limestone plateau split by river valleys, is divided into four areas. In **Périgord Blanc**, the white limestone soil supports cereals and dairy and veal herds; in **Périgord Vert**, woodland is interspersed with the lush green farmland of the Limousin; in **Périgord Noir**, thick oak and walnut forests cloak the country. The Noir is the land of the truffle, the coal-like fungus beloved of gastronomes. **Périgord Pourpre** covers the Bergerac region.

Quercy is also built on limestone, but here the rock is impermeable, unlike that of Périgord, where percolating water has created caves. Haut (Upper) Quercy consists of arid plateaus dotted with woodland. This is sheep-rearing country, in contrast to Bas (Lower) Quercy, with its vineyards and patchwork fields.

The limestone caves of Périgord sheltered human inhabitants during the Old Stone Age. Early exploration revealed stone tools and, in the early 1900s, the first cave paintings. In 1940 the superb paintings of the **Lascaux** cave were discovered. These rank alongside the great art from any age. Damage caused by lights and the breath of visitors has necessitated the closing of Lascaux, but an exact replica (Lascaux II) can be visited.

★★★
HIGHLIGHTS

Beynac-et-Cazenac
(►134)
Bonaguil, Château de (►135)
Les Eyzies-de-Tayac
(►141)
Gouffre de Padirac
(►146)
Hautefort, Château de (►142)
Lascaux II (►142)
Montpézat-de-Quercy
(►145)
Rocamadour (►147)
La Roque-Gageac
(►148)
Sarlat-la-Canéda (►150)

The Romans were drawn to the Dordogne region by the fertility of the soil. Later, in the early Middle Ages, the Dordogne saw cruel conflicts, some sparked by that same precious soil. The Albigensian Crusade, launched by the Catholic King of France against the Cathar heretics, was equally an invasion of the rich lands of the Dordogne and Languedoc. The Hundred Years War, between England and France, was also fought for control of the Dordogne, together with Anjou and Aquitaine. Both conflicts resulted in the construction of **fortresses** – medieval châteaux like Bonaguil and Castelnaud – and fortified hilltop villages known as *bastides*. When peace came, some of the castles were turned into châteaux, elegant mansions of the French nobility. Bourdeilles provides one of the best examples of the transition from military to domestic function.

Together, all these factors – wine, good food and a fine sense of history – make a visit to the Dordogne truly memorable.

CALENDAR OF EVENTS

JANUARY – Périgueux: **Epiphany Fair.**

LATE MAY – Sarlat: **Fête de la Ringueta,** traditional games (biennial – odd years).

MID-JUNE TO MID-SEPTEMBER – Beaulieu-en-Rouergue: **Contemporary Art Exhibition.** Carjac: **Contemporary Art Exhibition.**

JULY – Rocamadour: **Theater Festival.** Brive: **Folklore Festival.** Ribérac: **Festival of Words and Music.**

EARLY AUGUST – Bonaguil: **Music Festival.** Périgueux: **"Mimos" Mime Festival.**

EARLY SEPTEMBER – Notre-Dame-du-Capelou: **Annual Pilgrimage.** Rocamadour: **Festival of Poetry.**

LATE SEPTEMBER – Meyrals: **Wine Harvest Festival.**

CHRISTMAS EVE – **Midnight Mass** in the Occitan language ■

HENRI DE TOULOUSE-LAUTREC

Born in Albi in 1864, the son of a minor nobleman, Henri showed a talent for painting from an early age, but as a teenager his life was transformed by two freak falls that left him partially disabled and with shortened legs.

Henri went to Montmartre in Paris, in 1882, where he painted scenes of debauchery from his life in the city, interspersed with more sedate works completed in Albi and the well-known posters, for which he became famous and wealthy.

In 1899 he sought treatment for his alcoholism, but he soon returned to his old ways, and died in 1901, leaving behind his unique view of late 19th-century Bohemian Paris ∎

★★ ALBI *130C1*

"Red Albi" stands beside the Tarn river, which forms Dordogne's border with the parched plains of Languedoc. The town's nickname derives not from its bloody history, but from the red bricks of its buildings. Yet medieval history dominates Albi, the name forever linked to the Albigensian heresy of dualism and the crusade to crush it.

Soon after the last Cathar stronghold fell in 1255, a bishop was appointed to the new see of Albi. Bernard de Combret's first priority was to build a palace that was well defended against a resentful populace. Today the Palais de la Berbie houses a museum devoted to Albi's most famous citizen, the painter Henri de Toulouse-Lautrec.

Beside the palace is Albi's vast, fortress-like cathedral of Ste.-Cécile, begun by Combret's successor, who ruled Albi with an iron hand. The canopied porch is in Flamboyant Gothic style, dating from 1520. Inside lies a Gothic treasure, with delicately carved stonework, a sumptuous rood screen and a masterly fresco of the Last Judgment.

South of the cathedral is old Albi, a quaint district of brick-built and half-timbered houses. Beside the church of St.-Salvy are quiet and romantic cloisters dating from the 11th century, while in the road that bears his name stands the house in which Toulouse-Lautrec was born.

ALLASSAC *130B3*

In the early 20th century Allassac prospered through the local slate quarries, as witnessed by the roofs of its black-stone houses. Quite by contrast, the church's porch is built of pink rock. Allassac makes an excellent base for the exploration of Yssandon, an area of black schist and red

sandstone lying west of the Vézère river. In the Middle Ages, this was a region of vineyards and farmland. Today, orchards, cereal crops and vineyards are still separated by stands of walnut and oak trees. The area's villages are charming and full of interest; at Perpezac-le-Blanc you can visit an observatory and space center. For a fine view of the country, take the road from Perpezac to the ancient fortress ruins at the top of the Puy d'Yssandon.

ARGENTAT *130C3*

Gabardes used to carry goods from Argentat down the Dordogne as far as Bordeaux; one such flat-bottom boat floats beside the preserved quai Lestourgie, now a walkway flanked

by delightful houses. Another fine spot in this charming town is the place de l'Église, the center of the medieval town. Here the houses, many with roof tiles of split stone, reflect the town's historic river-trade prosperity. Close to Argentat are the Tours de Merle, a 12th-century ruin.

★ AUBUSSON 130C4

In the 14th century Flemish weavers were invited to set up craft workshops in this pretty village built on the banks of the Creuse river. A century later Aubusson was gaining a reputation for the production of fine carpets and tapestries. After a further century, France's finest weavers had studios in the town, several of them being given the title of Tapestry or Carpet Maker to the King. The town's most prosperous period was in the 18th century, when there was great demand for Aubusson's reproductions of old designs and interpretations of engravings or prints. Today the noble tradition lives on, with several weaving workshops still active: both the galleries of local work and workshops can be visited. Those with a special interest in the history of the craft can also visit the Maison du Vieux Tapissier, a beautiful 16th-century house that is now a museum dedicated to weaving. The Centre Jean-Lurçat exhibits the work of weavers and of Lurçat himself, who was inspired by Cubism. (See p.134 for a walk around the town.)

Tapestry detail. Flemish artisans brought the art of tapestry-weaving to Aubusson in the 14th century. Typical designs include stylized landscapes, and mythical or allegorical themes

THE DORDOGNE

WALK

AUBUSSON

From place Maurice Dayras, cross Pont-Neuf, and turn left along quai des Iles to rue des Déportes.

Cross into allée de l'Horloge, up steps to the Tour de l'Horloge, and when the path ends, turn right on rue de la Roche to the tourist office.

Turn right on rue Vieille to place de la Libération, then first left, sharply, on Grande Rue. Beyond the town hall, turn right up steps to place de l'Église, and then second left on rue de l'Est, then right down steps on rue Jean Jaurès.

Turn left, cross Pont de Juillet, and follow avenue des Lissiers to the Manufacture St.-Jean, beside the starting point ■

★ BEAULIEU-SUR-DORDOGNE   130C3

The town, "beautiful place" on the Dordogne, was named by the archbishop of Bourges after a Benedictine abbey had been founded here in the 9th century. The abbey church of St.-Pierre, dating from the 12th century, still survives and is famous for its doorway, the carvings of which are a masterpiece of early medieval art depicting the Day of Judgment. The church's treasury houses a 12th-century silver statue of the Virgin Mary, another superb Romanesque work. Clustered around the church is one of the best-preserved medieval towns in France, a tightly packed huddle of delightful stone houses.

★ BERGERAC   130A3

Most visitors to this large, elegant town assume that Cyrano de Bergerac, the large-nosed hero of Edmond Rostand's play, was born or lived here. In fact, the real Cyrano was a philosopher from northern France who probably never came this far south, and certainly was far from resembling the fictional hero. Not that Bergerac is anxious for you to know this, since the town has erected statues and named numerous restaurants and galleries for him.

Bergerac is the capital of French tobacco farming, and the Maison Peyrarède, a splendid early 17th-century house, now contains a museum dedicated to the tobacco trade. Close by there is a museum of wine making, vineyards now vying with tobacco fields as the main source of local prosperity. Both museums are set in the attractive old quarter, close to place du Dr. Cayla and place de la Myrpe, each lined with delightful half-timbered houses that are worth a look.

★★★ BEYNAC-ET-CAZENAC   130B3

The whole history of medieval Dordogne is invested in this majestic riverside castle, which all but overwhelms the limestone outcrop on which it stands.

The site's strategic value demanded a castle, and one existed by the time Richard the Lionheart arrived in the 12th century to pursue the Plantagenet war with Capetian France. After Richard captured the castle, it served as a base for local raids. Later, during the Albigensian Crusade, Simon de Montfort destroyed the castle to prevent it threatening his supply routes. The rebuilt castle saw action during the Hundred Years War (1337–1453), when it was held alternately by the French and the English. When peace finally returned, the castle became the seat of one of the four Barons of Périgord, rulers of Dordogne. From it, the view of the river is exquisite, but don't miss a chance to see the frescoed Last Supper in the baronial Hall of State.

The village below the castle is as elegant as a baronial capital should be, and includes a small museum and park that explore the history of the area from the Bronze Age to Roman times.

BIRON, CHÂTEAU DE   130B2

The seat of another Baron of Périgord, the castle of Biron also saw action during the Albigensian campaigns and the Hundred Years War. As it expanded across the bluff, the castle created a mass of thick walls and towers from which there are impressive views. Having been in the hands of the Gontaut family for over 800 years (one of its members, a former Governor of Burgundy, was beheaded when he plotted against Henri IV), the castle is now owned by the *département*.

★★★ BONAGUIL, CHÂTEAU DE *130B2*

Arguably the finest example of late-medieval castle architecture in France, Bonaguil was built for military purposes at a time when other châteaux in the Loire were constructed for purely ornamental and aesthetic reasons. Enlarged in 1445 around an existing central keep, Bonaguil had inner and outer towers, a barbican, and a moat and drawbridge. Though partially destroyed during the Revolution, it still impresses – a delight for all castle lovers.

BOURDEILLES *130A3*

Bourdeilles, a baronial capital of medieval Périgord, was used as an English base between 1337 and 1445 during the Hundred Years War. An elegant Renaissance château, it became the baronial home in later, more peaceful, times. In the interior of the château there is a superbly carved chimneypiece from the 16th century, a Gold Salon that was extravagantly decorated for Catherine de Médicis, and a magnificent bedroom named for the emperor Charles V.

Beynac castle looms over the river from a commanding cliff-top site. There are fine views from here of the tiny village that huddles beneath

★ **CADOUIN** *130A3*

The great Cistercian abbey became one of the most famous in France when, in the 13th century, the cloth reputedly used to wrap the dead Christ's head was "discovered" here. Pilgrimages were made throughout the Middle Ages, but in 1934 historians dated the embroidery to the late 11th century. The pilgrimages ceased, but research in 1982 suggested that the cloth might predate the embroidery. It can be seen at the museum in the chapter house. Also worth visiting are the fine Gothic cloisters and the village's bicycle museum, the most important of its kind in France.

★ **CAHORS** *130B2*

Delightfully positioned in a loop of the Lot river overlooked by rolling hills, this site was occupied by both Gauls and Romans, each of whom considered a spring here as holy. The Lot is crossed by a medieval fortified bridge, the Pont Valentré, its graceful arches holding aloft three square towers. The central one is known as the Devil's Tower: legend says that the devil agreed to help the architect in exchange for his soul, but lost out as the work neared completion when the man called for water to be brought in a sieve. Furious, the devil broke off the tower's topmost stone. All attempts to replace it failed, until a small devil was carved on a replacement. Close to the bridge is a moored mill boat, whose keel wheel was driven by the tide. At Cahors' cathedral look for the Renaissance cloisters. Nearby is a boulevard named for the town's most famous son, Léon Gambetta, French politician during the Third Republic. Old Cahors lies to the east of this boulevard, a network of alleys and quaint 16th-century houses.

The Cistercian abbey at Cadouin became a place of pilgrimage in the 13th century for a supposed relic of the Crucifixion that was found here. Today the abbey's Gothic cloisters have an air of tranquillity

BRANTÔME *130A4*

Life at court in the 16th century, with its soldiers and courtesans, is captured in the writings of Pierre de Bourdeille, a gentleman soldier and diplomat who retired from court to become the abbot here and took Brantôme as his pen name. The abbey, whose remains stand in an attractive setting beside the Dronne river, was founded by Charlemagne in the 8th century. The finest building is the Romanesque bell tower, built on a needle of rock. The earliest monks to occupy the site lived in caves (some beneath the bell tower), many of which were later used as dovecotes. The riverside village of Brantôme is delightful, with slate-roofed houses and a crooked bridge.

CARENNAC 130B3

François Fénelon, one of the great figures of medieval French literature, wrote his most famous book – on the adventures of Telemachus, son of Odysseus – while he was abbot of Carennac priory. In honor of their famous son, the townsfolk have changed the name of the nearby island in the Dordogne to Calypso's Island, and willingly point out the Tower of Telemachus to visitors. Here, they claim (with little evidence), Fénelon wrote his story. The tower is one high spot on a tour of this picturesque village, another being the Romanesque church with its beautiful carved doorway and elegant cloisters.

CASTELNAUD and FAYRAC 130B3

Across the river from the fortress of Beynac-et-Cazenac stand the castles of Castelnaud and Fayrac. Castelnaud, a tall, elegant pyramidal keep, is surrounded by equally tall walls, which afford good views across to Beynac castle. Fayrac, with its pepper-pot roofs, is reached by means of two drawbridges. Though much less impressive than Castelnaud, the view it offers is just as fine.

CORDES 130C2

Dominating the wine-growing region of Gaillac is the *bastide* town of Cordes, built by the Count of Toulouse in 1222 as a redoubt for the gentry of Languedoc, still outraged by the excesses of the Albigensian Crusade. The noblemen – whose fine houses make up the heart of Cordes – were not themselves heretics, but when Inquisitors came to root out the last of the Cathars, the nobles murdered them. The southern ramparts, looking over the gentle Périgord country, can be walked. In the steep narrow streets of medieval houses you'll find one that is a museum to the art of sculpting and spinning sugar.

★ CREUSE VALLEY 130C5

Rising in the granite hills east of Limoges, the Creuse river flows through Aubusson to reach its loveliest section, between the villages of Fresselines and Argenton-sur-Creuse. The Barrage d'Éguzon has created the Lac de Chambon, used for water sports, while downstream is Gargilesse-Dampierre, where the house of George Sand has been turned into a museum. Argenton itself is a charming place, best seen from the old bridge that spans the Creuse.

CUZALS 130B2

Lying on the northern side of the Célé Valley, about 40 kilometers (25 mi.) east of Cahors, the Musée de Plein Air du Quercy (Quercy Open-Air Museum) offers a fascinating glimpse of life in the Dordogne from the time of the Revolution through to World War II. The exhibits include furnished farmhouses, shops and agricultural machinery. In summer ox teams give rides to children.

TRUFFLES AND FOIE GRAS

Despite many attempts, the world-famous Périgord black truffle, which is a member of the fungus family, has resisted attempts at commercial cultivation.

Found underground in the local oak forests, it is sniffed out by dogs; pigs were once used, but they tended to eat what they found. The true, costly Périgord truffles are labeled *truffes du Périgord*.

A second Périgord specialty is *foie gras* (literally "fatty liver"), the livers being from geese or ducks that are maize-fed to reach a great weight. *Foie gras* is strictly labeled, too. The connoisseur eats it almost raw, but most people eat a pâté or *terrine* that is about 25 percent pork or veal ■

DRIVE

A PREHISTORIC TOUR AROUND THE DORDOGNE

383 kilometers/238 miles (allow 4 days)

This tour, which can be split in two by a short detour half way, explores the essence of the Dordogne: the fine towns of Bergerac and Périgueux, the scenic highlights of the valley from Rocamadour to Castelnaud, the famous cave paintings of Lascaux, and the golden building stone of beautiful towns like Sarlat and Domme.

The tour starts at Périgueux. The original center was by the church of St.-Étienne-de-la-Cité. After the Romans left, the town declined, to become prosperous again in the Middle Ages. A new town grew up closer to the river, with the cathedral of St.-Front at its heart.

Leave Périgueux along the N89 for Brive, then turn right on the D710. Next, go left on the D45, then right along the D47 to reach the Grotte du Grand Roc.

1 Grotte du Grand Roc

The view of the Vézère valley from the stairs leading to the cave is a joy in itself. Inside is a crowd of stalagmites and stalactites of amazing delicacy. Excavations at the Upper Laugerie Deposit have revealed numerous objects, including several skeletons.

Continue on the D47 to Les Eyzies-de-Tayac.

2 Les Eyzies

In the stunning Vézère Valley, rain and river water have formed a succession of caves in the limestone. Archeological finds have made this valley the most important in Europe for the study of man from paleolithic times to the Bronze Age. Although the

BERGERAC WINES

Although not as well known outside the region as neighboring Bordeaux wines, Bergerac wines can be very drinkable – and they are much cheaper.

Normal Côtes de Bergerac reds can be drunk quite young, but the Pecharmant wines should be racked for at least 4 years.

Monbazillac white is best served as an aperitif ■

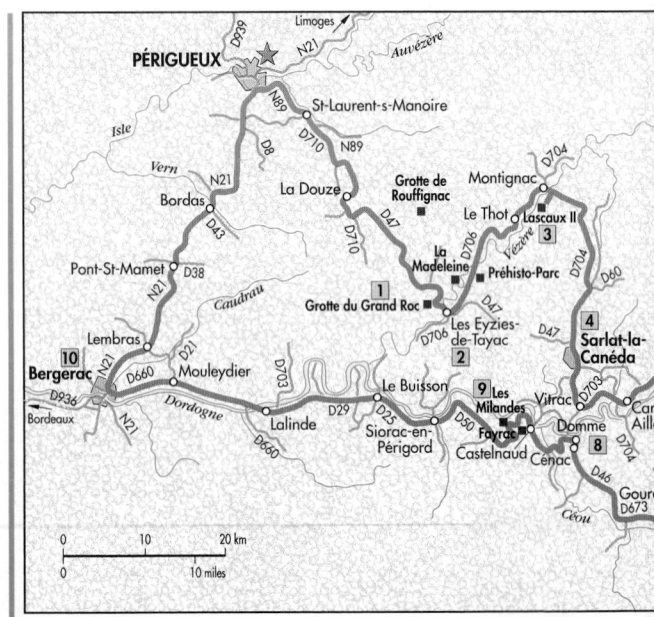

most important site is Lascaux, other caves have revealed objects of astonishing beauty, like the carved antler from La Madeleine cave. Many of the finds are displayed at the Musée National de la Préhistoire at Les Eyzies.

From Les Eyzies, take the D706 to Montignac, passing the Préhisto-Parc where 20 Neanderthal and Cro-Magnon sites have been skillfully reconstructed. Turn right on the D704, and right again to reach Lascaux II.

3 Lascaux II
The Lascaux cave, discovered in 1940, is among the world's foremost sites for the number and quality of its wall paintings. These paintings, which are believed to be about 16,000 years old, include various animals such as bulls, bison, deer, horses and a single painting of a man (being pursued by a wounded bison). Because of damage, the cave was closed to the public in

1963, however, an exact replica exists at Lascaux II.

Retrace the drive to Montignac and turn right on the D704 to Sarlat-la-Canéda.

4 Sarlat
Buildings of golden stone line the medieval streets of Sarlat, the loveliest town in the Dordogne. Of the streets the best is rue des Consuls, north of the cathedral, which runs into the place des Oies, itself equally charming. Nearer the cathedral, the Maison de la Boétie is probably Sarlat's most photographed building. At the Musée-Aquarium fish specimens from all over the Dordogne are on display.

Take the D46 for Vitrac, but in Vitrac-Port turn left on the D703 for Carsac-Aillac and Souillac.

5 Souillac
Set where the Corrèze meets the Dordogne, Souillac is famous for its abbey church and its museum of over 1,000 automatons, including a full jazz band.

The 12th-century church, a superb example of Romanesque style in southern France, has exceptional carvings near its doorway (note the lively figure of Isaiah).

Follow the D703 to Martel, then turn right on the N140 and left on the D70. Turn right along the D11 to Miers and left on the D91. Go left along the D60, right at a Y-junction by a stone cross, then right at a T-junction to reach the Gouffre de Padirac.

6 Gouffre de Padirac
First explored by Edouard Martel, father of speleology, Padirac

THE DORDOGNE RIVER

During the summer the shallow, slow-flowing Dordogne river is ideal for canoeing and kayaking, and rental outlets can be found every-where.

In winter, how-ever, it displays a different facet, with the possibili-ty of seasonal floodwaters mak-ing navigation a potential problem.

A major trade route since the earliest times, the river was used to transport wines, leather and cheeses down-stream to the Garonne and Bordeaux.

In order to cope with the vagaries of its variable flow the boatmen (*gabariers*) used flat-bottomed boats, which were known as *gabardes, sapines*, or *argentas* (after the town of the same name – see p.132) ■

JOSEPHINE BAKER AND LES MILANDES

Having already conquered Paris through her role in the legendary Folies Bergères, Josephine Baker bought the château of Les Milandes in 1936, when she was just 30 years old and at the height of her fame.

She converted part of it into a hotel and restaurant, adding a mini-golf course, tennis court and wax museum, and opened it to the public as the *village du monde*.

By the 1950s she had adopted a dozen children (mostly orphans) from around the world to live at Les Milandes, and over 300,000 people a year came to see her "model multicultural community" ■

contained animal bones dating from 200,000 years ago and human bones from some 50,000 years ago.

Today visitors marvel at the beauty of the cave's formations. The exciting tour involves a descent by elevator (or down 455 steps) and a boat trip along an underground river.

Follow the D90 to Padirac and turn right there on the road for Gramat. At Gramat, take the N140 towards Brive, then turn left along the D36. Turn left again along the D32 to Rocamadour.

7 Rocamadour

Rocamadour seemingly defies gravity as it clings to the side of a sheer cliff (view from the belvedere of L'Hospitalet on the D32). The village became an important medieval pilgrimage site in the 12th century.

Follow the D32 to Couzou and turn right on the D39, going through St.-Projet before turning right on the D1. Join the D673 to Gourdon, turning right for Sarlat, then right again for Salviac. Leave Gourdon on the D673. Turn right on the D6, which becomes the D46 to Cénac. Turn right on the D49 to Domme.

8 Domme

The strikingly situated Domme is a near-perfect *bastide*. Built by Philip the Fair in the late 13th century, the ramparts can still be walked. In the place de la Halle is a delightful covered market. The local folk museum throws light on life in a medieval hilltop village.

Return to Cénac and take the D50 through St.-Cybranet to

reach Siorac. In Pont-de-Cause, bear right for Castelnaud, and there go straight ahead for Fayrac and Les Milandes. Turn left on the D53 as for Siorac-en-Périgord, then, after a "virages" sign, turn sharp right uphill on the road to the Château des Milandes.

9 Les Milandes

Built in 1489, the château had its most famous period when it was owned by black American jazz singer Josephine Baker who, as *La Perle Noire*, captivated Parisian audiences in the 1920s and 1930s. Here Josephine set up her Village of the World, a foundation that cared for orphans from around the globe. Mementos of the singer can still be seen.

Continue along the road, then bear left as for Veyrines. Turn right on the D53, then take the D50 to Siorac-en-Périgord and the D25 to Le Buisson. Follow the signs for Lalinde, and then for Bergerac.

10 Bergerac

Despite the statue (and the various establishments named for him), big-nosed Cyrano de Bergerac had no association with this town.

Old Bergerac lies close to the Dordogne, a glorious array of narrow streets and delightful houses. Having prospered from tobacco farming, the town is now the center of an important wine-growing area. The Musée du Tabac traces the history of tobacco growing, and the Musée du Vin, de la Batellerie et de la Tonnellerie relates to wine, river shipping and cooperage.

From Bergerac, take the N21 to return to Périgueux.

★ DOMME   130B3

In a famous incident of the French Wars of Religion that occurred here in 1588, the Huguenot Captain Vivans led a group of men up the sheer rock face that protected the town's northern edge. Once inside, Vivans opened the town gates, letting in the remainder of the Protestant army.

For four years Vivans was governor of Domme, then, sensing the tide turning in favor of the Catholics, he agreed to sell the town to them – first demolishing most of the houses. What remains is worth visiting. The place de la Halle (old market place) is still overlooked by the governor's stern house. Another house on the square is home to the local folk museum, which explores the town's past.

★★★ LES EYZIES-   130B3
DE-TAYAC

From its source in Limousin, the Vézère river runs across sandstone and a belt of impermeable limestone to reach the soluble limestone of Périgord Noir. Here the river has cut a lush valley, and with the help of rain has eaten through the rock to create numerous caves. During the late Old Stone Age these caves were inhabited by humans; the excavated remains and wall paintings found in the caves have made this valley one of the most important prehistoric sites in the world. At its heart is Les Eyzies. The village's old castle, erected in the 13th century by the Barons of Beynac, is now the National Museum of Prehistory, guarded by a statue of Neanderthal man.

Close by are some of the valley's most important sites: at the Abri de Cro-Magnon were unearthed the finds that helped define Cro-Magnon man, while at the Font-de-Gaume cave there are some superb paintings. The

process of cave formation and the techniques of cave exploration are illustrated at the Musée de la Spéléologie in Tayac to the northwest of the village.

FIGEAC   130C2

Placed on the pilgrimage route from Le Puy-en-Vélay to Santiago de Compostela, Figeac has been important since the 9th century. An abbey established about then brought further prosperity. When the king wrested control of the town from the abbot in 1302, the traders, fearful of losing their livelihood, were calmed only by the king's grant of a Royal Mint; the Hôtel de la Monnaie now houses the tourist office and a museum of local history. At the place des Écritures is a huge replica of the Rosetta Stone, created in 1991 in honor of Jean-François Champollion, Figeac's most famous son and one of the world's greatest Egyptologists, who was born here in 1790.

At the entrance to the Museum of Prehistory at Les Eyzies stands a huge statue of Neanderthal man. The museum, housed in the village's former castle, displays the best of locally excavated finds

★★★ HAUTEFORT, CHÂTEAU D'   *130B3*

This magnificent château, which dominates the skyline of Périgord Blanc, is reminiscent of the great châteaux of the Loire, and dates from the same period. The château, reached by drawbridge, is set in 40 hectares (100 acres) of parkland laid out with terraces of flowers and trees. Inside, there is some beautiful woodwork and other fine treasures. Following a

formidable and elegant at the same time. It began life as a fortress of the Knights Templar, but over several succeeding centuries its form was softened by years of peace. Finally, the château was remodeled along lines that were to see their greatest flowering in the Renaissance châteaux of the Loire. Just enough of that style exists to take the edge off its harsher medieval origins.

Painting of the great black bull at Lascaux II. The drawings, some 25,000 years old, were reproduced by artist Monique Peytal using pigments and materials that closely matched the originals

disastrous fire in 1968, a vast amount of restoration work was required in order to return the château to its original glory – the result is a credit to the skilled artisans who worked on it.

JUMILHAC-LE-GRAND   *130B4*

Perched on Dordogne's border with Limousin, the village of Jumilhac is dominated by a château that manages to be both

★★★ LASCAUX II   *130B3* (GROTTE DE)

In 1940 four young boys were walking their dog when it disappeared into a hole in the ground. Unable to call it back, the boys returned with a lamp and clambered into the hole. Within minutes they stood before one of the world's foremost sites of prehistoric art. The boys told their teacher who, recognizing the significance of the find, contacted the Abbé Breuil, a leading French authority on the paleolithic era. It was the Abbé who gave Lascaux its nickname of the "Sistine Chapel of Périgord."

The cave was opened to the public in 1948, but by 1963 the breath of visitors, combined with the lighting, had resulted in serious damage due to moss, algae and bacteria. The cave was shut, but in 1983 Lascaux II was opened, an exact replica of the original chambers and paintings. The chambers were recreated by painstaking surveying using as far as possible identical pigments and materials. As a result of this reconstruction, visitors can again marvel at the great black bull, the wounded bison pursuing a man, and the other masterpieces created some 25,000 years ago.

★ LIMOGES   130B4
Although the art of enameling existed in the 6th century, it was at Limoges, in the 12th century, that the technique of *champlevé* was discovered. This involved applying successive coats of enamel onto copper, each coat fired at a lower temperature to give a characteristic deep luster. Limoges enamels, a marvel of their day, made the town the center of European enameled art. In the 18th century, fine clay was found nearby and a porcelain industry rapidly grew up. Today, both crafts are celebrated in two museums: the Musée Municipal, devoted to Limoges enamel, and the Musée Adrian-Dubouché, with its chinaware collections.

★ LOT, VALLÉE DU   130A2
The Lot river rises in the Massif Central, flowing through exquisite country and a cluster of delightful villages before reaching the Garonne. In its upper reaches the river passes through renowned vineyards. Legend has it that Czar Peter the Great drank, apart from vodka, only wine from the vineyards around Cahors. What is fact is that Eleanor of Aquitaine's dowry included the Lot vineyards when she married Henry II of England. In its course, the river carves through the Périgord limestone, creating spectacular cliff scenery. At Bouziès, east of Cahors, the caves in the cliffs were used by the English during the Hundred Years War. East again, at Cajarc, the Georges Pompidou Art Center is one of France's most important galleries of contemporary art.

★ MARTEL   130B3
Tradition holds that this town was founded in the 8th century by Charles Martel, at the spot where he gave thanks for having finally driven the Saracens out of France. True or not, the town is proud of its crest, three of Martel's war hammers. The old walls are now followed by wide boulevards, only the Tournemire prison tower now remaining.

★ MOISSAC   130B2
It is very likely that the great Benedictine abbey at Moissac, beside the Tarn river, was founded in the 7th century. Certainly by the 11th century it had become one of the most influential in France. The abbey church and cloisters survive; though badly damaged during the Revolution, they rank among the great artistic treasures of France. The jewel in the abbey's crown is the southern doorway, with its marvelous depiction of Saint John's vision of the Apocalypse, carved in the early 12th century. Almost as good are the carved capitals of the cloisters. The small museum attached to the cloisters has some of the best stonework from the old abbey.

PREHISTORIC SIGHTS
Although Lascaux is the Vézère Valley's most famous site, many other local caves have revealed finds of equal beauty and importance.

East of Les Eyzies, at Laussel, the best of the "Venus" figures (female forms clearly symbolizing fertility) was found, while the La Madeleine site, north of Les Eyzies, yielded a wonderfully vivid bull carved from deer antler.

The paintings at Pech-Merle and Font-de-Gaume are superb, while the engravings at Rouffignac and Les Combarelles reveal awe-inspiring talent.

Perhaps the most astonishing of all is the depiction of a bison, shown in profile and head-on, at La Grève ■

★ MONBAZILLAC, CHÂTEAU DE   *130A3*

The most famous Dordogne white wine is Monbazillac, a sweet aperitif or dessert wine. Visitors to the château, which stands at the center of the wine-growing area, can also explore a small wine museum, the building now being owned by the Monbazillac Wine Co-operative. The 16th-century castle stands stylistically on the border between medieval fortress and Renaissance château. The interior is well furnished, the Viscountess Monbazillac's bedroom being in resplendent Louis XIII style.

The vineyards of Monbazillac are renowned for producing a sweet white dessert wine. A tour of the château gives an insight into the techniques of its production, and includes a glass to restore you

★ MONPAZIER   *130B2*

This handsome *bastide* was begun in 1285 by Edward I of England. Built to control the Agenais plain, to the south of the Dordogne, it took the regular grid plan of its French counterparts, with one notable exception: all the houses were the same size, and were separated by an *androne*, a space that, it was hoped, would stop the spread of fire. Monpazier is one of the best-preserved of all the local *bastides*, and has many outstanding old houses. Perhaps the finest is the Maison du Chapitre, on the rue Notre-Dame, dating from the time of the original construction.

★ MONTAUBAN   *130B1*

In 1621, during the Wars of Religion, Montauban was a center of Protestantism and held out for three months when besieged by an army of 20,000 men commanded personally by King Louis XIII. The *bastide* town that withstood the siege can still be visited. The old town stands beside the Tarn and seems an age removed from the busy suburbs that make up modern Montauban. Pont-Vieux, a 14th-century bridge, crosses the river, and at the town end stands the Musée Ingres, an excellent fine arts museum. Not far off, the Ancienne Cour des Aides houses two more museums, one of natural history, the other dedicated to the old peasant lifestyle of Bas (Lower) Quercy.

★ MONTIGNAC *130B3*

As the closest town to Lascaux II, Montignac has prospered since the discovery of the original caves and the opening of the replica. But it has deserved to prosper, its neat houses lining the tidied bank of the Vézère in elegant style. Viewed from across the river, with the church and ruined castle rising above the red- and gray-roofed houses, Montignac is a captivating sight. The town's tourist office also houses a small museum devoted to Eugène Le Roy, a writer who died in 1907. His most famous novel, "Jacquou le Croquant," about a local peasant uprising, was made into a television series.

★★★ MONTPÉZAT-DE-QUERCY *130B2*

Half-timbered houses and arcades make Montpézat one of the most delightful villages of the Bas Quercy. At its heart is the collegiate church of St.-Martin of Tours, renowned for 16th-century tapestries illustrating the life of the saint, who left the army after giving half his cloak to a beggar, revealed in a dream to be Jesus. Inside, marble funeral figures depict the des Prés family of Montpézat, many of whom attained high office in the Church.

MONT RÉAL, CHÂTEAU DE *130A3*

This delightful and surprisingly home-like château shares a name with a more famous city in Canada. The derivation in each case is the same, both château and city being built on a Mont Réal, a royal hill. The coincidence goes further: one of the family that owned the château, Claude de Pontbriant, accompanied St.-Malo-born Jacques Cartier (who named both Canada and Montreal) on his second trip along the St. Lawrence River. Local legend has it that Cartier named the Canadian settlement after his companion's home rather than for the king. Another interesting legend says that the Chapelle de la Ste.-Épine at Mont Réal was built to house a thorn from Christ's crown of thorns.

MOUTIER D'AHUN *130C5*

Standing on the Creuse downstream of Aubusson, Moutier was the site of an abbey in the 10th century, a settlement that did not survive the constant pillaging of the Hundred Years War. The present church dates from the 15th century, a period of relative calm in the Dordogne. It is famous for its carved paneling and wooden sculptures, the work of master woodcarver Simon Baüer, from the Auvergne, who crafted the works in the late 17th century. The finest piece is a lectern formed from two lions standing on hind legs, back to back, supporting the lectern trays in their forepaws.

★ ORADOUR-SUR-GLANE *130B4*

On June 10, 1944 a group of 160 German S.S. troops arrived in this small village. D-Day had been just four days earlier and, to add further insult, two of the troops were shot by Resistance snipers. In retaliation the S.S. rounded up the village, putting the women and children in the church. The men were machine-gunned; the church was also raked with gunfire, then set alight. In all, 642 villagers were murdered, over 200 of them children. After the war it was decided that Oradour should remain as it was on that day. The ruins remain, charred and bullet-ridden. Automobiles still stand where they were, even the telegraph wires lie where they fell. Beside the ruins are the cemetery and the new village that has grown up since 1945.

BASTIDES

Centuries of bloody conflict, both religious and secular, produced a wealth of fortresses in the Dordogne, the best-preserved being Monpazier and Domme.

Though not unique to this part of France, *bastides* reached their zenith here. Built during the 13th and 14th centuries, they acted primarily as fortresses, protecting not only the lord and his family but also the local population.

Streets were laid out grid fashion with a central market area, and the whole was surrounded by ramparts that reinforced the natural hilltop defenses.

As peace slowly settled over the area, these castles evolved from medieval fortifications to elegant châteaux ■

DORDOGNE DOVECOTES

In medieval Europe the right to erect dovecotes was usually reserved for the nobility. One of the few exceptions was in the Dordogne, where families or whole villages often had their own.

These pigeon-houses were generally erected not for the collection of eggs or fat, young birds for the kitchen, but for the *guano* (pigeon droppings make good fertilizer). Local bakers also used the stuff, claiming that a sprinkling added piquancy to the smell of their bread!

The most common style of dovecote was set on columns to protect the birds from damp and predators ∎

★★★ PADIRAC, GOUFFRE DE   *130B3*

The Devil, returning to Hell with a sackful of souls, met Saint Martin riding a donkey. Being a gambling man, the Devil offered the saint the chance to win back the souls if he could make his donkey cross an obstacle of the Devil's choosing. If he failed, the saint's soul would be added to the sack. Saint Martin agreed and the Devil thumped the ground with his foot, creating a vast hole. Undaunted, Saint Martin urged his donkey forward, and the animal obligingly jumped across. Saint Martin took the sack while the Devil retreated down the hole he had created. This legend didn't discourage Édouard Martel, father of speleology, who explored these caves in the late 19th century. Today's explorer can follow in Martel's footsteps through a magical world of stalagmites, stalactites and rock formations. One, the Grande Pendeloque (Great Pendant), is 78 meters (256 ft.) long, almost touching the water where the boats pass.

PECH-MERLE, GROTTE DU   *130B2*

Although Lascaux is, justifiably, the most famous cave for prehistoric paintings, it is not unique. Another is Pech-Merle, carved in the same limestone but close to the valley of the Célé river. Its discovery in 1922, though less serendipitous, was also the work of young boys. At Pech-Merle the two boys were actually hunting for caves, encouraged by the local abbot, who was interested in both speleology and prehistory. What the youngsters found was a more impressive cave system than Lascaux, big enough to have flowstone formations as well as an array of wall paintings. Its

opening in 1949 led to the discovery of the entrance used by early humans, which was different from the one the boys had found. Since then visitors have gazed upon bison, horses, mammoths, and the equally fascinating outlines of the artists' hands and the petrified footprints they left in the mud floor.

★ PÉRIGUEUX   *130A3*

Inside a loop of the Isle river stands the capital of Périgord. Anyone looking for authentic truffles, *foie gras* or walnut-based delicacies need go no further. The city's history, from Roman days as Vesunna to thriving medieval center, was marked by barbarian invasions that left it ruined and deserted. As a result, today there are two old centers. Clustered around the huge church of St.-Étienne-de-la-Cité are the Roman remains of an amphitheater, a temple (the Tour de Vésone) and the old town wall. A 10-minute walk to the north east lies the cathedral of St.-Front, the medieval heart of Périgueux, rebuilt in the 19th century by the architect responsible for the Sacré-Coeur in Paris. A maze of alleyways links houses built from the 13th to the 15th centuries, when the city thrived on pilgrims journeying to the relics of Saint Front and was a market center for the fertile surrounding lands.

PUYGUILHEM, CHÂTEAU DE   *130A4*

In the early 16th century Mondot de la Marthonie, president of the parliaments of Bordeaux and Paris, built Puyguilhem above the valley of the Dronne river. Its elegance, like the great châteaux of the Loire, attracts admiration from architects and tourists alike. In part, that admiration is for the artisans who restored the dilapidated château after it was

acquired by the State in 1939. Inside, the carved chimneys (one decorated with carvings of six of the labors of Hercules) are remarkable. The château has been furnished in period style, giving an insight into the gracious living of 16th-century France.

PUYMARTIN, CHÂTEAU DE   *130B3*

With its square angles and rounded towers, its pyramidal and pepper-pot roofs, the whole built of golden stone atop a grassy hill, Puymartin is almost a fairy-tale castle. Inside, there are chairs in Louis XIII style and a Louis XV desk, and a remarkable set of Flemish tapestries illustrating scenes from the Trojan War.

★★★ ROCAMADOUR   *130B3*

To the southeast of Rocamadour, close to L'Hospitalet, there is a lookout beside the appropriately named Hôtel Belvédère. From here the view of Rocamadour – clinging vertiginously to the side of a cliff face as it stretches upwards – is truly breathtaking. It's easy to see why surveys suggest that this is one of the most visited villages in France. A chapel existed here from at least the 12th century, but in 1166 grave diggers unearthed the body of a man – and almost immediately, miracles started to occur near the site. By the 13th century the body was believed to be that of Zaccheus, the wealthy tax collector (by one tradition, married to Sainte Veronica), who climbed a sycamore to get a glimpse of Jesus, and gave away half his property after Jesus stayed at his house. The village's fame soon spread, with as many as 30,000 pilgrims arriving from all over France to attend *pardons* (religious festivals in honor of a saint) at the local church. It is said that when Protestants captured the village during the Wars of Religion their attempt to destroy the body was foiled when it refused to burn. Today's visitor can follow in the footsteps of the medieval pilgrims by climbing up through the village to the ramparts above, which afford a panoramic view. At the nearby Rocher des Aigles (Eagles' Rock) is a breeding center for birds of prey, with displays of falconry.

Old Périgueux. The capital of the Dordogne has two ancient centers, one medieval, huddled round the cathedral of St.-Front, and older, Roman remains, including a temple and vestiges of an amphitheater

La Roque-Gageac, sited below an oak-tree-covered cliff overlooking the Dordogne, is one of France's most picturesque villages. Its red-tiled houses built of honey-colored stone add to its charm

RODEZ 130C2

At the eastern edge of the Dordogne, where it merges with the Languedoc section of the Massif Central, stands Rodez, a fine city built around the huge cathedral of Notre-Dame. So large is the cathedral, and so intricate its stonework, that it took almost 300 years to complete. Old Rodez has many lovely old houses. Two of these are now occupied by the Musée Fenaille, housing a collection of medieval sculptures and furniture. The nearby Musée Denys Puech houses a collection of sculptures by the renowned local artist, who died in 1942.

★★★ LA ROQUE-GAGEAC 130B3

Surely one of the prettiest of all Dordogne's villages, La Roque-Gageac huddles below a massive limestone cliff.

Although all the houses are splendid, with their roofs of *lauzes* or red tiles, look out for the Manoir de Tarde, the twin-gabled manor house of the Tarde family, one of whose members was a famous 16th-century polymath.

In former times the village was a center for the transportation of salt and wood along the river. The Dordogne is placid here, and canoes can be rented near the

Château de la Malartrie, at the west end of the village. Despite its appearance, the château dates only from the early 20th century, imitating 15th-century style.

★★ ST.-CIRQ-LAPOPIE   130B2

Pronounce Cirq as "sear" and the locals will think you're one of them. This lovely village perches on cliffs above the Lot river and is surrounded by woods.

The name (and pronunciation) derives from Saint Cyr, killed thousands of miles away in Byzantium, but whose relics were brought here. The second part of the name is from the La Popies, lords of the area in the Middle Ages. A fortress at the village was built by an early member of the family, who served against the English. But the king feared its use by Huguenots during the Wars of Religion and ordered its demolition.

To see the ruins, take the steep path beside the town hall. The view of the village, the Lot and the limestone cliffs on the far side repays the effort of the climb. Back in the village, Maison Rignault houses a small museum of local furniture and some Chinese items, the bequest of a local painter for whom the house is named.

ST.-JEAN-DE-CÔLE   130A4

Film-makers are frequent visitors to this delightful village, attracted by the tiny hump-back bridge over the Côle river, by the collection of medieval houses built of glowing, golden stone, the church and the old castle. St.-Jean is an almost complete medieval village, and is officially listed as one of the prettiest in France. The castle, in part 12th century but extended and much modified, now houses a collection of old posters. The Romanesque church, with its curious bell tower, has some fine late-medieval woodwork.

ST.-JUNIEN   130B4

Famed for its paper- and glove-making, the latter of which is still an important local craft, St.-Junien is named for a 6th-century saint, one of those who have helped Limousin acquire its nickname of "Le Pays des Saints" (the land of saints). Saint Junien's remains lie beneath a 12th-century limestone tomb in the church that bears his name. The tomb, behind the altar, is lavishly worked, with relief figures of Christ, the Virgin Mary and the Evangelists being separated by carved, scrolled columns with elaborate capitals.

ST.-LÉON-SUR-VÉZÈRE   130B3

St.-Léon should be seen for its romantic setting in a loop of the Vézère, but also demands a visit for its Romanesque church, which many consider to be the finest in Périgord. It was built as the abbey church for a 12th-century Benedictine monastery, using the site of a Roman villa, the remains of one wall of which can still be seen on the river side of the church. The church is best viewed from the old cross in the square that fronts it, when the apse, semicircular side chapels and arcaded bell tower are seen to perfection. Close by are the Château de La Salle, a small 14th-century castle built – rather unusually – without mortar, and the later, more elegant Château de Clérans, at the river's edge.

ST.-LÉONARD-DE-   130B4
NOBLAT

St.-Léonard is famous as the home of Joseph-Louis Gay-Lussac, one of the greatest 18th-century French scientists. Born on December 6, 1778, Gay-Lussac made important discoveries in the fields of both chemistry and physics. He formulated the law governing the

WALK

LA ROQUE-GAGEAC

From the parking area near the river, walk eastwards along the road, passing tennis courts to reach a footpath to the left.

Follow this to a cross. Fork right, then left on the path for Gageac. To the left as you climb there's a *borie* (a stone hut for animals or storage).

At the next fork, near a large shed, go left through woodland. From this path there are excellent views of the village (perhaps the prettiest in the Dordogne) and of the river itself.

Follow the path through the village to reach steep steps that will return you to the parking area ■

WALK

SOUILLAC

From the abbey church, turn left, following signs for the swimming pool. Walk along boulevard des Molières to reach a lookout. Take the right fork down to the N20. Go under a railroad bridge and cross the Dordogne. Pass the campground, turning right on the D43, which follows a fine woodland edge. (The energetic can detour to the left, climbing to a television mast for superb views of Souillac – first settled by the Romans – and the river.)

Continue on the D43, fork right of the Château de Cieurac and turn right to the river. The pretty riverside path will take you back to the village ∎

volume and temperature of gases (though this is more commonly referred to as Charles's Law, after his contemporary, another French scientist) following observations he had made from a hydrogen balloon in which he ascended to a height of over 6,096 meters (20,000 ft.). This escapade alone, considering it took place in 1804, should be enough to secure Gay-Lussac a place in history. The village of the scientist's birth has a church with an interesting bell tower: a slender tower, square at the base, octagonal at the top and pierced by arcaded windows.

★★★ SARLAT-LA-CANÉDA *130B3*

The capital of Périgord Noir is one of the most attractive and best-loved towns of the Dordogne. At its heart is the almost complete medieval town that grew up as a prosperous market center in the late 15th century. A conservation program was initiated in 1964 to preserve Sarlat's exceptional heritage.

Many of the old houses, built of rich golden stone, are superb, some with attractive courtyards. Of all the houses, perhaps none is more appealing than the Maison de la Boétie, built in Renaissance style by the town magistrate in 1525. Étienne de la Boétie, son of the builder and himself a magistrate, who inspired Rousseau to write his "Social Contract," was born in the house. Elsewhere, the cathedral of St.-Sacerdos is a fine building, despite an odd mix of styles. Nearby is the curious Lanterne des Morts (Lantern of the Dead). Despite the name, the purpose of this 12th-century cylindrical building is not understood. North of the town the Musée-Aquarium specializes in all the fish species found in the Dordogne's rivers.

★ SOUILLAC *130B3*

Built at the confluence of the Corrèze and the Dordogne rivers, Souillac remains what it has always been, a busy commercial center. It's named for the marshland that once edged the river: today, one of the Dordogne's best campgrounds occupies land where wild boar were once free to roam. An abbey was established here in the 12th century, and the abbey church still stands, notable for its carved doorway: look out for the carvings of the prophet Isaiah, almost modern in its realism and fluidity. Close by is the National Museum of Automatons, which is dedicated to mechanical toys. One of the more unusual exhibits is a fully mechanized jazz band.

★ UZERCHE *130B4*

The "Pearl of Limousin" climbs up a rocky spur of land set in a curve of the Vézère. The gray-stone, gray-roofed buildings look a little grim from a distance, but are a delight at close quarters: following the narrow streets, you suddenly come upon a superb building or exquisite view. The church, crowning the spur, has beautiful capitals that are carved with plants and animals, while place des Vignerons, once the ancient fruit market, has several excellent houses. Nearby, Porte Bécharie is all that remains of the town's medieval walls.

★ VENTADOUR *130C3*

The wild ruins of this 12th-century fortress, perched above the Luzège gorge, can only be approached on foot, a journey rewarded by excellent views and a romantic setting. It's no surprise to learn that this is the birthplace of the troubadour Bernard de Ventadour, one of the best of that romantic breed of medieval singer-poets.

THE PYRÉNÉES

Although lower than the Alps, the
Pyrénées should not be overlooked
– what they lack in spectacular snow
and ice scenery they more than make
up for in accessibility

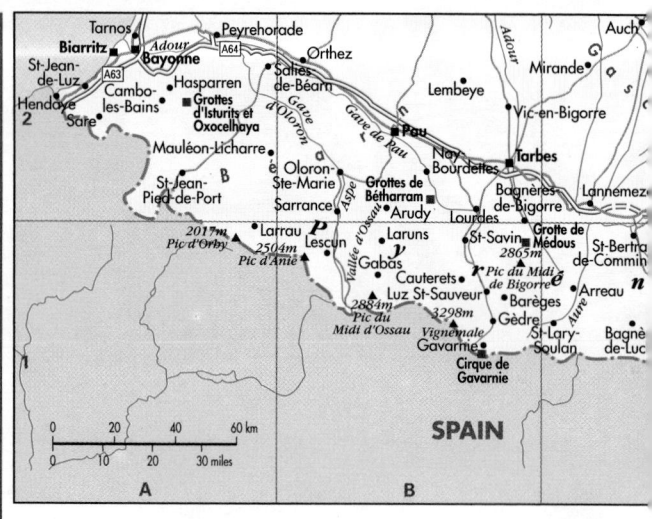

THE PYRÉNÉES

Rising abruptly from the plains of southwest France, the Pyrénées provide a natural and formidable barrier between France and Spain. They stretch for 400 kilometers (250 mi.) from the Bay of Biscay (on the Atlantic coast) to the Mediterranean. The highest peaks, rising to nearly 3,500 meters (over 11,000 ft.), lie in Spain, but for the most part the border keeps to the watershed ridge, encompassing, on the way, a third country   Andorra. There are glaciers, but these never approach the dimensions of those of the high Alps; the peaks above the tree line, though blasted clean by winter winds and snow, are accessible to the strong and determined walker.

The best of the mountain scenery is now protected by the **Parc National des Pyrénées**, which is continuous with Spain's Ordesa Park. Here the lucky visitor might spot ibex, isard (the Pyrenean chamois) and marmot. In the skies above, magnificent golden eagles wheel. Three types of vulture can also be seen: the Egyptian and griffon are relatively

common, but the lammergeier (or bearded vulture) is very rare. Even rarer are the Pyrenean brown bears, the last remaining ones being found to the west of the park.

Interestingly, not all of the best scenery is above ground. The limestone of the Pyrénées is honeycombed with **caves**. Some have revealed remarkable finds of prehistoric human inhabitants – the paintings in the Niaux Cave (Grotte de Niaux) are among the finest in the world, while others are fine show caves. One, the Gouffre de la Pierre St.-Martin, is among the deepest in the world.

> ★★★
> ## HIGHLIGHTS
>
> **Aure Valley** (►155)
> **Basque Country** (►156)
> **Carcassonne** (►157)
> **Gavarnie** (►163)
> **The High Pyrénées** (►163)
> **Niaux, Grotte de** (►165)
> **St.-Jean-Pied-de-Port** (►167)
> **St.-Martin-du-Canigou** (►168)

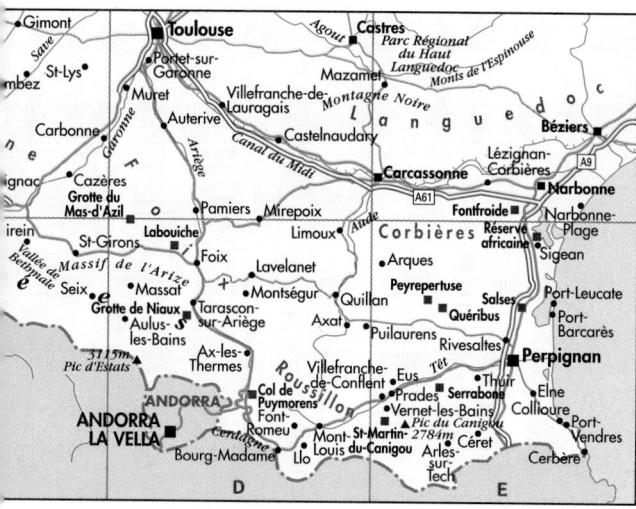

Culturally, the Pyrénées offer great contrasts. The western end is **Basque country**. The Basques are an ancient race, claiming to be the oldest in Europe. Their country has a distinct social and architectural feel: the villages are neat and pretty, the churches galleried. The Basques have a love of dancing, the dances being uniquely their own, and they play an equally unique game, *pelota*, claimed to be the world's fastest.

Moving east, the visitor arrives in an area that is clearly French. **Lourdes**, one of the world's greatest pilgrimage centers, lies here, while the most compelling mountain scenery lies to the south, where Vignemale is the highest peak of the French Pyrénées, and the Cirque de Gavarnie one of the most breathtaking features.

East again is **Andorra**, an enclave of duty-free prosperity

There are plenty of mountain trails in the Pyrénées to walk in the summer and ski along in winter. This is the place to come if you want to get away from the crowds and find hidden landscapes and unexplored territory

PLAYING PELOTA

The Basque national game of *pelota* embraces several variations on the game of *jeu de paume*, featuring a hard ball hit against a wall (*fronton*).

The fastest version (*cesta punta*) takes place in an indoor court (*trinquet*), with players wearing long, curved gauntlets (*chistera*) with which they catch the ball and return it.

At championship level this can be an exciting and graceful game to watch (most of the important matches are held in Biarritz).

On the village *fronton* children will often practice with their bare hands or with a wooden bat (*pala*) ∎

that is surrounded by mountains. Beyond Andorra is the land of the Cathars, medieval heretics whose improbable castles top the most inaccessible rocky pinnacles. And finally there is **Roussillon**, which, along with Languedoc, includes five *départements*, and now forms one of the regions of France. This is another area that is French only as an afterthought, for in ancient times it was part of Catalonia. The red-and-yellow Catalonian flag still flies from many of the buildings. Like the Basques, the Catalans have their own language and cuisine, and also their own dance: the *sardana*. You can see it being performed twice weekly in summer in the place de la Loge in Perpignan, the ancient capital of the Kingdom of Majorca.

★ ANDORRA *153D1*

No one is sure exactly who the Andorrans were or when they arrived in their mountain stronghold. One legend has it that they descended from a Gallic tribe that fought Hannibal as he crossed from Spain to France; others say that they are descended from Charlemagne or the Visigoths. From the early 12th century the country was ruled by Spain, but a convenient marriage gave the French an equal claim, and in 1278 a treaty divided control between the two countries. It remained in force until the referendum in 1993; Andorra then became an independent state, ruled by its own 28-member council. Being outside the European Union (E.U.), Andorra can offer duty-free goods, and this it does, growing prosperous on sales to Spaniards, French, and other nationalities alike. A visitor to Andorra la Vella, the capital, could be forgiven for believing that it is just a place to do some duty-free shopping –

one long street market. But that is a narrow view: make your way to Plaça de Pobles, a charming square on the western side of the town. The view past the church tower to the cliffs of Pic d'Enclar is stunning. Below the square is the Casa de la Vall, which is the seat of the Andorran government: its chambers are open to visitors.

ARLES-SUR-TECH *153E1*

The Vallespir, as the upper valley of the Tech river is known, was once an important iron-making center. At that time, Arles was the valley's unofficial capital, but now the iron-ore mines are closed. However, even before the iron-ore mining made it rich, Arles was a prosperous place, its wealth in medieval times being derived from pilgrims who were drawn to the town by the miraculous relics of two obscure Persian saints. Even more of a potent draw than the saintly relics was a white marble sarcophagus

called La Sainte Tombe (the Holy Tomb). This tomb was known to fill miraculously with liquid – in fact it does so to this day – and this was believed to cure various illnesses and complaints.

★★★ AURE VALLEY   *152C1*

The Aure rises close to the border ridge of the Pyrénées, its beautiful valley separated from the Spanish valley of the Rio Barrosa only by the 3-kilometer (2-mi.) Bielsa Tunnel. The Aure Valley is green and luxuriant, in sharp contrast to its Spanish counterpart, which is bleached and arid. The Aure flows through Tramezaïgues, a tiny hamlet, then on to St.-Lary-Soulan, one of the best Pyrenean ski resorts. Farther on is Arreau, which in ancient times was the capital of the local area, a fine market town full of narrow, medieval streets and half-timbered houses. Arreau stands at the confluence of the Aure and the Louron rivers; close to the latter is the Maison du Lys, a 16th-century house named for the Fleur-de-Lys carved on its timbers. At the Château des Nestes – *neste* means "river" in the Basque language – there is a fine museum dedicated to the old way of life in the mountains.

AURIGNAC   *153C2*

The Paleolithic period (Old Stone Age) that covers the time from 30,000 to 25,000 years ago is known as "the Aurignacian era," named for this Haute-Garonne hilltop village. The Musée de la Préhistoire traces the story of the discovery of a local cave in the 19th century and the excavations that led to a new understanding of prehistoric humans. Aurignac itself is a beautiful village of sand-colored stone houses, many dating from medieval and Renaissance times, each with an orange tiled roof. A fortified gateway topped by a bell-tower leads to the village church.

The hilltop village of Aurignac is known as the site of important archeological finds in the 19th century. A local museum explains their significance. The village also has many pretty old houses from medieval times

★★★ BASQUE COUNTRY *152A2*

The natives of Eskual Herria, the country of the Basques, claim to be the oldest race in Europe. Certainly they occupied the land that straddles the western end of the Pyrénées before the countries of Spain and France even existed.

Today a section of the Atlantic coast from St.-Jean-de-Luz to Biarritz, and the land eastwards toward Larrau, is the French Basque country – distinguishable by its long, tongue-twisting place-names. The Basques are also known for their love of traditional dances, which often include extremely energetic leaps. One of the oldest is the *zamalzain*, but the *fandago* and *arin-arin* are also popular. The most vigorous is the *saut basque*. Another unique feature of the Basque country is the game of *pelota*, one of the world's fastest games, played with a curved wicker scoop (*chistera*) that is used to hurl a ball against a high *fronton*, or wall. Of the towns in the French Basque country, the best-known is Biarritz, an elegant Atlantic resort (see p.102). The Hôtel du Palais, which overlooks the Grande Plage, was built for Napoleon III's Empress Eugénie, whose frequent trips put Biarritz on the visiting list of Europe's elite in the mid-19th century.

Basque folk culture is a rich and vibrant one, embracing dance, song, sport, food and costume. Several fêtes devoted to Basque tradition are held through the summer

★★ BAYONNE *152A2*

Bayonne, an old port on the Nive and Adour rivers, is the capital of the French Basque country. It is also renowned as a center of Basque gastronomy, as a walk along rue du Pont-Neuf or the neighboring streets will soon testify. Those interested in discovering more about the Basques should visit the Musée Basque, where the people's history is explored. The museum also has collections of traditional costumes and a fine display on the game of *pelota*. Another good museum is the Musée Bonnat, where the fine art collection includes works by Goya.

★ BÉTHARRAM, GROTTES DE *152B2*

Lying just 11 kilometers (7 mi.) west of Lourdes and sometimes overwhelmed by visitors, are the Grottes de Bétharram. The caves comprise a huge complex of underground chambers stretching for almost 5 kilometers (3 mi.). The stone formations are exquisite, but even better – particularly for children – are the travel arrangements for visitors. These start with a cable-car ride and continue with boat and train rides through the chambers. The cave's name derives from *Bét Arram*, mountain dialect for "beautiful branch." A local legend claims that a young girl who was drowning in the nearby Gave de Pau was saved when the Virgin Mary appeared and threw her a branch. The girl clung to it and was carried to safety.

★★ LA BIGORRE *152B1*

Bigorre is the Pyrenean region lying south of Tarbes, including Lourdes and one of the most spectacular sections of the high Pyrenean peaks. The Pic du Midi de Bigorre (2,865 m/9,387 ft.) is reached by cable car and offers, as you would expect, a fantastic panorama. The Bigorre also includes the famed Cirque de Gavarnie. The Cirque is breached by the Brèche de Roland, so called because of a legend that this natural gateway through the Cirque – which links France and Spain – was created when the knight Roland, a commander in Charlemagne's army, tried to break his magic sword so as to prevent it falling into enemy hands. Almost as famous is the Col du Tourmalet, at 2,115 meters (6,937 ft.) a landmark of Tour de France bicycle races.

★★★ CARCASSONNE *153E2*

Carcassonne lies at a bend in the Aude river, where the journey from the Atlantic coast to the Mediterranean coast is easiest. Such a strategic position has been defended from earliest times, even several hundred years before the Romans established their town of Julia Carcasso. Today Carcassonne is the most complete medieval walled city in France – indeed, in Europe – a fairy-tale place of walls and towers reached by a fortified bridge. Yet it is also an illusion, the work of Eugène Viollet-le-Duc

who reconstructed it from a ruined state in the mid-19th century. The reconstruction was painstaking, but there are certain inaccuracies – the pepper-pot roofs, for instance. Despite these minor lapses, Carcassonne is as close to authentic medieval as can be seen today – without the poor sanitation, filth and squalor, that is. La Cité, as the walled city is more correctly called in order to distinguish it from the larger, more modern part of the city at its feet, is a magical place. An outer wall surrounds it, and the land between that and the inner wall is known as Les Lices (the lists), where knights once practiced for tournaments and battle. Within the inner walls is the Château Comtal, the fortified heart of the old city which has now been converted into a small museum detailing its history.

CASTRES *153D2*

This large, industrialized city is worth visiting for its Musée Goya, and is also useful as a base for exploring the fine country of Midi-Pyrénées. The museum stands at the edge of the old town, a pleasant area that includes some attractive old houses. The Musée Goya has a small but very good collection of paintings by the great master, most of them portraits of aristocrats. There are also works by other Spanish artists. Beside the museum is Castres' cathedral, an imposing 17th-century building. Close to the town is the Haut Languedoc Regional Park, near Sidobrie, worth visiting for its unusual granite boulders. Natural erosion has created several *roches tremblantes* (shifting stones), which rock gently when touched. Legend has it that the movement of the stones can be used to predict the future, by anyone able to "read" the signs correctly.

BASQUE CUISINE

The Basques like strongly flavored foods and, being fond of eating heartily, also have a liking for dishes with heavy textures.

Typical ingredients of Basque cuisine are red and green peppers, garlic and onions. One favorite dish is *piperade*, a kind of omelet which combines all three of the above ingredients with tomatoes.

Near the coast a thick fish stew known as *ttaro* is based on conger eel or monkfish and is highly seasoned with garlic and onions.

Inland, chicken and kidneys are favored, each served *à la Basquaise* – that is, with a sauce of peppers, garlic, and onion.

For dessert, try *gâteau basque*, a heavy cake flavored with lemon and black cherries ■

WALK

ESTANY DE FONT VIVA

At the end of the road from Porté-Puymorens take the footpath 45 meters (148 ft.) to the north of the electricity company building. Follow it through pine trees beside a stream to reach a meadow.

Following the right edge, climb up to another meadow. Bear right and follow a path with yellow signposts to the Estany de Font Viva.

Follow the left edge of the lake to a col at the far end. Bear left here, descending into a valley. Go over a bridge and turn right when the path forks.

Follow the Lanòus stream, veering left when it enters a ravine to climb a grassy saddle marked by cairns. Continue down the path to return to the starting point ■

★ CAUTERETS   152B1

In the 10th century the Count of Bigorre established a monastery here, where mineral waters sprang from the rocks. By the 19th century Cauterets had become one of France's most elegant spa resorts, visited by royalty and nobility from all over Europe. The elegance remains, though now the town is a center for recreation. Trips to the nearby Parc National des Pyrénées are possible and there is a fine Park Information Center in the town. Other outings include a cable-car ride to the Cirque de Lys, for the most reliable snow in the Pyrénées, and Pont d'Espagne, from where paths lead to the top of the Vignemale, at 3,298 meters (10,820 ft.) the highest peak in the French Pyrénées.

CERDAGNE   153D1

Cerdagne is the name given to the upper valley of the Ségre river and the plateau that extends from it. At its heart is Font-Romeu, a ski resort built in the 1920s. Nearby, at Ermitage, a chapel marks the spot where an 11th-century farmer, seeing his bull pawing the ground, investigated and unearthed a statue of the Virgin, which was found to have miraculous powers. More earthly wonders can be seen at Odeillo. Here stands a gleaming solar furnace, the world's largest. Occasionally in summer the parabolic mirrors of the furnace are used for spectacular laser displays. Also worth visiting is the beautiful Carol Valley – which leads to the Col de Puymorens and Andorra – and Mont-Louis, a fortified village built by Vauban in the late 17th century. For the best views of all, take Le Petit Train Jaune, a train with red-and-yellow cars, which climbs over improbable viaducts and through stunning scenery.

★ CÉRET   153E1

Situated in the Vallespir in Roussillon, French Catalonia, this interesting village attracted artists during the early years of the 20th century and, consequently, became an important meeting place for leaders of the modern art movement. Its Musée d'Art Moderne reflects this role, with works by Chagall, Dali, Matisse, Miró and Picasso.

★ LE COMMINGES   152C1

In 72 BC Pompey founded the town of *Lugdunum Convenarum* on a hill at the entrance to the upper valley of the Garonne. Today this site is occupied by St.-Bertrand-de-Comminges, one of the chief archeological sites of the Comminges (as this section of the Garonne Valley is known). Nearby are the Gargas Caves, decorated with prehistoric paintings of deer, bison, horses and over 150 outlines of hands.

The prehistoric finds of the area are displayed at the Musée Comminges in St.-Gaudens. It is an apt place for such a museum, the village having been the home of Norbert Casteret, one of the greatest French cave explorers.

LE COUSERANS 153C1

Between the Pays de Foix (the country south of Foix) and the Comminges lies the Couserans, a region that is seldom explored, with quiet valleys and spectacular mountain scenery. At its heart is the Bethmale Valley. The valley was once famed for its bear trainers, but both the trainers and the bears have long since gone. It is also famed for its traditional native costume, which includes extravagantly pointed clogs. Legend has it that one young valley dweller used the points of his clogs as knives to kill his girlfriend after she had left him for another man. Local costumes are displayed at a museum devoted to Couserans arts and traditions, in Augirein. There is also an exhibition on the Guerre des Demoiselles, the "War of the Spinsters." This extraordinary 40-year feud started in 1829 when the local people rose up against the landowners who, despite the Revolution, still operated a feudal control over the valley. The name derives from the men's habit of wearing loose shirts held tight at the waist by a red belt. This fashion, giving the impression of a bust, made the men look like *demoiselles*, and, together with their blackened faces, helped preserve their anonymity.

East from Aigozein is Castillon en Couserans, overlooked by the ruins of a castle destroyed on the orders of Cardinal Richelieu, who feared it might be used as a Protestant stronghold. On the valley's eastern side is Seix, a center for canoeing and rafting.

The upper valley of the Ségre river is known as the Cerdagne; further west, it becomes the Cerdanya in Spain. The best view of the area is from Le Petit Train Jaune, one of whose cars is open-topped

DRIVE

THROUGH THE HIGH PYRÉNÉES

392 kilometers/243 miles (allow 4 days)

This tour explores some of the highest roads in the Pyrénées. As the Col du Tourmalet is rarely open before June (due to snow) it is a summer tour; to make the most of it wait for a day when there are no clouds surrounding the high peaks.

The starting point is Pau, a town with two interesting museums. The Musée des Beaux-Arts with a collection of works from Europe, and the Musée Bernadotte, exploring the life history of one of Napoleon's marshals.

MOUNTAIN CHEESE

Excellent sheep's cheese, *fromage de brebis*, is available throughout the Pyrénées.

Traditionally, this is made by Basque shepherds as they graze their sheep on the high mountain pastures during the summer months.

The importance of sheep to the Basques is highlighted by the Basque word for rich – *aberats* – which means "he who owns large flocks" ■

Leave Pau on the N117 to Tarbes (not the A64 autoroute).

1 Tarbes

Tarbes is busy and prosperous, and has many of the elegant features that would also be expected from a town of its status. The Jardin Massey is a quiet, attractive park with pools and statues among the trees. The open-air theater and bandstand are used during the summer for a varied range of programs of musical/theatrical/artistic events, the players often competing for attention with the cries of the park's peacocks. At the park's center is Musée Massey, which is housed in a 19th-century mansion. Here you can see a collection of paintings and an interesting display on the hussars, the elite French cavalry.

Leave Tarbes along the D935 to Bagnères-de-Bigorre.

2 Bagnères-de-Bigorre

The Romans were the first to exploit the thermal springs here, though the town's reputation as a fashionable spa reached its height in the 19th century. The history of the spa, and that of the local area, is explored at the Musée Bigourdon.

A different kind of outing is offered at the Grottes de Médous, where boats explore an underground section of the Adour river. Within the town, the white water of the Adour offers a challenging canoe course for experienced enthusiasts.

Leave Bagnères on the D938 as for Toulouse. Turn right along the D26, then go right again onto the D929 through Hèches. Now watch for a left turn, just as you see the sign for "Rebouc" over a railroad crossing. Take the immediate left, following the D26 again. In St.-Bertrand-de-Comminges turn right at the intersection, going uphill and along the D26.

3 St.-Bertrand-de-Comminges

The village and cathedral take their name from a 12th-century bishop, Bertrand de l'Isle, who was responsible for restoring both village and church after centuries of neglect following its sacking by Burgundian invaders in the 6th century. The cathedral in which Bertrand is buried is a magnificent edifice, surprisingly so for such a tiny village. The village itself, of medieval half-timbered houses, is charming and full of architectural interest.

Return downhill, then go straight ahead on the D26 through Valcabrère. Turn right on the N125, following signs to Luchon.

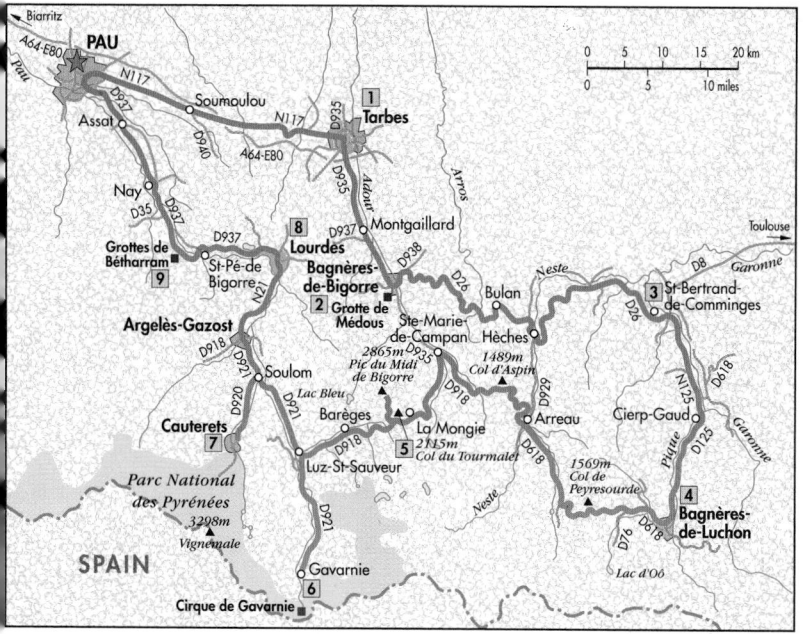

4 Bagnères-de-Luchon

Luchon for short, this is the most elegant of the Pyrenean spas, with its shaded boulevards and parks adorned with numerous statues. The great days of the spa, when the rich and famous came, are explored at the town's museum in Allées d'Étigny, the main boulevard, where patrons of sidewalk cafés sit beneath linden trees.

Luchon is now a center for leisure sports – hang gliding, climbing, mountain trekking, canoeing and river rafting – and also more relaxing ones such as clay pigeon shooting and archery.

Leave Luchon along the D618 over the Col de Peyresourde. In Arreau, go right on the D929, then (opposite the Esso gas station and not before) bear left (uphill) over the Col d'Aspin on the D918. Turn left in Ste.-Marie-de-Campan to follow the D918

in the direction of the Col du Tourmalet.

5 Col du Tourmalet

At 2,115 meters (6,939 ft.) the Col du Tourmalet is the highest pass in the French Pyrénées. The name of the *col* means "bad detour," and the cyclists who have to ascend its hairpin bends in the Tour de France (the Tour usually comes this way) must steadfastly agree. From the *col* the view is spectacular.

The Observatory on the Pic du Midi was built in 1882 and is in use all year round, the staff being transported by cable car from the ski resort of La Mongie when the road is blocked by snow during the winter months. (See also Walk on p.162.)

Immediately beyond the summit of the Col du Tourmalet, bear left through Barèges to Luz-St.-Sauveur. Turn left on the D921 in the direction of Gavarnie.

PYRENEAN PASTURES

The annual mass movement of livestock up to summer mountain pastures is a centuries-old tradition, though now most areas are accessible by truck.

However, the ancient rights governing grazing have changed little, with elaborate arrangements (*faceries*) ensuring that pastures are shared out fairly. The oldest *facerie*, between Roncal and Baretous, dates to 1375 and is still renewed annually with the payment of three white heifers ■

WALK

LAC DES COUBOUS

Starting at Pont de la Gaubie, about 8 kilometers (5 mi.) to the west of the Col du Tourmalet, walk along the D918 and then turn right onto a path that is signposted for Étangs d'Escoubous.

Follow the path to a track taken by footpath GR10. Now follow the track as it bears right to cross the Coubous stream and then zig-zags up to Lac des Coubous.

To get back, do not go down the zig-zags; continue ahead along a narrower path that crosses the hillside. When the path becomes faint, follow cairns below the marshy ground, then go downhill beside the ski tows to return to the start ∎

6 Gavarnie

The narrow road to Gavarnie is a dead end, making the journey a trial of patience and driving skill. But it is worth the effort to see the Cirque de Gavarnie, a superb mountain amphitheater. The Grande Cascade, tumbling down the Cirque's rock walls, has one of Europe's longest drops – 442 meters (1,450 ft.). The village of Gavarnie is quite charming; its Information Center on the Parc National des Pyrénées is a useful starting point if you plan on exploring the park.

Return to Luz-St.-Sauveur and take the D921 as for Lourdes. Immediately after leaving Soulom, turn left onto the D920 to Cauterets.

7 Cauterets

Cauterets also has an excellent information center on the Parc National des Pyrénées. This is particularly interesting for its details on the lammergeier. This bird, sometimes called the bearded vulture, is the largest of Europe's birds of prey. Once close to extinction, the bird is now slowly increasing in numbers – but it is still only the very lucky visitor who sees one. Cauterets, an elegant old spa, is a good base for exploring the high Pyrénées. From it the Pont d'Espagne can be reached, and from there paths lead to the summit of the Vignemale, at 3,298 meters (10,820 ft.) the highest peak in the French Pyrénées.

Return to the D921 and turn left to Lourdes.

8 Lourdes, Midi-Pyrénées

In 1858, 14-year-old Bernadette Soubirous saw a vision of the Virgin Mary at the Grotte Massabielle beside the Pau river. Over a period of time Bernadette had 18 visions, during one of which a spring miraculously began to flow. The water from the spring was found to have healing powers. During Bernadette's lifetime pilgrims visited the grotto in increasing numbers: today the town is a major world pilgrimage center, the miraculous waters from the spring having to be rationed.

The candle-lit pilgrimages to the site and the open-air Masses are memorable and very moving, however commercialization of the grotto in the nearby stores seems out of keeping with the spirit of the place. Within the town, the Musée Bernadette tells the story of the young girl's visions and includes a fascinating history of the pilgrimages undertaken here. Less crowded is the Musée Pyrénéen, a museum of the arts and traditions of the local area.

Leave Lourdes on the D937, following the signs for Bétharram. Go through St.-Pé-de-Bigorre, turn left, then left again, to reach the Grottes de Bétharram.

9 Grottes de Bétharram

Occasionally the Bétharram caves can be crowded with overspill visitors from Lourdes, but they are worth the wait that this can entail. The cave's name derives from an old legend about a girl who was drowning in the nearby Gave de Pau; she was apparently saved by a *Bét Arram*, which means "beautiful branch" in the mountain dialect, thrown to her by the Virgin Mary. The cave entrance is reached by cable car, and its immense complex of chambers can be explored both by boat and train.

Return to the D937 and turn left for Pau.

★★★ GAVARNIE   *152B1*

Occasionally known as the "Chamonix of the Pyrénées," the village of Gavarnie is the base for trips to the Pyrénées' most spectacular mountain feature, the Cirque de Gavarnie. Traditionally the Cirque is reached on horseback, a trip that takes about 20 minutes. On foot it is reached after an hour's steep walking. The Cirque is a vertical amphitheater of rock, created by glaciation. At its highest point it is about 1,400 meters (4,600 ft.) from rim to floor. Down the cliff tumble numerous waterfalls, one of which, the Grande Cascade, falls 442 meters (1,450 ft.), making it one of Europe's longest.

★★★ THE HIGH PYRÉNÉES   *152B1*

The high French Pyrénées lie south of Cauterets, following the border with Spain eastwards past the Cirque de Gavarnie and onto the Pyrenean National Park. This is a land of thermal spas – Cauterets itself, Luz-St.-Sauveur, and Barèges, the highest of the Pyrenean spas – and spectacular mountain scenery. The highest of the peaks in the French Pyrénées is Vignemale (although the border with Spain runs through the summit, so the Spanish can claim a share); there are higher peaks across the border. Vignemale is associated with the eccentric mountaineer, Count Henry Russell, whose statue can be seen near Gavarnie. Russell was born in 1834, the son of an Irish father and a French mother. After traveling the world he decided that the Pyrénées were the finest mountains on earth. He made the first ascent of numerous local peaks, but was fascinated with Vignemale to the point of obsession. He climbed it 33 times, the last time when he was 70. He was the first man to ascend it in winter, and he once had himself buried up to his neck on the summit overnight to see if he could see God. Though he did not, he said, he did claim to "feel His presence." Over the years Russell had several caves excavated on the peak's flanks, one just below the summit.

The Parc National des Pyrénées is continuous with the Spanish Ordesa Park, the two having been set up to preserve the landscape, flora, and fauna of the high peaks. The Park has helped to preserve the ibex and the isard, the Pyrenean form of the chamois, but has unfortunately failed to protect the Pyrenean brown bear. The bears, reduced in numbers to just a handful, live on in two valleys to the south of Pau; re-introduction has just begun to try to increase their numbers.

A statue of 19th-century explorer Henry Russell gazes towards Vignemale from beside the bridge at Gavarnie. When he died in 1909, he had climbed his beloved peak 33 times, the last time at age 70

PAS DE VOUS RENDRE   HEUREUSE DANS

ELLE NOUS SALUE ET NOUS SOURIT

VOULEZ-VOUS ME FAIRE LA GRACE DE VENIR ICI PENDANT 15 JOURS

ALLEZ BOIRE À LA FONTAINE ET VOUS Y LAVER

★ ISTURITS ET OXOCELHAYA, GROTTES D' *152A2*

The Pyrénées are composed chiefly of limestone, a rock that dissolves in the weak acid of rainwater. Faults in the rock allow rain to penetrate, and chambers are cut out by underground rivers.

Two such cave systems are Isturits and Oxocelhaya, to the east of Cambo-les-Bains in the French Basque country. The caves are set one above the other, and excavations have revealed that prehistoric peoples occupied them until about 10,000 years ago.

In the upper cave (Isturits) there is a superb reindeer carved from stone by these early cave-dwellers, while the lower cave (Oxocelhaya) has some excellent flowstone formations. Finds from the excavations of the caves can be seen at the entrance.

LABOUICHE CAVE *153D1*

Close to Foix lies another fine show cave, but here there is an added fascination: the formations can be viewed from the vantage point of a boat that travels along the same river that created the spectacular chambers.

★ LOURDES *152B2*

It is estimated that 4 million people visit Lourdes annually, drawn by hopes of a miraculous cure, by the need to redefine their faith, or out of curiosity. The pilgrims overwhelm Lourdes, both in sheer numbers and because, for the majority, the town is only the grotto. Yet there is more to see: start at the model village (in Avenue Peyramale), which shows the town as it looked in 1858 before Bernadette had her visions, then try the town museum (in Parking de l'Egalité), which brings old Lourdes alive with its fine collections. The local area, the Bigorre, is explored at

the Musée Pyrénéen in the excellent Château Fort. The collections include one on Pyrenean geology and another on the traditional costumes of the Bigorre region. There is also a display of the memorabilia of Count Henry Russell, the eccentric mountaineer.

★ LUCHON *152C1*

Bagnères-de-Luchon, called Luchon by locals and visitors alike, was first developed as a spa by the Romans, who preferred it to all their other Pyrenean spas. In the 19th century it was an elegant, stylish resort; with its tree-lined avenues and beautiful park, it has maintained much of that air of sophistication. Within the park stand the casino and the spa buildings.

Luchon is also an excellent base for excursions in the surrounding area. The best of these includes Superbagnères, a high peak that offers a fabulous view of the high summits.

★ LUZ ST.-SAUVEUR *152B1*

This little spa, set on the Gave de Gavarnie, makes an excellent base for exploring southward to Gavarnie and the high peaks, the Parc National des Pyrénées, and Lourdes and the Bigorre. It is a picturesque place with an unusual fortified church. This was built in the 14th century by the Hospitalers of St. John of Jerusalem, an order set up to protect travelers. Being fortified, the church could offer both spiritual comfort and physical protection to those in need.

★★★ NIAUX, GROTTE DE *153D1*

South of Foix lies one of the most important caves of prehistoric art to have been discovered in Europe to date. Niaux was no accidental discovery, the huge

BERNADETTE SOUBIROUS

Bernadette Soubirous was born in Lourdes in house No. 2 on the street that now bears her name.

In 1858, when she was a frail 14-year-old with tuberculosis, Bernadette saw a vision of the Virgin Mary in a grotto, Grotte Massabielle. Her parents were unimpressed and tried to prevent her from visiting the grotto again. But Bernadette persisted, and was visited by the Virgin 18 times in all. On one occasion a spring of water emerged from the cave wall; later it was found to have healing powers.

Bernadette died at the age of 37, and was canonized in 1933 ■

The grotto at Lourdes is a major world pilgrimage center. An underground church capable of holding 25,000 people was built here in 1958, on the centenary of the visions. Daily masses are held at the grotto

TALES OF PAU

When she was eight months pregnant, the future Henri IV's mother, Jeanne d'Albret, traveled from Picardy specifically to have her baby in Pau.

She sang him Bernaise songs whilst in labor, hoping this would make him strong and resilient, and the new born's lips were rubbed with garlic and Jurançon wine, as was the local custom.

The French throne fell to her son when the Valois line expired with Henri III in 1589, but finding the gates of Paris closed to him because of Jeanne d'Albert's adoption of Protestantism, he proved himself an able politician by renouncing his faith with the famously pragmatic words, "Paris is worth a mass" ∎

cave mouth having been known for centuries before it was first explored in 1906. To minimize damage to the paintings, visits are limited to small guided tours (in French only), which use hand-held flashlights. Advance reservations are essential. What the flashlights illuminate are depictions of mammoth, bison, and deer. In the Salon Noir, the magnificent bison and ibex paintings are in black. There is also a strange graffiti of dots and dashes, which some experts have suggested was an early form of writing.

Finally, preserved in what was the mud of the cave floor, you can see the footprints of the artists, dated to 11,000 BC.

★ OLORON-STE.-   152B2
MARIE and VALLÉE D'ASPE

Oloron-Ste.-Marie is a small market town famous for its chocolate and for the manufacture of the *bérets* that have come to epitomize the French. The town has two churches: Ste.-Croix has roof vaulting that is typically Spanish, while Ste.-Marie has a beautiful 12th-century marble doorway, carved with scenes from the Bible. Oloron stands at the confluence of the Aspe and Ossau rivers. Each valley region is excellent, the Aspe more scenic, the Ossau famous for its cheese. But at present the two valleys are the center of a dispute over the last remaining Pyrenean brown bears. These shy creatures are reduced in numbers to perhaps less than 10; even these are threatened by the plan to drive a tunnel into Spain beneath the Somport Pass, in the Aspe valley. The people of the Aspe Valley would like the road, to improve their standard of living by encouraging more tourists. However, conservationists want

to prevent the road from being built and to bring in bears from Cantabria (Spain) or eastern Europe to replenish the stock. This last idea is being implemented in spite of opposition from sheep farmers, who lose animals occasionally to the remaining bears.

★ OSSAU, VALLÉE D'   152B1

Along with its neighbor, the Aspe Valley, Ossau is at the center of the controversy over the remaining Pyrenean brown bears. The bears feature in the exhibitions of valley flora and fauna at the Maison d'Ossau at Arudy. Beyond Arudy there are two small spas with explicit names – Les Eaux-Chaudes and Eaux-Bonnes ("hot waters" and "good waters," respectively) – before you reach Gabas. Gabas is the center for the manufacture of *Ossau Brebis*, a famous sheep's milk cheese. The distinctive Pic du Midi d'Ossau offers a challenging but worthwhile hike – allow yourself about three hours to reach the summit.

★ PAU   152B2

Pau (pronounced Po) was the birthplace, in 1553, of Henri IV, one of the best-loved French monarchs. The king liked to be called "Le Béarnais" after the local region of Béarn, of which this town was once the capital. At the center of the town is a château, begun in the 13th century but heavily modified since. During the summer the château houses an exhibition of Henri IV's memorabilia, Second-Empire-style furnishings (including King Henri's tortoise-shell cradle), and a museum to the traditions of Béarn. The town also has two other excellent museums: the Musée des Beaux-Arts houses a collection of paintings by artists from all over

Europe and includes one fine work by Degas, while the Musée Bernadotte follows the career of Jean-Baptiste Bernadotte, one of Napoléon's marshals who, in 1818, became king of Sweden.

PIC DU CANIGOU *153E1*

This mountain, rising to 2,784 meters (9,132 ft.), so dominates the local peaks that for a long time it was thought to be the highest peak in the Pyrénées. The Catalans, who lived at its base, held it in awe. In 1276 King Pedro III of Aragon claimed to have climbed to the summit and to have found a lake there, from which came a dragon "which began to fly about and to darken the air with its breath." The mystery and awe have lessened somewhat over the years, Canigou having been ascended

frequently and in a number of irreverent ways – by bicycle, on horseback, even by automobile. To make your own relaxed, ascent, reserve a seat on the spectacular jeep ride from Prades or Vernet-les-Bains to Chalet des Cortalets. From there a two-hour walk along a clearly signposted track will take you to the summit.

★★★ ST.-JEAN-PIED- *152A2* DE-PORT

St.-Jean is a picturesque and charming Basque town, once an important stop on the pilgrimage route to Santiago de Compostela. The "Port" of its name means mountain pass, the full name of the town, therefore, recalling the pilgrims who arrived, on foot, to cross the mountains on the route of Saint John. The pilgrims walked down the still-cobbled rue

In the footsteps of ancient pilgrims. Approach the old part of St.-Jean-Pied-de-Port via Porte St.-Jean on the north side of the walls by the citadel. The views from all around are breathtaking

FORTRESSES AND CATHARS

Catharism arose in southern France in the late 12th century. The Cathars believed the Catholic Church to be heretical, and rejected the Mass, marriage, burial rituals, and organized religion.

Alarmed by the rise of Catharism, the French king invaded Languedoc in 1209. The first city attacked was Béziers, where the population, both Cathar and Catholic, was massacred.

The Cathars then retreated to impregnable castles built on the rocky peaks of Roussillon and the Pyrénées. Of these the finest are Montségur and Peyrepertuse, the latter built along a sharp ridge with sheer drops.

The last stronghold was Quéribus, though even it finally capitulated in 1255 ∎

de la Citadelle from Porte St.-Jean to Porte d'Espagne. They still do, as this old pilgrimage route is becoming popular again with walkers and the pious alike. The citadel (la Citadelle) of the pilgrim road's name was built by Vauban when relations between France and Spain became strained in the late 17th century.

★★★ ST.-MARTIN-DU-CANIGOU   153E1

From Vernet-les-Bains the road rises to Casteil – where there is an excellent museum exploring the geology, flora, and fauna of the local area – but then goes no further. To progress to the abbey of St.-Martin-du-Canigou it is now necessary to walk – allow at least 30 minutes for the steep ascent – or to find a seat on a tourist jeep. The abbey is extraordinary. It was built in the 11th century by way of a penance by Count Guifred of Cerdagne after he had killed his nephew. The buildings occupy the flat top of a rocky spur. Within the church is the tomb of Count Guifred. He reputedly laid the first stone of the abbey with his own hands, and spent the last 48 years of his life here.

★★ ST.-SAVIN   152B1

For over 500 years, from early medieval times, a mysterious group of outcasts who were called Cagots lived at various places throughout the Pyrénées, but chiefly near St.-Jean-Pied-de-Port. Almost nothing is known with certainty about these folk, other than that they were forbidden to marry anyone other than another Cagot, and could not attend church, live in the towns, or visit the mills. Of their origins there is only conjecture.

There is some proof that leprosy was at the root of the fear and isolation, and some evidence that Cagots were dark-skinned

dwarves. It is conjectured that the name derives from the old mountain word for "dog." Most historians believe that the church of St.-Savin is the only link with the Cagots. A low window, known as the Fenêtre des Cagots, is believed to have been built so that the unfortunates could stand outside and hear mass. Inside, a holy water stoup is supported by two crude granite figures – could they be Cagots?

★ SERRABONE   153E1

Reached by a tortuous road, the 11th-century priory of Serrabone stands below a peak called *Roque Rouge*, the red rock. It therefore comes as a surprise to discover that the rose-colored marble used to build the priory was imported from quarries on the Pic du Canigou, many miles to the west. The carvings on the tribune of the priory church are a masterpiece of the craftsman's art, the intermingling of Biblical scenes and mythical animals being characteristically Catalan.

★★ TOULOUSE   153D2

Long ago the capital of Languedoc, now capital of the Midi-Pyrénées region, Toulouse is a bustling, industrialized city and the gateway to the Pyrénées for those arriving by plane. Arrival by air is fitting, as Toulouse is the center of the French aviation industry. Most visitors come here seeking the stores, restaurants, and hotels that big cities have to offer, but there is more to see: with the Garonne river threading through it, Toulouse is an elegant place. In the city center there stands the beautiful basilica of St. Sernin, the old abbey of Les Jacobins, and the cathedral. The Musée St.-Raymond has displays illustrating the history of the city, while the Musée des Augustins has a remarkable collection of art.

PROVENCE
AND THE
CÔTE D'AZUR

Bordered by the Rhône to the west,
the rugged Alps to the north, and the
shimmering Mediterranean along its
coastline, Provence is an intoxicating,
sun-drenched corner of France that
has delighted visitors for decades –
if not centuries

CALENDAR OF EVENTS

EARLY FEBRUARY – Nyons: **Festival of New Oil**. Marseilles: **Candlemass Procession**.

FEBRUARY – Sunday before Lent, Graveson: **Carnival procession of floats** (*Corso Carnavalesque*).

MARCH OR APRIL – Easter weekend, Arles: **Easter Festival**.

PROVENCE AND THE CÔTE D'AZUR

Greek merchants and Roman conquerors were the first to colonize this land. The Romans stayed for six centuries, and left a heritage of well-preserved monuments that have no parallel outside Italy. The Greeks left the olive tree, whose wizened trunks are characteristic features of the Provençal landscape, together with vineyards, hillsides scented with wild herbs and succulent fruits and vegetables.

The Middle Ages also left their mark in the form of numerous ancient churches and castles –

not to mention the typical hilltop villages (*villages perchés*), which are found throughout the region.

Artists such as Vincent Van Gogh, Henri Matisse and Paul Cézanne have been beguiled by the region's dazzling light and colors, creating a rich legacy that is reflected in numerous world-class art museums and exhibition centers. Tourists have also been coming here for over 150 years, attracted by the Provençal *joie de vivre*, its warm sunshine, plentiful good food and wine, and the glitz of the Riviera resorts.

While Provence can offer sophisticated cities such as **Nice** and **Avignon**, where the cultural and intellectual life (and even the

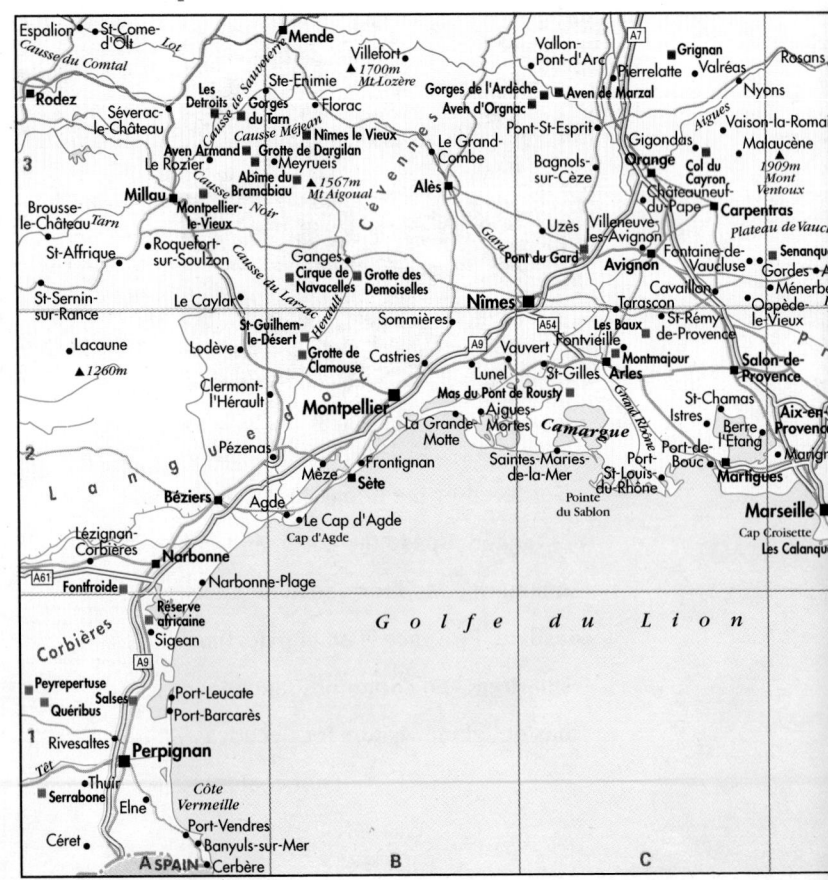

shopping) can match anything on offer in Paris, it also has wild and unspoiled areas, remote Alpine valleys, cool forests, spectacular gorges, and the marshy wastes of the **Camargue**. Escaping the hectic summer scene and the traffic jams of the coastal resorts is never difficult.

In many an inland village and town life still revolves around the agricultural calendar, and harvests are celebrated with boisterous *fêtes* involving colorful parades, outdoor banquets, music and dancing, and free-flowing wine and *pastis*. Traditions relating to Provençal legends, language and literature are also deep-rooted.

★★★ HIGHLIGHTS

Arles (►172)
Avignon (►173)
Les Baux (►174)
La Camargue (►175)
Cassis (►177)
Les Corniches (►77)
Gordes (►182)
Grand Canyon du Verdon (►182)
Nice (►187)
Nîmes (►188)
Orange (►188)
Pont du Gard (►189)
St.-Rémy-de-Provence (►190)

CALENDAR OF EVENTS

MID-MAY –
Le Beaucet:
Pilgrimage to the sanctuary of St.-Gentius.

JUNE 21 –
Courthézon: **Vine Stock Festival.**
Including a children's parade, dancing and singing.

JULY – Martigues:
Venetian Festival.
Parade of decorated floats at night.

AUGUST 1–23 –
La Roque-d'Anthéron: **Piano Festival at the Silvacane Abbey.**

LATE SEPTEMBER –
Nîmes: **Grape Harvest Festival.**

DECEMBER 24 –
Allauch: **Provençal Midnight Mass.**
Shepherds come down from the hills of Notre-Dame du Château ∎

WALK

AIX-EN-PROVENCE

Starting at the Grande Fontaine in place Général de Gaulle, follow cours Mirabeau on the right-hand side to appreciate the fine doorways of Aix's handsome 17th- and 18th-century mansions.

At the Fontaine d'Eau Thermale, cross to the old quarter, threading through the maze of old streets to place Richelme and place de l'Hôtel de Ville.

Continue up rue Gaston de Saporta to the St.-Sauveur cathedral, which has a 5th-century baptistry.

Make your way back via the place des Prêcheurs and the place de Verdun to a passageway that leads back to cours Mirabeau. A sign indicates the hat shop owned by Paul Cézanne's father ■

In the summer Provence is alive with **festivals** of all kinds, from the avante-garde to the Fête des Gardians (the Camargue cowboys), a cultural cornucopia embracing over 4,000 separate events. Out of season, life takes on a more sedate pace: sitting under a spreading plane tree in some peaceful village square, the only sound to disturb the silence will be the soft clunk of *boules* as the Provençals enjoy themselves in time-honored fashion.

AIX-EN-PROVENCE   170D2

Capital of Provence for many centuries, Aix is a prosperous city with a rich architectural and cultural legacy that has given it a character unique to the region. With its grand, post-Renaissance mansions, impressive avenues and charming squares complete with bubbling fountains, Aix has an elegant ambience that is reflected in its lively café life and thriving arts scene.

The focus of the city is the broad, tree-lined cours Mirabeau. Soothing fountains set along its length separate the chic cafés on the north side from the fine old mansions of honey-colored stone that line its south side. Behind them is the Quartier Mazarin, which has many 17th- and 18th-century buildings ornamented with finely carved doorways and wrought-iron balconies.

To the north of the cours Mirabeau are the busy, narrow streets of the atmospheric old quarter, Vieil Aix, where you'll find the imposing Hôtel de Ville, Aix's cathedral (St.-Sauveur), and several interesting museums (particularly unusual are the textile collections in the Musée des Tapisseries). Cobbled squares, colorful markets, open-air cafés, and intriguing stores for browsing in all make this the perfect area for leisurely strolling.

A short walk up the hill north of Vieil Aix takes you to artist Paul Cézanne's old studio and house, set in a peaceful little garden and left just as it was when he died.

★ ANTIBES   171F2

The ever-fashionable port of Antibes can boast as many yachts as its Riviera rivals, but in few others can you step behind the quayside to find such a delightful old town surrounded by ramparts and ancient gateways. There's a wonderful market (daily except Mondays), overflowing with local produce, which gives the cobbled backstreets a heady, all-pervading aroma (Antibes is the largest flower-growing center in Provence). Also not to be missed is the Picasso Museum, housed in a 13th- to 16th-century château where the artist once lived.

★★★ ARLES   170C2

Set on the banks of the mighty Rhône, Arles is a small town with an illustrious past reflected in its superb Roman monuments and medieval churches, excellent museums, and rich cultural heritage as the spiritual capital of Provence. Old folk traditions still survive today in the form of colorful festivals and other events such as the local version of a bullfight, the *Course à la Cocarde*.

At the heart of Arles' beautiful old town center is the animated place du Forum, with most sights within easy reach. First stop should be the remarkable Église St.-Trophime, whose elaborately carved portal and beautiful cloisters are both masterpieces of the Provençal Romanesque style. Just near here is the Roman theater, still impressive despite centuries of pillaging, and the even more spectacular Roman amphitheater (les Arènes), which can hold more than 20,000 spectators, as it often does today when bullfights are held. Other Roman monuments include the Alyscamps (an immense pre-Christian and early Christian burial ground) and the thermal baths.

Arles is well stocked with museums, most notably the Museon Arlaten (founded by the Nobel prize-winning poet Mistral, it has an extensive Provençal folklore collection), the Musée d'Art Chrétien (4th-century sarcophagi) and the Musée Lapidaire d'Art Païen (Greek and Roman sculpture and mosaics).

papal palace, and the enormous 4-kilometer (2½-mi.) walls that encircle the old town, isolating the center from the modern, sprawling city around it.

At the heart of Avignon is the place de l'Horloge, a large square surrounded by bustling outdoor cafés; to the north of here are most of the interesting sights, including the Palais des Papes itself (a "must" on any itinerary, its interior houses some splendid 14th-century frescoes as well as tapestries), the cathedral, several

Pont St.-Bénézet in Avignon was begun in 1177, and for over a century was the only stone bridge over the Rhône. In the 17th century, the floodwaters of the river swept away 18 of its original 22 arches

★★★ AVIGNON   *170C3*

This big, busy city rose to prominence in medieval times when it became the home of the Papal Court, who sought to flee political pressures in Rome during the controversial "Babylonian Captivity." Its former wealth and power is evident in the vast Palais des Papes, as much a fortress as

fine 17th-century mansions, and the Rocher des Doms gardens, which offer sweeping views over the Rhône below.

Jutting out across one branch of the river are the remains of the famous Pont St.-Bénézet, immortalized in the nursery song "Sur le pont d'Avignon," but with only four of its original 22 arches

CANNES FILM FESTIVAL

Each year in May, Cannes is transformed into Hollywood-on-the-Riviera as moviemakers, actors, producers, and agents descend in their thousands for the famous International Film Festival.

This two-week jamboree of wheeling and dealing is covered by around 3,000 journalists from all over the world, all eager to spot the hottest starlet from among the many hopefuls who stand posing for the cameras.

Hundreds of movies are screened around the clock, the most important being shown in the orange, bunker-like Palais des Festivals, all hoping to win the coveted Palme d'Or trophy.

Members of the public can buy tickets for some, though not all, of the screenings ■

now standing. Avignon also has numerous old churches and a handful of good museums, the most worthwhile of which are the Musée du Petit Palais (which has an extensive collection of medieval and Renaissance art) and the Musée Calvet (art and antiques across three centuries).

Avignon is famous for its annual Festival, established in 1947. It offers an extravaganza of drama, art, music, dance, and film and takes place from mid-July to mid-August. The city is also well supplied with good restaurants and cafés, chic stores (particularly in the rue Joseph Vernet) and quaint corners that merit a moment of quiet exploration.

★★★ LES BAUX   170C2

Perched on a rocky plateau with sweeping vistas all around, Les Baux was once the stronghold of a powerful dynasty of warlords who terrorized the surrounding regions during the early Middle Ages. Their citadel, an impregnable eyrie with walls rising dramatically from the sheer rock face, is now largely in ruins, but it remains a hauntingly atmospheric place.

The village below the citadel has many fine old mansions lining its cobbled streets and a plethora of art galleries, boutiques, and craft stores that are excellent places for browsing.

Just outside Les Baux is the Val d'Enfer (Valley of Hell), an evocative, boulder-strewn valley with several deserted sandstone quarries, one of which has been turned into the quite extraordinary Cathédrale d'Images, an underground sound-and-light show with a difference.

BEAULIEU-SUR-MER   171F2

Renowned for its mild microclimate (they grow bananas here) and prolific gardens, Beaulieu is a

charming old resort that offers several elegant hotels. On a headland just beyond the casino is the fascinating Villa Kérylos, a reproduction Greek villa that was built by the archeologist Theodore Reinach in 1908. It has been lavishly constructed using acres of marble, and is now a museum

★ BÉZIERS   170A2

Rising up from the surrounding plains on its hilltop site, Béziers was the scene of a dreadful massacre during the Albigensian Crusade in 1209, during which 20,000 people were put to death. The city recovered and rebuilt itself, and the results can be seen in the old medieval quarter that clusters around the top of the hill, crowned by its vast cathedral.

Despite the forbidding exterior, the cathedral interior has some lovely stained glass and fragments of frescoes. Nearby there is also a fine arts museum and a museum devoted to wine. Béziers has a good antiques and flower market on Fridays, but parking is a constant problem.

★ BIOT   171F2

This small town is famous for its ceramics and glassware, crafts that were introduced by the artist Fernand Léger in the 1950s. On the edge of Biot, Léger's own work (which also included stained glass, ceramics and mosaics) can be seen in the Musée Fernand Léger. More contemporary pieces can be bought at the Verrerie de Biot (glassworks), where you can also watch the glass being blown.

This appealing town is set on a small hill, and its old streets lead up past cafés and boutiques to the delightful place des Arcades, which is flanked by arcades that have unusual, irregularly shaped arches. Beyond the square, Biot's church contains 15th- and 16th-century paintings and altarpieces.

★★★ LA CAMARGUE 170C2

Forming a vast triangle across the greater part of the Rhône Delta, the Camargue is a unique environment of salt marshes, lagoons, canals, and seascapes inhabited by hundreds of species of birds and herds of wild horses and bulls. It is also the home of the famous Camargue cowboys (*les gardians*); horse riding is available at the many ranches throughout the area.

An extensive array of flora and fauna is supported by the terrain. For bird-lovers the Camargue is paradise, with some 400 species of birds (including 100 migrating species) taking advantage of this watery wilderness. The most spectacular are undoubtedly the famous rosy-pink flamingoes, with up to 50,000 present here during the spring and summer.

The main tourist center is the lively coastal town of Saintes-Maries-de-la-Mer, although Arles (see p.172) is also conveniently close. There is an excellent information center at La Capelière (northeast of Les Saintes-Maries), which is the headquarters of the Parc Naturel Régional de la Camargue. Other observation posts and sanctuaries are scattered around the main lagoons, and there is also a superb open-air museum, the Musée de la Camargue, at the Mas du Pont de Rousty.

★★ CANNES 171F2

Thanks to the annual Film Festival in May, Cannes is probably the most famous of the Riviera resorts. It is also one of the oldest, having been discovered by the English Lord Brougham in 1834; his patronage persuaded scores of English and Russian aristocrats to build elaborate mansions here for their vacations.

The long seaside promenade, La Croisette, is lined with palm trees and plush, elegant hotels, with the neatly swept beach in front divided up into private areas with their own expensive restaurants for lunch on the beach. Behind La Croisette there is a network of pedestrianized streets with numerous branches of chic designer boutiques. In a prime position is the hideous, orange-colored Palais des Festivals, just beside the port at the western end of La Croisette, with the old town (Le Suquet) rising up on the hill behind.

For a complete contrast to the glitz of Cannes itself you can take an enjoyable boat excursion to the small, offshore islands of St.-Honorat and Ste.-Marguerite, both of which are excellent places for walks and picnics.

White horses are a traditional feature of the Camargue, along with its agile cowboys (gardians) and herds of black bull. There are bird sanctuaries and observation posts scattered through the park

CAP D'ANTIBES   *171F2*

Jutting out from the coastline between Antibes itself and Juan-les-Pins, the Cap d'Antibes has long been one of the most exclusive addresses on the Riviera, with royalty and film stars alike building sumptuous mansions for themselves on this wooded headland. For the casual visitor there is little to see except massive, guarded gateways, but you can walk around part of the headland and there are also one or two good sandy beaches that are accessible to the public.

★ CAP FERRAT   *171F2*

This is another exclusive residential area reserved for the seriously rich, although the small port of St.-Jean-Cap-Ferrat is a pleasant place to visit. There are splendid views of the Riviera from its Corniche roads. The main reason for a visit to Cap Ferrat is the impressive Villa Ephrussi de Rothschild, which was built over a period of seven years by Baroness Béatrice de Rothschild to house her extensive art collection. Open to the public, it is surrounded by incredible gardens.

The attractive port of Cassis is a delightful base for making a boat trip to the picturesque calanques that lie to the west of town. These inlets cut into steep-sided valleys make sheltered bathing spots

CARPENTRAS 170C3

This likable town has a long history as a market center (the Greeks and Phoenicians came here to trade for wheat, honey, and goats); if you're a market-lover Friday is the best day to visit, when the entire town center is transformed into a huge, noisy, colorful bazaar.

There are many interesting backstreets to explore, with fine old mansions, fountains, and other curiosities. The cathedral is an eclectic blend of styles, but hidden away behind it is a Roman triumphal arch that has similar features to the one in Orange (see p.188). It's worth climbing up the Porte d'Orange for the views across to Mont Ventoux and the Plateau de Vaucluse. On no account should you miss the 18th-century pharmacy, which has been preserved almost intact, in the old Hôtel Dieu just to the south of the town center.

★★★ CASSIS 171D2

There's nothing the inhabitants of nearby Marseilles like better than to drive to this idyllic port on weekends and consume a mouth-watering seafood meal, washed down with the excellent white *vin de Cassis*, in one of the many fish restaurants that are clustered along the quayside. There's no better way to pass a sunny day in Cassis, and to work it all off afterwards you can walk to the scenic *calanques* that lie to the west of the port: these narrow inlets (which resemble miniature Nordic fjords) can also be reached by boat from the port.

CHÂTEAUNEUF-DU-PAPE 170C3

Wine buffs will certainly need no reminding that the vineyards around this village produce one of the world's most well-known and prestigious wines. With its many *caves* (cellars) lining the village

streets, you'd be well advised to spend the night – especially since Châteauneuf-du-Pape has one of the highest alcohol contents (12.5 percent) of any French wine.

Dominating the village is the ruined castle of the Avignon popes, who were the first to plant vines here. At one end of the village is a fascinating display on wine-making down the centuries in the Musée du Père Anselme.

★★★ CORNICHES, LES 171F3

Stunning views of the Riviera coastline are the reward for navigating the many *lacets* (hairpin bends) on the Corniche roads between Nice and Menton. From Nice the Grande Corniche climbs gradually and traverses the clifftops high above the blue Mediterranean, passing through La Turbie (see p.193) before descending in a series of dizzying turns to Menton.

The Moyenne Corniche is also spectacular – particularly above Villefranche. The Corniche Inférieure is less enjoyable and jammed with traffic in summer, but it allows access to the coastal resorts.

CÔTE VERMEILLE 170A1

Squeezed between Perpignan and the Spanish border, this 30-kilometer (19-mi.) section of coastline gains its name ("the Vermilion Coast") from the earthy shades of vermilion permeating the crystalline rocks beneath its olive trees. The principal resort is Collioure, with its market square, beaches, and 17th-century castle. The artist Henri Matisse stopped here briefly, painting the lovely church of Notre-Dame-des-Anges on the beach at Collioure.

Beyond here, Banyuls-sur-Mer marks the end of the coast, in a region that is noted in particular for its sweet dessert wines.

WALK

LES CALANQUES

Park at the beginning of the Calanque de Port-Miou (a favorite yacht berth) and climb over a ridge to the Calanque de Port-Pin, where you can swim from a small beach.

Continue upwards to a plateau, from where there is a wonderful panorama back toward the towering cliffs on the other side of the Bay of Cassis.

Ahead, the ground slopes gradually downward until you arrive at the edge of the magnificent Calanque d'En Vau, where the dramatic limestone cliffs plunge down into the azure waters below. Beyond, you can see the Riou archipelago shimmering in the distance.

Return to Cassis by the same route ■

DRIVE

EXPLORING THE CÔTE D'AZUR

233 kilometers/145 miles (allow 3 days)

Brilliant sunshine, lush vegetation, and vistas of azure-blue sea against a backdrop of serrated mountains continue to attract visitors to the French Riviera. The quality of its light and the vibrancy of its colors have inspired scores of artists. Hairpin bends on the Corniche roads between Nice and Menton offer panoramas along the coastline. Our tour begins on the Corniche Inférieure from Nice.

BIRTH OF THE CÔTE D'AZURE

It was a vineyard owner from Dijon, Stephen Liegeard, who first coined the phrase.

In 1887 he left the damp northern weather behind and drove down to the Mediterranean for a vacation. Alighting from his vehicle he exclaimed "côte d'azure!" (literally "azure coast").

When Liegeard returned home he published an illustrated book, "La Côte d'Azure 1888," extolling the virtues of this coastline, and the name stuck ∎

Leave Nice following the N98, the Corniche Inférieure, to Villefranche. Bear right for St.-Jean-Cap-Ferrat.

1 Cap Ferrat

As with neighboring headlands to the east (Cap Martin) and west (Cap d'Antibes), Cap Ferrat has long been a sought-after residential address, with property values here reflecting the exclusiveness of the numerous mansions and villas tucked away in their well-screened gardens. One that is open to the public is the former home of the Baroness Béatrice Ephrussi de Rothschild, an imposing, Italianate-style villa built across the saddle of the headland. It is surrounded by magnificent (not to say eccentric) gardens. It took seven years in all to complete the villa, which was designed as a showcase for the Baroness' impressive collection of around 5,000 art treasures. In 1934 the villa together with its contents were bequeathed to the Académie des Beaux-Arts, and now form the Musée de France.

Return to Villefranche-sur-Mer and bear right on the D125, then follow signs through Beaulieu for Monaco.

2 Monaco

Arriving in Monaco through the modern suburb of Fontvieille, your first impressions will bear little resemblance to the legends of wealth and glamour surrounding this principality. Traffic can be a problem here. Follow the road around into avenue du Port and continue straight into the underground parking lot that is sited beneath "The Rock," as old Monaco is known.

Emerging in the old town, you'll get a much better idea of the layout of Monaco, with the harbor area (La Condamine) spread out beneath you; exquisite yachts flank the harbor walls. Beyond, the headland rises up into the district of Monte-Carlo, with sumptuous belle-époque hotels and the famous casino dominating the view.

Leave Monaco on the N98 as for Menton. In Roquebrune bear right for Cap Martin. Follow Menton signs to the shore road, then keep right along the seafront in the direction of Menton.

3 Menton

One of the oldest paleolithic relics in France, the skull of "Menton man," was discovered here in the 19th century, perhaps proving that our ancestors knew a good spot when they saw one – much like today's visitors. Menton's sunny, sheltered position makes it an enjoyable place to visit, with some charming Italianate buildings, several lush gardens, a casino and a splendid baroque church (St.-Michel). Olive, lemon and orange trees give the town a pleasantly exotic and park-like

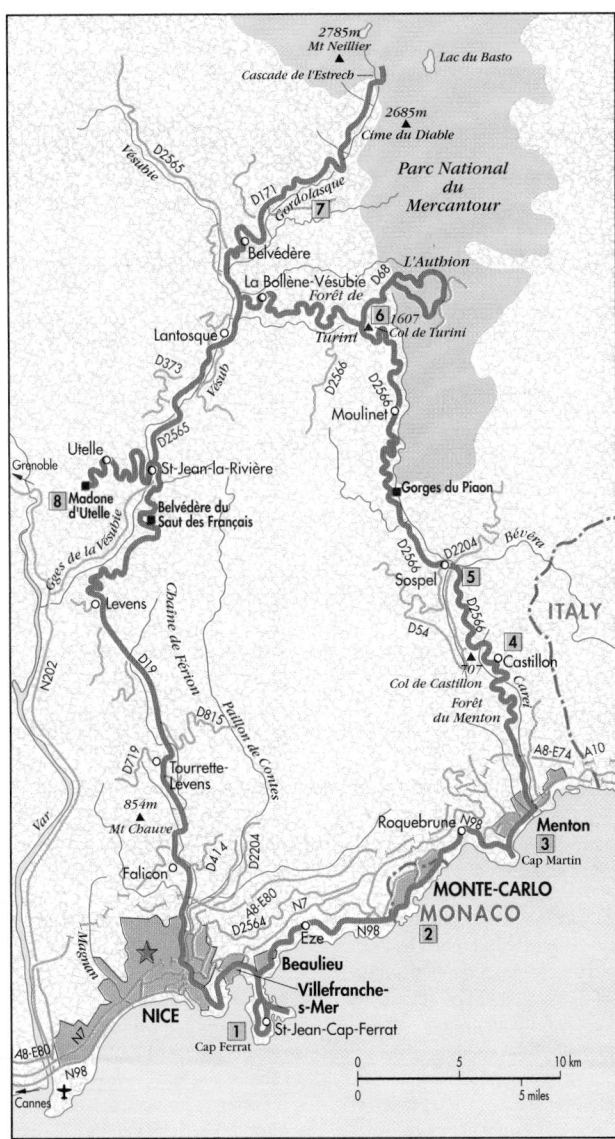

WRITERS IN PROVENCE

The allure of the sunny south has always attracted writers, poets, and painters to Provence.

Guy de Maupassant was one of the first to discover the charms of St.-Tropez (in the 1880s), and in the Roaring Twenties the Americans descended en masse, among them Ernest Hemingway and F. Scott Fitzgerald.

Menton became the favored place of Katherine Mansfield, and Colette and Anaïs Nin made St.-Tropez their home in the 1930s.

Graham Greene lived the last years of his life in Antibes, and Anthony Burgess was a resident of Monaco until his death in 1993.

Provence's home-grown authors include Frédéric Mistral (who won the Nobel Prize in 1904), Jean Giono, René Char and Marcel Pagnol ■

character. Housed in a 17th-century bastion between the town's two beaches is the Jean Cocteau Museum, which has a collection of the artist's paintings, drawings and stage sets.

Leave Menton on the D2566 as for Sospel. Look for the sharp right turn into Castillon.

4 Castillon

This interesting little place was destroyed by an earthquake in the 19th century, wrecked again during World War II, and has now been comprehensively rebuilt as a model Provençal village. From the town's minute square there is a beautiful view down the Carei Valley toward the glittering sea.

ALPINE ART

Sospel's fine collection of baroque buildings on the west bank surround the place St.-Michel, dominated by the vast Église St.-Michel.

Built in the 17th century, it incorporates a much older 12th-century belltower, but the interior is pure, sumptuous baroque, with elaborate cornices and gilded altarpieces.

The church also contains a magnificent altarpiece by François Bréa, one of the founders of the Nice School that flourished during the 14th and 15th centuries. At the time Nice belonged to Italy, and the northern Italian influence is evident in the many works which the Bréa family workshops produced at the time.

Paintings and altarpieces from the Nice School are scattered through the region in several churches and pilgrim chapels ∎

Turn right onto the D2566, bearing right on it to the Col de Castillon. Go through the tunnel and turn right in the direction of Sospel.

5 Sospel

For many centuries Sospel was an important crossroads on the old trading routes. The ancient tollgate still stands in the middle of the 11th-century bridge that joins the two halves of the town. On the east bank there is a fine collection of Italianate houses; on the west bank the old streets open out into a grandiose square, surrounded by baroque buildings.

Leave Sospel on the D2566 via Moulinet towards the Col de Turini.

6 Col de Turini

The highway follows the Bévéra river upstream, twisting and turning between high wooded bluffs that are at their most dramatic in the Gorges du Piaon.

At the intersection some 25 kilometers (15½ mi.) from Sospel, the small hamlet at the Col de Turini is surrounded by dense forests. Many of the trees here (such as maple and beech) are usually only found much farther north in Europe. Covering some 3,500 hectares (8,650 acres), the forest is refreshingly cool after the heat of the coast.

From the Col de Turini, an 18-kilometer (12-mi.) circuit takes you up to l'Authion, where pine and larch predominate, eventually giving way to alpine pastures. A war memorial beside the road commemorates the bitter struggle to oust the Germans in 1945, and at a height of 2,082 meters (6,830 ft.) there is a platform with breathtaking views over the peaks of the Parc National du Mercantour and the pre-Alps behind Nice.

Leave the Col de Turini on the D70 through La Bollène-Vésubie, where you make a sharp right following the sign for "St.-Martin." Go right on the D2565 as for St.-Martin Vésubie, then make a sharp right on the D71, follow signs to Belvédère and go right at the intersection for Gordolasque. This is the narrow D171. Follow it to a parking lot before the bridge where the public road comes to an end.

7 Vallon de la Gordolasque

This detour to the head of the valley follows the rushing torrent of the Gordolasque. It's worth stopping in Belvédère for a terrific view of the Vésubie valley and surrounding peaks. The road ends at the 1,700-meter (5,575-ft.) Pont du Countet, where the falls of the Cascade de l'Estrech drop down from a cirque surrounded by snow-clad peaks.

Return through Belvédère to the D2565 and turn left as for Nice. At St.-Jean-de-la-Rivière take the D32, the hairpin climb past Utelle. Go left on the D132 in the direction of Madonne d'Utelle.

8 Madonne d'Utelle

The hair-raising drive up to this isolated spot 1,174 meters (3,852 ft.) above sea level is well worth it, for once there you're confronted with an extraordinary 360-degree panorama of the Alps and the Riviera, with the coastline stretching away into the distance.

Return to St.-Jean-de-la-Rivière and turn right on the D2565. After a "Nice par Levens" sign, bear left on the D19 and follow the road back towards Nice.

ESTEREL, *171E2*
MASSIF DE L'

Bulging out along the coastline east of St.-Raphael, the Esterel Massif is one of the best-kept secrets on the Riviera. Most people drive right past or take the train along this craggy, rust-red coastline – which forms a dramatic contrast to the azure seas – without realizing that an unusual wilderness lies in the center of the mountains, a hidden world of deep red canyons and vividly colored rocks inhabited by wild boar and deer. Two of the most unusual ravines harbor flowers and plants unknown elsewhere in the Mediterranean, and are designated Biological Reserves. Both are easily reached along a network of paths (suitable for walking or mountain-biking) that criss-cross the whole area. In spring, the Esterel is a mass of wild flowers.

ÈZE *171F3*

Sited some 400 meters (1,300 ft.) above the sea, the ancient village of Èze clings to a rocky outcrop and draws visitors in their thousands to admire its tenacious, picturesque position overlooking the Mediterranean. It is the highest, and the most heavily visited, of the Provençal *villages perchés* (hilltop villages) and is awash with chic boutiques, galleries, and antique stores. Entering through the 14th-century gateway, make your way through the cobbled streets and old stone houses to a stunning panorama from the ruined château at the summit of the village.

FONTAINE-DE- *171C3*
VAUCLUSE

The limestone Vaucluse plateau is riddled with underground caverns and passages draining into the subterranean Sorgue river, which rises up from the depths and

disgorges a huge volume of water toward the spring for which this village is named. The *fontaine* is one of the most powerful resurgent springs in the world, and best seen in the winter when the flow is at its peak.

The poet Petrarch was much taken with this fascinating location, and there is now a small museum dedicated to him in the village. Along the 2-kilometer (1½-mi.) walk to the source itself there are also now a number of strangely disparate attractions, such as a museum of paper-making, a museum devoted to the subterranean world, a French Resistance museum, and a new museum displaying instruments of torture and death (exhibits include a genuine guillotine).

★ FONTFROIDE *170A2*

A delightful Cistercian abbey set amid luxuriant gardens, Fontfroide has been thoroughly restored to its former glory after it was destroyed and abandoned during the Revolution. It is less pure in style than other Cistercian monasteries in the region, but is nevertheless worth a detour from nearby Narbonne (see p.186).

FONTVIEILLE *170C2*

This little village happily thrives on its associations with the 19th-century novelist Alphonse Daudet, who is said to have been inspired to write "Lettres de Mon Moulin" ("Letters from My Windmill") by the ancient windmill that perches on a hillock just to the south of Fontvieille. Memorabilia of the author is housed in a small museum next to the windmill, and there is also an exhibition about his life in the nearby Château de Montauban.

★ FRÉJUS *171E2*

Just 3 kilometers (2 mi.) inland from the coast, Fréjus was

PROVENÇAL CUISINE

Olive oil, garlic, sun-drenched tomatoes, and aromatic herbs are some of the essentials of Provençal cuisine.

Fish and shellfish also feature. Bouillabaisse is a substantial dish that includes almost anything the fishermen may have brought to market. It is accompanied by a spicy red paste known as a *rouille*.

Lamb is usually grilled with savory herbs or stuffed *à la Provençale*.

***Aioli* is a thick garlic mayonnaise, often served with raw vegetables (*crudités*).**

***Salade niçoise* invariably contains tuna, tomatoes, black olives, anchovies and hard-boiled eggs.**

Local goat's cheeses are also worth trying, and as an aperitif, try some *pastis*, a potent, aniseed-flavored liqueur ∎

PERFUMES AND GRASSE

It takes over 8 million blossoms of jasmine or 900,000 rose buds to make just 1kg. (2.2 lb.) of perfume essence, the basis for creating the expensive scents for which France is renowned.

In the perfume factories of Grasse, the most important job is that of the head perfumer or *le nez* (the nose), as he or she is known. The perfumer's sensitive sense of smell makes a selection from around 3,000 different essences (around 300 of which may eventually be used) to create a fragrance – and this process may take many months.

There are only around 300 "noses" worldwide that are able to do this job, around 50 of whom work in the Grasse area ■

founded by the Romans and still has a few ruins from those days – most notably the arena (not as grand as others in Provence), a theater, and remnants of an aqueduct. But the real jewel is the medieval Cité Épiscopale, which includes a cathedral with a set of remarkable 16th-century carved walnut doors, a delightful cloister, and one of the oldest baptisteries in France.

Down on the coast the town's seaside suburb, Fréjus-Plage, has sandy beaches and is popular with families; nearby are a safari park and an aquatic theme park.

GIENS PENINSULA   171E1

This curious little peninsula juts out from the port of Hyères-Plage and is formed by two sandbars linking a wooded promontory to the mainland. From the village of Giens, boats depart for the offshore island of Porquerolles.

★★★ GORDES   170C3

Dominated by its 15th-century château, Gordes clings to a bluff on the edge of the Vaucluse plateau. The castle houses a permanent exhibition devoted to the works of the Hungarian geometric artist Victor Vasarely, and the cobbled streets of the village shelter a number of other artists' galleries and workshops.

Just outside Gordes is the peculiar Village des Bories, an unusual collection of drystone huts that is well worth visiting – though built in the 19th century, these are typical Mediterranean neolithic dwellings.

GOURDON   171E2

Another famous Provençal *village perché*, Gourdon sits high above the Loup river and has a stunning panorama down the coastline. At the heart of the village, the carefully restored 17th-century château contains a treasure trove

of armaments, 16th- and 17th-century furniture and art works in its Musée Historique, as well as a contemporary art collection. The château gardens were designed by Le Nôtre (of Versailles fame).

★★★ GRAND CANYON DU VERDON   171E2

Carved by the Verdon river out of the limestone plateau of Haute Provence, the Grand Canyon is one of the natural wonders of the region, a magnificent gorge rising 700 meters (2,230 ft.) above the emerald waters of the river.

You can drive most of its length between Castellane and Moustiers-Ste.-Marie, with fabulous views from the road on either side of the canyon – La Corniche Sublime is the route along the south bank, while La Route des Crêtes along the north bank links a series of stunning lookout points. Be warned, however, that in the summer months this classic excursion is also the goal of almost everyone who visits Provence, and the journey can be very slow. As an alternative, there are several walks down into the canyon and you can even rent a canoe or pedal-boat to explore the river where it disgorges into the Lac de Ste.-Croix.

Above the Lac de Ste.-Croix, Moustiers-Ste.-Maries is a pretty town that specializes in faience (glazed ceramics), but again the crowds can be insufferable during the high season.

★ GRASSE   171E2

Dubbed the "perfume capital of France," Grasse is surrounded by cultivated fields of lavender, jasmine, mimosa, roses, and other blossoms essential for the creation of the potent essences that form the basis of perfume. A tour of the famous factories here offers an intriguing insight into both old and new methods of creating perfume essences; the Fragonard *parfumerie* also has a superb museum with hundreds of antique *flacons* (perfume jars) from ancient times onwards.

Perhaps the most famous of Grasse's sons was Jean-Honoré Fragonard, the 18th-century painter who wittily depicted the frivolous gaity of court life. The Fragonard Villa-Museum contains a collection of his paintings.

Grasse's *vieille ville* (old town) is also worth a visit, particularly the place aux Aires; there's a colorful market every morning in this lovely old square, which is surrounded by 18th-century arcades and mansions.

GRIMAUD   171E2
Named after the Grimaldi family who owned it from the 10th century onwards, Grimaud is an attractive *village perché* with a Romanesque church, a ruined château, and lovely views over the Massif des Maures and the St.-Tropez gulf. In the bay, Port Grimaud is a purpose-built resort with canals for roads. It's worth a short visit, but very expensive.

HYÈRES   171E2
One of the first resorts on the Riviera, Hyères is now a major horticultural center and well known for its palm tree nurseries – the town has been rechristened Hyères-les-Palmiers. Surrounding the old town are several gardens that can be visited. The yacht marina at Port d'Hyères is a huge complex 4 kilometers (2½ mi.) away from town.

Offshore, the three Iles d'Hyères are renowned for their wild natural landscapes, spring flowers, and migrating birds; Porquerolles is the most popular, with cycling and walking tracks.

The Grand Canyon du Verdon is one of Europe's most dramatic gorges, extending some 26 kilometers (over 16 mi.). Two roads that follow the north and south banks of the gorge offer spectacular views

In a picturesque setting between mountains and sea, Menton's natural attraction lies in the warmth of its climate. An abundance of lush vegetation adds to its exotic aura

JUAN-LES-PINS   *171F2*

Juan-les-Pins was one of the first Riviera resorts to launch a summer season (up until the 1930s the coast was still a winter vacation destination); its success was boosted by the arrival of a coterie of well-known jazz musicians, giving rise to the International Jazz Festival, which still takes place in July each year. The nightlife here is legendary, so if you're planning on staying choose your hotel with care (soundproofing might help); the sandy beach is one of the best along this part of the coast.

★ LUBERON   *171D2*

On the southernmost edge of the *département* of Vaucluse, the Luberon became the "in" place during the 1980s. Most of this area is part of the Parc Régional du Luberon, and there are still many unspoiled villages and hidden wilderness areas here. The unofficial capital of the Luberon is Apt, a pretty town on the banks of the Calavon river.

★ MARSEILLE   *170D2*

Although it has none of the glamor of the Riviera resorts, Marseille is an intriguing city with a cosmopolitan atmosphere and a lively arts scene. Its reputation for crime and corruption may precede it, but in this respect Marseille is no better or worse than any other big city for the casual visitor.

The heart of the city is the old port, where fishing boats and yachts rub shoulders, and tourist boats set off for the Château d'If, the notorious island prison that Alexandre Dumas used as the setting for his novel, "The Count of Monte Cristo." From the port, the broad boulevard of La Canebière runs through the city center, with the art-deco Opera House off to one side. Of several museums in this area, the best are the Musée d'Histoire and the Musée Cantini.

A steep climb (or bus ride) up the hill above the city leads to the church of Notre-Dame de la Garde, with views over Marseille.

MAURES, MASSIF DES 171E2

This densely wooded, hilly region covers the hinterland behind Hyères and Fréjus. In the Dark Ages it was a notorious hide-out for Saracen raiders, who built forts on the hilltops and terrorized the surrounding countryside. It's an excellent area for touring, with several peaceful towns (such as Collobrières and La Garde-Freinet) tucked away amid the chestnut, oak, and pine forests; the most scenic drive is the 71-kilometer (44-mi.) Route des Crêtes.

MENTON 171F3

Protected by the mountains behind it, Menton has an unusually benign climate, with more than the average dose of annual sunshine.

In the 19th century artists and writers (such as Katherine Mansfield and Aubrey Beardsley) settled in Menton in the hopes that the weather would improve their health, a trend continued today by the many *retraités* (retired people) who live here. Don't let this mislead you into thinking Menton has little to offer; it is full of character and has a lively program of festivals (such as the Fête du Citron, the Chamber Music Festival, and a biennial art exhibition). It also has a good beach in front of the recently redeveloped seafront promenade.

★★ MONACO and 171F3 MONTE-CARLO

The tiny principality of Monaco, covering just 2 square kilometers (less than 1 sq. mi.), has been an independent state since the 14th century and has been ruled by the Grimaldi dynasty and their descendants ever since.

Squeezed between the mountains and the sea, Monaco has had to expand upward (hence the numerous skyscrapers) and outward, reclaiming more and more land along the shoreline. The old town, Monaco-Ville, sits atop a promontory to the west; here you can watch the changing of the guard outside Prince Rainier's palace, visit the tomb of Princess Grace (Grace Kelly) in the cathedral, and marvel at the strange species housed in the excellent Oceanographic Museum (one of France's most popular tourist attractions). There's an exuberant carnival in the old town each September.

Monte-Carlo is the name given to the district on the headland across the main harbor from the old town, with pride of place going to the famous *belle-époque* casino; around it there are many classic luxury hotels as well as the equally well-known Café de Paris, from where you can watch the action in the square outside the casino. Half the fun of Monte-Carlo is simply wandering around, trying to spot celebrities or eyeing the yachts in the harbor. The Grand Prix takes place in May.

THE MONTE-CARLO CASINO

Monte-Carlo's ornate casino was built to attract a wealthy clientele vacationing in the South of France, but word soon spread of fortunes to be won, and professional gamblers such as Charles Deville Wells soon began to arrive. Wells turned his initial $400 stake into $40,000 in a 3-day spree at the tables in 1891. Others, not so lucky, threw themselves off the cliffs behind the casino.

The American Room and the Pink Salon Bar are worth a look for their extravagant decor, but the real action takes place under the gilded chandeliers of the European Gaming Room

You must be over 21 and have a passport or other identification to visit the casino ■

WALK

GROTTE STE.-MARIE-MADELEINE

This shrine to Mary Magdalene is high up in the Ste.-Baume Massif behind Marseilles.

Start in the parking lot near the Hôtellerie de la Sainte-Baume, where a track leads up to the chemin des Rois, an ancient royal path. A series of oratories lines the gently sloping track that leads to the carrefour de l'Oratoire, beyond which there are 160 steps up to the top. Legend claims that Mary Magdalene spent the last years of her life in this cavernous grotto, now walled in as a chapel.

Back at the crossroads, turn left and descend down a series of stone steps through an ancient forest of ash, beech, holly and yew trees ■

MONTMAJOUR, ABBAYE DE
170C2

This wonderful old monastery, just 5 kilometers (3 mi.) outside Arles, was once one of the most powerful in Provence. Today most of it lies in ruins, but it is still an evocative place to visit. The 12th-century Upper Church is notable for the breathtaking purity of its structure; the attractive cloisters, richly decorated with detailed carvings, are a marvel of medieval sculpture. From the top of the mighty keep there are splendid panoramic views across the surrounding countryside.

★ MONTPELLIER
170B2

France's eighth-largest city, Montpellier is a lively place with a large student population as well as some of the south's most inspired modern architecture. Montpellier derived its fortunes from the spice trade in medieval times, with access to the sea via the Lez river. The first medical school in Europe was founded here in the 12th century, which achieved the status of university in 1289. Today, the focus is on industries such as computing, pharmaceuticals, and agronomy.

The heart of the city is the place de la Comédie, surrounded by busy cafés and somber 19th-century buildings; on the east side, the steel and glass Polygone building (housing stores and the *mairie* – town hall) leads through to Montpellier's boldest project, the Antigone housing scheme, surrounding a monumental plaza.

Walk north from the place de la Comédie and you'll come to another futuristic building, Le Corum, built for conventions. Head west, and the promenade du Peyrou leads up to a superb vista over the city. The Musée Fabre is worth a visit for its fine collection of old masters and 19th-century art.

MONT VENTOUX
170D3

Dominating the Rhône Valley and the Vaucluse plateau, Mont Ventoux is the highest peak between the Alps and the Pyrénées; "Ventoux" derives from the Provençal *ventour*, meaning windy – a designation you will readily appreciate once you get to the summit, where winds of 230 kph (143 mph) have been recorded. On weekends dozens of cyclists test their mettle on the long climb up, no doubt even more appreciative of the fabulous views once they get to the top. Parts of the mountain are a designated Biosphere Reserve, with unusual flora and several rare bird species.

MOUGINS
171E2

This immaculately restored medieval village in the hills behind Cannes is a popular dining spot, thanks to the presence of Roger Vergé, one of France's most famous chefs, who owns two restaurants here. Even if you haven't come to eat, it's a delightful place to wander around, admiring the old houses. There's a photographic museum, and art exhibitions in the summer.

NARBONNE and THE LANGUEDOC/ROUSSILLON COAST
170A2

Surrounded by the productive vineyards of the Languedoc region, Narbonne is an agreeable and prosperous town with a long history, several interesting monuments, a superb market (on Thursdays), and a city center filled with parks and greenery.

Narbonne's greatest curiosity is the unfinished cathedral of St.-Just, which was started in the 13th century but left half-finished in the 14th century because of a legal dispute; what remains, however, is a masterpiece of High Gothic design. Nearby is an excellent museum, the Musée d'Art et d'Histoire (with a mostly 17th-century collection), and the equally fascinating Musée Archéologique (which has Greek and Roman remains).

On both sides of Narbonne, the Languedoc-Roussillon coast is a patchwork of lagoons, sandy beaches, and marshes, with a few old fishing villages and several purpose-built resorts such as Narbonne-Plage, La Grande Motte, and Le Cap d'Agde.

(so named because it was funded by the English aristocracy who vacationed here in the 1820s), which runs right around the bay behind the pebbly beach. A few *belle-époque* buildings (such as the Hôtel Negresco) still grace the seafront, while others surround the place Masséna at the eastern end.

Behind place Masséna is the *vieille ville*, a fascinating area that has been redeveloped, although it has managed to retain much of

★★★ NICE 171F2

It may not be as flashy as Cannes or St.-Tropez, but Nice can hold its own in terms of sightseeing attractions, museums, shopping, dining, festivals, and sheer entertainment value. It's a characterful place with all the dynamism of a big city (in fact, Nice is the fifth-largest city in France), enhanced by its location on the wide, sparkling Baie des Anges – the Bay of Angels.

One of the best starting points for exploring Nice is the well-known Promenade des Anglais

its original character. Nice's lively daily market takes place on the cours Saleya, which lies between the old town and the sea. There are also several superb seafood restaurants along here.

Leading north from place Masséna, the broad Promenade du Paillon has become the city's civic showcase, lined with prominent new buildings such as the Museum of Modern and Contemporary Art (MAMAC) and the Acropolis convention center.

Art lovers will find plenty to fill their time in Nice, with numerous

The palm-fringed Promenade des Anglais is an excellent place to begin a stroll around Nice. Graceful buildings line the seafront, and the old part of the city below the castle hill has a lively air

PROVENCE AND THE CÔTE D'AZUR

WALK

PERPIGNAN

This short walk explores the heart of the capital of Roussillon, French Catalonia.

From place Arago, named for the astronomer François Arago (born locally in 1786), follow the street above the banks of the Basse river to Le Castillet – the last remains of the city's medieval walls. Turn right on a pedestrian-only zone to place de la Loge. To the right, the Loge de Mer was built in 1397 (now a fast-food outlet).

Turn left along rue St.-Jean to the cathedral, famed for its gilded wooden crucifix, Dévot Christ. Then return to place de la Loge to reach place Jean Jaurès. Turn left along rue Mailly, then right along rue de l'Ange to return to place Arago ∎

excellent galleries and museums including MAMAC, the Musée des Beaux-Arts Jules Chéret, several galleries devoted to individual artists (such as Raoul Dufy and Gustav-Adolf Mossa), not to mention the superlative collections held in the Chagall Museum and the Matisse Museum. These latter two are to the north of the city center in the chic suburb of Cimiez.

Nice's boisterous Mardi Gras carnival is still going strong, an event that exemplifies the warm-heartedness and high spirits of this attractive city.

★★★ NÎMES   170C3

Like Arles, its neighbor to the east, Nîmes was an important Gallo-Roman city and has retained some magnificent monuments from this era. In the 19th century it had a thriving textile industry and developed a hard-wearing blue serge that eventually became known as denim ("de Nîmes"). Languishing for much of the 20th century, it has now been re-invigorated with an imaginative program of bold contemporary architecture. It's an enjoyable city to visit, with fountains, lotus-shaded boulevards, quiet old backstreets, fashionable stores and a lively arts scene.

The most prominent Roman monument is the remarkable Arènes, built in the reign of Augustus in the 1st century AD and one of the best-preserved amphitheaters in Europe. The tiers of seats are divided into four sections to reflect the social status of the spectators, who could number anything up to 20,000; bullfights are held here in the summer months, when the amphitheater is frequently filled to capacity. Nîmes' other major landmark is the delightful Maison Carrée, a temple dating from the same period. Facing it on the

place du Forum is the Carré d'Art, housing a library and the Museum of Contemporary Art.

Also unmissable is the lovely Jardins de la Fontaine, a classic 18th-century garden on a hillside near the city center – this was France's first public garden.

★★★ ORANGE   170C3

The first major town heading down into Provence, Orange has been known as the gateway to the south since the Romans built their massive Arc de Triomphe on the old road (Via Agrippa) through the Rhône Valley in 20 BC. Traffic on the N7 still thunders past this impressive monument, with its three arches, unusual double attic, and well-preserved reliefs depicting Roman victories over their Gallic enemies.

The town center of Orange has been mostly pedestrianized, creating a peaceful environment with many pleasant, tree-lined squares and busy sidewalk cafés. Orange is principally a market town, but tourism has been a regular fixture since the 19th century thanks to the Arc de Triomphe and the superb Théâtre Antique, which has a massive, 36-meter (118-ft.) stage wall that is embellished with statues, mosaics, and columns. It is still in use today for festivals and concerts in the summer months.

PERPIGNAN   170A1

Despite being the unofficial capital of French Catalonia, Perpignan is a somewhat soul-less place that attracts little admiration – one can't fail to note that its most beautiful building, the Gothic Loge de Mer (a 14th-century trading house), has been turned into a burger café. The city is also the proud possessor of the oldest royal palace in France, the Palais des Rois de Majorque, which dates from the

13th century and was the seat of the little Kingdom of Majorca and Roussillon, created by the house of Aragon. Perpignan also has an unusual Gothic cathedral, finished in 1509, with an old ghetto area, the Quartier St.-Jacques, nearby.

PÉZENAS   *170B2*

Set in the middle of the rolling plains of the Hérault, Pézenas prospered in the Middle Ages as the seat of the États du Languedoc. The nobility and clerics who were based at the court constructed a host of fine buildings and churches, many of which still survive – the tourist office provides detailed information on walking tours around the 70 or so listed historical buildings in the old town center. Of particular note are the *hôtels particuliers* (private mansions) built in a style distinctive to Pézenas; the Hôtel Lacoste and Hôtel d'Alfonce are particularly fine examples.

The town's elegant streets are often used for historical movie sets, and the spirit of the "Golden Age" is maintained in a program of concerts, festivals, and exhibitions that carries on through most of the summer months.

★★★ PONT DU GARD   *170C3*

This majestic Roman aqueduct has long been considered one of the "Wonders of the Ancient World," an extraordinary engineering achievement that was part of a system bringing water to Nîmes from a source near Uzès, 10 kilometers (6 mi.) away. Built from masonry bricks weighing up to 6 tonnes each, its three tiers of arches span the Gard river, reaching a height of some 48 meters (157 ft.) above the river: you can now walk (but carefully!) along the top.

STE.-MAXIME   *171E2*

This sedate family resort lies across the Gulf of St.-Tropez from its better-known neighbor, and in front of the palm trees and casino on the promenade it has a sandy beach with plenty of watersports. The medieval Tour Carrée on the seafront has a local museum, but there's little else to see aside from the daily market.

Pont du Gard is one of antiquity's wonders, built in around AD 50. It formed part of a system that was 49 kilometers (30 mi.) in overall length, supplying the Roman city of Nîmes with its daily fresh water requirements

VAN GOGH IN ST.-RÉMY

Van Gogh arrived in Arles in 1888, and although at first he didn't like the city, he was captivated by the quality of light and the beautiful landscapes of Provence, and implored his Impressionist friends to come down from Paris and join him.

Paul Gauguin arrived, but decided he preferred Paris: humiliated, van Gogh threatened him with an open razor and then later cut off his own ear, which he gave to a prostitute. The artist finally admitted himself as a patient to the sanatorium of St.-Paul-de-Mausole in St.-Rémy, where he painted some of his most remarkable works ∎

ST.-PAUL   171F2

This overcrowded *village perché* is heaving with art galleries, boutiques, and bistros. A museum housed in a 12th-century keep next to the town hall displays scores of photographs of the celebrities who have graced St.-Paul with their presence, owing to the fame of a local restaurant, the Colombe d'Or, which was a favorite with artists such as Picasso, Matisse, Signac, and Bonnard in the 1920s; the owner wisely accepted paintings in lieu of payment for their checks, which means you can now dine here surrounded by priceless artworks. Just outside the village there is an exceptional collection of modern art and sculpture at Fondation Maeght, a purpose-built multimedia center that includes works by many of the most important and influential artists of the last 50 years.

ST.-RAPHAËL   171E2

Although it once played host to luminaries such as Guy de Maupassant, Hector Berlioz, and Alexandre Dumas, St.-Raphaël nowadays has no great cachet; despite that, it is a pleasant enough resort with a long, sandy beach. Behind the seafront there are some unusual 19th-century buildings (most notably the Byzantine cathedral and the Winter Palace hotel), and an interesting Romanesque church, the Église St.-Pierre.

★★★ ST.-RÉMY-DE-PROVENCE   170C2

Sheltering beneath the northern flanks of the Alpilles, St.-Rémy is one of the most characterful towns in Provence and makes an ideal base for touring the surrounding region. It has all the most delightful aspects of a traditional Provençal town – leafy, sun-dappled squares with cooling fountains, an excellent market, good restaurants and food stores – and yet it has remained relatively unaffected by the advent of tourism.

Within the town center there are many splendid mansions, such as the Hôtel Mistral de Mondragon (which now houses the Musée des Alpilles) and the Hôtel de Sade (where you'll find the archeological museum); another houses Le Centre d'Art Présence Van Gogh, which has contemporary art exhibitions and audiovisual displays on the life of the painter. After cutting off his ear, Van Gogh came to St.-Rémy to convalesce, staying at the asylum in the monastery of St.-Paul-de-Mausole outside of town.

Within walking distance of the town center are the excavated remains of the Greco-Roman town of Glanum, which include temples, houses, baths, a forum, and a sacred well. Opposite Glanum are an unusual commemorative arch and mausoleum, known simply as Les Antiques, which date from around 30 BC.

★★ ST.-TROPEZ   171E2

No trip to the Riviera is complete without a visit to St.-Tropez, this small port with a big reputation whose name has become a byword for fashionable opulence, hedonism, and the jet-set lifestyle. Unfortunately, on some days it seems like everybody on the coast has decided to visit at the same time – the traffic jams can be appalling.

Of course, if you arrive by speedboat or yacht you can moor up in the old port and be at the heart of the action right away. St.-Tropez's teeming port is a high-priced parade, a non-stop show, with everyone trying to spot celebrities in trendy dockside bars such as Le Gorille and Sénéquier.

It wasn't always like this, of course: St.-Tropez was a fishing village turned artists' colony until the arrival of Brigitte Bardot in the 1950s, and many of the best works of the fauvists and post-Impressionists who lived here are on display in the excellent Musée de l'Annonciade on the north side of the port. It is also worth the effort of climbing up to the old Citadel above the harbor. From here there are wonderful views over the rooftops of the town and beyond, to the Gulf of St.-Tropez and Ste.-Maxime.

St.-Tropez's beaches are around the headland from the town, spread around the broad Baie de Pampelonne. The first bamboo-and-thatch beach huts were built here in South Pacific style in the 1950s; the classy concessions that line the bay still bear names such as Tahiti-Plage and Bora Bora.

SÉNANQUE, ABBAYE DE   *170D3*

Sheltered in a peaceful, lavender-scented valley 4 kilometers (2½ mi.) outside Gordes, this beautiful 12th-century abbey is one of three Cistercian monasteries located in Provence.

These serene stone buildings echo the simplicity and purity of the Cistercian creed, and several monks have now moved back in to create a community here. There is a superb cloister and a lovely, weathered church.

The abbey at Sénanque was founded in 1148, and rejoices in a tranquil setting on the edge of the Vaucluse plateau. Its simple stone buildings create an atmosphere conducive to a life of contemplation

Rocher de Baume, Sisteron. The limestone beds of the Durance Valley were folded and shaped in the Quaternary period to create this dramatic glacial bar. The town itself is the northern limit of olive cultivation in Provence

SISTERON   *171D3*

Guarding the gateway to northern Provence, Sisteron's advantages as a strategic site are evident – the Durance Valley narrows down to less than a kilometer (½ mi.) wide at this point, with steep mountain slopes rising up on either side of the river. The ancient citadel still dominates the town (although much of it was damaged by Allied bombing in 1944); its walkways and defenses are well worth exploring.

Back down in the town, the central plaza is dominated by three 14th-century towers and the cathedral, and there are numerous shops, boutiques, and cafés that spread outwards into the surrounding streets and alleyways. The old town (*vieille ville*) is a pleasant maze of old houses and narrow passageways leading through to the place de l'Horloge, which is the setting for a colorful local produce market held here twice a week.

TARASCON 170C3

The Good King René spent his last years living in his fabulous castle at Tarascon, directly overlooking the Rhône river, with troubadours (medieval minstrels) and artists in attendance. The castle is one of the finest fortified medieval buildings in France, its sheer crenellated walls seemingly at odds with its fairy-tale interior – particularly the royal apartments, with their graceful balconies (from which the troubadours sang) and spiral staircases overlooking the cour d'honneur.

Tarascon was also home to the fictional buffoon Tartarin, created in the 1870s by the novelist Alphonse Daudet (who was also associated with the Provençal village of Fontvieille; see p.182). His exploits are remembered in the so-called Maison de Tartarin near the city center.

TOULON 171D2

Often dismissed as no more than a seedy port, Toulon is not the sort of place you'd choose for a vacation, but it's certainly worth a visit if you're staying nearby. As France's main Mediterranean naval port it has a long history, and naval enthusiasts will find much to interest them; many visitors will also enjoy a trip round the harbor to see the warships, submarines, and aircraft carriers of the Mediterranean fleet.

The town center, once a warren of dingy backstreets, has been redeveloped and is now a pedestrianized area with pleasant gardens, fountains, and little shops and restaurants. There are also several museums, the best of which is the Musée de Toulon, with an extensive contemporary collection as well as many works dating from the 17th century.

Rising up above the town and harbor, the summit of Mont Faron can be reached via a hair-raising drive or (far easier) by cable car; 542 meters (1,778 ft.) high, it has stupendous views as well as a museum dedicated to the Allied landings in the South of France at the end of World War II.

LA TURBIE 171F3

The unmistakable profile of the Trophée des Alpes rises up above this village on the flanks of the Maritime Alps, a colossus built by the Romans to celebrate their eventual victory over the Alpine tribes in 6 BC. An inscription on its base lists all 44 tribes conquered by Augustus: vandalized and quarried for stone over the centuries, the Trophy still stands 35 meters (115 ft.) high and is visible far out to sea. There's a small museum in the grounds, detailing its restoration.

La Turbie also has a baroque church that contains works from the schools of Brea, Raphael, Veronese, and Ribera.

★★ VAISON-LA-ROMAINE 170C3

This attractive town straddles the Ouvèze river, its two halves connected by a Roman bridge. There is always plenty to occupy the visitor in Vaison, whether it be indulging in a gourmet food festival, exploring the delightful vieille ville, shopping for arts and crafts, or dining out in one of the town's many fine restaurants.

Two of the most important areas of this once-thriving Roman town have been excavated. The quartier de Puymin includes the remains of several grand houses, walkways, and a theater (still used for summer performances); a small museum contains some fine statues. On the other side of the main street, the quartier de la Villasse has several more opulent villas with mosaics and formal gardens, Roman baths, and an arcaded shopping district.

OLIVES

Every market in Provence will have a special stall devoted to olives, with almost as many different varieties available as there are days in the month.

Introduced by the Greeks, the hardy olive thrives in the baking heat of the Provençal summer. A mature tree can yield up to 30 kg (66 lb.) of oil, and will carry on producing for up to 30 years. The harvest starts in November, and lasts in some areas through January. The old methods, whereby friends and family gathered up the olives as they were shaken loose from the tree, have largely been mechanized, but those with one or two trees in their garden can take their produce along to a nearby moulin à huile (olive mill) for processing into oil ■

PROVENCE AND THE CÔTE D'AZUR

FOLK TRADITIONS

Provence is rich in folk traditions, particularly the many different local festivals that take place in the summer months.

If you chance upon one of these you're likely to see women in traditional costume of black skirt and blouse overlaid with delicate lace embroidery, and the men in their velvet waistcoats, string ties, and black felt hats.

Young men and women perform the *farandole*, an ancient dance accompanied by the *tambourin* (a small drum) and *gaboulet* (flute).

The making of small figurines (*santons*, or "little saints") dates back to the 18th century: they are fashioned out of clay or wood, and their costumes from typically colorful Provençal fabrics ∎

In the old town, the cobbled streets lead up through the carefully restored houses to the ruins of an old château, from where there are fine views across the town and Mont Ventoux.

Vaison is also a convenient base for touring the vineyards and villages of the nearby Dentelles de Montmirail. You can make an interesting round-trip via Crestet, Malaucène, Le Barroux (where there is a partially restored 12th-century château), and on to famous wine villages such as Beaumes-de-Venise and Gigondas. This route completely circumnavigates the jagged peaks of the Dentelles, and if you branch off above Gigondas there's a walking trail that leads up to the heart of Col du Cayron at the center of these unusual limestone formations.

VALLAURIS 171F2

Picasso came here in the 1940s and quickly took to working in clay at a friend's pottery workshop. He stayed for 10 years, in the process re-invigorating a local trade that had existed as long ago as the Middle Ages. The town is now full of pottery and ceramic shops of all kinds, with some of Picasso's originals on view in the Municipal Museum inside a Renaissance château in the town center. Nearby, a deconsecrated chapel was decorated by Picasso in 1952 with his seminal work, "La Guerre et La Paix."

VENCE 171F2

Just 10 kilometers (6 mi.) inland from Nice, Vence is a lively place with a handsome *vieille ville*. Although it has always been a fashionable retreat for the well-to-do, it still gives the impression of being a typical Provençal town.

Most people, however, come here to see one of Matisse's most famous works, the interior of the Chapelle du Rosaire. Henri Matisse came here from Nice in 1941 to recover from a serious illness and was nursed back to health by Dominican nuns: although not religious himself, as a mark of gratitude he designed a new interior for this little chapel. Aged 80 when the work was completed, he achieved what is now considered to be one of his masterpieces: the simple, white-tiled walls of the chapel are covered in stark, black-and-white murals – the only color is supplied by light streaming in through the stained-glass windows.

The chapel is just outside the main town center, but it's worth taking the time to look around the old backstreets. There's a 450-year-old ash tree in the place du Frêne, opposite the Château de Villeneuve, and from here you can wander down the little rue du Marché (where tempting aromas waft across from food shops on either side) to the town's heart in the place du Peyra. On one side of the square, the Romanesque cathedral has a mosaic by Marc Chagall, and carved Gothic choir stalls from the 15th century.

VILLEFRANCHE 171F2

Just east of Nice, Villefranche is famed for its seafood restaurants, which line the quayfront with views over its scenic harbor and Cap Ferrat beyond. It's a superb place for a languid lunch, but Villefranche does have more to offer. Just behind the quay, steep steps lead up through the old town where there is an unusual vaulted passageway, the rue Obscure, little altered since it was built in the 13th century. There's an impressive citadel and a few museums, but the best surprise is the marvelous Chapelle St.-Pierre, decorated in 1957 by the artist Jean Cocteau in homage to the fisherfolk of Villefranche.

THE
MASSIF
CENTRAL

**For the adventurous traveler, much
of the Massif Central is a wilderness
just waiting to be discovered**

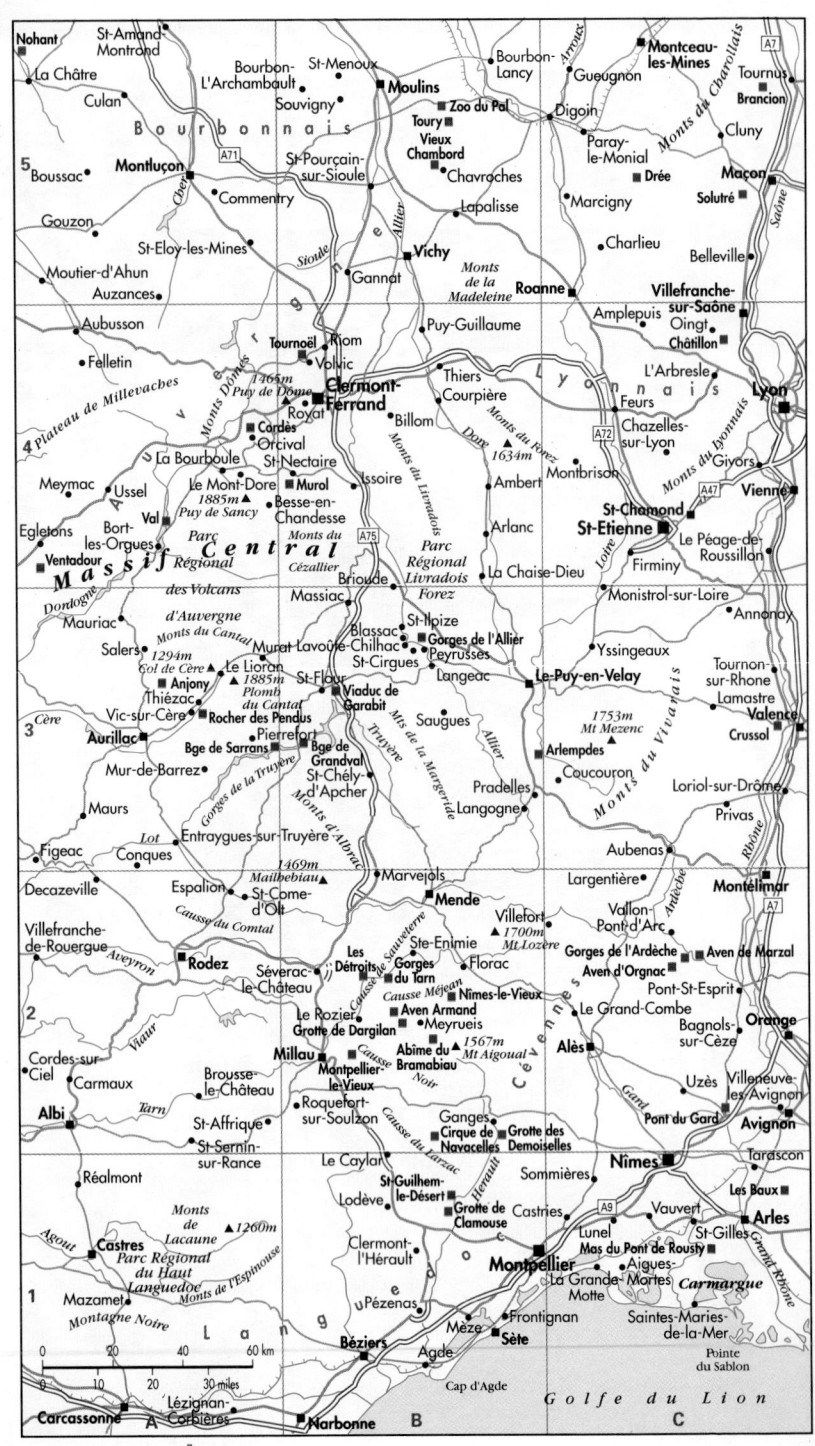

THE MASSIF CENTRAL

The Massif Central is a land-locked, mountainous region that rises up between the Alps and the Pyrénées and covers an astonishing one-sixth of the land area of France – astonishing, because for such a large area it is very little known, despite the diversity of attractions and the compelling landscapes it has to offer. For the visitor this is all to the good, and even though you may be limited in your choice of accommodations this is more than made up for by the wild scenery, the absence of mass tourism and industry, and a rural culture firmly rooted in the past.

At the heart of the Massif Central, the **Auvergne** is one of the better known areas, with its busy capital Clermont-Ferrand providing a convenient base from which to tour the surrounding unspoiled countryside. Much of the Auvergne is part of the Parc Naturel Régional des Volcans d'Auvergne, France's largest regional park, which is scattered with extinct volcanic cones (known as *puys*) and explosion craters filled with water. Streams and waterfalls tumble down along forested or grass-covered slopes into the lush valleys below, and lakes reflect the eroded peaks.

The variety of terrain makes this superb hiking country, and there are hundreds of kilometers of signposted footpaths for either day hikes or long-distance walking. Horse riding and, in winter, cross-country skiing are also popular. Barrages across rivers have created scenic lakes ideal for sailing and windsurfing, and the fishing is wonderful.

Tranquil villages and country *auberges* are also on the itinerary, enlivened by ruined strongholds and lovely old Romanesque churches. Mineral springs bubble up everywhere, giving rise to a number of spa towns (the best known of which is **Vichy**).

Farther south, vast upland plateaux (known as *causses*) are sliced through by rivers and riddled with some of the world's most extensive underground cave systems, and on the untamed streams canoeists can test their skills through spectacular gorges.

Some of these **gorges** are also drivable – notably the famous Gorges du Tarn – and there are superb walks above the canyons and valleys. However you see it, this virtually untouched region will not fail to affect you by its natural beauty.

★★★ HIGHLIGHTS

Les Causses (▶200)
Clermont-Ferrand (▶201)
Gorges de l'Ardèche (▶202)
Gorges du Tarn (▶202)
Monts du Cantal (▶207)
Le Puy/Parc Naturel Régional des Volcans d'Auvergne (▶208)
Vichy (▶210)

CALENDAR OF EVENTS

MAY – Clermont-Ferrand (Puy de Dôme) sees the **Festival of Notre-Dame du Port**.

JULY – Violet Fair at Ste.-Eulalie (Ardèche).

JULY TO SEPTEMBER – Vichy (Allier) plays host to the **Folk Festival**.

AUGUST – Clermont-Ferrand (Puy de Dôme) hosts a **Country Dance Festival** (*Bourrée*). ■

St.-Guilhem-le-Désert dates from the 9th century, when an abbey was founded here by Guilhem of Aquitaine. Its abbey church claims a relic of the True Cross

Inside Château d'Anjony are several art treasures that make a visit more than worthwhile. Its collection of period furniture, tapestries and portrait paintings is exceptional

★ ANJONY, CHÂTEAU D' 196A3

One of the most unusual châteaux in the Auvergne, Anjony overlooks the valley of the Dore and has been inhabited by the same family since it was built by Louis II d'Anjony (who fought alongside Joan of Arc) in 1449. The château is a strange-looking place, with a large central section surrounded by four tall, round towers, but it is well worth visiting for the many art treasures that have been acquired by the Anjony family over the centuries. The chapel (situated inside one of the towers) is decorated with fine 16th-century frescoes, while the other rooms contain wonderful period furniture, paintings, tapestries (including one from Aubusson) and other objets d'art.

AURILLAC 196A3

Lying at the foot of the mountains, Aurillac makes an excellent base for touring the Auvergne. The older part of town, with its narrow streets and historic houses, is on the west bank of the Jordanne river alongside the Pont Rouge – so called because there was once a red-painted wooden bridge here. There are some fine old houses in the vicinity, notably the Maison Consulaire (rue de la Coste), the Maison Noailles (5 rue de Noailles), and the Maison Meynard (rue Vermenouze).

Just next to the bridge, place Gerbert is named for Aurillac's most famous citizen, who became Pope Sylvester II in 999. There is a statue of him in the

square. Originally a shepherd boy, Gerbert was educated by local monks and then sent to Cordoba University, where he undertook the study of medicine and mathematics; he's credited with having invented the astrolabe, made the first clock using weights, and introduced Arab numerals to the European world. He eventually became the first French pope.

Aurillac has a surprising number of museums. The most interesting of these is the Maison des Volcans: housed in one wing of the Château St.-Étienne, it has numerous displays and films about volcanoes worldwide, as well as those of the surrounding region. There's also an art museum (Musée Hippolyte-de-Parieu), an archeological museum (Musée Jean-Baptiste Rames), and two museums of local ethnography (Musée de Cire, Musée du Vieil Aurillac).

Aurillac also has one or two fine old churches, principally the Église St.-Géraud (originally part of a Benedictine abbey founded in 916) and the Église Notre-Dame-aux-Neiges. Worth looking out for on Wednesdays and Saturdays is a wonderful market.

BESSE-EN-CHANDESSE 196A4
The picturesque hilltop town of Besse was fortified in the Middle Ages and most of it (including the town gate, church, and prison tower) was built from black lava. Some of the finer houses are along rue de la Boucherie, and the church is worth visiting for its medieval choir stalls.

Today Besse is a popular year-round mountain resort. To the southwest, Lac Pavin is one of the region's most attractive crater lakes: surrounded by dense pine forests, the lake forms an almost perfect circle and has a depth of some 90 meters (295 ft.).

Within reach of Besse there are several other pretty volcanic lakes, most notably the Lac du Chauvet, Lac de Montcineyre, and the Lac de Bourdouze.

★ BORT-LES-ORGUES 196A4
This small town on the banks of the Dordogne derives its name from the curious crystalline formation of the nearby cliffs, known as les Orgues ("the organ pipes"), which rise up in a series of dramatic 100-meter (328-ft.) volcanic pillars. Created by the cooling of phonolite lava, these unusual pillars can be reached on foot from a parking lot that lies just outside the village.

To the north of Bort-les-Orgues, the Lac de Bort is an artificial lake behind a massive hydroelectric barrage – the first in a series of five that control the water flow down the Dordogne (you can visit the powerhouse to see how it all works). With the flooding of this valley the 15th-century Château de Val was left marooned on a rocky islet on the west side of the lake, creating a picturesque setting, with the château's walls and turrets rising up from the water's edge. There are regular guided tours of the interior, and art exhibitions are held here in the summer.

LA BOURBOULE 196A4
Known as a spa town since the 15th century, la Bourboule has a sedate, restful atmosphere. There are several parks on either side of the river, where locals like to while away the hours in a game of *boules*. The town's arsenic-rich waters are said to help cure allergies. If the only thing you need is a dose of fresh air, you can take a gondola up to the Charlannes plateau above the village and take a pleasant walk back down through the forests and alpine meadows.

At 300 meters (over 1,000 ft.) deep, the Cirque de Navacelles is a dramatic natural amphitheater that marks the former course of the Vis river. On the valley floor a single-arched bridge leads to the pretty village

★★★ LES CAUSSES   196B2

Between the upper Lot Valley and the Mediterranean coast there is an immense limestone plateau, or *causse*, carved into four sections by the rivers that flow through it. The highest is the Causse Méjean, between the Tarn and Jonte rivers, which is above 1,000 meters (3,280 ft.) almost everywhere. Although seemingly desolate, it can be a beautiful place, with deep, wooded ravines and fields that are ablaze with poppies in the summer. Larzac is the best known of the *causses*, having become a cause célèbre (or even a causse célèbre) in the 1970s when the government tried to establish a vast military camp there: environmentalists and farmers protested, and the plan was dropped. The Causse Noir lies between the Dourbie and Jonte rivers; the Causse de Sauveterre (which is the most northerly) lies between the Lot and the Tarn rivers.

The Grands Causses have several unusual geological features, such as spectacular underground caves and bizarre rock outcrops. The best known are at Le Caylar, Montpellier-le-Vieux, and Nîmes-le-Vieux. Of the underground caves, the Aven Armand 11 kilometers (7 mi.) northwest of Meyrueis is exceptional; near Ganges, the Grotte des Demoiselles is another massive and inspiring cavern.

Another peculiarity of the region are the cirques, where rivers have worn vast natural amphitheaters out of the surrounding rocks – the most impressive is the Cirque de Navacelles, near Ganges.

CÈRE, VALLÉE DE LA   196A3

From its source at le Lioran in the heart of the Cantal mountains, the Cère river flows down a beautiful, lush valley, plunging through two narrow gorges (the Pas de Compaing and the Pas de Cère) on the way. The delightful old village of Vic-sur-Cère is an attractive base for exploring the area; it has some imposing 16th-century houses on the left bank of the river. From Vic-sur-Cère you can undertake a drive up to the Col de Curebourse and walk along the ridge to the Rocher des Pendus overlooking the valley.

★ LA CHAISE-DIEU   196B4

Set on an isolated granite ridge surrounded by the forests of the Parc Naturel Régional du Livradois Forez, this red-roofed village owes its origins to a monastery founded here in the 11th century – named Casa Dei, or House of God, the name became Chaise-Dieu in French.

The original monastery was replaced in the 14th century with the present towering church on the orders of Pope Clement VI, who had been a monk here. He commissioned Hugues Morel, who built the monumental Palais des Papes in Avignon. Inside, the church reflects the grace and simplicity of pure Gothic style. Clement VI's tomb is surrounded by elaborately carved 14th-century choir stalls and some remarkable tapestries; in the north aisle there's a famous fresco of the *Danse Macabre* dating from the 15th century.

★★★ CLERMONT-FERRAND   *196B4*

The largest city in the Massif Central, Clermont-Ferrand's most dominant landmark is its 13th-century cathedral, a fine example of early Gothic style. Not far from the cathedral is the equally striking Romanesque (11th- and 12th-century) church of Notre-Dame-du-Port.

The city also is well provided with museums, including the Musée du Ranquet (among the musical instruments and pottery items you'll come across an early calculator, made in the 17th century by Blaise Pascal, who was born here in 1623), the Musée Bargoin (devoted to archeology and art) and the Musée Lecoq (natural history).

One of the most enjoyable areas in Clermont-Ferrand is the old quarter in Montferrand, Clermont's twin urban center. Around the ancient Carrefour des Taules, most of the houses have been carefully restored: the tourist office will be able to provide you with a map to guide you around the best of them.

Clermont-Ferrand also has an opera house, theaters, galleries, sports facilities, and a Grand Prix racing circuit outside of town.

★★ CONQUES   *196A3*

One of the loveliest villages in the Aveyron region, Conques clings to the hillside above the Ouche Valley, its old houses clustered around the twin-towered church of St.-Foye.

Saint Foye was an early Christian martyr and pilgrims would often stop here on their way to the sanctuary of Santiago de Compostela, across the Pyrénées, allowing the monastery to accumulate enough wealth to build this imposing church in the 11th century. It has a splendid carved doorway and a gold- and jewel-encrusted statue reliquary of Saint Foye from the 9th century.

Aside from the church, there are many well-restored old stone houses to admire in this remote little hillside village.

★ GORGES DE L'ALLIER   *196B3*

Flowing north through the Haute-Loire, the Allier passes for some 30 kilometers (19 mi.) through somber gorges of dark volcanic rock to the west of le Puy. There's good trout fishing and canoeing on the river, and several attractive villages perched above the gorge.

One of the most picturesque is St.-Ilpize, which has the ruins of a 14th-century stronghold built on top of a rock spur, and a frail-looking bridge connecting it to the opposite bank high above the rushing waters. St.-Cirgues, Blassac and Peyrusses all have churches with ancient frescoes. At Lavoûte-Chilhac there's a ruined abbey, a Gothic church, and a 15th-century bridge.

Farther downstream, Brioude consists of a maze of narrow streets around its grandiose Romanesque church; the largest in the Auvergne, St.-Julien-de-Brioude honors a Roman soldier who was martyred for his faith.

BLAISE PASCAL

Born in Clermont-Ferrand in 1623, Blaise Pascal was one of the foremost French philosophers of the 17th century.

He was a math genius, and at the age of 19 he devised the world's first adding machine – largely because he wanted to help his father reduce the hours he spent on his business accounts.

At the age of 25, Pascal conducted experiments on the Puy de Dôme that showed how air pressure varies according to altitude; he correctly surmised that this would have an effect on weather prediction and the behavior of thermometers.

At 33, Pascal gave up science in favor of religious philosophy. He died at the young age of 39, and his "Pensées" ("Thoughts") was published after his death ■

THE MASSIF CENTRAL

MONTPELLIER-LE-VIEUX

The strange rock formations of Montpellier-le-Vieux were once thought by local shepherds to be a "petrified town" that had been cursed for its sins. It is a remarkable place, and there are several trails.

After entering the site, follow the path to the first intersection; turn right and take the next left: there's a fine view of the Causse du Larzac and Causse Méjean to the south and north respectively.

Farther on, you come to the Porte de Mycènes, a 12-meter (39-ft.) natural rock arch. The track goes past a formation dubbed "Cyrano's Nose" and a large cave (the Grotte de Baume Obscure), before returning to the parking lot ∎

★★★ GORGES DE L'ARDÈCHE   196C2

Between the Cévennes and the Rhône valleys, the craggy Ardèche mountains offer plenty of opportunities for hiking and mountain-biking. Canoeists head for the lovely Gorges de l'Ardèche, which slice through the mountains between Vallon Pont d'Arc and Pont St. Ésprit; the usual starting point is the natural archway at Pont d'Arc, 5 kilometers (3 mi.) from Vallon, where you can rent a canoe and be picked up by bus at various points downstream for the journey back.

Drivers can follow a scenic route along the top of the gorges, following the D290 from Vallon Pont d'Arc to its confluence with the Rhône.

★★★ GORGES DU TARN   196B2

Separating the Causse Méjean from the Causse de Sauveterre, this impressive canyon has been a tourist attraction for over a hundred years and is one of the few gorges where you can drive along the riverbank. Naturally enough, in July and August this means that the narrow D907b can become one long traffic jam.

The most dramatic stretch is between Le Rozier and Ste.-Énimie, with 500-meter (1,600-ft.) cliffs on either side and waterfalls tumbling from the rock face; every so often, natural rock amphitheaters and fertile valleys open out from the main gorge.

Ste.-Énimie is a charming village, somewhat swamped in summer, but with plenty of outlets for renting canoes or mountain bikes. If you're mostly interested in walking, there are excellent, though strenuous, routes from Le Rozier, where the Tarn is joined by the Jonte: well-marked paths lead up to stunning views above both rivers. At La Malène, about halfway between

the two villages, you can take a boat ride through Les Détroits (the Straits), one of the most scenic sections of the gorge.

★ GORGES DE LA TRUYÈRE   196A3

Rising in the mountains of Lozère, the Truyère is one of the main tributaries of the Lot river. It passes through countless gorges whose relative inaccessibility has made them less famous than the Gorges du Tarn.

One of the few routes to the river is the road from Pierrefort to the Barrage de Sarrans; boat trips also ply upriver from the Barrage de Grandval to Garabit. Spanning the gorge is a remarkable 19th-century railroad viaduct, built by Gustav Eiffel five years before he began his famous tower in Paris.

ISSOIRE   196B4

The ancient Protestant capital of the Auvergne, Issoire is today a prosperous industrial town with a noteworthy Romanesque church. It has some fine absidial chapels and the crypt (which was left untouched by garish 19th-century renovation) is worth a look.

LE LIORAN   196A3

This year-round resort is set amid pine forests just below the 1,294-meter (4,245-ft.) Col de Cère, with nearby Super-Lioran providing most of the skiing facilities (including 19 tele-skis and acres of *pistes*) in winter. During the summer the cable car from Super-Lioran carries hikers and hang-gliders almost to the top of the 1,855-meter (6,086-ft.) Plomb du Cantal, from where you can undertake day hikes.

★ LOT, VALLÉE DE   196A3

Running parallel to the Dordogne Valley, the Lot Valley is far less busy and has many appealing aspects: the prettiest section is in the middle, where the Lot meanders in great horseshoe bends between thickly wooded limestone hills.

The principal town in the valley is Cahors, enclosed in a tight loop of the river. Its most prominent landmarks are the 12th-century cathedral and the Pont Valentré, with its three fortified towers.

Upstream, the Grotte du Pech-Merle has, in addition to the usual stalactites and stalagmites, several chambers decorated with remarkable prehistoric drawings.

Elsewhere along the valley there are some lovely, unspoiled towns such as St.-Cirq-Lapopie, Puy l'Evêque and Luzech.

The natural arch of Pont d'Arc is the most popular starting point for canoeists along the Ardèche river. This vast bridge is 34 meters (111 ft.) high and spans the full width of the river

DRIVE

LAND OF THE QUIET VOLCANOES

335 kilometers/209 miles (allow 3 days)

Clermont-Ferrand may be a big, industrial town, but within striking distance is some of the loveliest countryside in the Massif Central, including the dramatic landscapes of the Parc Naturel Régional des Volcans d'Auvergne, and the forests of the Parc Naturel Régional du Livradois Forez.

The hill country around Clermont-Ferrand is made up of the relics of huge volcanic convulsions thousands of years ago, and there are some good walks with panoramic views.

The region's 20 mineral springs supply the whole of France – and beyond – with bottled water.

Leave Clermont-Ferrand on the N89 as for Tulle. Go right on the D767 then right on the D941c to Royat.

1 Royat

Set in a valley above its neighbor Clermont-Ferrand, Royat is an attractive old spa town whose thermal springs have been providing cures for numerous ailments since Roman times.

Leave Royat on the D68. Turn left on the D941a and immediately right on the D68. Go straight on to join the toll road to the summit of Puy de Dôme. Check for ouvert (open) sign.

2 Puy de Dôme, Auvergne

This volcanic summit is worth the steep climb up by automobile for the views over the volcanic peaks of the Parc Naturel Régional des Volcans d'Auvergne.

Access is by toll road, a legacy of the days when the summit was reached by steam train from Clermont-Ferrand. At the top, there are all the usual facilities as well as some fascinating reminders of the history of this ancient site.

The Celts knew it as Dumia, or royal mountain, and worshipped

MOUNTAIN CHEESES

The Massif Central does have excellent mountain cheeses.

Roquefort is a sharp, creamy, blue cheese made from ewe's milk.

St.-Nectaire is produced in the Puy-de-Dôme and Cantal mountains

Finally, there is Cantal, a hard cheese that is produced in and around Aurillac ■

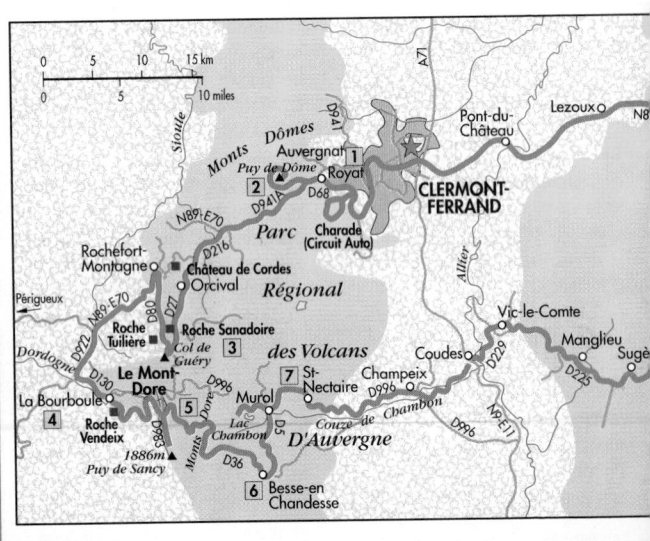

their various gods from its lofty summit.

The Romans turned it into a center of worship to Mercury and built a fabulous temple, said to have once been twice the size of the Maison Carré in Nîmes.

You can still see the base of the temple walls and part of the grand staircase – remains that were discovered when the observatory was built here in the late 19th century.

Turn right onto the D941a and turn right again. Go straight ahead on the D216 then on the D27 and the D983. Stop at a major parking lot just before the junction with the D80.

3 Col de Guéry, Auvergne

The Col de Guéry viewpoint encompasses two huge rocks standing like gateposts on either side of the densely wooded Cirque du Chausse, with the valley stretching away into the distance beyond them.

The two rocky outcrops (known as the Roche Tuilière and the Roche Sanadoire) are the remains of an ancient volcanic cone, and the valley between them was later sculpted further by retreating glaciers during the Ice Age.

Turn right onto the D80 to Rochefort-Montagne, then turn left and follow the N89, D922 and D996 to La Bourboule.

4 La Bourboule, Auvergne

This peaceful spa town has two thermal establishments for *curistes* (principally those seeking help for allergies) as well as a good range of sporting facilities. The town has several attractive, pastel-colored bridges spanning the Dordogne and some grand but faded *belle-époque* buildings.

Behind the Hôtel de Ville (town hall), the Parc Fenêstre is a pleasant woodland park with a lake and a narrow-gauge railway. The park is also the base station for the *téléférique* (cable car) that whisks you up to the Plateau de Charlannes above the town: at 1,250 meters (4,100 ft.).

Charlannes has some lovely walks through the woods, with superb views, and in winter you can ski.

Leave La Bourboule on the D130 to Le Mont-Dore.

5 Le Mont-Dore, Auvergne

Like its neighbor 7 kilometers (4 mi.) downstream, Le Mont-Dore was originally a Roman spa that became fashionable again in the 19th century. Comfortable hotels and good restaurants also make this an agreeable base for walking on the alpine meadows of the Puy de Sancy, accessible by cable car or by following the D983 out of Le Mont-Dore.

WALK

PUY DE DÔME

The highest point in the Monts Dôme range, the Puy de Dôme is well worth a visit for incredible views over the surroundings.

From the summit parking lot, follow the footpath up past a bust of Eugène Renaux (a pilot who made a record-breaking return flight to Paris in 1911) and the remains of the Temple de Mercure: the Romans built their own temple on a previously Celtic sacred site. The Roman temple was a large and beautiful building composed of at least 50 different types of stone and marble.

Continue up to the summit itself, which at 1,465 meters (4,800 ft.) offers an unsurpassable view of over 100 volcanic peaks ∎

THE LEGEND OF SAINTE. ÉNIMIE

In the church at Ste.-Énimie, a series of ceramic tiles relates the legend of the princess who gave the village its name.

Énimie lived in the 7th century and wanted to devote her life to God. Her brother, King Dagobert, insisted that she accept the hand of one of his barons, but Énimie contracted leprosy before the marriage could take place.

A vision told her to go south, where a fountain would heal her. Énimie recovered at the fountain of Burle, but the illness returned as soon as she tried to leave. Realizing that God wanted her to stay, she founded a convent (remains of which can still be seen), and stayed here until her death in 628 ■

In winter, this doubles up as a ski area. From the summit at 1,883 meters (6,180 ft.) there are breathtaking views over the Auvergne countryside.

Return on the D983 from the Puy de Sancy, then right on the road signed "Besse par Col-Croix St. Robert." Check ouvert sign. Follow the D36 to Besse.

6 Besse-en-Chandesse, Auvergne

This attractive town has many well-preserved 15th- and 16th-century houses and fortifications from the same period. There is also an unusual ski museum.

Some 7 kilometers (4 mi.) beyond the village is the ski station of Super-Besse, which is popular with walkers and skiers.

Leave Besse on the D5 to Murol then go right on the D996 to St.-Nectaire.

7 St.-Nectaire, Auvergne

Set in the wooded valley of the Courancon, St.-Nectaire is another renowned spa town.

You can sample the mineral waters in the parkland at Les Thermes, but if you're not here for your health the main attraction is the 12th-century church in the upper village of St.-Nectaire-le-Haut; its treasures include a 12th-century reliquary of Saint Baudime and a carved Virgin that also dates from the Romanesque period.

Continue on the D996 to Champeix. Follow signs to Coudes and Vic-le-Comte, then continue on the D225 and D996 (which is sometimes signed N496) to Ambert.

8 Ambert, Livradois Forez

This quiet town lies in a wooded valley watered by the Dore river. It is most notable for its unusual Hôtel de Ville (town hall), which is entirely circular and surrounded by arcades – it was originally built as a grain market. There is also a small museum devoted to cheese (tastings follow the tour).

Leave Ambert on the D57 for the Moulin Richard-de-Bas.

9 Moulin Richard-de-Bas, Livradois Forez

Ambert was once known as a center for paper-making, and one of the oldest mills in the area now houses a fascinating museum devoted to this ancient craft.

The Moulin Richard-de-Bas dates back to the 14th century but the displays inside hark back even further into the history of paper-making, starting with Egyptian papyrus and Chinese scrolls.

Return to Ambert and take the D906 then the N89 in the direction of Thiers.

10 Thiers, Livradois Forez

This is an appealing town to wander round, savoring the marvelous half-timbered and carved facades on its historic houses that survive along the steep streets of the old quarter.

At the heart of the town is the attractive place du Pirou. Thiers is a major center for the production of cutlery, and you can see many fine examples in the Maison des Couteliers.

Return from Thiers on the N89 and continue to Clermont-Ferrand.

MASSIF DE L'AIGOUAL 196B2

The forested slopes of Aigoual are often shrouded in cloud, obscuring the views from the 1,567-meter (5,140-ft.) summit, which are said to reach as far as Mont Blanc on a good day. But good days are rare – Mont Aigoual is one of the rainiest places in France.

The extensive plantations of beech and pine that blanket the steep sides of the mountain are relatively recent – in the 19th century the mountain was almost entirely deforested. Two roads and six long-distance footpaths converge at the summit, with an arboretum (Hort de Dieu) a little bit farther down.

Heading north in the direction of the Gorges du Tarn and Meyrueis, stop at the Abîme de Bramabiau, an awe-inspiring abyss that has been created by a small stream, the Bonheur, as it rushes down Mont Aigoual's slopes. There are guided tours of the underground course of the river in summer.

Meyrueis is well placed for tours to the Gorges du Tarn, the Gorges de la Jonte, and nearby caverns such as the Grotte de Dargilan and Aven Armand.

★ MONT-DORE 196A4

This old spa town sits at the head of the Dordogne, 7 kilometers (4 mi.) upstream from La Bourboule (see p.199). You can tour the *Établissement Thermal*, originally a Roman spa. Aside from the *curistes*, most people visit Mont-Dore for winter sports or as a base for hiking up to the "roof of the Auvergne," the upper slopes of the Puy de Sancy – also accessible by cable car.

★★★ MONTS DU CANTAL 196A3

To the south of the Monts Dore, the Cantal Mountains are the remnants of a once-massive volcano over 3,000 meters (9,800 ft.) high and more than 100 kilometers (62 mi.) around its base. Long since worn down by glaciers and climatic erosion, the volcano now consists of a number of high peaks such as Puy Griou, Puy Violent, Puy Mary, and Plomb du Cantal.

This is one of the loveliest regions in the Auvergne, with the spectacular conical peaks interspersed with lush valleys. There are many long-distance footpaths; bases for touring include Aurillac, Le Lioran, Thiézac, and Salers.

Puy de Dôme, viewed from the south. This is the highest of all the peaks that make up the landscape known as the Chaîne des Puys. From the summit there is a superb panoramic view over the city of Clermont-Ferrand as well as the surrounding area

Narrow streets of the village of Le Puy, set in an old volcanic crater basin. A massive 16-meter (52-ft.) statue of the Virgin and Child dominates the town atop another rocky outcrop

ORCIVAL 196A4

This attractive village to the west of Clermont-Ferrand has a well-preserved Romanesque church, Notre-Dame d'Orcival, which has been a pilgrimage site for centuries. Set against the hillside and completed in 1130, the church's side walls are reinforced by sturdy buttresses and immense arches. The church's 12th-century statue of the Virgin Enthroned, still with its original gilt decoration, is paraded through the streets on Ascension Day.

★★★ PARC NATUREL 196A4 RÉGIONAL DES VOLCANS D'AUVERGNE

The Parc Naturel Régional des Volcans d'Auvergne covers an area of some 3,500 square kilometers (1,350 sq. mi.) across most of the western Auvergne, a dramatic volcanic landscape of truncated peaks, crater lakes, lava plateaux and fertile valleys. It encompasses three main ranges: the Monts Dômes, Monts Dore, and the Monts du Cantal.

The Monts Dômes (also known as the Chaîne des Puys) are the youngest of the Auvergne volcanoes and form a north–south chain with some 112 small volcanoes (*puys*) rising from the lush surrounding countryside.

Adventurous hikers can walk along GR441 past over 40 extinct volcanoes on the Tour de la Chaîne des Puys; or you can drive up to the highest point at Puy de Dôme – 1,465 meters (4,800 ft.).

Farther south, the Monts Dore and Monts Cantal are much older, interspersed with volcanic lakes.

LE-PUY-EN-VELAY   196A3

Capital of the Haute-Loire, Le Puy is set in an old crater basin; giant outcrops of volcanic rock rise up from the town's streets.

The most prominent is the Rocher d'Aiguilhe, with the 11th-century chapel of St.-Michel-d'Aiguilhe perched on top. If you can manage the 268 steps, you'll see a building that follows the contours of the rock, decorated with Moorish-inspired mosaics.

Dominating the old town (and reached by a series of steep streets and steps), Le Puy's cathedral is also unusual, with a façade of colored stone and a vault with six oblong domes. The Moorish theme is continued in the arches and wrought-iron grilles of its beautiful cloister.

Behind the cathedral, a massive 16-meter (52-ft.) statue of the Virgin and Child sits on top of another volcanic outcrop. There is a viewing platform at the top, with a panoramic vista over Le Puy's extraordinary setting.

Elsewhere in the town there are plenty of opportunities for purchasing lace, for which Le Puy is renowned; lace-making has been widespread here since the 17th century. There's a wonderful collection of traditional lace and some intriguing 18th-century sample-books in the Musée Crozatier in the Jardin Vinay.

RIOM   196B4

Once the capital of the Auvergne (until it was overshadowed by neighboring Clermont-Ferrand – see p.201), Riom is a sedate town most notable for its Renaissance architecture and a good local museum, the Musée Régional d'Auvergne.

It's worth looking at the Église Notre-Dame-du-Marthuret (rue du Commerce), where there's an unusual 14th-century statue known as La Vierge à l'Oiseau, with the Christ child cradling a goldfinch.

ROYAT   196B4

On the outskirts of Clermont-Ferrand, Royat was a Roman spa town and still welcomes *curistes* today. Aside from the thermal springs it has a small museum (Musée du Passé), a casino and extensive sports facilities.

Its main historical interest is in the fortified Romanesque Église St.-Léger. There's also a stone-cutting workshop, the Taillerie de Pierres Fines, where you can buy semiprecious stones.

ST.-GUILHEM-LE-DÉSERT   196B1

Nestling in the gorge of the Hérault river with a ruined castle on the skyline above, St.-Guilhem-le-Désert is a charming village that owes its fortunes to Guilhem Court-Nez, a grandson of Charles Martel, trusted lieutenant of Charlemagne.

On the death of his wife, Martel renounced his soldiering career and turned to a life of spiritual contemplation. As a mark of esteem for his long-standing friend, Charlemagne gave him a fragment of the True Cross.

WALK

ST.-GUILHEM-LE-DÉSERT

Starting from the main parking lot, head toward the village and take the first left along the Grand Chemin du Val de Gellone for superb views.

At the top, bear right onto place de la Liberté. The present church dates from the 11th century and has a fine vaulted roof and fresco fragments. Only a small part of the adjacent cloisters has survived. The museum just beside the church contains some fine 12th-century sculptures, the church's altar (in marble with enamel inlay) and the sarcophagus of Saint Guilhem.

From place de la Liberté head back down the main street, passing the Tour des Prisons and the church of St.-Laurent to return to the parking lot ■

THE MASSIF CENTRAL

THE WATERS OF VICHY

Vichy started out as a spa under the Romans, and became a fortified town under the Bourbons: Louis XV's daughters, Victoire and Adelaide, "took the waters" at Vichy in the 18th century. Later, Emperor Napoleon created the Parc des Sources. But it was only after Napoleon III came here in the 1860s that Vichy knew real success.

Vichy's spring waters can be tasted in the Palais in the Parc des Sources. There are six different types; water from the Célestin source is the only one that is bottled (locals maintain that the others are only efficacious if taken at once). You can try the others here – each is said to be good for different afflictions ∎

Guilhem established a monastery in this remote valley and it became a popular place of pilgrimage. He was canonized on his death in 812, and buried in the church he had helped to build. By the 13th century there were over 100 monks at the monastery, but much was destroyed during the Wars of Religion (1562–98).

ST.-NECTAIRE   *196B4*
On the eastern approaches to the Monts Dore, St.-Nectaire is made up of the spa of St.-Nectaire-le-Bas and the old village of St.-Nectaire-le-Haut. The latter has a magnificent 12th-century Romanesque church noted for its finely carved capitals and a gold reliquary bust of Saint Baudime.

★ SALERS   *196A3*
This lovely old walled medieval town is a good base for exploring the northwestern corner of Cantal and the Monts Dore.

The narrow, cobbled streets are lined with 15th- and 16th-century houses ornamented with gables and turrets – most are built from the local black lava stone. There are good views over the Maronne Valley and the Cantal mountains from the end of the avenue de Barrouze, and the church (in rue du Beffroi) contains a 15th-century painted sculpture of the entombment of Christ.

SOUVIGNY   *196B5*
This peaceful little village was once an important pilgrimage center thanks to an abbey that was established to the monks of Cluny in the 10th century.

Inside this surprisingly capacious church (which is part Gothic and part Romanesque) there are several fine tombs,

including those of two Bourbon dukes. Opposite this church, the disused Église St.-Marc houses a small museum with a fascinating 12th-century octagonal calendar.

★ THIERS   *196B4*
Built on a small promontory above the rushing waters of the Durolle river, Thiers is a picturesque town with cobbled streets and some fine 15th-century timbered houses. For over 500 years it has been a major center for the production of knives and cutlery, and there are numerous traditional workshops that can be visited.

There's also a cutlery museum at the Maison des Couteliers.

★★★ VICHY   *196B5*
This aging spa town is famous not only for its sulfurous springs, but also for being the base from 1940 to 1944 of the puppet government under Marshal Pétain. Vichy was chosen by Pétain primarily because of the large number of hotels in the city, which enabled the regime to accommodate all the bureaucrats of the collaborationist government. Not surprisingly, little mention is made of this period today, even though Pétain's own offices were in the Pavillon Sévigné, the city's grandest hotel.

Vichy's success as a spa town dates from the late 19th century, when a casino and many grand hotels were constructed, and parks were laid out alongside the Allier.

Vichy still has a certain faded charm, as well as a young and lively population, who take full advantage of the extensive sports facilities and wide range of cultural entertainment (including opera and theater) available in the town.

THE ALPS AND THE RHÔNE VALLEY

Spectacular mountain scenery,
drives, walks and excursions
(although no guarantee of good
weather) sum up this
delightful area

THE ALPS AND THE RHÔNE VALLEY

France's "earthly paradise" (in the words of a great mountain explorer) is ruled by **Mont Blanc**, the highest natural citadel in Europe. The region has been tamed somewhat by roads and pylons, passes and tunnels, high-rise apartment buildings and all-weather sports arenas. Its torrents have been harnessed for hydroelectric stations and its livestock moved from pasture to pasture by truck or train rather than under the gentle hand of native shepherds. Yet it retains for the most part its essence: spectacularly wild and remote terrain, undiminished and only slightly disrupted by human activity.

With greater awareness of environmental issues, the region is facing up to the dangers of tourism for such a fragile ecosystem. The creation of national parks, uninhabited protected areas accessible only to walkers and climbers, as well as

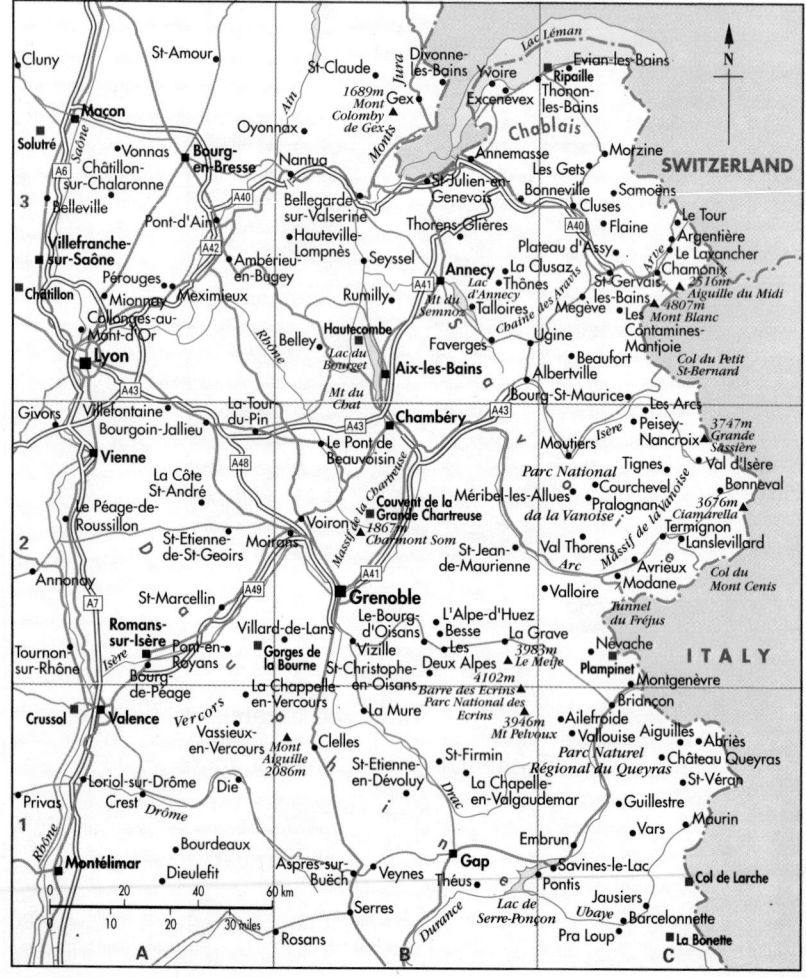

★ ★ ★
HIGHLIGHTS

Annecy, Lac d' (▶214)
Chamonix (▶218)
Écrins, Parc National des (▶219)
Lyon (old town) (▶220)
Mont Blanc (▶217)
Pérouges (▶226)
Queyras, Parc Naturel Régional du (▶226)
Vanoise, Parc National de la (▶228)

regional parks is a step in the right direction. So is the current effort that is being made to make the higher ski resorts more appealing in summer, and to improve their functional appearance. All of these promote controlled tourist development and the survival of rural industries and crafts.

Many of the extraordinary mountain-tops and passes are accessible to anyone who can afford the cost of a cable car (or who has the stomach for interminable hairpin bends engineered up the steepest peak). While contemplating pristine scenery from these heights, it is hard to combat the impression that all is well in this remote and awe-inspiring region. However, the haze above the valley floor by Chamonix is not a natural mist, but the result of pollution from traffic heading for the Mont Blanc tunnel.

From the tourist's point of view, it's important to remember that many of the area's river valleys are industrial and provide communication routes and

hydroelectric power. Elsewhere there's an enormous variety of relatively unspoiled scenery – from the glaciers and snow-white peaks that crown the lush and floral alpine pastures of the northern (Savoie) Alps to the remote, gray and forbidding rocky peaks and gorges of the southern (Dauphiné) Alps. The appeal of the towns, resorts, and villages in the two areas differs, too. In **Savoie** there are beautiful lakes encompassing popular spa resorts with well-developed facilities and no lack of charm (Aix-les-Bains, Évian-les-Bains, St.-Gervais-les-Bains), and several venerable towns of interest, including Annecy and Chambéry. In the less-developed **Dauphiné**, where getting around is not so easy, there are rugged mountain villages (notably in the Queyras) and fortified small towns (Briançon and Château-Queyras, for example).

If the **gastronomy** of the Alps is rarely considered as elevated as the terrain (it's simple mountain fare, with cheese, smoked ham, and potato dishes ranking among its specialties), that of the Rhône Valley enjoys the highest possible reputation. Indeed, it forms as good a reason as any to break a journey along

CALENDAR OF EVENTS

MARCH – The Café Theatre at St.-Gervais-les-Bains hosts the **Mont Blanc International Festival of Comedy**.

LATE JUNE/EARLY JULY – Cultural Europe can be experienced at the **European Theatre Festival** in Grenoble.

JULY – Annecy: the **Festival of the Old Town**.

AUGUST – Aix-les-Bains (Savoie) hosts a **Flower Festival**.

OCTOBER – Lyon Tennis Grand Prix.

NOVEMBER – **Beaujolais nouveau launch** in Villefranche – party begins at midnight ■

SCALING THE ALPS

The history of mountaineering in the Alps is peppered with the names of English explorers.

In the 18th century, Windham and Pococke were among the first people to describe the Chamonix Valley and the glaciers of Mont Blanc to the outside world; in the late 19th century, the golden age of alpinism, the most illustrious names were Whymper, Mummery and Coolidge. In 1857, the first alpine club was formed – in London.

Mont Blanc was first scaled in 1786; in 1787, the Swiss scientist De Saussure reached the summit without ropes (and dressed in a long-tailed silk coat).

Many resorts have "practice rocks," which are used for perfecting technique ■

the great thoroughfare of the **Autoroute du Soleil** – more tempting even than the handful of major sights along the river (generally concentrated in the ancient towns).

Lyon, a large city that is not unduly endowed with tourist appeal, has a fine Renaissance quarter, and more recommended restaurants than anywhere else in France, apart from Paris.

AIGUILLE, MONT *212B1*

This extraordinary flat-topped rock tower at the southern end of the Vercors provided one of the first mountaineering feats of the Alps, when King Charles VIII ordered it to be scaled (he wanted to establish the truth of rumors that it was inhabited by angels and fantastic animals).

One of Charles' captains, accompanied by six brave companions, duly set forth in 1492 to scale the height with the aid of ladders and ropes, but encountered nothing more fantastic than a flock of chamois.

AIX-LES-BAINS *212B3*

On the banks of the Lac du Bourget, this ancient spa resort, well known in Roman times, enjoyed a fashionable revival in the 18th century and continued to prosper, attracting French empresses and England's Queen Victoria. There are still some grand hotels, and of course a casino; the modern thermal establishment, surrounded by fine gardens, has some Roman remains within, and is also worth a visit.

As a spa Aix-les-Bains is somewhat past its heyday, but now offers more than curative treatments. There are plenty of opportunities for excursions on and around the lake, and the Dr. Faure museum contains some notable 19th-century paintings.

★★★ ANNECY, LAC D' *212B3*

A pretty-as-a-picture lake in a beautiful mountain setting, Lake Annecy naturally has long enjoyed great popularity and receives huge numbers of visitors, particularly in the fine old town of the same name that presides at its head. The towers of the former vast fortress still overlook the old town, which has a network of canals and bridges, heavy with flowers. In the remains of the castle are two regional museums (with displays of popular art and furniture respectively); and all along the lakeside are well-tended gardens and promenades, places for swimming and watersports, and plenty of boat trips available.

The surroundings of Lake Annecy are mountainous, wooded and beautiful, despite the influx of new villas. Boat excursions are available to leafy Talloires, overlooking the narrows

that divide the Grand Lac from the Petit Lac to the south. This is the lake's most fashionable and prestigious little resort, and a trip here offers the chance to see some of the delightful scenery, looking out over the lakeside to the Entrevernes mountains beyond, as well as the wooded promontory of the Château de Duingt (not open to visitors).

Excursions by automobile can include a drive up the wooded Semnoz mountain to the 1,699-meter (5,574-ft.) Crêt du Châtillon and back to the lake at Sévrier via the Col de Leschaux, from which the steep cliffs of Mont Veyrier (accessible by cable car from Veyrier), the jagged Dents de Lanfon, and the crags of La Tournette, 2,351 meters (7,053 ft.), can all be appreciated. To the south of the lake a forest road leads down the wooded Combe d'Ire, which ends in a nature reserve (footpath access only).

ARAVIS, CHAÎNE DES 212C3

The mountains of the Aravis, between Lake Annecy and Mont Blanc, offer some of the most pretty pastoral scenery of the French Alps: woods, high fertile pastures, and picturesque old wooden chalets hung with bright flowers. The mountain road just to the east of the lake, which crosses the Col de la Forclaz, offers fine views. Further north, the town of Thônes is renowned for its Saturday market, where you can buy the pungent local cheese – Reblochon. On the road towards Annecy there is a museum devoted to the Resistance movement.

Other excellent roads, with spectacular mountain views, include the Col de la Croix-Fry road, and the Col des Aravis, with views of Mont Blanc. La Clusaz is one of the oldest and biggest ski resorts in the area, and has plenty of sports facilities and walks.

Annecy's scenic lakeside setting is framed by rugged mountains. The old town, which has Gallo-Roman origins, spans the Thiou river as it runs from the lake. A network of canals and bridges decorated with flowers adds to its charm

Argentière is an important skiing resort to the northeast of Chamonix. All around are the snowy splendors of the Aiguilles de Chamonix, whose jagged peaks and needle-shaped granite ridges offer a challenge to skiers and mountaineers

★ ASSY, PLATEAU D' 212C3

On a ledge several hairpin bends above Le Fayet, the resort of Assy is of little interest to a casual visitor, but its modern church of Notre-Dame-de-Toute-Grace is well worth the drive, particularly on a sunny day, for it is the result of a unique collaboration between several of the great names in French art of the 20th century. Begun in 1937 and finally consecrated in 1950, it features an exterior mosaic by Léger, a tapestry behind the altar by Lurçat, windows by Rouault, and other works by Bonnard, Matisse, Braques and Chagall.

BARCELONNETTE and THE UBAYE 212C1

In one of the most remote valleys of the French Alps, the 13th-century mountain town of Barcelonnette provides an interesting contrast to its modern ski resort neighbors (Pra Loup and Le Sauze). The capital of the Ubaye district was laid out as a *bastide* in 1231, and many of its old houses are protected from heavy snowfalls by enormous projections. The Ubaye gorge itself can be followed into increasingly remote countryside, to the hamlet of Maurin at 1,903 meters (6,243 ft.).

★★★ BLANC, MONT 212C3

At 4,807 meters (15,770 ft.), this is Europe's highest peak, a majestic giant whose snowy profile crowns views for miles around, guarded by the Aiguilles de Chamonix, a series of jagged granite needle peaks that are a mere 3,000 meters (9,843 ft.) tall. The massif, on France's border with Italy, comprises three mighty glaciers, one of which, the 7-kilometer (4-mi.) Glacier des Bossons, hangs just above the valley floor, and can be seen peeping out between the trees. The longest glacier, the 14-kilometer (9-mi.) Mer de Glace, which moves at a rate of 90 meters (295 ft.) a year, is a popular tourist excursion; a rack railroad leads to a viewing platform, from where a cable car can be taken down to an ice cavern carved out of the glacier (the cavern is re-carved annually).

Some of the best views of Mont Blanc are from the opposite side of the Arve Valley: from the Brévent and Flégère mountains, which are accessible by cable car.

To the northeast of Chamonix, the resorts are more peaceful and the roads rather less busy. The hamlet of Le Lavancher offers superb views; Argentière is a major skiing resort; and the attractive old village of Le Tour lies up a little dead-end road just to the northeast of Argentière.

West of Chamonix lies the sedate old valley town and spa of St.-Gervais-les-Bains. From here, the Montjoie Valley leads up to the resort of Les Contamines-Montjoie, from where it is possible to take the walking Tour du Mont Blanc (marked TMB or GRTMB on maps), via Italy (Courmayeur) and Switzerland (Champex). The whole walk takes about 10 days, but hikers may choose to tackle only a section; there are refuges along the way.

★ BOURGET, LAC DU 212B3

Lacking the scenic variety of its rival, Lac d'Annecy, the popularity of the Lac du Bourget rests mainly on its chief resort, Aix-les-Bains. Long and thin, surrounded on both sides by high ridges, the lake was much admired in the 19th century by Romantic poets (notably Lamartine). The western side is more interesting in scenic terms. You can follow a road from Le-Bourget-du-Lac up the side of Mont du Chat, and then turn off to cross the Col du Chat. The road passes through farming countryside, with wide views.

On the western side of the lake and accessible by boat is Hautecombe Abbey, mausoleum of the Savoyard dynasty, largely redecorated in the 19th century in an elaborate Gothic style. The abbey has become popular for its services of Gregorian chant.

★ BRIANÇON 212C1

At 1,320 meters (4,330 ft.), this is the highest town in Europe. Of strategic importance since Roman times, its old town is still intact within the citadel walls built by the great engineer of Louis XIV, Sébastien Vauban.

CHAMBÉRY 212B2

Just to the south of the Lac du Bourget, Chambéry is a busy town that was once the capital of the kingdom of Savoy. Its most lasting image is an extraordinary fountain of massive elephants, which stands at one end of the arcaded rue de Boigne.

At the other end stands the ducal château, and the Gothic Sainte-Chapelle. The stone house called Les Charmettes was rented by Madame de Warens, protector and lover of Jean-Jacques Rousseau, who spent many idyllic years here. The house is now a museum, and has been kept as it was in the 1730s.

WALK

LAC DU BOURGET

This 1½-hour walk goes along the lip of the steep, wooded mountainside along the northeast side of the Lac du Bourget.

Start from the parking lot near La Chambotte, walk up to the Belvédère de la Chambotte, then take the path to the right of the first descending hairpin bend. At the end, join another path. Turn right, then after 50 meters (164 ft.) follow the path left onto a short uphill climb. A narrow path leads off to the right toward a clearing. The main path continues for about 200 meters (656 ft.), then right onto a wider track leading to another superb vantage point. Return to the main path, turn right, bear left at the fork, and descend into open countryside to the road just above La Chambotte ■

THE ALPS AND THE RHÔNE VALLEY

FLÉGÈRE

Summer walks from the middle station of the two-stage cable car from Les Praz de Chamonix offer excellent views of Mont Blanc.

The 8-kilometer (5-mi.) marked walk to the Lac Blanc and back takes about 3 hours. The route passes the Lac de la Flégère, and then a large cairn, which marks the entrance to the Aiguilles Rouges nature reserve. It then continues for about 300 meters (984 ft.), then up some rocky terrain to some steeper zig-zags that lead to an intersection.

Go left to another intersection, from where a short climb leads to the Lac Blanc, 2,352 meters (7,717 ft.), under the crags of the Aiguille du Belvédère ∎

★★★ CHAMONIX   212C3

Justifiably proclaimed world skiing capital, the bustling town and major resort of Chamonix attempts to cater to all comers – sedate and active, big spenders and backpackers – as well as provide for its own 10,000 inhabitants. It suffers from crowds, traffic, and pollution, but its natural assets cannot be disputed: the towering white mass of Europe's highest Alp, Mont Blanc, with an array of jagged rock needles (*aiguilles*) at its shoulders; tumbling glaciers; and every conceivable type of mountain terrain – for climbing, hang-gliding, skiing (cross-country, glacier, powder or heli-skiing), walking, or just admiring. Added to this are the resort facilities, with an extensive variety of sports ranging from golf to swimming, and plenty of nightlife of all kinds.

Chamonix offers one of the most exhilarating cable-car and telecabin routes of all – over the Mont Blanc massif to Italy, via the Aiguille du Midi, towering 2,500 meters (8,202 ft.) above the Chamonix Valley, and then six stages of ski-lifts; you return by bus through the tunnel. You'll need to take your passport with you. Caution is advised for those people who might be affected by rapid changes in altitude.

CHARTREUSE, MASSIF DE LA   212B2

This is a relatively small and thickly forested mountain area between Grenoble and Chambéry, rising abruptly from the valley floor, with several small winding mountain roads and forest tracks for confident drivers.

The heart of the massif is the Charmant Som, reached by a road from the Col de Porte to the hamlet known as Les Bergeries (from where a half-hour walk will take you to the top), one of the few areas of open pasture in the massif. From here there are wide views over the wooded terrain of the secretive Grande Chartreuse monastery (Couvent de la Grande Chartreuse), founded in 1084 by Saint Bruno in this valley setting, and famed for the potent liqueur formerly made by its monks. Visitors may see no farther than the entrance (at La Correrie).

DIE   212A1

Renowned for the local sparkling wine, Clairette de Die, the old walled town of Die lies in a pleasant, open, and fruitful valley at the southern edge of the wooded Vercors massif. A few fragments of Roman buildings and monuments can be seen, including a triumphal arch (Porte St.-Marcel) built into the ramparts at the southeast edge of town.

★★★ ÉCRINS,   212B1
PARC NATIONAL DES

This is one of France's largest protected areas, a region of outstanding natural beauty that includes several spectacular peaks, including the Barre des Écrins, 4,102 meters (13,458 ft.), La Meije, 3,983 meters (13,068 ft.), and Mont Pelvoux, 3,946 meters (12,946 ft.). There are no roads into the park, but access on foot is possible from the Oisans, the Valgaudemar, and from the Vallouise.

The former austere shepherds' hamlet of La Bérarde, in the steeply enclosed granite-walled Vénéon Valley that lies southeast of Le-Bourg-d'Oisans, is now a much frequented base in summer for mountaineers. (The access road from St.-Christophe may not open until May because of snow.) From here the 2,519-meter (8,265- ft.) Tête de la Maye, a relatively easy summit , is accessible; a walk into the National Park continues to follow the Vénéon up to the Plan du Carrelet, from where the views finally open out and include the Chardon glacier.

On the eastern side of the park a road goes up through the hamlets of Vallouise, Pelvoux, and Ailefroide – all of which offer facilities for mountaineers and walkers. The road continues up to the rocky Pré de Madame Carle. From the Pré, a mountain path continues on to the Glacier Blanc, amid awesome rocky scenery typical of the Dauphiné Alps.

In the south of the park, the torrent of the Séveraisse can be followed from the resort of La-Chapelle-en-Valgaudemar, past several waterfalls; from the end of the road, in a mountain cirque, a path (2½ hours round-trip) leads up to the Lac du Lauzon at 2,200 meters (7,218 ft.).

The Parc National des Écrins is one of the largest protected areas in France. Inside the park are a number of magnificent mountain peaks and tiny villages offering facilities for both hikers and climbers

WALK

LYON

The old town of Lyon, at the foot of the Fourvière hill, has several mansions dating from the 15th to the 17th centuries, built by wealthy traders, bankers, and civil servants. This walk takes in many of them, from Gothic (with inner courtyards) to Renaissance.

Start at the place du Change, take the rue de la Loge, then the rue Juiverie to the right (note Nos. 20 to 23, 13, 10, and 8). Turn right into place St.-Paul, then right again into rue Lainerie (Nos. 10, 14, and 18). Across the place du Change, take rue Soufflot (note Hôtel de Gadagne at No. 10) and rue de Gadagne, then rue du Boeuf (Nos. 1, 3, and 16). Off place Neuve-St.-Jean, take rue St.-Jean (Nos. 11 and 7), which leads you back to place du Change ■

★ **ÉVIAN-LES-BAINS** *212C3*

This once-elegant spa on the shores of Lac Léman (Lake Geneva), with a backdrop of the steep mountains of the Chablais, is one of the most well-known suppliers of mineral water. From relatively recent beginnings (in the late 19th century), when Évian acquired its baths, exotic domed casino, lakeside promenade, villas, and stately hotels, the spa has developed into a major conference center, which has ensured at the very least a regular and largely active clientele, if not quite the level of exclusivity to which it once aspired. Facilities, from sports to nightlife, are in abundance, and there are also good opportunities to take excursions into the mountains and on the lake.

★ **GRENOBLE** *212B2*

Capital of the French Alps, Grenoble is one of France's most lively college towns, upscale and confident, and with a multi-cultural population. Grenoble was in the forefront of the move toward modernization in the 1960s, when it was the venue for the Winter Olympics in 1968.

Still a dynamic city, Grenoble has acquired a reputation as one of France's leading centers of contemporary art (together with Bordeaux); its Musée des Beaux-Arts has an outstanding modern art collection.

Grenoble's location, at the confluence of the Drac and Isère rivers, ensured early settlement: from the Roman period onwards the town continued to expand. Now a gondola lift spans the river to the 16th-century Fort de la Bastille, from where there are fine views (as well as a vintage automobile museum). Paths lead down to the Musée Dauphinois, which features local history and crafts.

★ **LÉMAN, LAC** *212C2–3* **(LAKE GENEVA)**

This is France's largest lake, shared with Switzerland. It enjoys a mild microclimate (though its mists often inhibit views across).

On the southeastern part of the (French) shore, mountains rise steeply, providing the most interesting section of coastline. To the west of Évian is another, bigger spa – Thonon-les-Bains, the main town of the area; among vineyards to the east is the fine Château de Ripaille. There are a few swimming resorts, such as Excenevex, which has the best beach on the lake. The ancient little fortified riverside village of Yvoire is exceptionally pretty.

★★★ **LYON** *212A3*

Situated where the Rhône and Saône rivers meet, this is France's second city, for many years a powerful and wealthy place. In the Middle Ages Lyon was already famous for its trade fairs, banking, and its silk industry, and remains so to this day. The heart of the city, on a narrow peninsula between the two rivers, owes much to grand 18th- and 19th-century building programs, with monumental tree-lined squares (place Bellecour, place de la République, and place des Terreaux), and spacious shopping streets.

Even more charming is the restored Renaissance old-town area at the foot of the Fourvière hill (notably rue St.-Jean, rue de Gadagne, and rue du Boeuf), where tall Gothic mansions with their characteristic staircase towers now house restaurants, bistros, and designer boutiques.

At the top of the steep incline of Fourvière hill, easily reached by funicular, there are fragmentary remains of the Roman city and a vast yet distinctly unappealing late-19th-century basilica.

Lyon has many museums, some of exceptional interest, including the Musée Historique des Tissus, which features Lyon silk and material from all over the world; and the large Musée des Beaux-Arts. Other museums cover the history of the city (Musée du Vieux Lyon, which also features a puppet collection), the history of Roman Lyon (located near the ruins), and the history of silk in the city (Maison des Canuts, a small house in the former silk workers' quarter, Les Traboules, with a genuine loom).

Modern transport for a modern city: Grenoble has always been at the center of innovation and is known for its lively arts scene

DRIVE

A TOUR THROUGH THE PEAKS AND LAKES OF THE FRENCH ALPS

472 kilometers / 294 miles (allow 4 days)

This drive takes in some of the most spectacular features of the French Alps: beautiful lakes; the forests of the Chartreuse; the mountain passes of the Col de l'Iséran.

Start at Grenoble, capital of the Alps and one of France's most dynamic modern cities. Take the D512 on the north bank of the Isère, and continue in the direction of St.-Pierre-de-Chartreuse.

1 The Grande Chartreuse
This is the mother house of the Carthusian order, founded in the 11th century and isolated in the dark forests of the massif. There is a museum that explains the monastic life at La Correrie, just to the northwest of the town of St.-Pierre-de-Chartreuse.

ALPINE IBEX
Ski resorts and other developments have inevitably led to the loss of habitat for species such as the rare Alpine ibex, which lives high above the tree line for most of the year.

However, since the creation of the Parc National de la Vanoise, numbers have now crept back to over 500 of these sure-footed animals ■

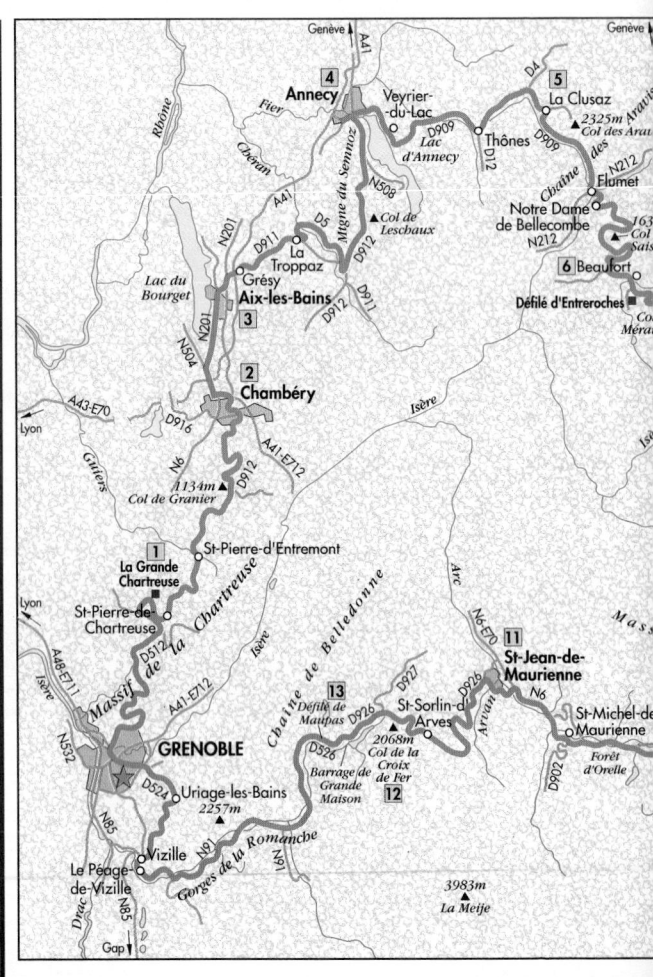

Rejoin the D512, then take the D912 over the Col du Granier to Chambéry.

2 Chambéry

This busy town, with its arcaded streets and a famous fountain, was the former capital of the independent duchy of Savoie.

Take the N201 in the direction of Aix-les-Bains.

3 Aix-les-Bains

On the banks of Le Bourget lake (the largest mountain lake in France), the old spa of Aix-les-

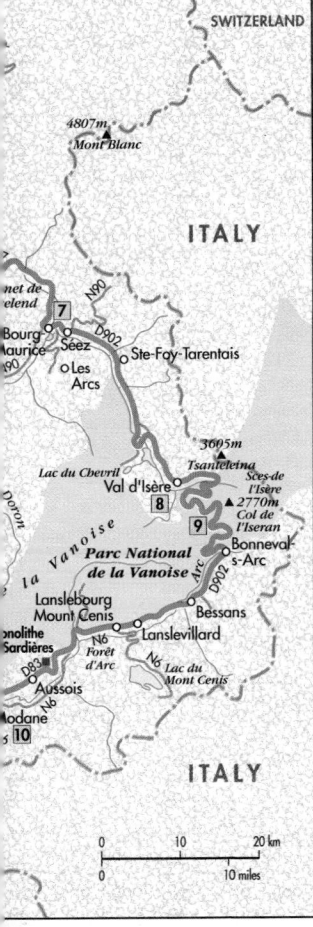

Bains – popular since Roman times – is still an elegant and stylish resort, situated at the foot of Mont Revard. Its heyday was in the 19th century, and some of the atmosphere of this period still pervades the resort today.

There are all kinds of activities, including boat trips, watersports, walks in the woods near the resort, and tours of the Roman remains, including the baths.

Continue north on the N201, then just outside Aix turn right onto the D911. After La Troppaz, take the D31 left, over the Cheran river, then turn right onto the D5. The D5 rejoins the D911; after 8 kilometers (5 mi.), take the D912, which ascends the Montagne du Semnoz and goes over the Col de Leschaux. Continue in the direction of Annecy.

4 Annecy

This beautiful old town has glorious lakeside gardens, a very animated little old town area with narrow streets and sidewalk cafés, horse-drawn carriages, and plenty of lake excursions.

Take the D909 to Thônes, and then to La Clusaz.

5 La Clusaz

This little ski resort does its best to entertain summer visitors, with canoeing, skating, riding, archery, fishing, and even grass-skiing and tobogganing on a metal piste. Reblochon cheese is made here.

Continue on the D909 over the Col des Aravis to Flumet; then go straight ahead on the D218B over the Col des Saisies and follow signs to Beaufort. Go through Beaufort in the direction of Bourg-St.-Maurice.

CHARTREUSE

The potent green liqueur known as Chartreuse is no longer produced as it was originally, at the monastery itself. It now comes from the small town of Voiron (northwest of Grenoble), where the vast cellars are open for visits, and free tasting is offered.

It is named after the Carthusian monks who made it, and who have never revealed the recipe – the elixir probably includes around 130 herbs and plants, added to brandy and honey.

Several other fruit- and plant-based liqueurs are also available (*myrtille, framboise*), in addition to the slightly less potent yellow Chartreuse ■

SKIING

Ski resorts in France are usually quite unlike those of its European neighbors.

Though leisure activity had been pursued in Switzerland in the 1920s and 30s, France joined the industry only after World War II. It set about building brand new high-altitude resorts – Courchevel, Les Menuires, Val Thorens, La Plagne, Tignes, Les Deux-Alpes, L'Alpe d'Huez, Les Arcs – in wide open terrain above the tree line. These resorts were designed to serve one purpose only – skiing.

This they still offer, generally on good snow (because of their altitude); but charm or village atmosphere was never their aim. Most are closed in the summer, as they have no local communities ■

6 Le Beaufortain

Beaufort is another cheese-making area. All around there is wonderful mountain countryside – the rock cleft of the Défilé d'Entreroches and the hairpin passes of the Col de Meraillet and the Cormet de Roselend, among steep torrents, scree slopes and snow-filled gullies, and occasional patches of green mountain meadow.

Continue to the town of Bourg-St.-Maurice.

7 Bourg-St.-Maurice

The valley town of Bourg-St.-Maurice, overlooked by cliffs, harnesses its waters with a hydroelectric system and offers white-water rafting and canoeing. Near Bourg-St.-Maurice lies the popular, modern ski center of Les Arcs.

Follow the signs, and the D902, to Val d'Isère.

8 Val d'Isère

This is one of France's major modern ski resorts, in a narrow valley setting, whose cable cars ascend spectacularly to great heights above. In summer there is little life, and less charm; but some tourist facilities are available, including horseback riding and mountain biking.

Continue on the D902 to the Col de l'Iséran.

9 Col de l'Iséran

At 2,770 meters (9,085 ft.), this is one of the highest roads in Europe, often impenetrable until mid-June. It took 20 years to build, in a setting of wild beauty, and offers superb views into the remote mountains of the Parc National de la Vanoise. The descent is on a better-surfaced road than the ascent.

Continue on the D902. In Bessans follow the Chambéry sign. Go through Lanslevillard, then, in Lanslebourg, join the N6 as for Chambéry. In Sollières, turn right onto the little D83 to Aussois, then go straight ahead on the D215 in the direction of Modane.

10 Modane

This is a major highway and railroad crossing that serves as an access point for several of the Vanoise mountain walks.

Take the N6 towards St.-Jean-de-Maurienne.

11 St.-Jean-de-Maurienne

This industrial valley town has a historic cathedral of great interest, with late-15th-century choir stalls.

Take the D926 for the Col de la Croix de Fer, through narrow wooded gorges.

12 Col de la Croix de Fer

As the road emerges from the five rock tunnels above the breathtaking Arvan gorge, it crosses alpine meadows before a narrow and dizzying zig-zag ascent to the summit of the mountain pass.

Continue down on the Grenoble road.

13 Défilé de Maupas

This route follows more dramatic gorges – the Combe d'Olle and the Défilé de Maupas – as it descends, finally skirting the Barrage de Grand' Maison.

Continue toward Grenoble. At Vizille, turn onto the D101, then take the minor D524 through Uriage-les-Bains back to the center of Grenoble.

★ MAURIENNE, LA *212C2*

The Haute Maurienne area, along the Arc Valley – historic thoroughfare from France to Italy via the Mont Cenis pass (Col du Mont Cenis) – has preserved many of its charming old villages. Unlike many other mountain regions, it has more to offer than just natural scenery. On a pilgrimage route, its village churches are adorned with frescoes and wood carvings, notably at Avrieux, Termignon, Lanslevillard and Bessans.

The local style of building reflects the bleak and often treeless surroundings and harsh winters. Buildings housed people and animals, under roofs made of large flat pieces of stone (*lauzes*) in order to withstand the heavy layer of snow that served as insulation. Particularly unspoiled stone-built villages include Bonneval, the last village before the tortuous climb to the high Iséran Pass, and those along the isolated Avérole Valley to the east of Bessans. The villages of Termignon and Aussois, just to the north of the river, give access to the Vanoise National Park.

The western Arc Valley is industrial, its sole interest for the tourist being a fine cathedral at St.-Jean-de-Maurienne.

MEGÈVE *212C3*

This is one of France's most fashionable and exclusive ski resorts, spread along a wide valley surrounded by gentle wooded slopes. It is also popular in summer; the prosperous and scattered chalets here are more inviting than many of the deserted alpine ski stations. It is well provided with almost every kind of sports facilities, including networks of gentle waymarked walks. A number of mountain excursions by cable car or telecabin are possible – for views, walks or leisurely contemplation in mountain restaurants.

MORZINE *212C3*

South of Lake Geneva, the relatively undramatic mountains of the Chablais, edged to the north by vineyard-covered foothills, have spacious pastures, verdant valleys, and wooded slopes. At the meeting point of no less than six valleys, Morzine is the capital of the area, spread around a large expanse of open countryside; it is both a winter and summer resort, with good sports facilities and extensive opportunities for driving and walking excursions, assisted by a variety of mountain lifts.

A typical dwelling in the Maurienne. Houses were built to contain animals as well as people, and roofs were constructed using large flat pieces of stone, strong enough to support heavy layers of snow that served as insulation

Fall colors in the Parc Naturel Régional du Queyras. The park has a wealth of flora and its remote, elevated setting enjoys a beneficial climate. There are good opportunities for walks amid lovely natural scenery

OISANS, L' 212B2

Consisting largely of the Massif des Écrins (see p.219), the area of the Oisans comprises also the Romanche Valley, busy and very industrial in parts, and the narrow Vénéon Valley, which leads into the heart of the Écrins. In the summer months, glacier skiing is possible from the high modern resorts to each side of the Romanche – L'Alpe d'Huez and Les Deux-Alpes – neither exactly brimming with charm. Beyond L'Alpe d'Huez, a steep mountain road leads (in summer only) over the Col de Sarennes toward the picturesque old villages of Clavans and Besse; here you can still find the sturdy mountain houses, with stone roofs and immensely thick stone walls, that are characteristic of the area.

One of the high peaks of the Écrins, the Meije, topped by a mighty glacier, can best be viewed from just above the large village of La Grave at the foot of the peak, on the road that leads to the village of Le Chazelet.

★★★ PÉROUGES 212A3

Northeast of Lyon, this extraordinary medieval fortified hilltop village, originally founded by Italians from Perugia, supports (as in the past) a thriving artisan community. The narrow cobbled streets, with a central drainage gulley, are shaded by overhanging roofs; the late-medieval houses – many with fine, spacious interiors – have mullioned windows and decorative arches. In the lovely central square there is an ancient hostelry (still plying its trade) and a 200-year-old linden tree.

★★★ QUEYRAS, 212C1
PARC NATUREL RÉGIONAL DU

This high and remote mountain area, bordered to the south and east by the 3,000-meter (9,843-ft.) peaks of France's frontier with Italy, and to the northwest by the narrow gorges of the Guil river, enjoys a sunny climate. A large part of the region is under the protection of a regional park and is rich in flora; high open pastures offer splendid walks.

The village of St.-Véran, lying at 2,000 meters (6,562 ft.), is the most attractively rustic old community of the area. Despite its location on a dead-end road (and the fact that no automobiles are allowed to travel through the village), its charms are now being sought by increasing numbers of visitors; somehow it still manages to keep the 20th century at bay. St.-Véran is a good place to see the traditional architecture of the Queyras region, as well as the typical decorative fountains, sundials, and crosses adorned with scenes of the Passion; one house is preserved as a museum.

From St.-Véran a beautiful mountain road continues to the pilgrimage chapel of Notre-Dame-de-Clausis, from where marked paths (for experienced walkers, in good weather) lead to the mountain crests and passes that serve as the Italian frontier.

To the north, the Guil Valley has some small summer and winter resorts – Aiguilles and Abriès – as well as a couple of old fortified towns, Château-Queyras and Mont Dauphin. From Abriès, a good road leads up into the bare hills around the walking base of L'Echalp, and then rises steeply toward the rocky pyramid of Monte Viso, stopping at the fine Belvédère du Cirque.

To the north of the Guil, the drive over the Col d'Izoard to Briançon is one of the most exhilarating in the Alps because of its savage scenery – a rocky, lunar landscape devoid of trees and vegetation – on the aptly named Casse Déserte.

SERRE-PONÇON, LAC DE   212B1

This enormous reservoir, some 20 kilometers by 3 kilometers (12 mi. by 2 mi.), at the meeting of the Durance and Ubaye rivers, is well provided with watersports facilities, particularly windsurfing. Embrun, a fine old town high on a ledge above the river, has a 12th-century Italianate cathedral.

Just off the road between Savines and le Sauze near Pontis, to the west of the Forêt de Boscodon (which is a reserve for chamois), you can see some of the strange *demoiselles coiffées* (bonneted maidens) or "fairy chimneys" (see picture on p.213). A phenomenon of the southern Alps, these are tall pillars of earth saved from erosion by a layer of rock forming a "hat." There's a bigger collection near Théus, up a steep road to Mont Colombis.

VALLOUISE, LA   212B–C1

This area, to the southwest of Briançon, forms the main gateway to the Écrins National Park (see p.219). Its chief resort is Vallouise, a charming old village with an information center about the national park; farther up the valley lies Ailefroide, full of walkers and climbers, at the foot of the towering Mont Pelvoux.

NAPOLÉON IN THE ALPS

In a daring bid to regain power after being exiled to the island of Elba, Napoléon stormed through the Alps on his way to Paris in March 1815.

Landing 1,026 soldiers on the coast at Golfe-Juan, Napoléon made the 350-kilometer. (218-mi.) journey to Grenoble in just 6 days, often struggling in deep snow.

At the village of Laffrey, south of Grenoble, his route was blocked by troops. Throwing open his coat, Napoléon challenged them with the following words: "Soldiers! I am your emperor! If anyone among you wishes to kill me, here I am!" Officers ordered the soldiers to fire, but instead they cried "Vive l'Empereur!" and joined him in a triumphal procession into Grenoble.

Later he wrote in his memoirs: "As far as Grenoble, I was merely an adventurer. At Grenoble, I became a prince" ■

RHÔNE GASTRONOMY

The Lyonnais has long been thought of as the high temple of French gastronomy.

Its reputation was probably founded on the cooking of a series of women chefs (known as "Les Mères") over 200 years ago.

Paul Bocuse's Auberge, near Lyon, started up in 1765; he is the seventh generation to follow in the family profession, while Georges Blanc is the fourth generation of chefs at Vonnas.

***Cuisine moderne* was started here by Fernand Point in the 1950s. Point's restaurant at Vienne is still a gastronomic highlight; as are those of Pic at Valence, Chapel at Mionnay, Blanc at Vonnas, and Bocuse at Collonges-au-Mont-d'Or. But be warned: such luxury does not come cheap ■**

★★★ VANOISE, PARC NATIONAL DE LA   212C2

The great rocky peaks of the Vanoise massif are now part of France's oldest national park, founded in 1963. Wild and remote, with wide glaciers and high valleys, the area contains a mixture of charming old valley villages and some of France's most dynamic modern ski resorts, from where high incursions can be made (on skis, at least) to the very summits of the peaks.

The already extensive network of interconnecting ski lifts grows wider every year; several resorts within the park (Courchevel, Méribel, Les Menuires, and Val Thorens) are linked in what is claimed to be the greatest skiing domain in the world. The glaciers provide summer skiing, too – near the peaks of La Grande Motte and the Aiguille de Péclet (reached from Tignes and Val Thorens respectively).

In summer, more appropriate and lower-altitude bases can be found for exploring the many hiking trails that cut across the park (sturdy walking shoes are recommended). Along the park's southern edge are the attractive hamlets of the Arc Valley (see la Maurienne, p.225), including the villages of Aussois, Termignon, and Bonneval. On the western side, the steeply enclosed climbers' resort of Pralognan, 1,400 meters (4,600 ft.), and the little town of Champagny-en-Vanoise (a great cheese-making center) are lovely old places, as is the village of Peisey-Nancroix in the Ponturin Valley to the north.

Visitors with automobiles can take the steep and winding road that goes into the park from Termignon to Bellecombe, 12 kilometers (7½ mi.), from where there are many walks along the little Leisse Valley.

★ VERCORS, LE   212A1

A limestone mountain massif, forested with pines and with a green and gentle interior, the Vercors is notable for its deep and tortuous gorges, where torrents carve their way through the rock and roads are cut precariously into cliff faces. It is also remembered as a major citadel of the French Resistance during World War II. Several monuments commemorate those who lost their lives, including one at the Grotte de la Luire, south of La Chapelle-en-Vercors. At the rebuilt village of Vassieux-en-Vercors, a small museum explores these wartime events.

The resort of Villard-de-Lans makes a suitable base for leisurely walks, and for drives along some of the gorges. The most spectacular are the dark and forbidding Grands Goulets – very narrow, with the road hewn alarmingly into the overhanging rock; and the Combe Laval, yet another precarious road high above the Cholet river.

VIENNE   212A2

This old and busy Rhône town has much of interest for sightseers. The sights fall mainly into two categories: remains of the city's Roman past, which include a fine Corinthian temple, restored in the 19th century, and a huge theater, which is used for summer drama; and several interesting churches, two of which date from very early Christian times (St.-Pierre, which now houses a museum of Gallo-Roman works; and St.-André-le-Bas, which has a fine cloister). The cathedral of St.-Maurice is constructed in Romanesque and Gothic style, and has a wealth of beautiful carvings.

On the western side of the river, the excavations of the Gallo-Roman town can be visited.

BURGUNDY, ALSACE-LORRAINE AND THE NORTH

Head southeast from the
magnificent cliffs and Gothic
cathedrals of the north to the rich
wines of Burgundy and soft
mountains of the Jura

CALENDAR OF EVENTS

APRIL TO MAY – Strasbourg (Bas-Rhin) hosts a **Spring Fair** between these two colorful months.

MAY TO SEPTEMBER – Domrémy (Vosges): **Festival of the Maid of Orléans.**

JUNE – The **French Grand Prix** is held at Dijon (Côte d'Or) drawing crowds from around the world. Wissembourg (Bas-Rhin) puts on a **Costume Festival.**

JULY TO AUGUST – The **North Burgundy Festival** at Châtillon-sur-Seine with music and dance.

JULY TO SEPTEMBER – All over Burgundy, tours are organized through the illustrious vineyards ■

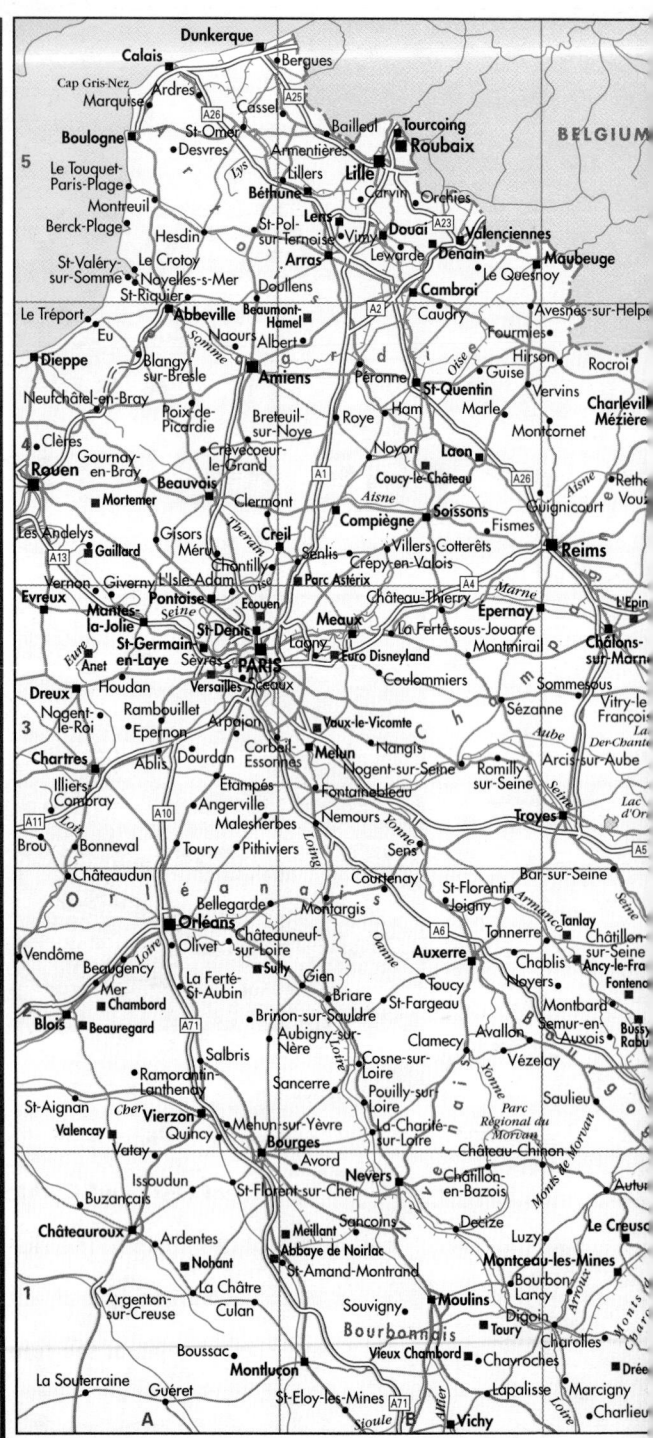

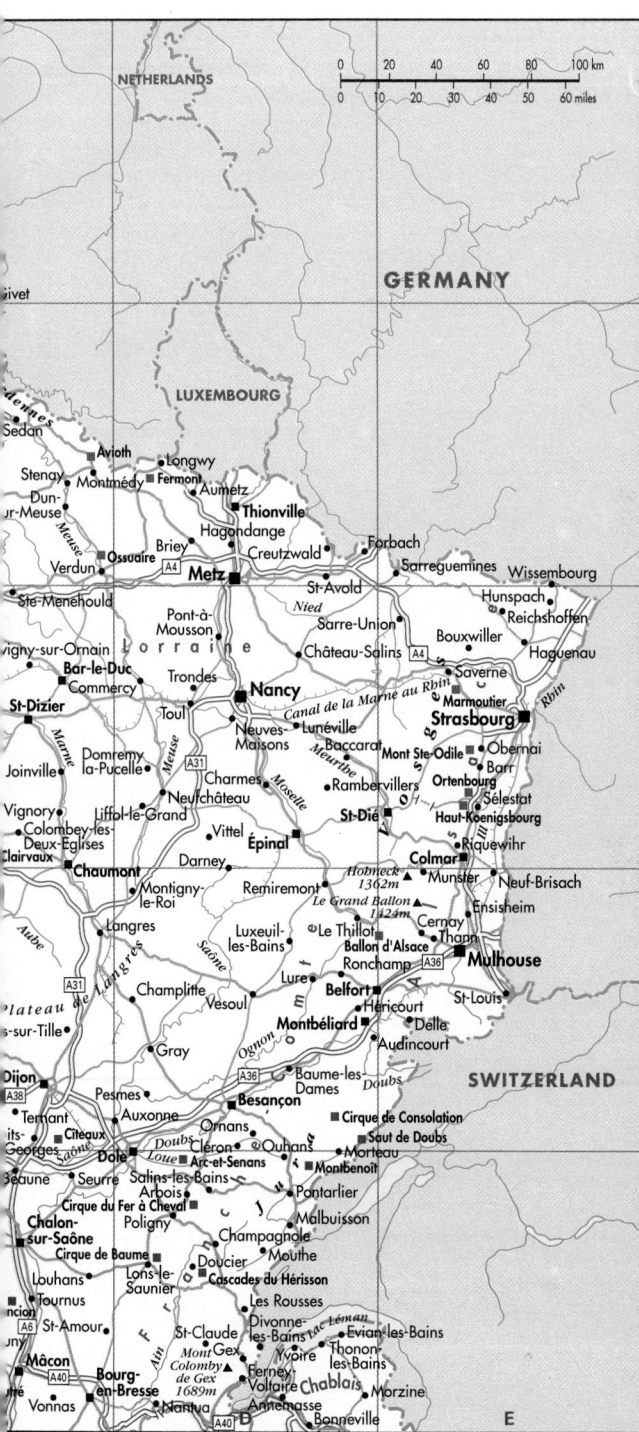

AUGUST –
A **Fishermen's Festival** is celebrated at this time of year in Auxerre (Yonne). Chaon (Doubs) holds a **Lake Festival** in this summer month. A **Horseman's Festival** takes place at Maiche (Doubs).

SEPTEMBER 1 AND 2 – The **Mystery of Sainte Reine** at Alise-Sainte-Reine is a reconstruction of the saint's martyrdom.

OCTOBER –
Hot-air Balloon Meeting during the first weekend at Auxerre.

OCTOBER 31 TO NOVEMBER 12 – See the **International Gastronomic Fair** held in Dijon.

NOVEMBER –
On the fourth Sunday the **Wine Festival** takes place in Chablis including wine tasting and the crowning of the Harvest Queen. **Beaujolais nouveau** is released on the third Thursday in November ∎

WALK

AMIENS

Start at the cathedral (France's largest), and head down rue Henri IV. Turn left onto rue des Sergents, then continue to rue des Trois Cailloux. Turn right and, at place Gambetta, turn left onto rue de la République, which brings you to the Musée de Picardie.

Return to place Gambetta and turn right onto rue des Trois Cailloux. Heading toward the 104-meter (341-ft.) Tour Perret, make a sharp left onto rue Victor Hugo at place René Goblet.

At rue Adéodat Lefèvre, turn right, behind the cathedral, then left onto rue des Augustins. At Port d'Amont, turn right and cross the river.

From here it's an easy 15-minute walk back to the cathedral ∎

BURGUNDY, ALSACE-LORRAINE AND THE NORTH

Every year, millions of visitors travel through the north of France on their way to and from the Channel ports or the Channel Tunnel. Few take time to visit the north coast, splendid examples of Gothic architecture, or the vast, silent war cemeteries.

Noted now for its World War I battlegrounds, the north was, in the Middle Ages, home to great trading towns, and the wealth they spawned led to the building of majestic cathedrals, many of which are still exactly as they were hundreds of years ago.

Slightly better known is **Alsace-Lorraine**. As French as anywhere else in the country, the region was for centuries battled over by France and Germany. It retains an interesting mixture of dialects, cuisine, wine, and architecture that wouldn't look out of place across the border in Germany. **Strasbourg**, vital to the running of the affairs of the European Union, typifies this with its unusual blend of mansard roofs and timber-framed houses. Take time to visit the harmonious ancient capital of Lorraine – **Nancy** – with its marvelous architecture and enlightened 18th-century town planning.

Burgundy has long been known for its world-famous wines. The region is much more than just its vineyards, however, with charming villages scattered across the rolling countryside, and food that is easily equal to the celebrated wines. Visit **Beaune**, in the heart of the wine industry, and home to the elegant Hospice (Hôtel Dieu). The architecture and concentrated wealth of **Dijon** are testimony to the faded greatness of the dukes of Burgundy, who were once a match for the French

Crown itself, and who built themselves impressive castles and palaces to prove it.

Farther southeast are the hidden valleys, remote forests, deep lakes and quiet mountains of the **Jura**, where cheese-making and gentle tourism go hand in hand. The Jura was long famous for its rebellious and anarchic population; even now you'll find the people rugged and independent, though often more welcoming of foreigners than visitors from the capital.

AIN VALLEY   231D1

The Ain river runs a 190-kilometer (118-mi.) course from its source near Champagnole in the Jura to its confluence with the Rhône, 20 kilometers (12½ mi.) east of Lyon. Hydroelectric dams along the upper section have created a series of spectacular narrow lakes, south of which you can see the impressive Gorges de l'Ain.

Near Doucier, not far from the river's source, you should visit the river's main claim to fame: the Cascades du Hérisson ("Hedgehog Waterfalls"). These remarkable falls can be reached by driving along the D326 from Doucier, then on foot. But note: in very hot weather this part of the river may dry up.

★★ AMIENS   230A4

Although more than half of Amiens was destroyed during World War II, and in spite of the fact that it is now a busy city of 130,000, the glorious Gothic cathedral still dominates both the old and new towns. The 112-meter (367-ft.) spire crowns France's largest cathedral, whose harmonious appearance owes much to the relatively short period of its construction (it was almost entirely completed within the 13th century).

Over 700 years later the extraordinary display of sculpture on the west front is as impressive as ever, and provides an appetizer for the sheer immensity of the interior. The old town also boasts the fascinating Musée de Picardie and a local history museum (in the 17th-century Hôtel de Berny), but perhaps more interesting are the old market gardens, known as *hortillonnages*, which were originally cultivated on the islands of the Somme. Many of the plots are accessible only by boat, and the produce used to be brought into town on immense barges. The gardens are only a short 15-minute walk from the cathedral.

★★★ ANCY-LE-FRANC,   230C2
CHÂTEAU D'

The lovely château of Ancy-le-Franc lies on the outskirts of the village, roughly halfway between Dijon and Troyes. It was built in the middle of the 16th century by the Clermont-Tonnerre family (who still own it) and remains one of the best examples of Italian Renaissance architecture in France. Less showy than the châteaux of the Loire, the inner courtyard and finely decorated apartments belie the somewhat sober exterior. This is one of the treasures of greater Burgundy.

ARBOIS   231D1

Famous for the pursuits of pasteurization (Louis Pasteur lived here, and his riverside house is now a museum) and wine-making (plenty of tasting opportunities), Arbois is an engaging town set among some of the most attractive Jura scenery.

The old and expensive Vin Jaune, which keeps longer than any other French wine, has an unusual flavor, but almost all palates will find the delicate Rosé agreeable. Try the local dishes, such as *poularde au vin jaune*.

Arbois: pretty houses overhang the Cuisance in the Jura region. Louis Pasteur had strong links with the town, and the house that used to be his father's tannery has been turned into a small museum

BURGUNDY WINES

As renowned as Bordeaux clarets, Burgundy wines come from vines grown from the island outpost of Chablis in the north to almost as far as Mâcon in the south.

The most famous of all come from the Côte d'Or, a long, narrow ridge that runs from Dijon to Beaune via Nuits–St.-Georges.

Beaune is very much the capital of the wine trade, even though Dijon is the capital of Burgundy. Try to stop in at one of the hundreds of properties where older and younger varieties of the same wine can be tasted. In October at harvest time, the area smells of crushed grapes ■

★ ARC-ET-SENANS *231D1*

In the days when salt was both more important and less easy to obtain, royal saltworks were started at Arc-et-Senans, near Salins-les-Bains, in the heart of the Jura. Architect Claude-Nicolas Ledoux was responsible for the plans for this town. Its housing is ranged in concentric circles around the salt evaporation halls, and are now used for exhibitions.

★ ARDENNES *231C4*

Spreading across the Franco-Belgian border, the Ardennes is a large forested upland region full of deer and wild boar. The Meuse river threads its way through the forest, and a boat trip along the river is recommended.

Enclosed in a loop of the Meuse is the area's major town, Charleville, which has a grand Renaissance square. Poetry lovers should note that Charleville was both the birthplace and resting place of Arthur Rimbaud.

★★★ ARRAS *230B5*

If it weren't for the extraordinary Grand'place and the place des Héros, Arras would probably be bypassed on your way somewhere else. As it is, the two squares are exquisite: unmissable examples of 18th-century northern European architecture, with narrow brick and stone town houses topped with Flemish gables and supported on sandstone colonnades. Underneath are the famous cellars, in some cases several stories deep, historically used in wartime to shelter the population.

★★ AUTUN *230C1*

The town of Autun may be tiny, but the early 12th-century cathedral of St.-Lazare is simply glorious. The tympanum, above the porch, is one of the best pieces of medieval stone carving and, unusually, it is autographed on the lintel by its sculptor, Gilbertus. Inside, look for the carved capitals and climb the bell tower for a fine view over the town. Autun also has a small collection of ancient remains. Most evocative are the ruins of the Roman theater, which show how important the town was.

★ AUXERRE *230B2*

Millions of Parisians race past Auxerre on the A6 (Autoroute du Soleil), but it's worth stopping here, the gateway to Burgundy. Ancient cobbled streets surround the 12th-century cathedral, which has lovely 13th- and 16th-century stained glass. It also flaunts some 11th-century frescoes in the crypt (look for the one showing Christ riding an unusual white horse).

Some 300 meters (984 ft.) north, up the rue Cochois, in the even older (9th-century) crypt of the Abbaye St.-Germain, you'll find frescoes depicting the life and death of Saint Stephen.

★ AVALLON *230B2*

Avallon comes in two parts: the modern town outside the old walls, and the ancient fortified town inside them. Fortunately the new town does not impinge on the old, and views from the south and west show the ramparts and towers to their best advantage. Inside the walls, a ramble through the convincingly ancient cobbled streets is worth making time for; you'll take in details such as the damaged 12th-century door to the church and the 15th-century watchtower that spans the main street just around the corner.

AVIOTH, BASILICA   231C4

Nestled into a fold of the Belgian border, the Basilica of Avioth is an ostentatious Gothic church with original 14th-century stained glass, lying 8 kilometers (5 mi.) north of the citadel town of Montmédy. A visit is worthwhile if your trip coincides with the annual pilgrimage on July 16.

BALLON D'ALSACE   231E2

At the southern end of the Vosges mountains there are several distinct round-topped peaks, known locally as Ballons, which contrast with the more rugged peaks of red sandstone further north. The Ballon d'Alsace is perhaps the most distinctive of these, and marks the corner of Alsace, Lorraine, and Franche-Comté. At 1,250 meters (4,100 ft.) the hill is over 750 meters (2,460 ft.) above the Belfort plateau, and makes for a pleasant excursion from Belfort.

BAR-LE-DUC   231C3

The market town of Bar-le-Duc is dominated by the church of St.-Étienne, on place St.-Pierre, at the edge of the upper town. There are good views of the town, the Ornain river and the Marne–Rhine canal from here and from the ramparts below. Inside

the church is "le Squelette," a skeletal statue carved in memory of the Prince of Orange, who wanted, in a rather macabre way, a memorial that would look as though he had lain dead for three years already. He got it.

★★★ BEAUNE   231C1

Heart of the Burgundy wine trade and home to the Hospice (Hôtel-Dieu), Beaune is one of the best bases for trips into the vineyards of the Côte d'Or.

If you visit only one place in Burgundy, make it Beaune. The Hôtel-Dieu saw continuous service from its founding in 1443 until 1971, and now has the main ward, with its famous curtained double-occupancy beds, open to visitors. Roger van der Weyden's famous polyptych, the "Last Judgement," originally the altarpiece here, is now on display in a separate part of the museum and should not be missed. Take the guided tour, which also allows you to visit the pharmacy and kitchens.

Beaune is also a great place to eat out, and, of course, to sample some of the excellent Burgundy wines – don't miss the opportunity of a wine-tasting at the Marché aux Vins across the street from the Hôtel-Dieu.

The Hôtel-Dieu in Beaune served as a hospital for over 500 years from 1443 to 1971. Its elegant exterior, with multicolored tiles and exquisite architectural detail, gives it the appearance of a splendid palace

BURGUNDY APERITIFS

A traditional regional aperitif is *kir*, made from a mixture of Bourgogne *aligoté* (white wine made from the inferior aligoté grape) and *crème de cassis* (blackcurrant liqueur) from Dijon.

The drink was invented by Canon Kir, mayor of Dijon during the 1940s, who served it at all public functions in order to boost its sales ■

BELFORT   231D2

Divided neatly into the old town on the east side of the Savoureuse river and the new town on the west side, Belfort is a major hub of light industry and a transportation nerve-center, since it lies at the corner of Alsace, Bourgogne, and the Jura.

The town's hallmark is the huge sandstone lion, 22 meters (72 ft.) long, 11 meters (36 ft.) tall, that stands near the château at the summit of the old town. The lion was the work of the sculptor Bartholdi, who also made his mark with the Statue of Liberty. The pleasantly restored streets leading up to the château on its 70-meter (230-ft.) crag merit a stroll, and show Belfort's historical importance as guardian of the Belfort Gap, the main route from the Vosges to the Jura.

★ BERGUES   230A5

Just inland from Dunkerque, the small town of Bergues remains trapped in a defensive past, surrounded by old fortifications, protective walls and elaborate moats. The harmonious yellow-brick houses date mostly from the 17th and 18th centuries, though many had to be rebuilt – as was the 54-meter (177-ft.) watchtower – after 1944.

★ BESANÇON   231D2

Capital of Franche-Comté since the end of the 17th century, Besançon was, in the days before digital watches, the French capital of watchmakers. The city now has a number of good museums, all of which are in the older part of town, almost surrounded by the Doubs river and cut off by the citadel to the southeast.

The Beaux-Arts Museum features an excellent, if eclectic, collection ranging from Rubens and Titian to Matisse and Picasso. Take the elegant, if sometimes forbidding, Grande Rue to the cathedral of St.-Jean, which sports a Roman altar, a 19th-century astronomical clock and a noteworthy "Virgin and Saints" by Fra Bartolomeo (1512). Other museums include a natural history museum, a museum dedicated to the Resistance and a museum of agricultural exhibits.

★ BOULOGNE 230A5

Most attractive by far of the big Channel ports, and the European Union's largest fishing port, Boulogne has to some extent been deserted by tourists, since the ferry services now mostly go to Calais, 35 kilometers (22 mi.) away. But the walled old town alone makes Boulogne worth a visit, and you should definitely make the effort to walk up from the port and around the medieval rectangular ramparts, stopping in at the somewhat overblown 19th-century cathedral. The new aquarium, Nausicaa, on the beach (across the river from the ferry terminal) is France's largest, and well worth the detour.

BOURG-EN-BRESSE 231C1

Visited mainly for the monastic church of Brou (see below), on the southeast side of the city, Bourg-en-Bresse nonetheless merits a visit of its own, and you should certainly stop for a meal – the cuisine is not only excellent, but outstanding value for money. The center of town is dominated on Wednesdays and Saturdays by an exceptionally good and colorful market. Take time, if you're already here to visit Brou, to explore the narrow streets and admire the chic town houses, if only to work up an appetite.

LA BRESSE 231C1

The rolling pastures and small woods of the Bresse region (around Bourg-en-Bresse) are famed mainly for the quality of the chickens that are bred here – make sure you try the excellent *poulet de Bresse* while you're visiting. Look also for the traditional farmhouses and barns, many of which have remained unchanged since the early 17th century, with their wide roofs and distinctive saracen chimneys. If you aren't on a fixed budget, stop in at Georges Blanc's wonderful little restaurant in the small town of Vonnas – it's one of the top 20 in all of France, with a wine cellar (and a price tag!) to match.

★★ BROU 231C1

The monastic church at Brou (now part of Bourg-en-Bresse) is one of the treasures of late Gothic architecture. Completed in 1532, the church is near perfect, with 74 exquisitely carved choir stalls, a magnificent rood screen, glorious stained glass, and the three marble tombs of Philibert II of Savoy, his mother (Margaret of Bourbon), and his wife (Margaret of Austria). The monastery next door now houses an interesting regional museum.

BUSSY-RABUTIN, CHÂTEAU DE 230C2

Some 60 kilometers (38 mi.) northwest of Dijon, and only 4 kilometers (2½ mi.) from the village of Alise Ste.-Reine (site of Alésia, the scene of the defeat of Vercingetorix by Julius Caesar in 52 BC), lies the 16th-century château of Bussy-Rabutin.

In 1659, Roger de Rabutin, the satirical writer, wrote a parody on the young Louis XIV's love affairs. This earned him a spell in the Bastille, before he was exiled to his château here. You can see a fine portrait of him by Le Febvre.

EXPERIENCING THE SEA

More than just an aquarium, Boulogne's enormously successful National Marine Center, Nausicáa, has now been in existence for over five years.

During that time more than 3 million people have passed through its doors to savor this unusual experience, where New-Age "sea music" filters through half-lit rooms, illuminated only by aquarium tanks, where you find yourself having eyeball-to-eyeball encounters with fish and other creatures.

More than 6,000 fish live in Nausicáa's 27 aquariums, which jointly hold over 1.5 million liters (220,000 gal.) of water.

The relationship between humans and the sea is explored via various inter-active terminals, including touch-tanks and a mock-up of a fishing trawler ■

CHANNEL TUNNEL

Since the 16th century, engineers and visionaries have dreamed of a way of connecting England and France that didn't rely on taking boats across often unfavorable seas.

In Victorian times great plans were drawn up for bridges, tunnels, and pontoons, but all were deemed to be politically dangerous, and it wasn't until 1966 that a serious plan for a tunnel was considered in earnest. However, funding problems from the British side meant that work didn't start until 1986.

Opened in 1993, the 52-kilometer (33-mi.) tunnel runs 30 meters (98 ft.) under the sea bed and the journey from Folkestone to Calais takes about 35 minutes. Paris to London by rail on the Eurostar takes about 3 hours ■

CALAIS 230A5

France's busiest passenger port was almost completely destroyed during World War II, and was hastily rebuilt afterwards in unsophisticated concrete – so don't expect too much in the way of classic architecture or streets with any real character. Since the completion of the Channel Tunnel and the new expressway into the docks, drivers have had to make a detour to visit the center, which has made the town both less crowded and more pleasant.

If you don't see them here, outside the town hall, do at least try to see Rodin's "Burghers of Calais" in the Rodin Museum in Paris (see p.39). The statue depicts the offer by six of the city fathers to sacrifice themselves in exchange for the freedom of the city from the English siege of 1346–7; though emaciated, the figures are certainly not humble.

Across the road, in the Parc St.-Pierre, a former German bunker has been converted into a war museum. The beach in Calais (across the harbor from the ferries) is surprisingly pleasant, considering nearby heavy traffic, and it's worth strolling along the grassy sand dunes to the western end, where you'll find a couple of good seafood restaurants.

CAMBRAI 230B5

Cambrai, famous since medieval times for its fine linen, Cambric, was almost entirely destroyed in 1918 during the German retreat, although the fine town hall on the Grand'Place shows what the city used to be like. Watch the figures of Martin and Martine strike the hours on the great bell here. In the nearby church of St.-Géry, look for the Rubens painting of the burial of Christ. It may not give you an appetite for traditional Cambrai tripe and sausages, but you should try them anyway.

★★ CASSEL 230B5

The small, self-contained town of Cassel epitomizes Flemish life, and has the advantage of a wonderful location. Perched on a 176-meter (577-ft.) hill above a plain that is almost at sea level, the site offers fantastic views east across the border into Belgium, north to the Channel and south and west over the Flanders fields made infamous during World War I.

There is a good statue of Maréchal Foch, who made this his headquarters in 1914–15, at the top of the hill.

Walk from here down through the narrow, sloping streets of this elegant town, stopping to admire the charming, elongated cobbled Grande Place.

CHABLIS 230B2

The little town of Chablis is responsible for one of the world's most famous wines. Far closer to Champagne than the heart of Burgundy, the absorption of the commune into Bourgogne in 1477 has meant that the wine, in spite of everything, is a Burgundy. Small vineyards are scattered among the forests, which were planted here during the decline of the wine before it experienced its re-emergence over the last two decades, and there are many pleasant country walks. The town itself was mostly destroyed in 1940, but the church of St.-Pierre, just outside, dates back to the 12th century.

CHÂLONS-SUR-MARNE 230C3

A mix of ancient and modern, Châlons-sur-Marne lies on the east bank of the Marne and is worth visiting if you're interested in wines (champagne) or religious architecture.

Half-timbered houses cluster near the city's churches, the most famous of which is Notre-Dame-

Rodin's "Burghers of Calais" (1895) stands in front of the town hall in Calais. This group of bronze figures demonstrates the sculptor's hugely expressive talent; copies of the work can also be seen in London, Paris and Los Angeles

en-Vaux, with its four towers and 56-bell carillon. Inside there is excellent stained glass (from Troyes), and in the museum, housed in the cloisters to the left of the church, you can see a marvelous collection of statues and sculpted capitals from the old Romanesque cloisters.

The great Gothic cathedral of St.-Étienne also has good stained glass and a particularly gaudy treasury. The church of St.-Jean is the oldest in the city, with an 11th-century Romanesque nave.

★ CHÂTILLON-SUR-SEINE   230C2

The main attraction in this small town is the treasure from Vix, which can be seen in the museum.

Most striking of the artifacts excavated from the grave of a Gallic princess is a huge bronze urn dating from the 6th century BC. The urn stands nearly 2 meters (7 ft.) tall, weighs over 200 kg (440 lb.), and has a magnificent frieze of warriors and horse-drawn chariots around its neck.

Also not to be missed here is the church of St.-Vorles, a Romanesque treat from the 10th century (the tower is slightly more recent, having been added in the 13th century). The tourist office will happily tell you how to get to the source of the Douix on foot; the short walk is well worth the effort on a hot summer's day, as the river springs from the rock here in cool, leafy surroundings.

SNAILS

Everywhere you go in Burgundy (and now in the rest of France) you'll see *escargots* (snails) on the menu.

Many visitors never try this specialty, in spite of its mouth-watering sauce of parsley and garlic butter.

It's true that eating snails at their worst can be likened to chewing on small pieces of rubber, but at their best they are tender, flavorsome, and simply delicious. Try them! ∎

WALK

NOYELLES-SUR-MER

Start at the railroad crossing in Noyelles. Walk up the main street, then turn right onto rue de l'Église. Turn right at the next intersection, cross the street, and take the rue du 8 Mai.

Leave the village, past the sports stadium; follow a path to the left downhill, passing a quarry, and at an intersection take the main track to the left. Soon you will see the gateway to the Chinese Cemetery. Follow the path around to the right, then turn left; a track leads to the cemetery. Continue down the road into Nolette and follow the sign to Ponthoile.

Carry on to the picnic area, cross the river and turn left along a track beside the river. The track soon gives way to open fields, then becomes a road which leads back to the railroad crossing ■

CLUNY *231C1*

In 1798, after the Revolution, the abbey church of St.-Pierre-St.-Paul was destroyed completely as part of the systematic suppression of the Cluniac order. All that can be seen today of what was for centuries the largest, most important and most influential church in Christendom is something of the groundplan, a single tower of the transept, and a flour store (*farinier*).

Cluny is still worth a visit, however, for the remnants (the collection of carved capitals in the *farinier* is simply magnificent), and to learn more about the historical importance of the Cluniac order, whose abbots at one time wielded more influence than the popes. To see a smaller, period replica of the lost church of Cluny, visit Paray le Monial.

★ COLMAR *231E3*

Colmar is the archetypal Alsatian city, with high-gabled, half-timbered houses lining the old streets and squares of the picturesque city center. Look in particular for the old Customs House, with its timber gallery and staircase tower, and the Maison Pfister, which has frescoes and a pyramidal roof. Take time to walk down across the river into the charming Quartier de la Krutenau, Colmar's "Little Venice."

To avoid disappointment in the Unterlinden Museum, which bills itself as France's most popular outside Paris, it's worthwhile seeing everything else you want before finishing with Mathias Grünewald. His magnificent "Issenheim Altarpiece" was completed in 1512 for the chapel of the Antonites' convent in Issenheim, south of Colmar. After this you may be in the mood for a good meal: Colmar is a pleasing place to sample the best of Alsatian cuisine.

COLOMBEY-LES-DEUX-ÉGLISES *231C3*

The small village of Colombey-les-Deux-Églises (population 660) was put on the map by Général de Gaulle, who lived here from 1946 to 1958 and died here in 1970, just one year after retiring from political life.

The first floor of his house is now open to visitors and you can see how simply this most famous of French soldiers and politicians actually lived. Many visitors will also want to visit de Gaulle's burial plot in the village graveyard, and nobody will be able to miss the 44-meter (144-ft.) memorial cross of Lorraine, which looks out over the surrounding countryside.

★ COUCY-LE-CHÂTEAU *230B4*

All that is left now of one of the greatest medieval castles is the extensive ramparts and heaped ruins that completely surround this town. These, ironically, were in much better shape before they were subjected to heavy damage during World War I by the retreating German army.

★★★ DIJON *230C2*

The underrated capital of Burgundy is often overlooked in favor of the smaller and more charming Beaune, but Dijon has plenty of attractions in the cheerful town center, and boasts a whole host of superb restaurants for every budget.

The enormous Palais des Ducs now houses the Museum of Fine Arts, which has a good permanent collection of sculpture and also puts on occasionally brilliant temporary exhibitions. The cathedral has a lovely colored tile roof, and sits above an interesting 10th-century round crypt, but is overshadowed somewhat by the outstanding front of Notre-Dame, with its rows of Gothic gargoyles.

Walk the narrow streets behind Notre-Dame for something of the atmosphere of 16th-century Dijon, without, you'll be glad to hear, the authentic smell and noise of genuine 16th-century life.

DIVONNE-LES-BAINS 231D1

Completely dominated by the wealth of Switzerland less than a kilometer away, Divonne has little left of the charm T. S. Eliot found here in the 1920s, and the casino now has the highest turnover in France. The baths and hot spring waters, thought to be beneficial since Roman times, have been superseded by pursuits such as gambling and golf, though the village itself has a thriving Sunday market, and has been gentrified somewhat by the municipality. The lake has a good artificial sandy beach and offers pleasant swimming in summer.

DOLE 231D1

Usurped by Besançon as capital of the Comté in 1674, Dole still has the feel of an old regional capital with its fine houses (note the carved doorways) and narrow streets. The engaging old town surrounds the 16th-century church of Notre-Dame, which, though somewhat dour on the outside, is delightfully spacious inside, and has an elegant tower 75 meters (246 ft.) tall.

One street away, running parallel to the Doubs river and the Rhône–Rhine canal, is the rue Pasteur. The house where Louis Pasteur was born is now a museum to his achievements, even though Pasteur left Dole when he was just five. Also worth visiting is the Hôtel de Froissard, a former Carmelite convent.

DOMRÉMY-LA-PUCELLE 231D3

This tiny village (pop. 182, and falling) is nonetheless the most celebrated in Lorraine: Jeanne d'Arc was born here. Her extraordinary – and extraordinarily short – life (she was burned at the stake when just 19 years old) is celebrated here in the house in which she was born and in the church where she was baptized. Her parents' house is now a museum and shows just what Joan achieved between 1425, when as a 13-year-old she heard the famous voices telling her it was up to her to liberate France, and May 1431, when she was finally burned as a heretic for refusing to renounce her beliefs. Military commanders don't come much more heroic, glamorous, or interesting than this.

WALK

DIJON

Start from the center of town, at the place François Rude. Head due north, crossing rue Musette, and enter the superb market hall with its rich array of stalls. Return to rue Musette and turn left, noting the façade of Notre-Dame, with its mechanical clock from 1383. Go behind the church into rue de la Chouette and look for the tiny, carved, stone owl on the church wall. The streets behind here are Dijon's oldest.

Turn right on rue Lamonnoye to place du Théâtre. Turn right again to place de la Libération. Farther along rue de la Liberté return to place François Rude ■

Detail of the main gateway to the Palais des Ducs, Dijon. The palace was restored and adapted in the 17th century and is now home to a fine arts museum

DOUAI 230B5

Battered successively by both World Wars, Douai still retains enough of its original 17th- and 18th-century houses in the center of town, on the right bank of the Scarpe river, to merit a visit. The 64-meter (210-ft.) Gothic bell-tower (Beffroi) is one of the best in the north of France.

Some 8 kilometers (5 mi.) from Douai, at Lewarde, is the Centre Historique Minier, which gives a horrifyingly accurate picture of what mining life was like before the invention of new machines and drilling equipment.

★ DOUBS VALLEY 231D2

The source of the Doubs and its confluence with the Saône are just 90 kilometers (56 mi.) apart, but the river manages to wind its way for over 430 kilometers (270 mi.) between the two points. The upper reaches of the river are scenic, and run through an area of outstanding natural beauty, particularly where the river marks the Franco-Swiss border.

The Saut du Doubs is a spectacular 30-meter (98-ft.) waterfall, near Morteau, best

Downstream from Villers-le-Lac, the gorges of the Doubs river mark the boundary with Switzerland. The scenery here is especially pretty, with limestone cliffs and verdant upland pastures creating an air of tranquility

seen from a boat (downstream), and marks the beginning of the Doubs Gorges. The limestone gorges are renowned among fly-fishermen and canoeists, and also offer some good rock-climbing.

Between Pontarlier and Morteau stop off at Montbenoît, whose abbey church has superbly carved 16th-century choir stalls.

★★★ ÉPERNAY/REIMS 230B3/C4

Twin hosts to the sound of popping corks and fizzing glasses, Épernay and Reims have entirely made their fortunes on the accidental invention by the monk Dom Perignon of the champagne-making process.

In spite of the unforgettable champagne connection, Reims is very much worth visiting on its own account; Épernay, on the other hand, is champagne city, with its network of limestone tunnels, its cellars, monuments, and museums all single-mindedly celebrating the millions of bottles of bubbly that are produced in and around the town each year.

Reims, six times larger and coronation city for most of the French kings, is home to some of

the most prestigious of the champagne houses (including Krug, Lanson, Taittinger and Veuve Clicquot). But it also has the cathedral of Notre-Dame (with some wonderful stained-glass windows by Chagall), the excellent Musée St.-Denis (tapestries and paintings), the 12th-century Basilica of St.-Rémi, and the Musée Hôtel le Vergeur (sculpture, engravings and paintings).

ÉPINAL   231D3

Located on the western edge of the Vosges mountains, Épinal stands on both sides of the Moselle river, with the old town on the right bank. Many of the buildings here date back to the Middle Ages: of special note are the Basilica of St.-Maurice (13th century) and the colonnaded place des Vosges.

On the west bank (actually an island), don't miss the Musée des Vosges et de l'Imagerie – Rembrandts vie for attention here with Épinal's most famous export: garish 18th- and 19th-century pictures on the subjects of virtue and piety.

★ L'ÉPINE   230C3

Since the Hundred Years War, when the Virgin Mary was spotted burning in a thorn (*épine*) bush here, this has been a major pilgrimage site. The 16th-century church is a triumph of Flamboyant Gothic architecture. Inside, the choir is an interesting mixture of Gothic and Renaissance. L'Épine is 9 kilometers (5½ mi.) east of Châlons-sur-Marne, and can easily be combined with a visit to Châlons (see p.238).

FONTENAY, ABBAYE DE   230C2

The abbey at Fontenay is one of the best surviving examples of Cistercian simplicity, and is an example of how unadorned architecture dominates the great abbeys, while more decorative styles prevail in the great Gothic and Renaissance churches.

Although heavily restored at the beginning of the 20th century, nothing distracts from the harmonious lines and elegant architecture of the monastery.

HAUT KOENIGSBOURG   231E3

There has been a castle at the site of Haut Koenigsbourg for the best part of a thousand years, but, following repeated destructions and rebuildings, the one you see today is a 1908 reconstruction of the 1479 version built for the Count of Thierstein. The castle is the largest in Alsace, and stands, at 755 meters (2,477 ft.), far above the Rhine plain.

The views from up here are splendid. The triple ramparts, sandstone walls, and massive towers lend the castle a feudal air, though this is spoiled slightly by the dormer windows Kaiser Wilhelm II had put in the roofs – this area was part of Germany from the Franco-Prussian War of 1870–1 until 1918. He apparently regretted the addition later.

CANALS OF BURGUNDY

Wherever you travel in Burgundy you'll see the famous canals that run across the region and form part of the grand connection that allows boats to get from the North Sea to the Mediterranean without ever having to venture into the Atlantic.

One of the best ways of seeing them is to rent a longboat or small cruiser (these are available at many locations, for anything from half a day to a month) and travel up and down the canals.

Apart from the fun involved, you also get to see the countryside from a very different perspective ■

BURGUNDY, ALSACE-LORRAINE AND THE NORTH

Laon's cathedral of Notre-Dame was completed in 1235 and is one of France's most formidable Gothic edifices. Many of the ideas used here can be seen in later churches, such as Notre-Dame in Paris

GOTHIC CATHEDRALS

The Gothic style can be seen all over northern France, and can be divided very roughly into the early, flowering, and Flamboyant periods.

The cathedral at Laon is one of the best examples of early Gothic. By the 13th century the style had flowered, and with the aid of flying buttresses it became possible to build churches with lighter, more spacious interiors. Notre-Dame in Paris and Amiens cathedral are both fine examples.

Decoration and the sculptors' skill assumed greater importance over time. The church at L'Épine is a fine example of the Flamboyant style ■

★ LANGRES *231C2*

Standing right on the edge of one plateau and looking down onto another, Langres is a superb little fortified town that has remained for the most part unrestored and undeveloped. Its ramparts, which run 4 kilometers (2½ mi.) around three sides of the town, give fine open views over the valley of the Marne river.

The towers and gateways along the way offer good vistas, and provide a distinct contrast to the picturesque Renaissance houses inside the walls. One of these now houses the Musée du Breuil de St.-Germain, which includes a collection of furniture; one room is dedicated to the writer and philosopher Diderot, born in Langres in 1713.

★★ LAON *230B4*

With its unrivaled ridgetop location, the old walled city of Laon is visible from miles around. Its cathedral is one of the finest medieval Gothic churches in France. Special features include extremely deep-set porches on the west front, seven towers, a tremendously long, 118-meter (387-ft.) four-story nave, and a pair of near-perfect rose windows at either end of the transept. The 13th-century cloisters can be visited via the chapterhouse.

The old town is full of lovely streets that have survived almost unscathed over the centuries. Given Laon's steep position, leave your automobile at the bottom of the hill and take the automatic monorail into the town.

★ LILLE 230B5

The huge industrial center that Lille has become since World War II has made the city the capital of the north. Find your way into the city's cosmopolitan heart and you are rewarded with fine architecture in the well-restored quarter of Vieux Lille, and the superior Musée des Beaux-Arts – its collection runs from Flemish Masters to the Impressionists.

The enormous pentagonal citadel, on the northwestern edge of the old town, was designed by the military architect Vauban for Louis XIV, and is a masterpiece of defensive engineering.

LONS-LE-SAUNIER 231D1

The quiet capital of the Jura makes a pleasant stopover on your way through the region. The main attraction is the rue du Commerce, with its 18th-century arcades. Claude-Joseph Rouget de Lisle, composer of the "Marseillaise," the French national anthem, was born at No. 24 in 1760, and the clock tower at the end of the road chimes out part of the tune on the hour, every hour. Lons has been a spa town since Roman times, and the curative waters are still used in the local swimming pool.

LOUE 231D1

At its most attractive just down-stream from Ornans, the Loue river was made famous in Paris by the painter Courbet in the 19th century. It has a charming air, and two natural widenings of the river – the Miroir de la Loue at Ornans, and the Miroir de Scey just above Cléron – will make you stop to gaze at the beautiful reflections.

You can visit the source of the river in a big cave near Ouhans, or travel down the Gorges de Nouailles by canoe if you dare; most visitors will be content just to look into the steep valley.

LUNÉVILLE 231D3

Like Versailles, Lunéville is a town dominated by its immense château, which was built in the early 18th century. The palace was home to the dukes of Lorraine until 1737, and must have been magnificent at the time – Voltaire described it as the Versailles of Lorraine. With its bare interior and dusty rooms, the palace is now unfortunately only a shadow of its former self.

Often overlooked by visitors to Lunéville is its bicycle and motorcycle museum, which has an unrivaled collection of more than 200 pre-war machines, many of which look impossible to ride, downright dangerous, or both.

MÂCON 231C1

Nestled on the west bank of the Saône, at the end of an original 14th-century bridge, Mâcon marks the southern end of the Burgundy wine region and is host to big wine sales in May. Look for neighbors of the now overpriced Pouilly-Fuissé, which comes from the Mâconnais region: Pouilly-Vinzelles and Pouilly-Loché are excellent alternatives.

Admirers of the Romantic writer Lamartine can see the house where he was born and follow a "Circuit Lamartine" around the town.

★ MARMOUTIER 231E3

The Benedictine monastery of Marmoutier, 7 kilometers (4 mi.) south of Saverne, was founded in the 6th century, and visitors still come to the small town to see the old abbey's rather austere-looking church. Built in red Vosges sandstone, the masterful 12th-century west front is one of the most perfect examples of Romanesque architecture in Alsace. If you're looking for a place to dine, try the Aux Deux Clefs if you get the chance.

ALSACE WINE

Unlike the great châteaux of Bordeaux or the complex classification of Burgundy, Alsace wines are both refreshing to drink and refreshingly simple in nomenclature.

Only 47 vineyards in Alsace have the *Grand Cru* status that allows them to put their name on the bottle; most of the others are bottled by the name of the grape from which they are made.

These fall broadly into one of four categories: Riesling (strong and dry); Gewürztraminer (faintly spicy, heavier); Tokay d'Alsace (properly known as Pinot Gris, slightly smoky, nutty); and Sylvaner (fresh and simple wines) ∎

WALK

NANCY

Start at the cathedral, visiting the splendid baroque interior, before walking down rue Maurice Barrès to place Stanislas.

This square houses no fewer than five palaces (the largest is now the town hall), along with two fountains, a wealth of gilded railings, and a triumphal arch on the north side. Stop in at the Musée des Beaux-Arts.

Through the arch, find your way onto place de la Carrière, with its splendid houses; this leads to the Palais du Gouvernement, flanked by colonnades.

You can take a detour here, to the left, to visit the Ducal Palace and the Lorraine museum, or turn right, to enter the Parc de la Pépinière. Take the southwestern exit from the park to return you to place Stanislas ■

★ METZ   231D4

The lively city of Metz was only returned to France after World War I, in 1918, after being part of Germany for nearly 40 years. Many of the buildings – the train station is a good example – reflect German rather than French architectural sensibilities.

The most obvious exception to this is the lovely 13th- and 14th-century sandstone cathedral of St.-Étienne, a harmonious testament to the vision of the great Gothic cathedral builders. Inside, the nave is among the tallest in France, at 42 meters (138 ft.), and there is over half a hectare (1½ acres) of stained glass to admire. Most of this is original 13th-, 15th- and 16th-century work, but new windows have been added by 20th-century artists, such as Marc Chagall.

Explore the city's river banks, taking in the impressive defensive gateway known as the Porte des Allemands, on the Seille, before it joins the Moselle, and the attractive Esplanade, on the Moselle itself, with views across to the Ile de Saulcy. Note also the 4th-century church of St.-Pierre-aux-Nonains, one of the oldest in France, the medieval arcades of the old town, and the Museum of Art and History.

MEUSE   231C4

The Meuse flows for 500 kilometers (312 mi.) of its 950-kilometer (594-mi.) length through France, before crossing Belgium and Holland on its way to the North Sea. On its way it passes across some of France's most famous battlefields (Sedan and Verdun, in particular), and in parts the river is now heavily industrialized, but none of this detracts from its natural beauty, particularly where it is guarded by the towering limestone hills of the Côtes de Meuse.

MOSELLE   231D3

From the tumbling mountain stream that is the Moselle river at its source (high in the Vosges, near the Col de Bussang), to the grand industrial waterway it becomes around Thionville, the Moselle is a study in contrasts. At its most enchanting in the upper reaches, as far down as Épinal, it flows through attractive farmland. Farther down its course, great laden barges carry their goods into Germany, along the border with Luxembourg, before the river joins the Rhine at Koblenz.

MOULINS   230B1

Five hundred years ago, as the capital of the dukes of Bourbon, Moulins was an important city wielding influence as far away as Spain and Holland. The market town is now off the beaten track, though, and makes a pleasant detour into provincial France.

Walk along the rue d'Allier to see the best of the 15th- and 16th-century town houses here, and stop in at the cathedral of Notre-Dame, three blocks north, to see the striking triptych and the superior stained-glass windows in the apse. On your way you will have passed the Jacquemart, the old town clock with its mechanical figures that strike the hours. The Art and Archeology Museum, located behind the cathedral, has a very good medieval collection as well as some interesting china.

★★ MULHOUSE   231E2

It's unlikely that you would visit the industrial city of Mulhouse if it weren't for its first-rate collection of museums. The enormous Musée du Chemin de Fer (the biggest railroad museum in Europe) features magnificent French steam engines to brilliant scale models and a whole miniature railroad network.

The Automobile Museum features a wonderful collection of 440 vehicles, from the very first models of the 19th century through to some of the most famous racing automobiles ever built. Collected over many years by the Schlumpf brothers, they are all still in working order.

It's also worth investigating the Fabric Printing Museum (Musée de l'Impression sur Étoffes), and the Alsace Ecomuseum (11 km/7 mi. north), which gives some impression of local domestic life through a series of traditional buildings. If you're after the outdoors, then you should head for the southeast corner of the city, to the well-maintained botanical gardens and zoo.

MUNSTER 231E2

Famed primarily for its production of one of France's strongest and most pungent cheeses, the small town of Munster and the Munster Valley in the southern Vosges also have lovely vineyards and woodlands, small hotels and good, well-marked walking trails. The trek up to the 1,267-meter (4,157-ft.) summit of the Petit Ballon is hard work, but is well worth the effort, as the views from the top are magnificent.

★★★ NANCY 231D3

Tossed back and forth for centuries between the French and the dukes of Lorraine, Nancy finally became French for good on the death of Stanislas, the last duke, in 1766. Stanislas is the man to thank for the beauty you can see in modern-day Nancy, and was responsible for the unsurpassed combination of elegance and harmony in the place Stanislas, with its five palaces, two fountains, a wealth of gilded railings, and a triumphal arch. Also to be visited are the cathedral, with its magnificent

baroque interior, the Fine Arts Museum, with its collection of paintings from the Old Masters right through to the 20th century, the Ducal Palace, and the Lorraine historical museum.

You won't want to miss the nearby Parc de la Pépinière, a pleasant garden that has a good display of rose beds, a small zoo, and a tropical aquarium.

NANTUA 231D1

The small town of Nantua ought, somehow, to be more popular than it actually is. Sitting at the head of a pretty 3-kilometer (2-mi.) long lake in an attractive valley halfway between Geneva and Bourg-en-Bresse (see p.237), the town markets itself as a small vacation resort, but is now completely dominated by the new expressway that flies across the valley above the town and plunges into the cliffside tunnel. If you do make it here, it's worth the effort and the 2½ hours it takes for a healthy clamber up to the summit of the Monts d'Ain, at 1,127 meters (3,697 ft.).

see p.237

ART NOUVEAU IN NANCY

In the 1900s, Nancy developed into an important center for the decorative arts when Emille Gallé founded his École de Nancy, a forerunner of the artnouveau movement. Gallé excelled in making exquisite vases as well as designing extravagant furniture ■

Munster cheese, renowned for its characteristically pungent aroma, was first made by Irish monks, who settled in the area in the 7th century. It is delicious with fresh bread

WALK

ORTENBOURG AND RAMSTEIN

Start from the parking lot at the *auberge* in Huehnelmuehl. The path zigzags up through the forest before reaching a plateau near a sign to Ortenbourg (Ramstein is to the right, but there is no public access).

A flight of steps leads up to the base of Ortenbourg's walls. The stone castle dates from 1258, but was destroyed in 1633. After seeing the ruins, walk ahead from the gateway onto a signposted path. You'll soon see an unmarked path to the right that comes out of the forest onto a path above a vineyard. Turn right. The path joins a sur-faced road, bend-ing to the left. Continue into more woodland to return to Huehnelmuehl ■

NEUF BRISACH *231E2*

The perfectly preserved octagonal fortress town of Neuf Brisach, on the west bank of the Rhine, was designed by Sébastien Vauban, Louis XIV's brilliant military architect, in 1697, after the French lost Alt Breisach, across the river. The small town makes a pleasant stopover if you're traveling along the Rhine, and the walls, moats, and ramparts are evocative of other, grander times.

★ NEVERS *230B1*

Although it has been accused of a certain grayness, Nevers, on the upper Loire, has a collection of worthy monuments and a surviving industry in spun glass and porcelain – you can see this being made at several factories in just the same way as it was 500 years ago. The cathedral is famous for having a Romanesque apse at the west end and a Gothic one at the east end.

The Ducal Palace, across the square and facing down onto the Loire, is a superb example of Renaissance architecture with a lovely spiral staircase tower flanked by two octagonal towers at the corners. A kilometer away, to the northeast, stands the harmonious 11th-century Cluniac church of St.-Étienne.

Nevers is also close enough to the villages of Pouilly-sur-Loire and Sancerre to be a good place to taste their excellent white wines. It is also worth seeking out the rarer, smaller, Quincy and Menetou-Salon wines.

★ OBERNAI/ MONT SAINTE ODILE *231E3*

The attractive town of Obernai lies on the Route du Vin at the foot of Mont Sainte Odile, itself one of the high points of any visit to the Vosges. Both are liable to be very busy with tourists, but are worth visiting all the same.

Obernai is just what an Alsatian wine village should look like: crumbling ramparts, timber-framed houses, and old, narrow streets. Far above it, on the ridge of Mont Sainte Odile, walk around inside the great ruins of the Pagan Wall, and visit the convent of Ste.-Odile at the summit. Many of the visitors – practically all on December 13, the saint's day – are actually pilgrims rather than tourists.

★★★ OPALE, CÔTE D' *230A5*

The 50-kilometer (32-mi.) coastal road (*corniche*), from Boulogne-sur-Mer to Calais, takes in along the way some of France's most spectacular clifftop scenery and passes the famous Cap Gris-Nez and Cap Blanc-Nez.

For a taste of the wind, stand on Cap Gris-Nez and look south to Boulogne, across the Channel to England, some 35 kilometers (22 mi.) away, and up the coast to Cap Blanc-Nez. The view from Cap Blanc-Nez is easily worth the steep walk up to the 134-meter (440-ft.) summit – the highest point on the cliffs. Between the two caps there is a long, windswept beach. Farther up the coast, Blériot Plage is named for Louis Blériot, the first man to fly across the Channel, in 1909.

ORNANS *231D2*

Primarily of interest to devotees of Gustave Courbet, the little town of Ornans was the birth-place of the great painter and was one of his greatest inspirations – he returned here frequently to paint the local landscapes and village scenes.

The museum dedicated to him here is good but not first class, mainly because the painter's best canvasses are in the Louvre in Paris. The finest views of the town are from the bridge across the Loue river; a very attractive effect is created by the wooden balconies on the row of dilapidated houses that overhang the waters of the river.

★ LE QUESNOY *230B5*

Public gardens in the small town of Le Quesnoy surround the well-preserved fortifications built here in the 17th century, once more testifying to the military brilliance of the ubiquitous Vauban. The scale of the moats and bastions show just how vulnerable to attack France's northern border was thought to be.

LES RECULÉES *231D1*

Unique to the Jura, the Reculées are the distinctive V-shaped limestone valleys that are found from Lons-le-Saunier to Arbois. Each one culminates in a *cirque*, which is a steep-sided glacial river source, at the bottom of which are usually deep caves. The most spectacular is the 200-meter (650-ft.) Cirque de Baume, just east of Lons-le-Saunier, which offers sensational views of the gorge from the top of the cliffs.

Take the steep path down to the caves at the bottom, which erupt in a waterfall after heavy rains. Another *cirque* that is well worth a visit is the Cirque du Fer à Cheval, which marks the end of the Reculée des Planches, running southeast from Arbois, and which contains the source of the Cuisance river.

★★★ RONCHAMP, *231D2*
NOTRE-DAME DU HAUT

Built on a spectacular hilltop site west of Ronchamp, the little church of Notre-Dame du Haut is arguably the most atmospheric and interesting of all post-1945 churches. The site had been a place of pilgrimage for centuries, and so it remains today. The new church, built here from 1950 to 1954, was designed by Le Corbusier and features the work of many other famous artists, including Marc Chagall and Henri Matisse. Deeply set stained-glass windows keep the inside mysterious, while on the outside the sweeping ark-like roof is unlike anything you've ever seen.

These pretty, wooden houses overhang the Loue river at Ornans. They will be immediately recognizable to anyone who is familiar with the work of the artist Gustave Courbet, Ornans' favorite son

LA ROUTE DU VIN/ 231E3
LA ROUTE DES CRÊTES

Alsace has two excellent tourist routes that are really designed with the driver in mind. Through the valleys, and passing through some of the most attractive towns and villages of Alsace, is the Route du Vin. This well-marked 180-kilometer (113-mi.) itinerary is best taken at a leisurely pace, stopping off for wine-tastings and sightseeing. Be warned, though, that the most famous of the villages, such as Riquewihr, are so popular in summer that they can become unpleasantly crowded.

Running from the German border to the Belfort Gap, the Route des Crêtes was built during World War I as a supply line for the French army. It now serves as an excellent drive through some of the best walking country France has to offer, and has magnificent views in places that extend from the Black Forest in Germany to the Swiss Alps.

ST.-CLAUDE 231D1

Tucked away in a valley in the Jura that seems on the way to nowhere, St.-Claude is famous for the unlikely and seemingly incompatible pursuits of pipe-making and diamond-cutting. More than 3 million tobacco pipes are made here each year from imported briar roots – this town of 12,000 in the heart of the Jura managed to corner the Corsican briar market during the mid-19th century.

There's a rather cute little pipe museum displaying everything you need to know about their manufacture, and next door there's a gem collection which is more interesting than you'd expect. Across the street is the cathedral of St.-Pierre, which used to be an abbey and boasts superbly crafted choir stalls.

The tiny town of Riquewihr on the Route du Vin is renowned for its Riesling. Pretty, half-timbered houses decked with flowers line its narrow streets; some date as far back as the end of the 15th century

LES ROUSSES 231D1

Popular as both a winter and summer resort, Les Rousses is situated at 1,100 meters (3,609 ft.) and is surrounded by some of the best soft mountain scenery in the Jura. The lovely lake marks the start of the Vallée de Joux, which runs into Switzerland after 10 kilometers (6 mi.). In the winter it's worth coming here for the excellent cross-country skiing and reasonably easy downhill resorts nearby. In summer take advantage of the lake and the plentiful opportunities for walking and cycling are available in the area. The dairy, where you can see the tasty local cheese being made, is well worth a visit.

★ ST.-OMER   230A5

Until not long ago, the elegant little town of St.-Omer was the busy first stop for southbound travelers from Calais, but since the expressway has been built the town has calmed down and is now hardly visited by tourists.

The basilica of Notre-Dame stands impressively on the west side of town, next to the lovely public gardens, and has an exceptional collection of religious art and artifacts. The tower is English perpendicular and would almost look more at home across the Channel. About 180 meters (591 ft.) from the basilica is the Hôtel Sandelin, which houses a strong collection of Delft ware and local ceramics, and the remarkable gilded 12th-century cross of Saint Bertin.

ST.-QUENTIN   230B4

Driving north along the A26 toward Calais, St.-Quentin's solid, grand basilica is an impressive landmark off to the right not long after you've passed Laon on its crag to the left. The town was almost completely destroyed during World War I, and hasn't been as well rebuilt as it might have been, but the 15th-century (parts date back to the 12th century) basilica is well worth a visit, and inside it's much brighter and more open than you'd expect from the dense exterior.

Butterfly collectors should not miss the specimens on display in the Entomology Museum (in the library, open only in summer).

★ ST.-RIQUIER   230A5

The village of St.-Riquier is dominated by its Benedictine abbey church, which dates back to the 15th century. Built in the Flamboyant Gothic style, it has the scale and presence of a cathedral, with a huge tower and a quiet, dignified interior.

SAULIEU/MORVAN NATIONAL PARK   230C2

Situated on the old N6 (which has now been superseded by the A6 expressway), Saulieu has forever been an *Étape Gastronomique*, famous for the quality of its food and accommodation on the route from Paris to Lyon and the south. Eat at the Côte d'Or if you can afford it – it's one of the top 20 restaurants in France; you can complain about anything here except the price. The lunchtime menu will give you a good taste of what the world's best cooking is all about. Before your meal have a stroll around the town, taking in the sculptor Pompon's famous bronze bull and the 12th-century basilica of St.-Andoche, with its beautiful carved capitals.

West of Saulieu is the Morvan National Park, Burgundy's wild outdoors antidote to the regimented vineyards and neatly partitioned farmland to the east. Here there are rocks for rock climbers, fast-flowing rivers for canoeists, lakes for anglers, and hills and forests for walkers.

SÉLESTAT   231E3

Invisible, long-demolished walls surround the tight network of medieval streets in the center of Sélestat and contain a wealth of ancient architectural details; look carefully at the doors, window casements, towers, and houses that line the narrow streets.

Drop in at the Bibliothèque Humaniste to see the collection of books and manuscripts from the 7th century on – this was the library of the school of Humanism that made Sélestat so famous in the 15th century. Sélestat also boasts two excellent churches, the Gothic church of St.-Georges, and the Romanesque abbey church of Ste.-Foy, which has only just managed to survive 19th-century restoration work.

JURA CHEESES

The Jura is one of the great cheese-making regions of France, and there are several places (notably at Les Rousses, and at other towns along the N5 from Dole to Gex) where you can see the complete process and try different varieties.

A whole range of Comtés vary from the young, sweet, smooth cheeses to the older, stronger, drier cheeses that are kept for up to five years before being sold.

Try Morbier, with its distinctive blue stripe through the center and its slightly bitter taste, and Bleu de Gex, which resembles the English Stilton cheese in flavor and texture ■

BATTLEFIELDS AND WAR CEMETERIES

Blood has been spilled on the fields of northern France since time immemorial (great battles of the Hundred Years War such as Crécy and Agincourt were fought here), but nothing has ever compared to the bloodletting that took place in the four years from 1914 to 1918.

After the war, monuments were put up and cemeteries were laid out, and these are worth a visit.

A preserved section of the trenches can be seen at Beaumont-Hamel. The largest cemeteries are those near Albert, north of the Somme, where nearly 600,000 soldiers perished in 1916. There are also monuments near Verdun and at Vimy Ridge ∎

SEMUR-EN-AUXOIS   230C2

Caught in a loop of the Armançon river, Semur-en-Auxois is one of the prettiest fortified towns in the area. Walk along the Promenade des Remparts for a lovely view down to the river. Cross the isthmus into the heart of the old town and visit the 13th-century Gothic church of Notre-Dame (restored in the 19th century by the much-vilified Viollet le Duc), not forgetting to take a look at its impressive treasury. Walk down to the river, to the Pont Joly, from where there are lovely views.

★ SENS   230B3

Home of the first pure Gothic cathedral in France, Sens is a medium-sized town at the northwestern edge of Burgundy, on the Yonne river. Bypassed by the N6 to the north and the A6 to the south, the town makes an attractive provincial stopover on the way into the heart of Burgundy. As you go into the cathedral, note the damage wreaked during the Revolution to the statues around the main doorway. Inside, take a look at the excellent medieval and Renaissance stained glass, which includes a dramatic portrayal of the death of Thomas à Becket in Canterbury Cathedral in England, on the north side of the choir. The treasury is unusually rich, and contains a fine collection of embroidered vestments.

SOLUTRÉ   231C1

A few kilometers west of Mâcon, and overhanging the great vineyards of Pouilly-Fuissé, is the distinctive rock of Solutré.

At the foot of this rock the bones of over 100,000 prehistoric horses were found, leading to speculation that this was probably a site where wild horses were driven off the cliff 15,000 years ago, prior to being served up to early devotees of horseflesh (although less common in France than in neighboring Switzerland and Belgium, there are still plenty of *boucheries chevalines* in France, with the distinctive horse's head above the door or on the window).

The best artifacts found at the Solutré site are in the museum in Mâcon, but the village also has its own little museum.

★ SOMME   230A4

The Somme flows quietly down its 245-kilometer (153-mi.) course, repudiating its part in the misguided Somme offensive that took place from July to October 1916. The lives of 276,000 Germans and a similar number of allies were exchanged futilely here for gains of territory that never exceeded 10 kilometers (6 mi.) in either direction.

The river reaches the sea, after passing through Amiens and Abbeville, at the wide Baie de la Somme, where it is flanked by the small ports of Le Crotoy to the north and St.-Valéry-sur-Somme to the south. Both towns serve up good seafood platters.

★★★ STRASBOURG   231E3

Like Paris, Strasbourg was originally built on a defensive island in the middle of a river, but has since expanded to many times its original size (nearly half a million people now live in the area). As well as being the showy capital of Alsace, Strasbourg is also one of the major centers of the European Union (see p.256), home to both the Council of Europe and the European Parliament. The old town, dominated by the asymmetrical 142-meter (465-ft.) spire of the great medieval cathedral, is a picturesque mixture of half-timbered houses and classic

Alsatian sidewalk café culture, and should not be missed.

Inside the cathedral, look for the three-story Angel Pillar, which shows the Last Judgment in graphic Gothic detail. The great astronomical clock in the cathedral draws crowds at noon.

As you'd expect in a city this culturally aware, Strasbourg also has a fine collection of museums, ranging from the bright and noisy collection of the Musée d'Art Moderne (European, from the postimpressionists onwards) to the dulled, quiet medieval faces on the Gothic sculptures at the Musée de l'Oeuvre Notre-Dame. At the western end of the island, where the Ill river divides, is Petite France; pretty, flower-bedecked galleries of timber-framed 16th-century houses overhang the small canals and quays of the Ill.

★ TANLAY *230C2*

The glorious Renaissance château of Tanlay, 10 kilometers (6 mi.) east of Tonnerre, is the real reason for visiting this village. The château was built around 1550 and was a Protestant stronghold during the wars of religion. It is set in a lovely park and has round towers, bell-shaped domes, a superb courtyard, and swans in the moat. Take one of the guided tours around the sumptuous interior, where you'll be able to see some good period furniture, great fireplaces, and a particularly attractive *trompe l'oeil* gallery.

TERNANT *231C2*

You'd never know it, as you come to this village church in the middle of nowhere between the Loire and the Morvan, but inside there are two gorgeous wooden triptychs. They were donated to the church in 1435 by Philippe de Ternant, the court chamberlain to Philip the Good. Ternant may

have been generous, but he didn't fail to take the opportunity to have himself painted into immortality in both works of art.

★ THANN *231E2*

Graced with the finest spire in Alsace, and dominated by the medieval ruins of Engelsbourg castle (destroyed in 1673), the little industrial town of Thann marks the southern end of both the Route du Vin and the Route des Crêtes (see p.250).

As you go into the church (locals will direct you to the "cathedral"), look for the beautifully sculpted porch. Inside, you will see more fine carving on the choir stalls. The "Madonna of the Vineyards," a painted wooden Virgin and Child, serves as a useful reminder that there is plenty of excellent Alsace wine-tasting in the town.

The astronomical clock inside the cathedral of Notre-Dame in Strasbourg dates from 1838. Death himself sounds the hours, while at noon crowds gather to watch the entire group of figures ringing out the time

WALK

THE CÔTES DE TOUL

This 10-kilometer (6-mi.) walk, Le Circuit de la Linotte (Linnet Walk), should take around 3 hours.

Start in Trondes, a village on the Côtes de Toul wine route. Go down the rue des Thermes and cross the main street. Turn right along rue de la Neuveville. The path carries on beside a forest. At the foot of the Bois de Raumont, turn left. The path rejoins the D192, then continues to La Neuveville-derrière-Foug. Leave the village, turn left at the rue des Paquis, and out into fields.

Round a knoll there is a view of Boucq (the 14th-century towers of the château and the church tower make this village distinctive). Take the track to the right, past Faux Moulin farm and on to Renard Moulin. Pass the farm to a sharp bend in a road, where an arrow points left. Follow the road (D101) through La Tuilerie de Trondes, back to Trondes ∎

TONNERRE   230C2

The small town of Tonnerre spans the Armançon river and the Canal de Bourgogne, and is worth a short visit. The old hospital, which was founded in 1293, is the town's most interesting attraction; its 80-meter (262-ft.) infirmary has a splendid vaulted wooden roof. The Fosse Dionne, 5 minutes away, is a tamed spring that runs into a pool, and used to be the communal laundry area, until washing machines took over.

TOUL   231D3

Toul has long outgrown its nine-pointed, moated 17th-century fortress, but that's where its heart still is. The bastions and ramparts are well worth investigating, as is the original Porte de Metz, designed by Vauban, on the north side of town. The 14th-century cathedral of St.-Étienne has a very fine west front and two 65-meter (213-ft.) octagonal towers, and gives access to Renaissance chapels off the nave, and lovely cloisters. Even better cloisters can be seen at the smaller, simpler church of St.-Gengoult, which also has some good examples of 13th-century stained glass. Several 14th-century houses can be seen in the rue du Général Gengoult. Try some of the local wine, the Côtes de Toul.

★ LE TOUQUET-PARIS-PLAGE   230A5

Hugely popular with the English upper class from the end of the 19th century to the beginning of World War II, Le Touquet was originally designed as the self-styled "Paris Beach" of its title. Before vehicle ferries were invented in the late 1950s, the airfield at Le Touquet gained brief popularity as being the cheapest place to which you could fly your automobile over to France for the start of a European tour.

Now, its glories somewhat diminished, the town still has what it has always had: a lovely 12-kilometer (7½-mi.) sandy beach. Given the weather on the English Channel it is more likely that you'll come here to promenade than to swim or improve your tan, but behind the somewhat faded, rectilinear streets of the main town there are lovely villas set back in specially planted pine forests.

★★ TOURNUS   231C1

Halfway between Mâcon and Chalon-sur-Saône is the enchanting town of Tournus. Monks on the run with the bones of Saint Philibert settled here in the 9th century, and built what is arguably the finest of France's Romanesque churches.

The original 9th-century façade and 10th-century crypt are the oldest parts of the church, but the whole has an immensely calm, aged feel to it, and the huge, unadorned pillars, stretching roofward, support unusual transverse barrel vaults.

Stop at Tournus for the night on your way south, and stroll in the evening along the Saône and

across the bridge for a beautiful sunset over the town with the silhouette of the abbey to your right. Some 15 kilometers (9 mi.) to the west of Tournus is the fortified village of Brancion.

★★ TROYES   *230C3*

Famous through the centuries for its great fairs, Troyes has a lot to see, from the cathedral and a number of fine churches to an assortment of museums covering everything from carpentry tools to modern art. Until recently the city of 60,000 was the heart of the French bicycle components industry, but it has now been displaced almost entirely by imports from Japan.

The old town, running east from the train station to the cathedral, has a wealth of cobbled streets, narrow medieval alleys, and the famous half-timbered houses that give it so much of its charm (these were, oddly, until only about two decades ago, covered in plaster for the most part). The cathedral of St.-Pierre and St.-Paul, begun in 1208, is quite simply magnificent. It is best visited on a sunny day when the light falling through the brilliant 13th- and 14th-century stained glass is at its best. Back across the canal is the almost as impressive basilica of St.-Urbain, an architectural masterpiece of the 13th century.

★★ VERDUN   *231C4*

It is impossible to go to Verdun without being forcefully reminded of the 18 months of bloodshed that occurred here from February 1916 to October 1917, when the German High Command attempted to bleed France dry. More than 800,000 men died in the fruitless battles, and even now, several decades later on, there are still places where even the toughest weeds won't grow. The area is littered with monuments to the great battle and to the futility of war. You should make a trip to see the ossuary at Douaumont, where the tall white Tower of the Dead stands as a memorial guard over the endless ranks of graves.

The site of the village of Fleury (totally destroyed by shelling) is now occupied by the Mémorial-Musée de la Bataille de Verdun.

★ VÉZELAY   *230B2*

In one of history's earliest-known marketing coups, the tourist office of Vézelay let it be known that it was in possession of the

The picturesque village of Vézelay is built on a ridge first settled by the Celts. An abbey was founded here in the 9th century, and Vézelay fast became a major pilgrimage center

THE BATTLE OF VERDUN

Verdun (and neighboring Vaux and Douaumont) were heavily fortified after the 1870-1 war with Germany, and these forts were the key to France's north-eastern defences.

On February 21, 1916, the Germans began an artillery barrage which started this bloody battle, but 18 months later they had still only advanced to within 5 kilometers (3 mi.) of Verdun ■

EUROPEAN UNION

France is home to the European Parliament and the Council of Europe (in Strasbourg); it has made its borders among the most open in the European Union, and it co-hosts the European Center for Nuclear Research (CERN). With millions of other Europeans traveling to (and through) France every year, and strong trade links with the other European nations, France is very much dependent on the other nations' goodwill. Not surprisingly, France was among the first to ratify the Treaty of Maastricht, pledged to further fiscal and political unity throughout Europe ■

relics of Mary Magdalen, and pilgrims on their way to Santiago de Compostela flocked to pay their respects. It was only after the later discovery of the bones of Mary Magdalen (authenticated by the church) in a cave in Provence that Vézelay declined as a pilgrimage center. The church at the top of the single street is now visited by throngs of tourists who come to see how well Viollet le Duc restored the dilapidated 12th-century church (the debate continues), although the carved capitals are beyond criticism.

If you're a gourmet, then a trip 3 kilometers (2 mi.) down the road to St.-Père may prove even more rewarding – here you'll find l'Espérance, one of France's top 20 restaurants. You'll have to reserve your table well in advance, take your time (this isn't fast food), and be prepared for the size of the check.

VITRY-LE-FRANÇOIS   *230C3*

Heavily bombarded during World War II because of its strategic location at the intersection of the Marne–Saône and Marne–Rhine canals, the town of Vitry-le-François was fortunate enough to be rebuilt afterward according to the original elegant groundplan, as laid out by François I.

Stop in the beautifully proportioned place d'Armes in the center of town and walk to the unassuming exterior of the 18th-century church of Notre-Dame. Inside, the ceiling seems to rise up forever; if you're lucky the organ will be playing, to heighten the atmosphere further still.

VOSGES   *231E3*

The low mountains of the Vosges run for about 120 kilometers (75 mi.) from La Moder in the north to Belfort in the south, and divide Alsace from Lorraine, with the Rhine Valley to the east and the

Moselle and Saône valleys to the west. The northern Vosges has been declared a nature park, but it is the southern Vosges, with its distinctive round-topped ballons contrasting with the more rugged forms of outcrop in the north, which provides the highest summits. Le Grand Ballon, at 1,424 meters (4,672 ft.), is the highest of all, but there are also fantastic views from the Ballon d'Alsace (see p.235), above Belfort, and the Petit Ballon, above Munster (see p.247).

There are excellent walking trails waymarked along the whole length of the Vosges, and with the pleasant villages in the valleys convenient for night-stops, the whole area makes an ideal place for a hiking vacation.

★★ WISSEMBOURG   *231E4*

Right up against the German border, the almost too pretty town of Wissembourg is the ideal base from which to explore northern Alsace. Old houses, ancient ramparts, and an attractive location on the Lauter river all conspire to make visitors stay a little longer than they'd intended.

Take time to venture to some of the many villages in the area – you'll be pointed in the direction of the bucolic little Hunspach, with its timber-framed houses and long-handled pumps, but you may want to investigate less well-known, but equally pretty villages. On your travels you'll also notice dilapidated castles frowning down at you from the heights; these almost always reward further investigation.

At the Maginot Line you'll be as sad as the French were to find that these vast, costly defenses were simply outflanked by the advancing German army some 50 years ago, who went through the Ardennes to the north instead.

TRAVEL
FACTS

All you need to know to make
your trip as comfortable as
possible: how to get around,
what to take, where to go for
entertainment, and even what to
do with the children

TRAVEL FACTS

CONTENTS

BEFORE YOU GO

AIRLINES

The national French carrier is **Air France**, tel: (800) 237-2747. Its flights link Paris with New York, Chicago, Washington, D.C., Los Angeles, Miami, San Francisco, and Houston. Inside France, the airline links many smaller French cities with Paris. If you're planning to stay in a smaller city, you may be able to arrange the entire trip using an Air France connection to the city of your choice.

Some 90 percent of U.S. airline passengers now pay less than full coach fare. So unless you always fly with one particular airline, aim for the lowest convenient fares to France. Lowest fares are most likely on flights that start from a hub city like New York, Atlanta, or Chicago. Avoid the period June through early September, and avoid weekends if you are trying to get a low-cost fare.

A good travel agent should be able to help with best fares. So may a charter ticket resale company like Council Charter, 205 E. 42nd Street, New York, NY 10017, tel: (800) 800-8222.

New Frontiers, the U.S. division of France's largest tour operator, offers a wide variety of flights, packages, train passes, and fly-drives (tel: (800) 366-6387).

ARRIVING
By air

Almost all scheduled flights from the U.S. fly into Paris. Paris has two airports. The main one handling transatlantic flights is **Aéroport Roissy-Charles de Gaulle**, about 26 kilometers (16 mi.) northeast of the city. Its passenger information service is at 01 48 62 22 80. The message begins with an answering machine speech in English and French, telling you which details to have ready. You then wait for an operator.
• **Taxi:** A taxi from Charles de Gaulle to central Paris costs approximately 50FF (280FF at night), plus 15 percent tip.
• **Train:** Take a shuttle train to Roissy station and get the city train from there. Presently it costs about 45FF one-way.

It is possible to catch TGVs (fast inter-city trains) from Roissy-Charles de Gaulle too, but you will need to have reserved your tickets in advance. Look for directions from Terminal 2.
• **Buses from Roissy-Charles de Gaulle airport:** The Roissy bus runs from Gate 12, Terminal 2D every 15 minutes between 6 a.m. and 11 p.m. It currently costs 45FF one-way.

Paris's other airport is **Orly**, which is about 11 kilometers (7 mi.) south of the city; tel: 01 49 75 15 15.
• **Taxi:** Between Orly and the center of Paris, a taxi costs approximately 130FF (200FF at night).
• **Train:** To get into Paris by train, go from Orly Airport train station; the fare from there to the center of Paris is 28FF.
• **Bus:** Take a shuttle from Gate C or D at Orly South (Sud) or Gate E at Orly West (Ouest) to the Air France city bus stop. See *Public Transportation* on p.269 for information about other French city airports.

Travelers to France from other European countries often take the bus or train.

By bus

Many British companies offer cheap bus/ferry trips to France, crossing via Channel ferries. Contact Eurolines, 52 Grosvenor Gardens, London SW1W 0AU (tel: 0171 730 8235) for details of buses from Britain to over 50 French cities.

Eurolines also offers bus services from many cities in mainland Europe. Major offices are in Amsterdam, Holland (tel: 020 560 87 87), Brussels, Belgium (tel: 02 203 07 07), Munich, Germany (tel: Deutsche Touring, 089 54587000), and Rome, Italy (tel: Lazzi Express, 06 884 08 40).

Senior citizens' and young people's discounts are usually available on buses, but they depend on the ticket price. When you call, ask the company if they are currently running any special price offers.

By train

France has good train connections, and trains are a pleasant, friendly way to travel in from other European countries. Trains from Britain and continental countries terminate at one of Paris's six main

TRAVEL FACTS

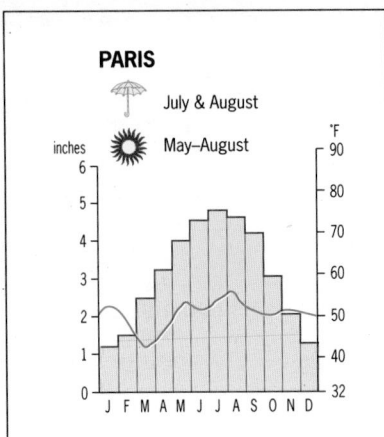

PARIS

July & August

inches   May–August   °F

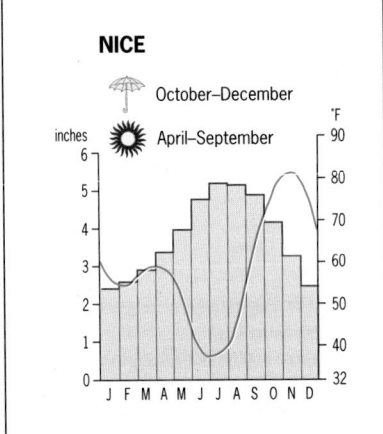

NICE

October–December

inches   April–September   °F

stations: Gare du Nord, Gare d'Austerlitz, Gare de l'Est, Gare St. Lazare, Gare Montparnasse and Gare de Lyon. All these stations are in central Paris and are well served by the Paris Metro system.

From Britain, Eurostar offers a train service via the Channel Tunnel to Paris Gare du Nord (and to Lille, in northern France).

Both first and second (standard) classes are comfortable. Check in 20 minutes before departure at Waterloo station in central London. The trip takes three hours to the center of Paris (Lille: two hours). Book in the U.S. via your travel agent or Rail Europe (tel: 800-EUROSTAR); Eurotunnel Customer Service Central, P.O. Box 300, Folkestone, Kent CT19 4QW (tel: 0990 353 535). (See *Public transportation* on p.269).

By sea
Cunard (28 Jackson Avenue, Long Island, New York, 10017, tel: (718) 361-4000) operates frequent transatlantic cruises between New York and Southampton, England. After arrival in Southampton you can continue to France by ferry, bus, plane, or train.

Other cruise lines sometimes cross the Atlantic when repositioning ships. Also, many cruise ships include stop-overs in French ports such as Marseilles. As cruise itineraries change, consult your travel agent or the travel pages in your local newspaper to check out current offers.

Contact major shipping companies if you wish to ship your automobile to France. The cost involved is unlikely to make this a viable option for a vacation.

CLIMATE AND WHEN TO GO
Climate
France has several different types of climate. Generally, the farther south you go the warmer it is in both summer and winter. Travel down through the whole country and you'll notice how the vegetation and style of rustic architecture change to reflect different climates.

Spring, summer, and fall all offer good weather, especially in southern regions.

The south of France (Provence area) has a Mediterranean climate, with long, hot, dry summers, occasional violent thunder-storms, and mild, pleasant winters. (There's a relentless, dry wind called the *mistral*, too, which blows mainly in cooler months.)

Summers in the northwest (Normandy, Brittany area) can sometimes be cool. Expect rain at any time. Stormy westerly winds are always a possibility. May and September often see the north's most settled and pleasant weather.

The northeast of France (Alsace region) has a Continental climate, more extreme than coastal areas, with hot, sometimes stormy summers and cold, snowy winters.

The Alps region to the east usually has delightful springs, pleasant, warm and sunny summers, and is blanketed in deep snow for the winter months.

Paris is generally temperate, and so prone to showers at any time of year. It is especially pleasant in the spring.

When to go

France will appeal at any time of year, but June, July, and September are considered the best months for visiting. If you time it right, you'll catch the festivities for Bastille Day on July 14 (see *National Holidays* on p.264). Summer is also a great time for the cultural and artistic festivals of which the French are so fond.

The French themselves go on vacation in August, so many stores and businesses close for the entire month.

Accommodation prices are higher in August at beach resorts, lakes, vacation villages, and other places where the French themselves like to go on vacation.

Fahrenheit/Celsius

To convert Celsius into Fahrenheit: multiply by 9, divide by 5, and add 32.

To convert Fahrenheit into Celsius: subtract 32, multiply by 5, and divide by 9.

Sounds easy, huh? Here are a few of the kinds of temperatures you will probably encounter, in both Celsius and Fahrenheit:

```
 0 F = minus 18 C
32 F =    0 C
39 F =    4 C
50 F =   10 C
61 F =   16 C
70 F =   21 C
79 F =   26 C
```

CUSTOMS AND QUARANTINE

• **Before you go:** Make a list of serial numbers of expensive items (such as cameras, jewelry, watches) which you plan to take to France, and get the list stamped by the customs office before you leave the U.S. This avoids the risk of being taxed for these items when you leave France.

• **Entering France:** Mark prescription drugs and keep a copy of your prescription handy, to show the customs officer if required.

• **Leaving France:** U.S. citizens may bring home $400 worth of goods tax free every 30 days. The next $1,000 is subject to a 10 percent tax. You cannot bring liquor into the U.S. unless you are over 21. It is forbidden to import certain items – particularly food items. The U.S. Customs Service *Know Before You Go* leaflet has full details. It also offers information on mailing gifts from

France to the U.S. (Box 7407, Washington, D.C. 20044, tel: (202) 927-6724).

• **Canadian citizens** can bring in C$300 worth of goods per annum. Goods of higher value attract a 12 percent tax. For more information contact Canadian customs on (800) 461-9999.

• **Reclaiming French Value Added Tax:** Value Added Tax (TVA in French) is a European sales tax. It is included in the price of goods sold. The French rate is 20.6 percent on everything except food, medicine, and books, which are subject to a reduced rate.

Non-European Union (E.U.) citizens can get a refund of France's Value Added Tax provided that (a) they are over 15, (b) they are staying in France for less than 6 months, and (c) they have spent at least 2,000FF in a single store offering duty-free items (look for the sign saying *vente en détaxe*).

Present your passport at the time of purchase and ask for the three-page export sales invoice (*bordereau*) and stamped envelope which the store will supply. Fill in the *bordereau* and keep it until you are leaving France. (Note: Some stores may refund slightly less than the full 20.6 percent tax, so check at the time of purchase how much they will refund.) When you leave France, show the *bordereau* and your purchases to the French customs official and he or she will stamp it and retain the two pink sheets, leaving you with a green sheet as your receipt. One pink sheet is sent to the store, who will mail you your refund (often only after several months).

Certain stores offer a **quick tax reclaim** for those due to fly from Orly or Charles de Gaulle airports. (Check if this service is offered at the time of your purchase.) To claim the instant refund, take your *bordereau*, passport, air ticket, and purchases to the customs office (don't put what you've bought in with your checked luggage).

The Aéroports de Paris information counter (ADP) will examine the figures and stamp the documents again and you can collect your refund from the airport's CCF (Change Bureau).

Allow 3 hours before departure to finish this IN ADDITION to normal check-in time.

• **Crossing into France from another E.U. country:** Adult visitors to France can bring duty-free allowances from other E.U. countries, as follows:

Tax paid in the E.U. (that is, bought in a regular store): 300 cigarettes or 150 cigarillos or 75 cigars or 400 grams of tobacco; 5 liters of table wine and 1.5 liters of alcohol over 22 percent volume (spirits), or 3 liters of alcohol under 22 percent or 3 more liters of table wine; 90 ml perfume, 375 ml toilet water and other goods to the value of 2,400FF.

Items from tax-free E.U. stores or from outside the E.U.: 200 cigarettes or 100 cigarillos or 50 cigars or 250 grams tobacco (double these if you live outside the E.U.); 2 liters of wine, 1 liter of spirits, 2 liters of alcohol under 22 percent volume or 2 more liters of wine; 60 ml perfume, 250 ml toilet water and other goods to the value of 300FF.

Quarantine regulations

It is not recommended to bring your pet with you for just a few weeks as it will undoubtedly find the traveling stressful. If it weighs over 5 kg (about 10 lb.) it must fly in a crate in the hold without you for the entire duration of the flight. Dogs under 5 kg can be carried in the cabin, but they must be confined in a crate. Crates may be obtained at the airport.

There is a tax of around $60 on pets brought into France, and pets aged under 3 months are not permitted to travel.

(For more information on bringing dogs into France see *Seeing-eye dogs* below.)

TRAVELERS WITH DISABILITIES

France is making efforts to accommodate people with disabilities, and most modern buildings are wheelchair-accessible – but facilities are not always as good as they should be, especially in cities and some smaller villages with narrow streets.

Tourist offices can provide you with local information about accessibility in specific places.

The French Government Tourist Board in the U.S.A. can also help. (See *Tourist Information Offices in the U.S.* on p.264 for details of addresses and phone numbers.)

Car rental

Hand-control rental vehicles are not offered by the major companies, but shift-stick vehicles that have been specially adapted for use by disabled people are offered by Intertouring Service, 117 boulevard Auguste Blanqui, 75013 Paris; tel: 01 45 88 52 37.

Wheelchair rental

Information on renting a wheelchair throughout France is available free from the Comité National Français de Liaison pour la Réadaptation des Handicapés (CNFLRH), who can also give advice about facilities for people who are blind or deaf, and accessibility to and within theaters, movie theaters, and other leisure attractions. Some English is spoken, though most of the literature is in French. The CNFLRH is located at 236 bis rue Tolbiac, 75013 Paris; tel: 01 53 80 66 66.

Seeing-eye dogs

Seeing-eye dogs may be unhappy about traveling (see *Quarantine regulations* above) but if you do need to bring one, make sure it has an international certificate of rabies immunization that is dated more than 30 days and less than 1 year from your departure date. Contact the American Foundation for the Blind for more details (tel: (212) 502-7600).

Other useful addresses for travelers with disabilities

• **The Society for the Advancement of Travel for the Handicapped** offers advice on planning specific trips (347 Fifth Avenue, Suite 610, New York, NY 10016; tel: (212) 447-7284).

• **The Disability Bookshop** (P.O. Box 129, Vancouver, WA 98666-0129; tel: (800) 637-2256) has a catalog that includes various helpful books about aspects of foreign travel for disabled people.

• **The Travelin' Talk network** offers advice and has a quarterly newsletter for disabled travelers (P.O. Box 3534, Clarksville, TN 37043-3534; tel: (615) 552-6670).

• **Mobility International** lists hotels, travel programs, camps, tours, andl access guides (P.O. Box 10767, Eugene, OR 97440; tel: (503) 343-1284; fax: (503) 343-6812).

• **Hexatours** at 45 E. 34th Street, Suite 500, New York, NY 10016-4313 (tel: 212/683 8719) organizes tours to Lourdes and also services for handicapped people in Paris.

• **Association des Paralysés de France** is a French organization; its accommodation guide, *Où ferons-nous étape?*, indicates disabled facilities. Symbols are used for non-French speakers. Head office is at 22 rue du Père Guérin, 75013 Paris; tel: 01 44 16 83 83 (French only).

DRIVING
Driver's license and age required to drive in France
If you plan to rent an automobile in France you'll need to bring along your driver's license plus an International Driver's Permit (IDP). Get an International Permit via your AAA local office, or write to AAA Florida, Travel Agency Services Department, 1000 AAA Drive (mail stop 28), Heathrow, FL 32746-5080; tel: (800) 222-4357.

Keep the automobile's ownership papers in the vehicle at all times. By law you must carry personal identification always, even when you're in a vehicle.

The minimum driving age in France is 18. (For further information, see *Driving Details* on p.266.)

Car rental details
Your U.S. travel agent should have lots of information on car rental. Packages that include car rental frequently offer the best deals. If you're hiring independently, use a multinational and pay in advance in dollars. **Hertz** (tel: 0990 996 699), **Avis** (tel: 0990 900 500), or **Budget** (tel: 0541 565 656) have many outlets throughout France.

You can rent an automobile once you're in France, but you'll probably find it pricier than in the U.S., unless you encounter a special offer. (For more information see *Driving Details* on p.266.)

ELECTRICITY
France runs on 220 volts at 50 Hertz AC, so use an adapter for American electrical goods. Certain adapters burn out small electrical items like razors and tape recorders, so ask for advice from your local travel store before buying. Take care when dealing with electric sockets in France: the outlets give a much stronger shock than North American ones do.

HEALTH
Medical insurance before you go
Medical insurance is vital, but don't pay for what you don't need. Americans should examine their own medical insurance policies before taking out extra medical insurance. Travel Guard International offers various insurance plans (1145 Clark Street, Stevens Point, WI 54481; tel: (800) 782-5151). Study the options to make sure you are covered in all circumstances, such as if you plan to do some diving or skiing.

Canadians should check to confirm that their provincial health plan will cover them abroad for up to 90 days.

Vaccinations
No special vaccinations are needed for entering France. It is recommended that you have been inoculated against polio, tetanus, and diphtheria. Arrange these shots several weeks before you travel.

INSURANCE
If you have a pre-existing medical condition check the fine print of any policy!

You may have a certain amount of travel insurance already, but please do compare a comprehensive travel insurance policy to check that you are fully covered. For instance, so-called "free" travel insurance may cover only low-risk/unlikely possibilities such as death occurring during the trip itself! A good policy will offer adequate coverage against cancellation, luggage loss, delays, theft, accident, medical emergencies, damage, or loss or theft of valuables, third-party, and legal expenses.

Some helpful addresses are:
• **AAA**, 1000 AAA Drive, Heathrow, FL 32746; tel: (800) 222-4357;
• **Access America**, Inc., P.O. Box 11188, Richmond, VA 23230; tel: (800) 284-8300;
• **Carefree Travel Insurance**, P.O. Box 310, 120 Mineola Boulevard, Mineola, NY 11501; tel: (800) 323-3149;
• **Travel Guard International**, 1145 Clark Street, Stevens Point, WI 54481; tel: (800) 782-5151.

NATIONAL HOLIDAYS

On national holidays in France, museums, banks, and nearly all stores close. Many restaurants, cafés, movie theaters, and some bakeries stay open. If the holiday falls on a Thursday or Tuesday, an extra day off is sometimes inserted to make up a long weekend.

Everything stops for **Bastille Day**, France's national day commemorating July 14, 1789, when French peasantry stormed the Bastille prison in Paris and the French Revolution began. On July 14 everywhere is decked with the national flag, and there are all types of enjoyable special events.

Many smaller stores and businesses close down throughout the whole of August, the French vacation month.

National holiday dates

- **January:** January 1, New Year's Day (*Jour de l'An*)
- **Late March or April:** Easter Sunday (*Pâques*), Easter Monday (*lundi de Pâques*)
- **May:** May 1, May Day (*Fête du Travail*); May 8, Victory Day (*Victoire 1945*); 40th day after Easter, Ascension Day (*Ascension*)
- **Mid-May to mid-June:** (7th Sunday after Easter) Pentecost (*Pentecôte*); (Monday after Pentecost) Whit Monday (*lundi de Pentecôte*)
- **July:** July 14, Bastille Day (*Fête Nationale*)
- **August:** August 15, Feast of the Assumption (*Assomption*)
- **November:** November 1, All Saints' Day (*Toussaint*); November 11, Armistice Day (*Armistice 1918*)
- **December:** December 25, Christmas Day (*Noël*)

PASSPORTS AND VISAS

U.S. and Canadian citizens do not presently need a visa for visits to France of up to three months as tourists. For longer stays, or if you want to work in France, apply at least four months before your proposed visit to the nearest French consulate. You should, however, note that most types of long-stay visas are difficult to obtain unless you are a European Union citizen.

There are several French consulates in the U.S. Look for your nearest one in the phone book or inquire at the New York consulate (address below).

- **French Embassy and Consulate, New York:** 934 Fifth Avenue, New York, NY 10021; tel: (212) 606-3688 (general number). For visa queries, tel: (212) 606-3644.

TIME

France is on Continental Time. That is, 1 hour ahead of Greenwich Mean Time in winter (2 hours ahead in summer), 6 hours ahead of New York and 9 hours ahead of the U.S. West Coast. When it's noon in Paris, it's 11 a.m. in London, 6 a.m. in New York, and 3 a.m. in Los Angeles.

France uses the 24-hour clock, not a.m. or p.m. Therefore, 1 a.m. is written as 1h, 12 noon is 12h, 1 p.m. is 13h, and midnight is 24h. For example, 10:15 a.m. is 10h15, and 4:30 p.m. is 16h30.

TOURIST INFORMATION OFFICES IN THE U.S.A.

- **New York:** French Government Tourist Office, 444 Madison Avenue, 16th Floor, New York, NY 10022.
- **Chicago:** French Government Tourist Office, 676 North Michigan Avenue, Suite 3360, Chicago, IL 60611.
- **Los Angeles:** French Government Tourist Office, 9454 Wilshire Boulevard, Beverly Hills, CA 90212.

The nationwide public information number, "France on Call," is a 900 number and costs 50¢ a minute. Dial (202) 293-6173.

TRAVEL AGENCIES

Many agencies specialize in Europe – look for their advertisements in your local paper's travel section. A specialist agency will have access to packages to France. It can access latest bargains, give information on a wide range of hotels, rooms, and room vouchers, and it can also fix up car rental arrangements and fly-drive vacations.

Learn more about evaluating travel packages by requesting a free brochure, *Tips on Travel Packages*, from the Council of Better Business Bureaus Inc., 4200 Wilson Boulevard, Arlington, VA 22203.

WHAT TO TAKE
Clothing

The clothing you bring depends of course on what you plan to do, at which time of year you are traveling, and which region of France you're going to visit. Clothes for traveling should be comfortable, easy to wash, and easy to keep wrinkle-free.

It's a good idea to start listing what you think you'll need about two weeks before you go. Most of us prefer to be comfortable on vacation, but if you plan to socialize with French people, think in somewhat more formal terms than you would in the U.S., and pack accordingly. For example, French people would wear shorts on the beach or for participating in sports, but even on a scorching Saturday afternoon they wouldn't wear shorts to visit a colleague's home.

Weather conditions in France aren't too extreme, but in winter bring sweaters, an overcoat, and an umbrella or waterproof jacket. In summer, or in the snowy winter regions, sunglasses are vital. Southern France gets hot in summer, so plenty of suntan lotion is necessary. Some country areas, notably the marshy Camargue, have problems with mosquitoes, so take along supplies of tried-and-tested bug repellent.

Clothing sizes

Clothing sizes don't convert exactly between French and American. Always try on goods before you buy them!

Women's tops and dresses

U.S.	France									
6	36	8	38	10	40	12	42	14	44	
16	46–48	18	50	20	52	22	54	24	56	26 58

Men's shirts

To change U.S. shirt sizes to French shirt sizes, multiply the American shirt size by 2 and add 8. To change French shirt sizes to American, subtract 8 from the French shirt size and divide by 2.

Men's suits

To change American suit sizes to French suit sizes, add 10 to the American suit size. To change French suit sizes to American, subtract 10 from the French suit size.

Shoes

Shoe sizes in France do not convert exactly to American ones. Again, the rule is try before you buy! Approximate conversions:

U.S.	France								
6	38	6	39	7	40	8	41	9	42
10	43	10	44	11	45				

Electronic equipment

Anything essential can be bought in France. However, you may prefer to bring certain things with you from the U.S. These could include appropriate adapters/transformers for electrical goods (see *Electricity* on p.263). Specialist items like camera batteries may not be available in rural areas.

Personal items

Always bring photocopies of important documents (to be kept separately from the documents themselves), and a copy of prescriptions for glasses. You should also take supplies of routine medication, sunscreens, cosmetics, and bug repellents.

If you can, bring or buy lightweight picnic implements. France is a great place for picnics.

Finally, if you are traveling with children, you might want to bring some of their favorite foods.

Recommended reading

France has always been a favorite with writers and photographers, and it's only possible to mention a few of the hundreds of books written about the country.
• **Fiction:** Georges Simenon's "Maigret" thrillers are set in Paris and are full of atmosphere. Ernest Hemingway's "A Movable Feast" is set in bohemian prewar Paris. Peter Mayle's "A Year in Provence" has been criticized for its patronizing tone, but it's readable and amusing nonetheless.
• **Non-fiction:** "Culture Shock – France" by Sally Adamson Taylor gives an American's practical suggestions about coping with the country. "The French" by Theodore Zeldin is an encyclopedia of a book that illuminates numerous aspects of French life and culture. "Portraits of France" by Robert Daley offers glimpses of French life and society. "Wild France" is part of a Sierra Club series of books that details sights for nature lovers exploring the countryside.
• **Photography books:** In "The French Café," Marie-France Boyer's intelligent text and Eric Morin's evocative photos create a fine portrait of this very French institution. Look for books by French photographers, including the veteran Henri Cartier-Bresson, one of the century's greatest observers of both French and foreign cultures.

GETTING AROUND

CYCLING

France is a favorite with foreign touring cyclists, and attitudes toward two-wheeled travelers are generally very favorable, as you might expect of a country that hosts the annual Tour de France cycle race. Many of its small, uncrowded roads run through lovely villages and scenery.

Taking your own bicycle

Airlines usually carry bicycles – for packing requirements contact individual airlines. Most trains transport cycles; the service is provided free on slow local trains. On inter-city routes you'll need to box and register the bicycle (for which a charge is made); it will then be transported free. Depending on the route to your destination your bicycle may go via Paris and take several days to catch up with you. TGV's don't carry cycles. SNCF's *Guide du Train et du Vélo* leaflet gives details (with an English translation) and is free at rail stations.

Most French towns have bicycle shops, but French cities generally lack cycling routes. The same applies to busy cross-country roads. It's compulsory to use cycle routes if they do exist alongside roads.

Renting a bicycle

Bicycle rental from SNCF costs from around 50FF a day and up (you may also need to pay a deposit or give your credit card number as guarantee). Insurance is not included, so do check your own travel insurance policy to see if you're covered. Some tourist offices as well as bicycle shops also rent out cycles. Inquire at rail stations or local tourist offices.

One of the best guides to France's many cycling opportunities is Susi Madron's "Cycling in France" (available for $12.00 including postage – payable by credit card – from Susi Madron, 2 Birch Polygon, Rusholme, Manchester M14 5HX, U.K.).

The French cycling organization **Fédération Française de Cyclotourisme (FFC)** focuses on club touring. It can supply helpful details and material (some in English). Write to the FFC at 8 rue Jean-Marie Jégo, 75013 Paris.

DRIVING
Accidents

If you are in an accident, you must stop. If the accident is minor, fill out the form called *Constat à l'amiable d'Accident Automobile*, which you'll generally find with your rental car's papers. Both you and the other driver sign and keep a copy of the document. You can complete this form in English, but if your French isn't fluent get a translation before you sign, to ensure you understand what the other driver has written.

If the accident necessitates calling the police, don't move the vehicle, but leave it exactly where the accident happened.

For both accidents and breakdowns you must set up your warning triangle on the highway so that oncoming vehicles can see it in time to avoid you.
• **Highway Information**, tel: 01 48 94 33 33.
• **Autoroute Information**, tel: 01 47 05 90 01.

How to be a local driver

French drivers are decisive, though not particularly aggressive. Some older French roads, especially in developed areas, are narrow and twisting. This may lead to problems when, say, three vehicles try to fit into a space only big enough for two. Keep calm, be assertive, and don't get angry. You will quickly understand why many old towns ban or severely restrict traffic.

One of the strangest French traffic rules is the *priorité à droite*. This means that vehicles coming from the right have priority at intersections unless there is a sign to the contrary. (This applies even if you are on a big street or highway, and traffic is coming from the right off a smaller section of road.)

Because of increasing traffic speeds, a new system has been introduced. A yellow diamond with a white border, or a triangle showing a minor roadway crossing a main roadway, indicates that those driving on the main roadway have priority.

France also has "rotaries," in which several routes join at a traffic circle. Vehicles join the circulating flow and exit when they reach the turnoff for the roadway they require. Note that *priorité à droite* does NOT apply at rotaries. If a driver flashes his lights at you, it signifies that he believes he has priority. Let him go first!

Age required to drive
See *Driving* on p.263.

Breakdown
If your vehicle breaks down, try to get it off the street or highway. Put your warning triangle out so that oncoming traffic can take avoiding action. There's no equivalent to the AAA in France, so make sure you have adequate breakdown insurance cover.

On toll expressways (*autoroutes*), call the breakdown emergency service from the nearest roadside telephone.

On other roads, dial 17 for the police, or (preferably) find a nearby garage yourself. Garages are more likely to cope if you're driving a French make of automobile.

Drinking and driving penalties
The current laws on driving while intoxicated are so strict that they have even been blamed for the decline in business for French bars! The limit is now just 0.50 ml per liter of blood.

French police are allowed to conduct random breath tests and the fines can be fairly heavy depending on the seriousness of the offence.

Fines
French traffic police can give on-the-spot fines for traffic violations. Tourists must pay up immediately, to avoid the risk that they will leave the country without paying.

Traffic violations punishable by a fine include:
• Not carrying a warning triangle and/or not having working hazard lights.
• Not wearing seatbelts. Seatbelts should always be worn by the driver and by all passengers.
• Allowing a child under 10 years old to ride in the front of the vehicle (unless the child is in a specially approved backward-facing fitted child seat).
• Stopping on the open road outside a town without first getting your vehicle off the road, out of the way of oncoming traffic.
• Overtaking under any circumstances while driving on a road that has a solid single line down the middle.
• Not coming to a complete halt at a stop sign. Edging slowly over the line without stopping is penalized.
• Driving with faulty lights. You are obliged immediately to get any light faults fixed, even if you are in a rented vehicle.
• Speeding or driving while drunk.
• Driving when under 18 years old or on a provisional license. (See *Driving* on p.263.)

Fuel
Gasoline (*essence*) is more expensive in France than in North America. Gas stations at *autoroute* rest stops are open 24 hours, but they charge more than hypermarkets. French gasoline is sold in liters, not gallons. To convert from liters to gallons, divide by 3.79.

Most French gas stations willingly accept credit cards, but you occasionally find some rural places that won't, so it's advisable to have some cash handy. Don't try and use a U.S. gas-company card; it won't work.

Parking
Major tourist sights usually have adequate lot parking. But finding space in some older cities can be difficult. If a place looks congested, it's worth considering parking just outside the city limits, and walking in or taking a local bus.

Parking (if you can find any) in villages and small towns may be free for short periods, but ensure you're not accidentally parked in a no-parking zone or at a bus stop – it's not always clear.

Tow-away, no-stopping zones are indicated by circular red signs with blue centers. They may not be visible in the actual spot where you wish to park, but you'll have passed them as you entered the zone. On exiting the zone, you'll see a black-and-white picture of the sign, crossed out.

In some places vehicles are parked on alternate sides of the streets, depending on what day of the month it is. These areas are marked by blue and red no-parking signs as described above, stamped with white numerals indicating the days of the month when parking is forbidden (*interdit*).

Solid yellow or dotted yellow curbside lines indicate parking restrictions. Yellow zig-zag curbside lines indicate bus stops.

Parking lots cost up to 10FF an hour and are shown by a white letter "P" on a blue background. Most cities also have street parking meters. The time limit is often a couple of hours. Meters vary, but normally take 2FF coins. Usually you pay, press a button, and the machine ejects a ticket showing what you paid and the exact time when the meter runs out. Leave the ticket visible inside the windshield.

Blue parking zones (*zones bleues*) are signposted. In these, you need to display a payment disc in the vehicle. You can get discs from the police or from tourist offices.

If the worst happens and you get a parking ticket, pay it immediately. Fines increase sharply if you don't pay. You'll need to buy a tax stamp (*timbre fiscal*) for the appropriate amount at a *tabac* (a store that sells cigarettes, etc.). Stick the larger section onto your parking ticket, and mail it to the address shown on the ticket.

Rental
(See *Driving* on p.263 for further car rental information.)

Make sure that your rental car contains the compulsory accident hazard warning triangle. Check what your rental agreement says about breakdown and accident, and ask about anything you are unsure of. You are legally obliged to have working lights at all times, so see if the vehicle has a spare set of lights. In case of breakdown, note that more garages carry parts for French automobiles (including Citroën, Peugeot, Renault), so try and rent a French make.

Road signs
Written signs include:
gravillons (loose road surface), *chaussée déformée* (uneven road edgings and temporary surface), *nids de poules* (holes in the pavement), *ralentir* (slow down), *serrez à droite/à gauche* (keep right/left), *cédez le passage* (yield), and *déviation* (diversion).

Road types (including toll roads)
• *Autoroutes*/toll roads: *Autoroutes* are toll expressways, and are marked with blue-and-white signs. There is an extensive network of *autoroutes* that centers on Paris. Tolls (*péage*) can be expensive, and toll booths accept most credit cards.

On maps, *autoroutes* are prefixed with an "A."
• *Routes Nationales*: *Routes Nationales*

form a large network of good highways. They are often only three lanes wide, with the middle lane used for overtaking. You'll see red-and-white markers along them, marking off the kilometers. *Route Nationale* numbers have an "N" prefix.
• *Routes départementales*: These are less important roads with yellow-and-white kilometer markers along their length, and their road number is prefixed with "D."

Safety belts (seatbelts) and restraints
Must be worn wherever fitted. Children under 10 years of age using the front seat MUST sit in a special child seat attachment.

Speed limits
Unless otherwise posted, the speed limit in France is 50 kph (31 mph) in developed areas. Slow down to this speed when passing the white sign showing the name of the village or town. The limit remains in force until you reach the sign at the other side of town, which shows the town name crossed out with a red line.
• **Other limits are** (a) 90 kph/55 mph (or 80 kph/49 mph on wet road surfaces) on two-lane undivided highways whose number is prefixed by "N" or "D," or on urban *autoroutes*; (b) 110 kph/68 mph (90 kph/55 mph in the rain) on divided highways; and (c) 130 kph/80 mph (110 kph/68 mph in the rain) on *autoroutes*.

There is also a minimum speed limit of 80 kph (50 mph) when driving on the outside lane of highways, in good visibility, in dry conditions, and on a level surface. A speed limit of 50 kph (31 mph) is applicable on highways in foggy conditions, when visibility is less than 50 meters (164 ft.).

Speeding fines are decided by the courts and depend on the excess speed.

HITCHHIKING
France is not a particularly dangerous country, but hitching is not recommended, especially for women traveling alone. If you really need to hitch, choose a spot just outside the city limits where vehicles can stop safely. Hitching on *autoroutes* is illegal. Try *autoroute* rest stop exits instead.

Student or youth accommodations often have notice boards offering shared rides: this is a safer option than hitching.

MAPS

The "AA Road Atlas France" is a large-format book that has details of the whole French road network. The "AA Glovebox Atlas France and Benelux" contains major roads in a handy format.

In France, buy various road and city maps at tourist offices, *Maisons de la Presse* (newspaper stores), and bookstores. The best-known French hiking maps are Didier et Richard's 1:50,000 trail maps, and Institut Géographique National (IGN) maps. The latter are available from the IGN Paris store at 107 rue la Boëtie, Paris 75008 (tel: 01 42 56 06 68).

Also try U.S. mail-order book service Forsyth Travel Library, P.O. Box 2975, Shawnee Mission, KS 66201; tel: (800) 367-7984, which sells a wide variety of worldwide maps by mail order.

ORGANIZED TOURS

The French Government Tourist Office has a list of specialist tour operators offering a good selection of themed tours, including ones geared toward archeology, military history, art history, golf, skiing, wine and gourmet foods, painting, prehistoric caves, and much more. Local tourist information offices and hotels can recommend many one-day or half-day tours taking in local attractions.

For bus tours around Paris, contact Paris Vision, 214 rue de Rivoli, Paris 75001; tel: 01 42 60 31 25, or Cityrama, 4 place des Pyramides, Paris 75001; tel: 01 44 55 61 00. A Paris tour currently costs 150-220FF.

French Heritage Trails

The Caisse Nationale des Monuments Historiques et des Sites (CNMHS) is the French organization responsible for historic monuments and sites.

It has created a range of heritage trails throughout France, based round architectural, historical, artistic, and other themes. An illustrated brochure giving details of the trails can be obtained from CNMHS at 62 rue St.-Antoine, 75004 Paris; tel: 01 44 61 20 00.

Regional and local tourist offices will also be able to supply further information about tourist routes that highlight places of especial interest.

Wine tours

Various regions of France have signposted wine tours, which take in the main wine-producing areas and cellars (*caves*). This can be an enjoyable as well as satisfying way of getting to know more about the wines themselves, and you may even be tempted to purchase wines direct from the grower. Look out for signs indicating local tastings and sales (*dégustation-vente*).

PUBLIC TRANSPORTATION
Air

You can reserve Air France internal flights from the U.S., either direct or through a travel agent. Once in France, use a French travel agent.

France has not benefited from the deregulation that has reduced fares in North America, so air fares within the country are relatively expensive.

Certain people qualify for discounts: senior citizens, students under 27, adults under 25, married couples traveling together, and families with children under 25 may all qualify. If you don't qualify, and if you have a rail pass, do examine the cost and time differences between taking a plane and taking a train. Trains may offer the better deal pricewise, and perhaps even timewise too.

There's a good network of regional airports; the main ones are listed below.
• **Nice-Cote d'Azur airport:** 6 kilometers (4 mi.) west of Nice center; tel: 04 93 21 30 30 and 04 93 21 30 12. Taxis from town cost around 150FF (extra at night and on Sundays). The bus between the airport and place Leclerc costs 45FF. There's not much luggage room available.
• **Lyon-Satolas airport:** 26 kilometers (16 mi.) east of Lyon center; tel: 04 72 22 72 21. Taxis to town cost about 230FF; buses cost 150FF. Buses connect with Lyon's two main train stations, Perrache and Part-Dieu.

Road

• **Local buses:** Most city buses are marked with the route number and the major stops. They run during the day and evening (Paris has special night services). Find timetables at bus stops. Tickets are bought on board (except Paris), or use a pass or *carnet* (block of 10 tickets).

• **Long-distance buses:** Long-distance country buses in France are efficient, but, except in mountainous areas, trains are more popular. Buses are generally cheaper and slower than trains. Local tourist offices can provide you with bus timetables.

• **Taxis:** French taxis can seem expensive. Taxis accept up to three people. It's best to phone, or get your hotel to phone for one. They can be hailed on the street, but can be hard to spot since they lack a standardized livery or design. Fares vary between cities, and are metered. They usually include a standing charge and an extra 6FF per luggage item. Fares rise at night, and, in some places, on Sundays. Ask the estimated cost in advance.

Train

The French national railroad network (SNCF) has a frequent, efficient service in both first and second class.

Rail passes

Rail passes make sense if you are planning to take several train trips. Young people can get special youth passes; senior citizens qualify for a card called *Carte Vermeil*. Call Rail Europe on (800) 438-7245 (in the U.S.), or (800) 848-7245 (in Canada), or write to the Reservation Center at 2100 Central Avenue, Boulder, CO 80301 for full details of all passes available.

• **Francepass:** Useful if you're traveling only in France. It lets you ride for between four and nine days within a one-month period. The days need not be consecutive, and the passes presently cost $145 second class (three days), with up to six additional days at $30 each (first class also is available). A surcharge applies for reserving a seat or *couchette* (sleeping-seat) in advance. Children four through eleven pay half fare. (A Métro pass from the airport to the center of Paris is included in this pass.) More expensive versions of the pass include car rental and domestic French airline travel options.

• **Europass:** This allows 5 to 15 days of travel in France, Germany, Italy, Spain, and Switzerland within a 2-month period.

• **Eurailpass:** If you are planning to travel 2,414 kilometers (1,500 mi.) or more by train, in several European countries, it may be worth investigating the purchase of a Eurailpass, valid in 17 countries.

Rail passes are not usually refundable or transferable, so take as much care of your pass as you would of your passport or money. Consider loss insurance. Examine the pass carefully before accepting it, to make sure there are no mistakes in your details. If the pass details don't match those on your other papers, even by a small amount, you could run into trouble if you encounter an over-zealous official.

If you plan just one single-destination train journey, buy the ticket in advance in the U.S. from a travel agent or Rail Europe. (All single-destination – also known as point-to-point tickets – cover TGV fast train surcharges.) Tickets purchased in North America don't need validation on the station platform (see below under *Validation*). However, you do need to validate a rail pass before you travel in France. Get the clerk to validate it for you before you try to use it. Don't try and put a pass into a validation machine (see below).

Validation

Point-to-point tickets bought in France must be validated on the platform. Put the ticket into the machine marked *compostez votre billet*. This stamps the date on it. Keep your ticket; you may need to show it to a ticket inspector on the train. Validate the ticket again if you rejoin the train after a stopover. Non-validated tickets attract fines.

TGV (High-Speed Train)

TGV (*train à grande vitesse*) trips of up to about 480 kilometers (300 mi.) can be faster by train than by air, once you've allowed for the check in and getting to the airport. Booking and advance seat reservation are compulsory on a TGV.

Whatever train you use, bring some food and drink. Train refreshments are expensive and train restroom water is not drinkable.

Motorail and overnight traveling

Traveling overnight can work if you want to save daytimes for sightseeing.

Second-class sleeping compartments may involve sharing with strangers of either sex. They're unlikely to bother you (or even speak to you), but you may prefer to sleep fully dressed and keep valuables with you in your bunk.

Family trains

These are great if you have young children. They operate on 11 long-distance routes, mostly from Paris. Each has a playroom (with play equipment) where you can sit and watch your child, and there are electric outlets for bottle warmers.

There's no extra charge for family trains, and under-4s travel free if they don't occupy a seat.

Paris Métro and RER trains

The Métro is the quickest, cheapest way to get around Paris. Route maps of the Métro, plus suburban lines (RER), are available free at stations.

Stations are marked with a big yellow "M" or "Métropolitain" sign.

To use the system you first buy a ticket. Métro stations sell individual tickets, weekly or monthly passes, or *carnets*, which are blocks of 10 tickets.

You can also buy *carnets* at *tabacs* (tobacco shops). Métro tickets and passes are valid for Métro, bus, and RER trains within Paris.

Find the station you want on the map and note the last station on that line. Métro lines are numbered and color-coded on maps, and they are named according to the last station on the line.

If you need to change trains, look when you change for a sign bearing the name of your destination line. The sign will direct you to the correct corridor.

There are four suburban rail lines, labeled A, B, C, and D. There are few RER stations in the center of Paris. You can interchange with RER trains at certain Métro stations, marked on the map, but RER lines are most useful for longer journeys.

Note that *Sortie* means "Exit."

The system opens at 5:30 a.m. and closes at 1:15 a.m. Check times of first and last trains from your station. Some stations, especially on Lines 2 and 13, have a reputation for being seedy at night, but in general the Metro is a fairly safe way of traveling in Paris.

Travelers with disabilities

• **Buses:** French buses are not usually practicable for wheelchair users.
• **Trains:** All TGV's accommodate wheelchairs, and seeing-eye dogs are transported free of charge (dogs are not authorized on the Eurostar Channel Tunnel trains, however). Slower trains ask wheelchair passengers to use a special compartment, and offer help with boarding.
• **RER (Paris suburban trains) and Paris Métro:** The RER has facilities at some stations for boarding wheelchair passengers, but the Paris Métro is not very accessible for wheelchair users. Passengers who are able to walk to and from the platforms can take advantage of special disabled persons' seats once inside the trains.

WALKING

Most of France developed in the age before automobiles, so towns and cities are often more suited to walking than driving.

There's a large network of signposted hiking trails. Long-distance trails are marked with red-and-white stripes. They link different areas of France, and some will even continue into other continental countries.

Shorter trails that are marked in yellow and red usually end at their original starting point. They may take several days to complete.

You don't need permits for hiking, but camping is confined to authorized campgrounds.

We have included some rural and urban walking suggestions in each regional section of this guide. See the contents list for details.

CRUISING INLAND

Two operators offering cruises on French waterways are **French Cruise Lines**, tel: (800) 346-6525 (East) or 800/858 8587 (West), and **Hotel Barge Cruises**, tel: (800) 234-4000.

SKIING AND MOUNTAINEERING

For information contact the Club Alpin Français at 24 avenue de Laumière, 75019 Paris; tel: 01 53 38 88 61.

DAY TO DAY

ACCOMMODATIONS

(See also the list of hotels and restaurants that begins on p.283.)

Most times of year it's easy to get a room in a hotel, but reserve ahead for the French vacation period (mid-July to end of August). Local tourist offices have lists of hotels.

Hotels vary from cozy family-run inns to magnificent châteaux or modern chains like IBIS. Smaller, older accommodations (even châteaux) typically lack certain conveniences. Few have air-conditioning. Some may lack en-suite bathrooms, in-room TVs and mini-bars. However, they may be exquisitely beautiful, furnished with priceless antiques and have wonderful restaurants! Modern French chain hotels aren't special, but are relatively cheap, clean, and convenient (sometimes a bit too convenient) for the highway.

Bed and breakfast/guesthouses

Look for the words *chambres d'hôte*. They are usually run by local people making use of their spare bedrooms. They're more common in country areas than in cities, and can offer a unique insight into French lifestyles. Sometimes the hostess will offer home-cooked meals at reasonable prices.

Camping, trailer sites

There are plenty of campgrounds in France. *Campings municipaux* (town campgrounds) are very reasonable, costing about 20FF a night. For longer stays try *campings 4 étoiles*, which offer better amenities, including restaurants and sports facilities.

Campings à la ferme

These are farm campgrounds, and they usually lack facilities. Don't camp anywhere that is not a campground. There are some-times discounts on fees if you produce a *camping carnet* insurance card. It's a good idea to have the insurance, and it doesn't cost a lot. It can be purchased through AAA.

It's possible to rent small RVs/trailers through the big car rental companies, but huge American-style RVs are impractical in France. They'd be impossible to maneuver down the narrow French country roads!

Apartments, villas, gîtes

For information on renting a city apartment, villa or *gîte* (cottage), contact the French Government Tourist Offices in the U.S. They have many leaflets and photographs, and also offer a list of operators offering personally inspected properties.

Staying with a family

Staying with a family can make a vacation special and may lead to long-term friendships. Tourisme Chez L'Habitant (tel: 01 34 25 44 44) arranges homestays. Bed and breakfast in Paris costs 1,400FF for one week, 1,200FF for subsequent weeks, plus 285FF annual subscription. (Various plans are available.)

Youth hostels

Auberges de jeunesse cost up to 125FF per night. They're most popular with young budget travelers, but older people and families also stay (no under-5s).

There's dormitory accommodations, usually meals, and often a kitchen. The hostels aren't usually as comfortable as American ones, but many of them look very attractive and they are an excellent way of meeting other friendly travelers.

The largest French hostel organization is FUAJ, 27 rue Pajol, Paris 75018; tel: 01 44 89 87 27. The *International Youth Hostel Handbook*, which lists the world's hostels, sells in some U.S. bookstores (or contact your local AYHA hostel for an address to purchase).

CHILDREN

The French don't have many special facilities for children, but well-behaved varieties are welcome everywhere, including in bars.

Hotels generally supply baby furniture for a small extra charge, but check in advance if yours will. It's fine to ask the owners of family hotels if they'll listen for your children when you're out at night. If they agree, it's on the basis of no legal liability. French people may assume your kids will be willing to eat quite fancy and formal food, so bring along supplies of any just-can't-do-without foods for them, because most brand-name American foods are unavailable in France. You can often find a McDonald's, which will likely amaze you with its high prices, and most cities harbor fast-food joints.

Places to take children

Most French beach resorts are well organized and refreshingly free of tackiness. They're geared to families doing things together, so often don't provide many exclusively-for-kids activities; instead, they offer child-size versions of grown-up facilities. The seacoast is at its liveliest during August.

Paris's *guignols* (puppet shows) are popular with adults and children alike. They're easy to understand even if you don't speak French. Contact the local tourist information office for venue details.

Three of the best theme parks

• **Disneyland Paris:** Despite its well-publicized early difficulties, this is now a huge attraction for European families, so schedule visits for midweek when the lines are shorter. If you and your kids loved Disneyland or Disney World, you'll love Disneyland Paris too. Apart from a certain French tinge, it's almost like America – even down to the food!

Technologically it's well up to the standard of its U.S. counterparts, and magnificently themed rides include one or two special French ones. The Sleeping Beauty Castle isn't much like a real French *château*, but it's visually spectacular and the huge dragon in its basement is surely one of the finest animatronic figures you'll ever see!

Food and souvenir prices are higher than in the U.S., reflecting the different costs of living. There are several themed hotels at Disneyland Paris, ranging from the 5-star Disneyland Hotel to the budget Hotel Cheyenne.

A one-day park pass costs 160FF (under 11: 130FF) in low season, 200FF adult/ 155FF child, high season. High season is from April 1 through October 1, and Christmas/New Year. For reservations in the U.S. and Canada, tel: (800) 647-7900; in France, tel: 01 60 30 60 53 (English spoken).

To get there from Paris, take the A4, leave at Exit 14, and follow the signs, or take the RER line A4 to Marne-la-Vallée.

• **Futuroscope:** Futuroscope is a marvelous and visually striking attraction that's unique and unlike anything else in the world. It combines a science park and a theme park, and its amazing architecture shelters the world's largest collection of big-screens, including the unique IMAX "Magic Carpet," an IMAX SOLIDO theater that views rapidly alternating images through liquid crystal glasses to create state-of-the-art 3-D, plus several other IMAX, OMNIMAX, and simulator theaters. English translations are available for most movies.

Hands-on attractions with a science theme provide active fun elsewhere.

There's a delightful restaurant, and snack bars offering good-quality food.

Futuroscope rides don't attract very young children, although imaginative play facilities are provided for them.

You can stay in several reasonably priced modern hotels on site. Reservations: Boîte Postale 3030, 86130 Jaunay Clan; tel: 05 49 49 30 10 (English is spoken).

The park is 324 kilometers (201 mi.) from Paris: take signposted exit 18 off the A10 Paris–Bordeaux *autoroute*.

• **Parc Astérix:** Astérix the Gaul is the French child's equivalent of Mickey Mouse. Everyone in France knows him and his crazy friend Obélix.

Parc Astérix is an authentic French theme park that also caters to non-French speakers (park maps and events programs are available in English). The park's rides also include Europe's current largest roller-coaster.

More uncommon things to see include artisans at work (from lace-makers to glass-blowers) and swordfights by the "Three Musketeers." The Little Gauls' Carnival gives youngsters the chance to don traditional costume and parade through the park with Astérix and Obélix.

Restaurants and food stands offer better fare than you'd expect.

The park is open April through October, and is signposted 38 kilometers (24 mi.) from Paris off the A1 Paris–Lille *autoroute*. Tickets can be obtained at the gate.

For more information, tel: 01 44 62 16 34 (English spoken), or write to Boîte Postale 8, 60128 Plailly, France.

COMPLAINTS

It helps to understand that most French systems are tightly organized, and flexibility in interpreting rules in the interests of good customer relations is not necessarily encouraged. Don't waste time with subordinates – go straight to the boss. You have the best chance of success if you are formal, well organized, and know what the rules should be.

Keep calm, state your case clearly, and aim for a resolution that is reasonable for everyone. Making a complaint will be much easier if you can find a fluent French speaker to help you negotiate. Some people may refuse to consider your complaint if they cannot fully understand what you're saying.

The French tend to argue and shout, though this doesn't usually mean that they are about to come to blows, and you will gain respect (and likely results) if you try to find a constructive way around the problem.

Don't over-react to the French tendency to shrug and raise their eyebrows when presented with a difficulty. It's easy to interpret this as an insulting "Who cares?" approach, but it probably only means that the person really is at a loss and cannot think how to help. Suggest the result that you would like to see, and ask the person's advice on how this can be made possible.

CRIME

France is quite a safe country, but there is inevitably some crime, of course, and so you should take precautions, especially in city areas like the 9th, 18th, 19th, and 20th Paris *arrondissements*.

Watch out for theft – pickpockets and automobile thieves particularly. As you must always carry identity in France, you'll probably have your passport with you; keep it and other valuables in a money-belt inside your clothes.

Lock vehicle doors and don't leave valuables lying around hotel rooms. Label bags and cameras with your name and contact address. Keep copies of valuable documentation like passports and air tickets in the hotel safe. Never leave bags unattended – in airports and public places you may find that the police remove them as a "security risk."

CONVERSION CHART

miles	kilometers	mph	kph
1	1.609	70	112
0.6214	1	43	70

inches	centimeters		
0.3937	1		
1	2.54		

feet	meters	yards	meters
1	0.3048	1	0.9144
3.281	1	1.094	1
sq. feet	**sq. meters**	**sq. meters**	**sq. yards**
1	0.0929	1	1.196

pounds	kilograms	ounces	grams
2.2	1	1	28.35
1	0.4536	0.0353	1

ETIQUETTE
How to be a local

The French are formal in everyday life, and you'll often find they react best if you're a bit formal, too. If they seem suspicious of your friendly approach, try not to get angry or upset: when you get to know French people you'll find them as kind as anyone else.

As in most places, those who live in the country are more relaxed than city people about dress and "image." Use "Madame" or "Monsieur" when addressing a person you do not know. On entering a small store, greet the storekeeper with "Bonjour, Monsieur/Madame." When leaving, say "Au revoir, Monsieur/Madame."

If you decide to practice your French, never address adults you don't know well using the informal *tu* and *ton* until they invite you to do so – instead you should use the more formal *vous* and *votre*. The *tu* form is used only between friends, relatives, and with children and animals, so using it inappropriately is taken as an insult.

The French aren't that comfortable about falling into conversation with strangers in public places. Chat with the bartender and hope he'll introduce you to the others. Once you're introduced, don't ask strangers what they do for a living, or discuss money. It's considered intrusive.

The French gesticulate a lot and hands are part of their expressive vocabulary. For this reason it is considered polite to keep them in view when eating (though don't put your elbows on the table). Likewise, remove hands from your pockets while chatting. If you are invited over by a French person, bring a gift, like an extremely good bottle of wine or bunch of flowers. Never offer chrysanthemums; they are reserved for burials, and will cause serious offense.

FESTIVALS
France is abuzz with festivals and sports events. Get a complete listing from the French Government Tourist Office. Some annual events to look for include:
- **January:** Monte-Carlo rally (Monte-Carlo)
- **February:** Carnival (Nice)
- **March:** Salon du Mars modern art festival (Paris)
- **April:** Open Tennis Championships (Monte-Carlo)
- **May:** Cannes Film Festival (Cannes)
- **June:** Le Mans automobile rally (Le Mans); Tour de France cycle race – end of June, early July throughout France; Roland Garros Tennis Championships (Paris)
- **July:** Festival month! Tour de France continues; Bastille Day (July 14); and many city festivals throughout France
- **August:** Mime Festival (Périgueux)
- **September:** Vendanges – harvest festivals (wine regions)
- **October:** Prix de l'Arc du Triomphe horse race (Paris)
- **November:** Les Trois Glorieuses wine festival (Burgundy)
- **December:** Christmas festivities, particularly good in Paris
(For a fuller list of events, see the beginning pages of each region in this guide.)

HEALTH MATTERS
(See also *Opening Hours* on p.279, and *Emergencies – Medical Care* on p.282). The American Hospital is at 63 boulevard Victor Hugo, Neuilly-sur-Seine, near Paris (tel: 01 46 41 25 25). It may recommend an English-speaking doctor at a hospital near you. In the U.S., the IAMAT, 417 Center Street, Lewison, NY 14092 (tel: (716) 754-4883) offers lists of well-qualified, English-speaking physicians abroad who accept set

fees. You get good quality medical care in France, but you'll need medical insurance.

Drugstores
Drugstores abound. Every district should have a drugstore on call at night. The French have a tradition of homeopathic care, and most drugstores will stock homeopathic products or are near specialist homeopathic stores. The latter can advise about finding local homeopathic doctors.

LANGUAGE
The French language sounds nasal and has some unfamiliar sounds, so try and hear some French before you arrive in France, perhaps from a language tape. The "r" is rolled slightly in the back of the throat, and the "j" is pronounced like "s" in "leisure." The last consonant of many words is hardly pronounced at all.

It is courteous to try to speak French to French people and your efforts can create a favorable impression. Always use "Madame" or "Monsieur".

Useful French phrases:

good morning	**bonjour**
good afternoon	**bonjour**
good evening	**bonsoir**
good night	**bonne nuit**
goodbye	**au revoir**
yes/no	**oui/non**
please	**s'il vous plaît**
thank you	**merci**
you're welcome	**je vous en prie**
Do you speak English?	**Parlez-vous anglais?**
I don't understand.	**Je ne comprends pas.**
Where is…?	**Où se trouve…?**
Where is the U.S./ Canadian/British embassy?	**Où se trouve l'ambassade américaine/ canadienne/ de Grande Bretagne?**
How much is…?	**Combien coûte…?**
I'd like…	**Je voudrais…**
Excuse me	**Pardon/ Excusez-moi**
Where are the restrooms?	**Où se trouve les toilettes?**
What time is it?	**Quelle heure est-il?**

Help!	**Au secours!**
where	**où**
when	**quand**
how	**comment**
yesterday	**hier**
today	**aujourd'hui**
tomorrow	**demain**
left	**à gauche**
right	**à droite**
straight ahead	**tout droit**
cheap	**bon marché**
expensive	**cher**
good	**bon**
bad	**mauvais**
hot	**chaud**
cold	**froid**
old	**vieux (m)/vieille (f)**
	vieil (m) if
	followed by a
	vowel or a silent
	"h"
new	**nouveau (m)/**
	nouvelle (f)
open	**ouvert(e)**
closed	**fermé(e)**
early	**tôt**
late	**tard**
in front of	**devant**
before	**avant**
behind	**derrière**
near	**près**
here/there	**ici/là**
breakfast	**le petit déjeuner**
lunch	**le déjeuner**
dinner	**le dîner**
entrance	**entrée**
exit	**sortie**
stores	**les magasins**
market	**le marché**
bakery	**la boulangerie**
butcher	**la boucherie**
pharmacy	**la pharmacie**
fishmonger	**la poissonnerie**
railroad station	**la gare**
railroad platform	**le quai**
gas station	**un poste à**
	essence
bus station	**la gare routière**
bus stop	**l'arrêt du bus**
parking lot	**le parking**
Please write it down.	**Veuillez me l'écrire,**
	s'il-vous plaît.
Do you take	**Acceptez-vous les**
credit cards/	**cartes de crédit/**
travelers' checks?	**les chèques de voyage?**
The check, please. (in a restaurant)	**L'addition, s'il vous plaît.**

DAYS OF THE WEEK

Sunday	**dimanche**
Monday	**lundi**
Tuesday	**mardi**
Wednesday	**mercredi**
Thursday	**jeudi**
Friday	**vendredi**
Saturday	**samedi**

NUMBERS

1	**un/une**
2	**deux**
3	**trois**
4	**quatre**
5	**cinq**
6	**six**
7	**sept**
8	**huit**
9	**neuf**
10	**dix**
11	**onze**
12	**douze**
13	**treize**
14	**quatorze**
15	**quinze**
16	**seize**
17	**dix-sept**
18	**dix-huit**
19	**dix-neuf**
20	**vingt**
21	**vingt-et-un**
22	**vingt-deux**
30	**trente**
40	**quarante**
50	**cinquante**
60	**soixante**
70	**soixante-dix**
80	**quatre-vingt**
90	**quatre-vingt-dix**
100	**cent**
1,000	**mille**
one million	**un million**

MEDIA
Newspapers and magazines

Newsstands in major population centers generally sell English-language papers. You also find this applies in areas with large British populations, like Provence. Most papers are British, a day or two out of date. The *International Herald Tribune* and *U.S.A. Today* can also be found, plus magazines like *Newsweek*, *The Economist*, and *Time*. Some small English-language papers are published in Paris for English-speaking people (Anglophones) living there. These publications can be purchased in Parisian bookstores and newsstands. Also look out for *Pariscope*, a weekly that contains Paris entertainments listings.

Television

Bigger hotels usually have satellite or cable channels that get CNN and frequently the British channel Sky. MTV and BBC World Service television services are also sometimes available. Pre-recorded videocassettes in France will have been recorded using the French television system, SECAM, which is not compatible with the system used in North America, nor in fact with most other countries' systems. You can use French blank tapes in your own video camera, though.

Radio

• **AM & FM:** Voice of America Europe broadcasts in France on 1197 kHz AM. BBC for Europe transmits on 648 kHz. The BBC World Service is available 24 hours a day on 648 kHz AM.

Also in Paris, Radio France International broadcasts nearly an hour of world news in English at 4 p.m. on 738 kHz AM.

In southern France, Riviera Radio on 106.5 and 106.3 MHz FM broadcasts BBC news on the hour.

You can pick up the BBC Radio 4 station on 198 kHz in some areas, particularly in the north west. Radio 4 has an interesting mix of arts, political features, and plays.
• **Scan the short-wave frequencies** for other English broadcasts. Voice of America broadcasts on 3980, 6040, 9760, 11970, and 13205 kHz. Radio Canada International broadcasts at various times through the day; contact the Canadian Embassy.

Minitel

Minitel is a national computerized information system linked to the French phone system. As a visitor, you probably won't use the domestic system, but you will find simpler and more limited public versions in post offices and train stations. You can then access train timetables and phone directories free of charge. You may find it easier (and quicker) than using phone information services, and they are useful if you don't speak French.

MONEY MATTERS

The currency unit is the French *franc* (FF). There are 100 *centimes* in every franc. Coins come in denominations of 5, 10, 20, and 50 centimes (50 centimes is marked "½ franc") and 1, 2, 10, and 50 francs. Banknotes are issued in denominations of 20, 50, 100, 200, and 500 francs.

Credit cards and ATM's

The cheapest and most convenient way of organizing your money is to use cards in stores and withdraw cash from ATM's using either credit cards or bank ATM cards. (If you use a bank ATM card make sure that it and the machine both carry the Cirrus sign.)

The card company will convert the sum you draw into dollars (at good rates, usually) and deduct it from you at home. Charges vary, and are usually reasonable. Ask your own card company or bank about charges before you go.

The vast majority of French businesses take major cards, but small provincial businesses may only accept cards for purchases above a certain value (usually 100FF). Some French establishments refuse American Express because they consider the charges too high. If you have difficulty obtaining card authorization for any reason, you may have to call the company (possibly even in the U.S.) to work things out. Always ensure that you have access to money in some form other than plastic.

Travelers' checks

These can be purchased at your bank or at American Express. If you lose travelers' checks they can be replaced quickly as long as you have the serial numbers. However, you'll sometimes have to pay a high commission when buying or selling them. (Check before buying to see if and when your own bank waives commission.) Although it is now difficult to cash travelers' checks as most French banks have stopped this service, they are accepted in shops. It's advisable to get travelers' checks in French francs. You'll be less likely to be asked for hefty commission payments when cashing them. It has been known for some businesses to charge nearly one-fifth of face value for cashing non-franc checks! If you plan to use travelers' checks in small stores, especially those in rural areas, confirm before you buy that they will be accepted. Some businesses may be wary, even if the checks are in francs. The American Express emergency number in France is 08 00 90 86 00 (toll free).

Cash

It's obviously not a good idea to carry lots of cash, but bring at least $100 in francs with you to France to cover initial expenses, especially if you are going straight to a country area where there may not be many ATM's. French banks offer fair exchange rates for selling francs. Post offices charge a 1 percent transaction fee. Check you get fair rates if you use currency exchange booths or hotel exchange facilities.

For changing money out of hours in Paris the currency exchange at the Gare de Lyon is open daily, 6:30 a.m. to 11:00 p.m. (See also *Opening Hours* on p.279.)

NIGHTLIFE AND ENTERTAINMENT

The best way to make a quick assessment of the current theater, movies, opera, and cabaret scene is to ask the tourist information office for brochures. In Paris, buy *Pariscope* magazine.

Getting tickets

Buy tickets in advance from the box office, or at the door on the night. If there's a popular show you especially want to see, contact a major ticket agency in the U.S. to inquire about getting tickets in advance.

FNAC, 1 rue Pierre Lescot, is a Paris ticket agency for major shows; tel: 01 40 41 40 00.

If you're looking for half-price theater tickets, try the Kiosque-Théâtre at 15 place de la Madeleine, 75008 (no phone inquiries). The kiosk disposes of unsold tickets for upcoming performances and opens at 12:30 p.m. Tuesday through Saturday, but be there earlier for the best bargains. Consult floor plans before you buy, especially if you hope to purchase cheaper seats.

Paris opera and theater are often performed in old buildings, which are full of atmosphere; but the cheaper seats sometimes lack comfort, have restricted views, or may fail to meet modern acoustical expectations.

Theater and opera

France puts a high value on culture so there are plenty of regional theatrical and musical events, especially during the summer festival months. Paris, however, is the theater and opera center of France.

Movies

France has a thriving movie industry. If you speak French this is a great opportunity to brush up on it.

Many Paris movie theaters run English-language films with subtitles, and you can usually keep up with recent American films. There are also some unusual, tiny movie theaters. The one at the famous Pompidou Center attracts movie buffs who appreciate its many obscure French and foreign movie screenings.

Music

Paris has thriving jazz, rock, and classical scenes. For concert information and tickets contact FNAC Musique, 24 boulevard des Italiens, 75009; tel: 01 48 01 02 03.

Also seek out the many inexpensive lunchtime concerts and small artistic events that are typically held in churches.

Nightclubs and cabarets

The Paris cabaret scene, immortalized by the paintings of Toulouse-Lautrec, now caters mainly to affluent foreign tourists.

The Moulin Rouge at place Blanche, 75009 (tel: 01 46 86 00 19) and the Crazy Horse Saloon at 12 avenue George V, 75008 (tel: 01 47 23 32 32) offer phone reservations during the day for their professional (but pricey) shows.

France doesn't have much of a lively club scene. French people prefer sophisticated (and expensive) nightclubs. Most are often members-only.

Café life

French cafés are a great institution, and offer a window on the French way of life. You'll discover an infinite variety of cafés selling an interesting selection of drinks, for instance *citron pressé* (fresh lemonade), anise-flavored *pastis* or imported beers. Higher prices are charged for customers who occupy tables rather than standing up to drink. Cafés in popular or fashionable locations charge more – sometimes much more – than cafés in back streets.

OPENING HOURS
Banks

Banks are open on weekdays from 9:30 a.m. to noon and 2:30 to 4 p.m. (in many provincial towns they open Tuesday through Saturday, same hours). The day before a public holiday, they close at noon.

Museums and sights

Museums generally shut Mondays or Tuesdays, and sometimes close for an hour or two at lunchtime. It's best to check exact opening hours of local tourist sights. They often follow the same pattern as museums.

Post offices

Post offices open Monday to Friday 8 a.m. to 7 p.m., and 8 a.m. to 12 noon Saturdays. They may close for lunch in rural areas, or operate for slightly shorter hours. Paris has a 24-hour post office at 52 rue du Louvre, near the Louvre Museum.

Restaurants and bars

Many restaurants are closed on Sunday, although you'll usually be able to find a snack bar or pizza parlor. There's never a shortage of places to eat in Paris.

Stores and drugstores

Larger stores and drugstores hours are usually from 9 a.m. to 6:30 p.m. Some close for an hour at lunchtime (exact times of opening vary between stores). Huge supermarkets are now popular in France and may stay open seven days a week (10 a.m. to 9 p.m. or similar hours). If you need one of these so-called *hypermarchés*, ask locally for directions to the nearest one that stays open, otherwise you could spend a long time driving around uninspiring commercial areas. Most of those delectable little French food stores you'll notice are family businesses. They open six days a week, approximately from 9 a.m. until 6 p.m. Some still take the traditional two-hour lunch break, and if they do they'll stay open until about 8 p.m. They're usually closed on Sundays, but sometimes close Mondays instead (or as well).

PHONES

All phone numbers in France comprise 10 digits. The first digit will be a 0 in all cases, and in Paris it is followed by a 1. In order to phone France from the U.S., dial 011-33 followed by the last 9 digits of the phone number, omitting the initial 0.

To phone the U.S. from France, dial 00, wait for the tone, then dial 1 followed by the area code, city code, and number.

For directory assistance for French numbers, dial 12, then wait, or use a Minitel (see p.277). For assistance with overseas numbers, dial 19-33 12 + country code.

Public phones

France has a good public phone service. Most phone booths use pre-paid phone cards (*télécartes*), which you can buy at post offices and tobacco stands (*tabacs*); the cards cost 40FF for 50 units, 96FF for 120 units.

French phone calls are charged per unit, not per minute. One unit pays for 6 minutes' worth of local calls, or less time if you are phoning a long-distance or international number. (For example, 120 units are equivalent to about 12 minutes' connection to the U.S. and Canada.) You can also use your own U.S. calling card; follow its instructions for making international calls. Note that it may not be cheaper than using a phone card from a public phone once you have considered access and initial connection charges. The cheap rate for phone calls within France is 10:30 p.m. to 8 a.m., and from 2 p.m. on Saturday for the weekend. To North America the cheap rate is 8 p.m. to 2 a.m., noon to 2 p.m., and Sunday afternoons.

• **Toll free:** Emergency numbers (medical: 15; Police: 17; fire: 18) and toll-free numbers (beginning with 05) can be dialed free of charge from public phone booths.

Using the phone

The phone LCD displays in phone booths have instructions in French. *Hors service* means "not in use", *décrochez* means "pick up the phone", *introduire carte* means "put in the card", *patientez s.v.p.* means "wait". The French ringing tone sometimes begins with a flurry of short beeps, followed by a series of long beeps; at other times you hear only the long beeps. A busy signal is indicated by short beeps similar to the U.S. busy signal.

PLACES OF WORSHIP

About 80 percent of French are Catholics. There are also about 700,000 Jews, 1 million Protestants and 3 million Muslims.

The main places of worship in Paris can suggest how to find appropriate places of worship in specific provincial areas.

The American Church in Paris has Protestant services and is a contact and information point for travelers: services 9 a.m. to 10:30 p.m. (7 p.m. on Sunday); 65 quai d'Orsai, Paris 75007; tel: 01 47 05 07 99.

The English-speaking Catholic Church is at 50 avenue Hoche, Paris 75008. Mass is celebrated in English daily and several times on Sunday (tel: 01 42 27 28 56).

To obtain information on mosques, tel: 01 45 35 97 33. The main mosque is on place du Puit de l'Hermite, Paris 75005, tel: 01 45 35 97 33.

The main Synagogue holds services on Friday and Saturday and is at 44 rue de la Victoire, Paris 75009, tel: 01 42 85 71 09.

POST OFFICES

• **Paris:** the main post office in Paris is open 24 hours a day, 7 days a week; 52 rue du Louvre, Paris 75001; tel: 01 40 28 20 20, 01 49 52 53 54.

• **Lyon:** the main post office is at 10 place Antonin Poncet, Cedex 69002 Lyon; tel: 04 72 40 65 22.

• **Nice:** the main post office is at 23 avenue Thiers; tel: 04 93 82 65 00.

• **Marseilles:** the main post office is at 1 place de l'Hôtel des Postes, Cedex 13001 Marseilles; tel: 04 91 15 47 19.

• **Strasbourg:** the main post office is at 5 avenue Marseillaise, 67000 Strasbourg; tel: 03 88 52 31 00.

• **Nantes:** the main post office is at place de Bretagne, Cedex 44038 Nantes; tel: 02 40 12 60 00.

• **Toulouse:** the main post office is located opposite 7–9 rue La Fayette, Cedex 31000 Toulouse; tel: 05 62 15 30 00.

Poste restante

If you aren't planning to have a fixed address in France, arrange to get your mail *poste restante*.

Under this system, the post office will keep the mail until you pick it up. They charge a flat fee of 110FF per period of 3 months plus 3FF for every item of mail, and will require to see your ID before releasing it. Mail is filed alphabetically, so anyone who writes to you *poste restante* in France must put your family name/surname first, in capitals, followed by your first name or initials (such as: SMITH, Jane A.). If the person writing to you addresses mail in the American way ("Jane A. Smith") the post office will file the letter under the first name shown. On the next line of the address, the person writing should put "Poste Restante," followed by the post office address. If you have a choice of post offices, choose the main one in the city. Mail will automatically end up there if your correspondent makes mistakes in the address.

Letter rates

Current airmail rates to North America are 4.40FF for postcards/letters up to 20 grams. (Weigh letters at the post office.)

Aerogram forms presently cost 5FF worldwide. Allow about a week for mail to get home. Use airmail stickers when mailing items to North America. Express airmail is available but it is expensive. FedEx is not well known in France, although courier services do exist.

RESTROOMS

The modern automatic restrooms now seen on many Paris sidewalks are state of the art and extremely clean, but the same cannot always be said of older public restrooms.

Most modern hotels and stores have conventional, pleasant modern restrooms, marked *toilettes* or *WC* (pronounced "Twa-let" or "DOObla-vay say"). Some older public restrooms and those in some cafés and bars may still have the so-called "Turkish" style fixtures, which consist of a hole in the ground with footrests on either side. Stand well clear when flushing.

The French are not particularly modest about bathroom matters, so expect occasionally to find public restrooms where men's urinals are in full view of both sexes.

Toilet tissue is sometimes in short supply in public restrooms, so carry a small supply yourself. Restrooms don't always have washing facilities immediately available, but there's usually a basin somewhere nearby. French hotel bathrooms usually contain a hand-basin, a tub, sometimes a shower plus a WC and bidet.

SHOPPING

Paris is famous for its top-quality goods and it offers window shopping to die for. Prices, however, are high and far from heavenly!

You'll find antiques and galleries on the Left Bank; adventurous designer boutiques on Le Marais, and highly creative couture on place des Victoires. Some of the world's top couturiers cluster in the avenue Montaigne.

Paris's three main department stores are in the place de l'Opéra area, you'll find less astronomically priced shopping opportunities in the Champs-Élysées, and tourist stores abound.

It seems that every French town has an open-air food **market** with stands displaying local and international fruits, vegetables, and flowers. The different Paris districts also have their own street fairs and markets. These markets rarely operate continuously, so inquire locally to find out which day of the week the market is open. Get there early for the best variety, but if you are looking for bargains try the end of the day when stall-holders sometimes sell off unsold produce at lower prices.

Each French region has its regional shopping specialties, which make ideal **souvenirs**. For example, Provence offers hand-made soaps, perfumes, and all kinds of lavender-scented goods. Alsace-Lorraine has clocks and wood carvings. Brittany and Normandy are the home of folksy Quimper pottery, traditional sweaters, and lace. Local tourist offices can direct you to where you can find the best buys in their region.

Any shopping spree in France is likely to include wonderful **food** and fine **wines**, but make sure you check U.S. regulations in advance if you're planning to bring edible souvenirs back home. (See *Customs and Quarantine* on for more details p.261.)

SPECTATOR SPORTS

• **Soccer:** Soccer is known as *le foot* or *le football*. (American football is not very well known.) The season runs all winter, with a break between Christmas and the end of January. Paris's main stadium, home of First Division team Paris-SG, is the Parc des Princes at 24 rue du Commandant Guilbaud, in the 16ème; tel: 01 42 88 02 76.
• **Tennis:** The French Open is part of the Grand Slam of top tennis tournaments, and is held in Paris in late May/early June at Roland Garros stadium, avenue Gordon-Bennet, 75016 Paris; tel: 01 47 43 48 00.
• **Cycling:** The Tour de France is one of the world's great races, and is held for three weeks in late June and July over a grueling 4,000-kilometer (2,500-mi.) route, ending up at the Champs-Élysées in Paris.

TIPPING

Restaurant service is usually included (*service compris*), but it is customary to leave small change for the waiter. Give tips for outstanding service. If service is not included (*service non compris*), tip 15–20 percent. Give 15 percent to hairdressers, taxi drivers, and other staff. Theater and movie theater ushers get 5FF, tour guides 10FF; bellboys get 2FF per bag.

TOURIST INFORMATION OFFICES
Main offices
• **Paris:** 127 avenue des Champs-Élysées, east of the Arc de Triomphe; tel: 01 49 52 53 54, fax: 01 49 52 53 20.
• **Nice:** Next to station; tel: 04 93 87 07 07.
• **Lyon:** South of place Bellecour; tel: 04 78 42 25 75, fax: 04 78 37 02 06.
• **Marseilles:** Next to the old port at 4 la Canebière; tel: 04 91 13 89 00. There's also a tourist office at the station.

WATER

French tap water is safe and drinkable everywhere. French mineral water (Évian, Vichy, Perrier) are readily available in stores.

EMERGENCIES

EMBASSIES AND CONSULATES

Consulates can supply information on local doctors, dentists, and other specialists, and can give advice in case of injury or serious illness (though you are responsible for medical costs). If you lose your money they may be able to help you to contact people back home, and they can also issue a replacement passport if yours is stolen.

An information leaflet can be obtained by sending a SASE to the Bureau of Consular Affairs (CA/PA) Room 5807, Department of State, Washington, D.C. 20520.

U.S. Embassy and Consulates in France

If you are a U.S. citizen vacationing for several weeks without a contact address, consider registering with the U.S. Consulate. In an emergency, your family could contact the Citizens' Emergency Center at (202) 647-5225. The Center will contact the U.S. Consulate in France, which will do its best to find you.
• **Paris:** The U.S. Embassy is at 2 avenue Gabriel, Paris 75008; tel: 01 43 12 22 22 (off place de la Concorde). The U.S. Consulate in Paris is at 2 rue St.-Florentin; tel: 01 40 39 84 11. Closed on both American and French holidays.

The Canadian Embassy and Consulate in Paris are both at 35 avenue Montaigne, Paris 75008; tel: 01 44 43 29 00.
• **Lyon:** Canadian Consulate: tel: 04 72 77 64 07.
• **Marseilles:** U.S. Consulate: tel: 04 91 54 92 00.
• **Nice:** U.S. Consulate: tel: 04 93 88 89 55.

EMERGENCY PHONE NUMBERS

In emergencies dial the following numbers (all toll free, except for the Poisons Hotline):
• **Ambulance:** 15
• **Police:** 17
• **Fire Brigade:** 18
• **Mountain rescue and coastguard:** 17
• **Poisons Hotline:** 01 40 05 48 48
An English-speaking crisis line in Paris operates at 01 47 23 80 80. It is open between 3 and 11 p.m., and offers practical advice in English on a range of problems. (You can dial it from outside Paris, too.)

LOST PROPERTY

If you lose something in a French city, visit the city Lost and Found Office (*Bureau des Objets Trouvés*) to see if it has been handed in. Inquire in person; there are forms to fill in. The Paris office is at 36 rue des Morillons, 75015 (Metro: Convention).

MEDICAL CARE

Phone 15 for emergency medical care. (There's also a non-toll-free number, 01 45 67 50 50.) Your call will reach an organization called SAMU – there is generally someone there who can speak English. SAMU will send appropriate help – a doctor, an ambulance with paramedics, or a mobile intensive care unit. In emergencies, payment is taken care of after treatment. Otherwise you should pay right away.

Prescriptions

Every Paris *arrondissement* is expected to have one drugstore on call, day or night. Phone the police for details of drugstores on call.

POLICE

There are two separate French police forces, the *Police Nationale* and the *Gendarmerie Nationale*.

Police uniforms are blue, with flat caps or characteristic peaked *gendarme* caps. Traffic policemen wear white gloves, and all police uniforms have shoulder tags indicating the policeman's affiliation.

Military police wear green tags. Riot (security) police, the CRS, are usually only found in troubled and unsettled areas. PAF are the border police. There are also mountaineering police in alpine areas.

French law is NOT based on the assumption that you are innocent until proven guilty, so the police can demand ID (you must carry ID on you, by law) and are also allowed to search, question you, and seize your possessions if they think fit. Don't get angry or argue with them; be polite, respectful, and cooperative.

HOTELS AND RESTAURANTS

A recommended guide to some of
the best places to stay and eat in
France, from a luxury hotel in Paris
to a rural family-run hotel in the
Pyrénées, and from bouillabaisse
to French bread
and cheese

ACCOMMODATIONS

Our recommendations in this guide include some of the most comfortable, interesting and welcoming places to stay in the country, in every corner of the land and to suit every pocket. They also cover every type of accommodation available.

AAA DIAMOND RATING

Diamond ratings are on a scale of one to five and range from a simple accommodation to the most luxurious hotel.

The hotel ratings here are based on the system used by the official French tourist office. Due to cultural and social differences, however, direct point-by-point comparisons cannot be made, but the ratings do indicate the relative value of each establishment.

◆ **one-diamond hotels** are usually small, with good, simple furnishings and facilities. These hotels often have a more personal atmosphere than you might find in larger hotels.

◆◆ **two-diamond hotels** are generally small to medium size. They usually have more facilities than one-diamond establishments, such as TVs and telephones in all rooms and at least half offering en-suite (private) bath or shower.

◆◆◆ **three-diamond hotels** are usually medium size, with more spacious rooms than one or two diamonds. They often have a full reception service as well as a more formal restaurant and bar facilities. All rooms should have en-suite (private) bath or shower.

◆◆◆◆ **four-diamond hotels** are larger and more spacious. All rooms will have en-suite (private) bathrooms and most hotels offer private suites as well. Porters, room service and a formal reception will be available. There is often a choice of restaurants. High standards of comfort and cuisine are expected.

◆◆◆◆◆ **five diamonds** denotes luxury hotels offering the highest international standards of facilities, services and cuisine.

TYPES OF ACCOMMODATIONS

Château hotels

Found at the top end of the scale, many grand mansions and châteaux have been converted into hotels with varying degrees of luxury – in some you may be able to stay in converted outbuildings, therefore saving on costs while still enjoying the ambience of the château and its grounds.

Meals are generally taken *en famille* and the cuisine is usually of a high standard. Some châteaux offer a bed-and-breakfast option. Many of the deluxe properties belong to the Relais et Châteaux organization, whereas 75 of the more moderately priced historic homes are covered by Château Accueil.

Grand hotels

Major cities and big resort areas also have their share of grand hotels, such as the famous palace-type hotels of Paris, Nice and Cannes. Prices are usually astronomical.

Hotels

Almost every town and village has a traditional family-run hotel, usually with a bar full of locals, a busy dining room, and a relaxed, family-oriented atmosphere. The plumbing might not be ultramodern but this is usually more than made up for by picturesque charm and ambience.

Many of the simpler family-run hotels (one or two stars), mainly in rural areas, belong to the Logis de France organization (its 4,000 properties are distinguished by a yellow fireplace logo); following inspection they're classified with one, two or three chimneys.

A recent phenomenon in the French hotel industry has been the appearance of prefabricated, box-like hotels by the side of busy main roads and freeways, such as the Formule 1 chain; these are really basic, no-frills motels, often unstaffed (all transactions are automated by credit card) with many rooms but no en-suite (private) facilities. Popular with French traveling salesmen, they're useful if you've been driving too long and just need one thing – sleep.

Better facilities are available in two-star chain hotels (such as Ibis, Interhotel, Climat de France and Campanile) or three-star chains (such as Mercure/Altea or Novotel), and in many children may be allowed to stay in your room free.

Self-catering

France is very good for self-catering, simply because so many French people have second homes (ski chalets, beach villas or even city apartments) that are rented out.

Self-catering is also available in *gîtes*. These are rural holiday cottages, often converted from old farm buildings. Around 40,000 of these are inspected and graded through the Gîtes de France organization. The best properties should be booked well in advance.

Food

One thing to bear in mind is that for some hotels the restaurant rather than the accommodation is the main attraction. Similarly, upmarket restaurants may offer rooms as an ancillary service – often at prices far below what you would expect from the restaurant itself.

Costs

By law hotel tariffs must be clearly visible in the reception area and in each bedroom. Prices are usually quoted per room and do not include breakfast – which is a good thing, since you will usually find that your morning croissant and coffee are a better value in the local café or *pâtisserie* than in the hotel itself.

In high season many resort hotels will insist on *demi-pension* (half board), which provides an all-inclusive rate for room, breakfast and evening dinner.

In this guide we have used the following abbreviations for the major credit cards:

AE   American Express
DI   Diners Club
MC   MasterCard
VI   Visa

For our recommendations the following price bands apply for a twin or double room in high season (in French francs):

(F)   under 450FF
(FF)   450–750FF
(FFF) over 750FF

PARIS

ler arrondissement
Hotel Agora (FF) ◆◆
7 rue de la Cossonerie
Tel: 01 42 33 46 02
Fax: 01 42 33 80 99
Convenient location in city center. Satellite TV. Central heating. 29 rooms. AE/MC/VI

Hotel Louvre-Forum (FF) ◆◆
25 rue du Bouloi
Tel: 01 42 36 54 19
Fax: 01 42 33 66 31
Cheerful small hotel in center of Paris, close to sights. Comfortable rooms. Breakfast served in historic vaulted cellar. 27 rooms. AE/DI/MC/VI

Relais du Louvre (FFF) ◆◆◆
19 rue des Prêtres St.-Germain-L'Auxerrois
Tel: 01 40 41 96 42
Fax: 01 40 41 96 44
In the center of Paris, dating to the 18th century with beautiful rooms. No restaurant. 21 rooms. AE/DI/MC/VI

4ème arrondissement
Castex Hotel (FF) ◆◆
5 rue Castex
Tel: 01 42 72 31 52
Fax: 01 42 72 57 91
Convenient city-center location. No smoking. English spoken. 27 rooms. MC/VI

Hotel du Jeu de Paumé (FFF) ◆◆◆◆
54 rue Saint-Louis-en-l'Ile
Tel: 01 43 26 14 18
Fax: 01 40 46 02 76
Delightful, refined small hotel carved out of a 17th-century royal tennis court. Tasteful rooms with beams and marble bathrooms,

some duplex suites. 32 rooms. AE/DI/VI

Hotel de la Place des Vosges (FF) ◆◆
12 rue Biragué
Tel: 01 42 72 60 46
Fax: 01 42 72 02 64
Charming 17th-century town house on a quiet street close to the place des Vosges. Basic comforts and excellent location. Satellite TV. 16 rooms. AM/DI/MC/VI

Hotel Sansonnet (FF) ◆◆
48 rue de la Verrerie
Tel: 01 47 87 96 14
Fax: 01 48 87 30 46
Comfortable 17th-century building with soundproofed rooms. Convenient location to explore the city center. Satellite TV. 25 rooms. MC/VI

5ème arrondissement
Grands Hommes (FF–FFF) ◆◆◆
17 place du Panthéon
Tel: 01 46 34 19 60
Fax: 01 43 26 67 32
An 18th-century building, once a popular meeting place for artists in the 1920s. Friendly service. Satellite TV. 32 rooms. AE/DI/MC/VI

Hotel de L'Espérance (FF) ◆◆
15 rue Pascal
Tel: 01 47 07 10 99
Fax: 01 43 37 56 19
Charming small hotel near the picturesque Quartier Latin. Rooms offer high standard of comfort. Breakfast in delightful garden. 38 rooms. AE/DI/MC/VI

Hotel de Notre-Dame (FF) ◆◆◆
19 rue Maître-Albert

Tel: (01) 43 26 79 00
Fax: (01) 46 33 50 11
Rustic beams and old furniture bring charm to this hotel. Comfortable with modern facilities. Satellite TV. 34 rooms. AE/MC/VI

Hotel des Trois Colléges (FF) ◆◆
16 rue Gujas
Tel: 01 43 54 67 30
Fax: 01 46 34 02 99
Convenient and comfortable hotel with views of the Sorbonne. Spacious lounge serving delicious breakfasts and afternoon teas. 44 rooms. AE/DI/MC/VI

6ème arrondissement
Chaplain (FF) ◆◆
11 rue Jules Chaplain
75006
Tel: 01 43 26 47 64
Fax: 01 40 51 79 75
Attractive hotel in quiet street near Montparnasse area. Comfortable public rooms for relaxation. Satellite TV. 25 rooms. AE/DI/MC/VI

Le Clos Médicis (FFF) ◆◆◆
56 rue Monsieur-Le-Prince
Tel: 01 43 29 10 80
Fax: 01 43 54 29 90
Conveniently located 18th-century residence with a Provençal-style interior. Bar. Delightful garden. Satellite TV. 38 rooms. AE/DI/MC/VI

L'Hotel (FFF) ◆◆◆◆
13 rue des Beaux-Arts
Tel: 01 44 41 99 00
Fax: 01 43 25 64 81
A Parisian legend redolent of Oscar Wilde's last days. Kitsch piano bar, restaurant, and some superbly furnished rooms. Satellite TV. Air conditioning. 27 rooms. AE/DI/MC/VI

Hotel d'Angleterre

(FFF) ◆◆◆
44 rue Jacob
Tel: 01 42 60 34 72
Fax: 01 42 60 16 93
The former British embassy, with pretty garden patio and spacious rooms where Ernest Hemingway once stayed. Bar and piano lounge. Reserve well in advance. 27 rooms. AE/DI/MC/VI

Hotel des Marronniers

(FFF) ◆◆◆
21 rue Jacob
Tel: 01 43 25 30 60
Fax: 01 40 46 83 56
Named for the chestnut trees that dominate the garden. Elegant interior with floral decorations, oak-beamed rooms, and vaulted cellars converted to lounge areas. Reserve well in advance. Air-conditioned rooms. Satellite TV. 37 rooms. MC/VI

Sainte-Beuve (FF–FFF) ◆◆◆

9 rue Sainte-Beuve
Tel: 01 45 48 20 07
Fax: 01 45 48 67 52
Exclusive establishment between the heart of Montparnasse and the Jardin du Luxembourg. Period antiques mix happily with modern furnishings. Tasteful and imaginative extras. Satellite TV. 23 rooms. AE/MC/VI

7ème arrondissement

Hotel du Nevers (FF) ◆◆
83 rue Bac
Tel: 01 45 44 61 30
Fax: 01 42 22 29 47
This former 18th-century convent is situated close to the major tourist sights. Modern amenities. 11 rooms. No credit cards.

8ème arrondissement

Bristol (FFF) ◆◆◆◆
112 rue du Faubourg St.-Honore
Tel: 01 53 43 43 00
Fax: 01 53 43 43 01
Elegant hotel in the prestigious Faubourg area. Satellite TV. Indoor pool, sauna, solarium and gymnasium. Outstanding cuisine. 195 rooms. AE/DI/MC/VI

New Hotel Roblin

(FFF) ◆◆◆
6 rue Chauveau-Lagarde
Tel: 01 44 71 20 80
Fax: 01 42 65 19 49
Situated close to the Louvre, Opéra and the Champs-Élysées.Tastefully decorated rooms with air conditioning. Luxurious restaurant. Satellite TV. 77 rooms. AE/DI/MC/VI

Hotel Étoile (FFF) ◆◆

3 rue de Ponthieu
Tel: 01 42 25 73 01
Fax: 01 42 56 01 39
Enchanting art-deco interior and comfortable rooms with air conditioning. Close to historic sights. Satellite TV. 25 rooms. AE/DI/MC/VI .

9ème arrondissement

Hotel Riboutte Lafayette
(FF) ◆◆
5 rue Riboutté
Tel: 01 47 70 62 36
Fax: 01 48 00 91 50
Peaceful small hotel in the center of the city. Satellite TV. Good amenities and well-furnished public areas. 24 rooms. AE/MC/VI

11éme arrondissement

All Suite Hotel
(FF) ◆◆◆
74 rue Amelot
Tel: 01 40 21 20 00
Fax: 01 47 00 82 40
Convenient location near city center. Air conditioning in rooms, some reserved for nonsmokers. Satellite TV. Parking. Restaurant. 289 rooms. AE/DI/MC/VI

12ème arrondissement

Hotel Claret
(FF–FFF) ◆◆◆
44 boulevard de Bercy
Tel: 01 46 28 41 31
Fax 01 49 28 09 29
A former inn that retains its original charm while offering a good level of comfort. Parking. Restaurant. 52 rooms. No credit cards.

13ème arrondissement

Holiday Inn Garden Court
(FF–FFF) ◆◆◆
21 rue de Tolbiac
Tel: 01 45 84 61 61
Fax: 01 45 84 43 38
Convenient location near city center and the Seine. Air-conditioned rooms. Satellite TV. Parking. 71 rooms. AE/DIMC/VI

16ème arrondissement

Hotel Keppler (FF) ◆◆
12 rue Keppler
Tel: 01 47 20 65 05
Fax: 01 47 23 02 29
Charming small hotel in the heart of Paris, close to the main sights. Satellite TV. Cozy atmosphere and modern facilities. 49 rooms. AE/MC/VI

18ème arrondissement

Eden Hotel (F) ◆◆
90 rue Ordener
Tel: 01 42 64 61 63
Fax: 01 42 64 11 43
Attractive, comfortable hotel in a picturesque neighborhood at the foot of Montmartre, close to Sacré-Cœur. Parking. Satellite TV. 35 rooms. AE/DI/MC/VI

HOTELS

Prima Lépic (F) ◆◆
29 rue Lépic
Tel: 01 46 06 44 64
Fax: 01 46 06 66 11
Attractive hotel in center of Montmartre. Comfortable accommodation and trompe-l'oeil decor resembling a flower garden. 38 rooms. MC/VI

OUTSIDE PARIS

SEINE-ET-MARNE
77630 Barbizon
Hotellerie du Bas-Breau (FFF) ◆◆◆
22 rue Grande
Tel: 01 60 66 40 05
Fax: 01 60 69 22 89
Former hunting lodge beside Fontainebleau forest area. Sophisticated, comfortable interior. Restaurant with terrace. 19 rooms. AE/MC/VI

77300 Fontainebleau
De l'Aigle Noir (FFF) ◆◆◆◆
27 place N. Bonaparte
Tel: 01 60 74 60 00
Fax: 01 60 74 60 01
Surrounded by forest, this old country house offers a pool, fitness room, and a terrace for dining. Satellite TV. Air conditioning. Good restaurant. 57 rooms. AE/DI/MC/VI

NORMANDY

CALVADOS
14117 Arromanches
D'Arromanches (FFF) ◆◆
2 rue du Colonel René Michel
Tel: 02 31 22 36 26
Fax: 02 31 22 23 29
Comfortable accommodation in town center. Good restaurant managed by the proprietor. 9 rooms. MC/VI

14400 Bayeux
Château de Bellefontaine (FF) ◆◆◆
49 rue de Bellefontaine
Tel: 02 31 22 00 10
Fax: 02 31 22 19 09
In a park, this 18th-century château offers reservations for nonsmokers (unusual in France). Air conditioning. 15 rooms. No restaurant. AE/DI/MC/VI

Grand Hotel du Luxembourg (F–FF) ◆◆◆
25 rue des Bouches
Tel: 02 31 92 00 04
Fax: 02 31 92 54 26
In the heart of the city with access to a tennis court (1km), golf course (10km) and fishing. Satellite TV. Fine restaurant. 22 rooms. AE/MC/VI

14800 Deauville
Normandy (FFF) ◆◆◆◆
38 rue Jean Mermoz
Tel: 02 31 98 66 22
Fax: 02 31 98 66 23
Attractive waterfront location. Indoor pool. Suitable for visitors with disabilities. Parking. Good restaurant. 308 rooms. AE/DI/MC/VI

Royal (FFF) ◆◆◆◆
boulevard Cornuché
Tel: 02 31 98 66 33
Fax: 02 31 98 66 34
Interesting surroundings offering a pool, a charming terrace for dining, and an agreeable restaurant. Satellite TV. 245 rooms. AE/DI/MC/VI

14600 Honfleur
La Chaumière ◆◆◆◆
route du Littoral
Tel: 02 31 81 63 20
Fax: 02 31 89 59 23
Historic Norman farmhouse in peaceful rural setting close to the sea. Restaurant offers regional cuisine and outstanding wines. 9 rooms. AE/MC/VI

14340 Notre-Dame-d'Estrées
Au Repos des Chineurs (FF) ◆◆
chemin de l'Église
Tel: 02 31 63 72 51
Fax: 02 31 63 62 38
Charming 17th-century hotel in Auge countryside, ideal for a relaxing stay. MC/VI

EURE
27210 Beuzeville
Auberge du Cochon d'Or (F) ◆◆
place du Général de Gaulle
Tel: 02 32 57 70 46
Fax: 02 32 42 25 70
Convenient location, comfortable rooms, garden with a terrace, and an excellent restaurant. 20 rooms. DI/MC/VI

De la Poste (F) ◆◆
60 rue Constant Fouché
Tel: 02 32 57 71 04
Fax: 02 32 42 11 01
This hotel offers a garden, children's playground and bicycle rental. Commendable restaurant. 16 rooms. AE/DI/MC/VI

MANCHE
50300 Avranches
Abrincates (F) ◆◆
37 boulevard du Luxembourg
Tel: 02 33 58 66 64
Fax: 02 33 58 40 11
Comfortable establishment in historic town. Excellent regional dishes served in the restaurant. 29 rooms. MC/VI

50270 Barneville-Carteret
Les Isles (F) ◆◆
Tel: 02 33 04 90 76

Fax: 02 33 94 53 83
Situated close to the beach. Comfortable accommodation and fine views. Garden. Restaurant has a good seafood menu. 32 rooms. AE/MC/VI

50220 Courtils
Manoir de la Roche Torin
(F) ◆◆◆
La Roche Torin
Tel: 02 33 70 96 55
Fax: 02 33 48 35 20
Friendly hotel in rural seacoast setting. Restaurant has a tantalizing menu and fine views. 13 rooms. AE/DI/MC/VI

ORNE
61300 L'Aigle
Hotel du Dauphin
(F–FF) ◆◆◆
place de la Halle
Tel: 02 33 84 18 00
Fax: 02 33 34 09 28
Conveniently located, this historic 17th-century building offers a beautiful lounge with fireplace. Satellite TV. Restaurant. 30 rooms. AE/DI/MC/VI

61200 Fontenai-sur-Orne
Le Faisan Doré (F) ◆◆
Tel: 02 33 67 18 11
Fax: 02 33 35 82 15
Attractive timbered inn set amid landscaped gardens. Cozy well-equipped rooms. Bar. Restaurant offers delicious specialties. 15 rooms. AE/MC/VI

SEINE-MARITIME
76790 Étretat
Donjon (FF) ◆◆◆
chemin de St.-Clair
Tel: 02 35 27 08 23
Fax: 02 35 29 92 24
Small hotel set in parkland overlooking the coast. Outdoor pool. Restaurant

features traditional cuisine. 10 rooms. AE/DI/MC/VI

76000 Rouen
Climat de France (F) ◆◆
55 avenue de la Libération
Tel: 02 35 73 42 42
Fax: 02 35 72 06 00
Close to Rouen's historic center, this attractive establishment has pleasant rooms. Parking. Restaurant offers regional specialties. 49 rooms. AE/MC/VI

Hotel de Dieppe (FF) ◆◆◆
place Bernard Tissot
Tel: 02 35 71 96 00
Fax: 02 35 89 65 21
A pleasant hotel offering good value in this charming town. 41 rooms. Restaurant. AE/DI/MC

76540 Sassetot-le-Mauconduit
Château de Sassetot (F) ◆◆
Le Mauconduit
Tel: 02 35 28 00 11
Fax: 02 35 52 85 00
Town-center location, convenient to the sea and countryside. AE/DI/MC/VI

BRITTANY

CÔTES D'ARMOR
22600 Loudéac
Des Voyageurs (F) ◆◆
10 rue de Cadélac
Tel: 02 96 28 00 47
Fax: 02 96 28 22 30
Town-center location near lake, with individually styled rooms. Seafood specialties in the restaurant. 28 rooms. AE/DI/MC/VI

FINISTÈRE
29950 Bénodet
Armoric (FF) ◆◆◆
3 rue de Penfoul
Tel: 02 98 57 04 03

Fax: 02 98 57 21 28
Near yacht harbor, with terrace views over parkland. Casino. Heated outdoor pool. Restaurant. 30 rooms. AE/DI/MC/VI

29110 Concarneau
Des Sables Blancs (F) ◆◆
plage des Sables Blancs
Tel: 02 98 97 01 39
Fax: 02 98 50 65 88
Offers a garden and a restaurant. 48 rooms. AE/DI/MC/VI

29430 Plouescat
La Caravelle (F) ◆◆
20 rue du Calvaire
Tel: 02 98 69 61 75
Fax: 02 98 61 92 61
Set in a small seaside village near the Roscoff ferry port. Good restaurant. 17 rooms. AE/DI/MC/VI

29120 Pont-l'Abbé
Château Hotel de Kernuz (FF) ◆◆
route de Penmarc'h
Tel: 02 98 87 01 59
Fax: 02 98 66 02 36
Historic 16th-century residence set in secluded grounds near the sea. Outdoor pool. Restaurant serves a range of meals. 24 rooms. MC/VI

ILLE-ET-VILAINE
35800 Dinard
Hotel Amethyste (F) ◆◆
place du Calvaire
Tel: 02 99 46 61 81
Fax: 02 9946 96 91
Welcoming hotel in the town center, close to the river. Modern facilities. Bar and ice-cream parlor. 20 rooms. AE/MC/VI

Roche Corneilée (FF) ◆◆◆
4 rue Georges Clemenceau
Tel: 02 99 46 14 47

Fax: 02 99 46 40 80
Elegant hotel in charming surroundings. Restaurant serves enjoyable meals. 28 rooms. AE/MC/VI

35000 Rennes
Hotel Lecoq-Gadby
(FF) ◆◆◆◆
156 rue d'Antrain
Tel: 02 99 38 05 55
Fax: 02 99 38 53 40
Near town center, elegantly furnished. Restaurant offers a range of meals. 11 rooms. AE/DI/MC/VI

35400 St.-Malo
Central (FF–FFF) ◆◆◆
6 Grande rue
Tel: 02 99 40 87 70
Fax: 02 99 40 47 57
Centrally located with parking. Air conditioning. Restaurant. 46 rooms. AE/DI/MC/VI

Grand Hotel Thermes
(F–FFF) ◆◆◆◆
100 boulevard Hébert
Tel: 02 99 40 75 75
Fax: 02 99 40 76 00
Beside sandy beach. Sea-water health center. Indoor pool. Parking. Satellite TV. Restaurant. 189 rooms. AE/DI/MC/VI

35500 Vitré
Hotel Perceval (F) ◆◆
Aire d'Erbree
Tel: 02 99 49 49 99
Fax: 02 99 49 30 22
A modern hotel in a rural setting. Attractive restaurant offers regional specialties using local produce. 46 rooms. AE/DI/MC/VI

LOIRE-ATLANTIQUE
44000 Nantes
Hotel Le Jules Verne
(FF) ◆◆◆
3 rue du Couédic

Tel: 02 40 35 74 50
Fax: 02 40 20 09 35
Cozy hotel in the heart of Nantes close to the sights. Air conditioning. 65 rooms. AE/DI/MC/VI

MORBIHAN
56340 Carnac
Le Diana (FF–FFF) ◆◆◆◆
21 boulevard de la Plage
Tel: 02 97 52 05 38
Fax: 02 97 52 87 91
Attractive setting opposite the beach. Terrace. Satellite TV. Suitable for visitors with disabilities. Fresh seafood specialties in the restaurant. 32 rooms. DI/MC/VI

56800 Ploërmel ◆◆◆
Golf Hotel du Roi Arthur
(F) ◆◆◆
Le Lac au Duc
Tel: 02 97 73 64 64
Fax: 02 97 73 64 50
Comfortable hotel set in extensive grounds. Golf. Indoor pool. Leisure facilities. 46 rooms. Restaurant. AE/DI/MC/VI

56290 Port Louis
Du Commerce (F) ◆◆
1 place du Marché
Tel: 02 97 82 46 05
Fax: 02 97 82 11 02
Situated in historic town, near the beach. Modern facilities and delightful garden. Good restaurant. 36 rooms. MC/VI

THE LOIRE VALLEY AND THE ATLANTIC COAST

CHARENTE-MARITIME
17150 Mirambeau
Château-Hotel de
Mirambeau (FFF) ◆◆◆◆

route de Montendre
Tel: 05 46 70 71 77
Fax: 05 46 70 71 10
Château dates to the 12th century. Sauna, tennis, heated indoor and outdoor pools. Satellite TV. Suitable for visitors with disabilities. Good restaurant. 48 rooms. DI/MC/VI

17940 Rivedoux-Plage
Rivotel (FF) ◆◆◆
154 avenue des Dunes
Tel: 05 46 09 89 51
Fax: 05 46 09 89 04
Modern hotel close to the beach. Excellent facilities, sea and garden views. Outdoor pool. Restaurant serves seafood specialties. 35 rooms. AE/MC/VI

17200 Royan
Novotel (FFF) ◆◆◆
boulevard Carnot
Tel: 05 46 39 46 39
Fax: 05 46 39 46 46
Near sea-water health center. Air conditioning. Pool, terrace. Satellite TV. Suitable for visitors with disabilities. Good restaurant. 83 rooms. AE/DI/MC/VI

17100 Saintes
Relais du Bois St.-Georges
(FFF) ◆◆◆
rue de Royan
Tel: 05 46 93 50 99
Fax: 05 46 93 34 93
Set in beautiful surroundings outside the town center. Indoor pool. Parking. Air conditioning. Satellite TV. Suitable for visitors with disabilities. Light meals available in the restaurant. 30 rooms. AE/DI/MC/VI

CREUSE
23350 Genouillac
Le Relais d'Oc (F–FF) ◆◆
Tel: 05 55 80 72 45

Historic house in small village, adorned with period furniture. Comfortable rooms. Garden. Traditional cuisine served in restaurant. 7 rooms. No credit cards.

23300 La Souterraine
De la Porte St.-Jean
(FF) ◆◆
2 rue des Bains
Tel: 05 55 63 90 00
Fax: 05 55 63 77 27
Comfortable hotel in pedestrianized area of historic town, close to gardens. Parking. Restaurant. 32 rooms. AE/DI/MC/VI

GIRONDE
33120 Arcachon
Le Nautic (F) ◆◆
20 boulevard de la Plage
Tel: 05 56 83 01 48
Fax: 05 56 83 04 67
In town center beside marina and beach. Range of leisure facilities nearby. Comfortable rooms. Parking. 44 rooms. AE/DI/MC/VI

33300 Bordeaux
Grand Hotel Français
(FF) ◆◆◆
12 rue du Temple
Tel: 05 56 48 10 35
Fax: 05 56 81 76 18
One of Bordeaux's finest buildings, a 17th-century residence providing elegant accommodation. Air conditioning. 35 rooms. AE/DI/MC/VI

33290 Le Pian-Médoc
Le Pont Bernet (F) ◆◆◆
route du Verdon
Tel: 05 56 70 20 19
Fax: 05 56 70 22 90
Set in parkland close to vineyards. Heated outdoor pool. Leisure facilities. Good restaurant. 18 rooms. AE/DI/MC/VI

HAUTE-VIENNE
87510 Nieul
La Chapelle St.-Martin
(FFF) ◆◆◆◆
Tel: 05 55 75 80 17
Fax: 05 55 75 89 50
Splendid residence set in private parkland. Outdoor pool. Tennis. Fishing. Sauna. Inventive cuisine served in restaurant. 12 rooms. AE/MC/VI

INDRE-ET-LOIRE
37800 Sainte-Maure-de-Touraine
Le Cheval Blanc (F) ◆◆
On N10
Tel: 02 47 65 40 27
Fax: 02 47 65 58 90
Former inn near village. Restaurant offers regional cuisine. 12 rooms. MC/VI

37000 Tours
Moderne (F) ◆◆
1–3 rue Victor Laloux
Tel: 02 47 05 32 81
Fax: 02 47 05 71 50
Convenient town-center location near main transportation facilities. Cozy, rustic interior. Restaurant. 23 rooms. AE/MC/VI

LANDES
40130 Capbreton
L'Océan (F) ◆◆◆
85 avenue G. Pompidou
Tel: 05 58 72 10 22
Fax: 05 58 72 08 43
Attractive hotel in town center, close to marina and beach. Terrace with sea views. Restaurant. 27 rooms. DI/MC/VI

40100 Dax
Jean le Bon
(F) ◆◆
12–14 rue Jean le Bon
Tel: 05 58 74 29 14
Fax: 05 58 90 03 04
Peaceful accommodation in

popular spa town. Heated outdoor pool. Parking. Restaurant offers delicious regional cuisine. 27 rooms. AE/MC/VI

LOIR-ET-CHER
41000 Blois
Holiday Inn Garden Court
(FF) ◆◆◆
26 avenue Maudoury
Tel: 02 54 55 44 88
Fax: 02 54 74 57 97
Traditional hospitality and excellent facilities offered in town-center location. Parking. Elegant accommodation. 78 rooms. AE/DI/MC/VI

LOIRET
45190 Beaugency
Hotel de l'Abbaye
(FF) ◆◆◆
2 quai de l'Abbaye
Tel: 02 38 44 67 35
Fax: 02 38 44 87 92
Former abbey building in a quiet location beside the Loire. Parking. Restaurant offers traditional cuisine. 18 rooms. AE/DI/MC/VI

45160 Olivet
Rivage (F–FF) ◆◆◆
635 rue de la Reine Blanche
Tel: 02 38 66 02 93
Fax: 02 38 56 31 11
Charming establishment in attractive riverside setting. Tennis. Restaurant has fish and game specialties. 17 rooms. AE/DI/MC/VI

45000 Orléans
Terminus (F) ◆◆◆
40 rue de la République
Tel: 02 38 53 24 64
Fax: 02 38 53 24 18
Situated in historic center close to sights and stores. Comfortable rooms with modern facilities. 47 rooms. AE/DI/MC/VI

MAINE-ET-LOIRE
49100 Angers
D'Anjou (F–FF) ◆◆◆
1 boulevard Maréchal-Foch
Tel: 02 41 88 24 82
Fax: 02 41 87 22 21
Elegantly furnished hotel in town center. Parking. The restaurant is one of the best in Angers. 53 rooms.
AE/DI/MC/VI

PYRÉNÉES-ATLANTIQUES
64250 Aïnhoa
Argi Eder (FF) ◆◆◆
Tel: 05 59 93 72 00
Fax: 05 59 93 72 13
Idyllic setting at the foot of the Pyrénées. Outdoor pool, tennis court. Air conditioning. Reputable restaurant. 36 rooms. AE/DIMC/VI

64100 Bayonne
Loustau (F) ◆◆◆
1 place de la République
Tel: 05 59 55 08 08
Fax: 05 59 55 69 36
Located on the banks of the Adour, this establishment offers a good value. Air conditioning. Sauna. Suitable for visitors with disabilities. 44 rooms. AE/DIMC/VI

64200 Biarritz
Café de Paris (FF–FFF) ◆◆◆
5 place Bellevue
Tel: 05 59 24 19 53
Fax: 05 59 24 18 20
In the center of Biarritz next to the beach. Spacious rooms with sea views. Bistro and restaurant. 19 rooms. AE/DI/MC/VI

Au Temps de la Reine
Jeanne (F) ◆◆
44 rue Bourg Vieux
Tel: 05 59 67 00 76
Fax: 05 59 69 09 63
Convenient town-center location. Restaurant. 20 rooms. AE/MC/VI

64000 Pau
Gramont (F–FF) ◆◆◆
3 place Gramont
Tel: 05 59 27 84 04
Fax: 05 59 27 62 23
Former inn located in town center, offering a warm welcome. Attractive, homey rooms. Parking. Bar. 36 rooms. AE/DI/MC/VI

64500 St.-Jean-de-Luz
Parc Victoria (FFF) ◆◆◆◆
5 rue Cépe
Tel: 05 59 26 78 78
Fax: 05 59 26 78 08
A 19th-century residence in an attractive fishing port. Heated outdoor pool. Garden. Rooms decorated in 1930s style. Restaurant. 12 rooms. AE/DI/MC/VI

64310 Sare
Arraya (FF) ◆◆◆
Tel: 05 59 54 20 46
Fax: 05 59 54 27 04
Relaxing accommodation with traditional Basque-style decor. Air-conditioned rooms. Renowned restaurant offers regional specialties. 21 rooms. AE/DI/VI

SARTHE
72000 Le Mans
Vidéotel (F) ◆◆
avenue Paul Courboulay
Tel: 02 43 24 47 24
Fax: 02 43 24 58 41
Pleasant hotel in town center offering good service. Parking. Gourmet cuisine and regional specialties in the restaurant. 91 rooms. AE/DI/MC/VI

VENDÉE
85110 Chantonnay
Le Moulin Neuf (F) ◆◆
On N137
Tel: 02 51 94 30 27
Fax: 02 51 94 57 76
Splendid lakeside position, ideal for relaxing. Leisure facilities. Heated outdoor pool. Sauna. Fish specialties served in restaurant. AE/DI/MC/VI

85330 Noirmoutier-en-l'Île
Bois de la Chaize (FF) ◆◆◆
Tel: 05 13 90 05 63
Fax: 05 13 97 73 98
Island setting on the Baie de Bourgneuf. Heated indoor and outdoor pools. Tennis. 37 rooms. AE/MC/VI

THE DORDOGNE

CORRÈZE
19800 Gimel les Cascades
L'Hostellerie de la Vallée (F) ◆◆
Tel: 05 55 21 40 60
Fax: 05 55 21 38 74
Comfortable accommodation in picturesque village near waterfalls. Air conditioning in rooms. Restaurant. 9 rooms. MC/VI

DORDOGNE
24100 Bergerac
Bordeaux (F–FF) ◆◆◆
38 place Gambetta
Tel: 05 53 57 12 83
Fax: 05 53 57 72 14
Peaceful accommodation close to the historic quarter. Pretty gardens. Outdoor pool. Bar. Restaurant. 40 rooms. AE/DI/MC/VI

24530 Champagnac-de-Belair
Moulin du Roc (FF–FFF) ◆◆◆◆
Tel: 05 53 02 86 00
Fax: 05 53 54 21 31
Riverside setting and lavish interior. Fishing. Sauna. Indoor and outdoor pools. Restaurant offers tantalizing cuisine. 14 rooms. AE/DI/MC/VI

24120 Coly
Manoir d'Hautégente
(FFF) ◆◆◆
Tel: 05 53 51 68 03
Fax: 05 53 50 38 52
*Ideal touring base in rural
location. Cozy, elegant
establishment. Heated out-
door pool. Fishing.
Restaurant includes regional
specialties. 14 rooms.
AE/MC/VI*

24510 Limeuil
Beau Regard et Les
Terrasses (F) ◆◆
route de Trémolat
Tel: 05 53 63 30 85
Fax: 05 53 24 53 55
*Set in open countryside, an
ideal base for touring and
leisure pursuits. Restaurant
offers good food. 8 rooms.
MC/VI*

24290 Montignac-Lascaux
La Roserai (F) ◆◆◆
place d'Armes
Tel: 05 53 50 53 92
Fax: 05 53 51 02 23
*Set amid parkland, a com-
fortable 19th-century man-
sion in the historic center.
Outdoor pool. Parking.
Restaurant. 14 rooms.
MC/VI*

24800 Thiviers
Château de Mavaleix
(F) ◆◆◆
Tel: 05 53 52 82 01
Fax: 05 53 62 03 80
*Handsome medieval build-
ing that once provided rest
for pilgrims. Set in parkland.
Fishing. Outdoor pool.
Restaurant. 15 rooms.
MC/VI*

24340 Vieux-Maruil
Château de Vieux Mareuil
(FF) ◆◆◆
Tel: 05 53 60 77 15
Fax: 05 53 56 49 33

*Magnificent 15th-century
residence offering fine
views and a high level of
comfort. Heated outdoor
pool. Leisure facilities. Good
restaurant. 14 rooms.
AE/DI/MC/VI*

24200 Vitrac
De Plaisance (F) ◆◆
Le Port
Tel: 05 53 28 33 04
Fax: 05 53 28 19 24
*Cozy accommodation in hill-
side village. Outdoor pool.
Tennis. Well-prepared cui-
sine in restaurant. 42 rooms.
AE/DI/MC/VI*

LOT
46000 Cahors
Climat de France (F) ◆◆
Rond Point de Régourd
Tel: 05 65 30 00 00
Fax: 05 65 22 56 19
*Modern hotel near town
center. Parking. Restaurant
and buffet. 68 rooms. MC/VI*

46110 Carennac
Hostellerie Fenelon (F) ◆◆
Tel: 05 65 10 96 46
Fax: 05 65 10 94 86
*Charming hotel in village
center. Heated outdoor
pool. Parking. Good restau-
rant. 15 rooms. MC/VI*

46100 Figeac
Château du Viguier du Roy
(FFF) ◆◆◆
52 rue Émile Zola
Tel: 05 65 50 05 05
Fax: 05 65 50 06 06
*In historic center. Parking.
Heated outdoor pool. Air
conditioning. Suitable for
visitors with disabilities. 20
rooms. AE/DI*

46500 Rocamadour
Beau Site (F) ◆◆◆
Cité Medievale
Tel: 05 65 33 63 08

Fax: 05 65 33 65 23
*In town center. Parking.
Terrace. Restaurant. 43
rooms. AE/DI/MC/VI*

LOT-ET-GARONNE
47000 Agen
Hotel Château des
Jacobins (FF) ◆◆◆◆
1 ter place des Jacobins
Tel: 05 53 47 03 31
Fax: 05 53 47 02 80
*A converted château sur-
rounded by a garden.
Parking. Air conditioning.
Suitable for visitors with dis-
abilities. 15 rooms.
AE/MC/VI*

47190 Aiguillon
Le Jardin des Gygnes (F) ◆◆
route de Villeneuve
Tel: 05 53 79 60 02
Fax: 05 53 88 10 22
*Outside the town center.
Terrace. Parking. Outdoor
pool. Suitable for visitors
with disabilities. Restaurant.
24 rooms. AE/MC/VI*

TARN
81000 Albi
St.-Antoine (FF–FFF) ◆◆◆◆
17 rue St.-Antoine
Tel: 05 63 54 04 04
Fax: 05 63 47 10 47
*Peaceful former 18th-cen-
tury monastery. Pool and
tennis courts nearby.
Parking. Air conditioning.
Excellent restaurant.
Suitable for visitors with dis-
abilities. 44 rooms.
AE/DI/MC/VI*

81800 Rabastens
Du Pré Vert ◆◆
54 promenade des Lices
Tel: 05 63 33 70 51
Fax: 05 63 33 82 58
*Located outside the town
center. Parking. Terrace.
Restaurant. 27 rooms.
AE/DI/MC/VI*

THE PYRÉNÉES

ARIÈGE

09110 Ax-les-Thermes
L'Auzéraie (F–FF) ◆◆
promenade du Couloubret
Tel: 05 61 64 20 70
Fax: 05 61 64 38 50
Located in peaceful spa resort. Parking. Restaurant. 33 rooms. AE/MC/VI

09190 Lorp-Sentaraille
Horizon 117 (F) ◆◆
route de Toulouse
Tel: 05 61 66 26 80
Fax: 05 61 66 26 08
Rural establishment with well-equipped rooms. Garden. Outdoor pool. Tennis. Sauna. Restaurant offers regional specialties. 20 rooms. AE/DI/MC/VI

GERS

32003 Auch
Hotel de France
(F–FFF) ◆◆◆◆
2 place de la Libération
Tel: 05 62 61 71 71
Fax: 05 62 61 71 81
Former inn. Spacious rooms. Parking. Elegant restaurant. 29 rooms. AE/DI/MC/VI

HAUTE-GARONNE

31360 Boussens
Du Lac (F–FF)
7 promenade du Lac
Tel: 05 61 90 01 85
Fax: 05 61 97 15 57
Peaceful lakeside position. Terrace. Restaurant offers regional dishes. 12 rooms. AE/MC/VI

31800 St.-Gaudens
Hostellerie des Decres
(F–FF) ◆◆◆
Villeneuve-de-Rivière
Tel: 05 61 89 36 00
Fax: 05 61 88 31 04
Rural location. Outdoor pool. Leisure facilities. Terrace. Satellite TV. Restaurant. 24 rooms. AE/MC/VI

31000 Toulouse
Hotel des Beaux-Arts
(FF–FFF) ◆◆◆
1 place du Pont Neuf
Tel: 05 61 23 40 50
Fax: 05 61 22 02 27
Situated beside the Garonne river. Elegant air-conditioned rooms. Parking. 19 rooms. AE/DI/MC/VI

Videotel (F) ◆◆
77 boulevard de L'Embouchure 31200
Tel: 05 61 57 34 77
Fax: 05 61 23 54 74
Near town center. Air-conditioned rooms. Terrace. Parking. Restaurant. 90 rooms. AE/DI/MC/VI

HAUTES-PYRÉNÉES

65130 Capvern-les-Bains
Bellevue (F) ◆◆
route de Mauvezin
Tel: 05 62 39 00 29
Peaceful location outside town center. Suitable for visitors with disabilities. Light meals available in the restaurant. 33 rooms. MC/VI

65110 Cauterets
Club Aladin (FF) ◆◆◆
11 avenue du Gén. Leclerc
Tel: 05 62 92 60 00
Fax: 05 62 92 63 30
Breathtaking scenery. Organized skiing and hiking trips. Indoor pool. Parking. Satellite TV. Restaurant. Suitable for visitors with disabilities. 126 rooms. DI/VI

65100 Lourdes
America Hotel (FF) ◆◆◆
6 rue de la Rine Astrid
Tel: 05 62 42 25 25
Fax: 05 62 94 71 69
Modern hotel with good facilities. Air-conditioned rooms. Satellite TV. Parking. 127 rooms. VI

PROVENCE AND THE CÔTE D'AZUR

ALPES-DE- HAUTE PROVENCE

04160 Château-Arnoux
Bonne Étape
(FF–FFF) ◆◆◆◆
chemin du Lac
Tel: 04 92 64 00 09
Fax: 04 92 64 37 36
An 18th-century inn set in Provençal countryside. Heated outdoor pool. Air conditioning. Restaurant offers outstanding cuisine. 18 rooms. AE/DI/MC/VI

04300 Forcalquier
Hostellerie des Deux Lions
(F–FF) ◆◆◆
11 place du Bourguet
Tel: 04 92 75 25 30
Fax: 04 92 75 06 41
A 17th-century inn near the historic center. Traditional hospitality and elegant rooms. Reputable restaurant. 16 rooms. AE/MC/VI

ALPES-MARITIMES

06430 La Brigue
Le Mirval (F) ◆◆
Tel: 04 93 04 63 71
Fax: 04 93 04 79 81
Delightful hotel in a historic village. Garden. Restaurant. 18 rooms. AE//MC/VI

06400 Cannes
Hotel de l'Olivier
(FF–FFF) ◆◆◆◆
5 rue des Tambourinaires
Tel: 04 93 39 53 28
Fax: 04 93 39 55 85
Charming hotel in the old quarter, close to beach. Air-conditioned rooms. Garden

and terrace. Outdoor pool.
24 rooms. AE/DI/MC/VI

Hotel de Paris
(FF) ◆◆◆
34 boulevard d'Alsace
Tel: 04 93 38 30 89
Fax: 04 93 39 04 61
In town center close to
beach. Traditional hospitality
with modern facilities. Bar.
Turkish bath. Outdoor pool.
50 rooms. AE/DI/MC/VI

06670 Castagniers
Servotel (F) ◆◆
1976 route de Grenoble
Tel: 04 93 08 22 00
Fax: 04 93 29 03 66
Modern hotel situated in a
large park. Outdoor pool.
Leisure facilities. Reputable
restaurant. 44 rooms.
AE/MC/VI

06360 Èze
Château Eza (FFF) ◆◆◆◆
rue de la Pise
Tel: 04 93 41 12 24
Fax: 04 93 41 16 64
Attractive building with stunning views over the Côte
d'Azur. Elegant air-conditioned rooms. Outstanding
restaurant. 10 rooms.
AE/DI/MC/VI

06220 Golfe Juan
Beau Soleil (FF) ◆◆◆
impasse Beau Soleil
Tel: 04 93 63 63 63
Fax: 04 93 63 02 89
Between Cannes and
Antibes, close to the beach.
Air conditioning. Outdoor
pool. Tennis. Restaurant. 30
rooms. AE/MC/VI

06000 Nice
Acropolé-Nice-Hôte
(FF) ◆◆◆◆
25 boulevard Dubouchage
Tel: 04 93 80 57 33
Fax: 04 93 62 69 11

Elegant establishment in the
heart of Nice, close to
beaches and gardens.
Comfortable air-conditioned
rooms. Good breakfasts.
130 rooms. AE/DI/MC/VI

Splendide (FFF) ◆◆◆◆
50 boulevard Victor Hugo
Tel: 04 93 16 41 00
Fax: 04 93 16 42 70
Central location with rooftop
pool and terrace. Parking.
Air conditioning. Satellite TV.
Suitable for visitors with dis-
abilities. Restaurant. 128
rooms. AE/DI/MC/VI

06750 Thorenc
Auberge les Merisiers (F) ◆◆
24 avenue du Belvédère
Tel: 04 93 60 00 23
Fax: 04 93 60 02 17
Near to the Côte d'Azur in a
beautiful setting surrounded
by mountains Terrace and a
restaurant. 12 rooms.
AE/MC/VI

06140 Vence
Mas de Vence (FF) ◆◆
539 avenue Émile Hugues
Tel: 04 93 58 06 16
Fax: 04 93 24 04 21
Close to the town center.
Terraces. Outdoor pool.
Parking. Suitable for visitors
with disabilities. Regional
specialties in restaurant. 41
rooms. AE/DI/MC/VI

BOUCHES-DU-RHÔNE
13100 Aix-en-Provence
Mas de La Bertrande
(F–FF) ◆◆◆
Beaurecueil
Tel: 04 42 66 75 75
Fax: 04 42 66 82 01
A Provençal farm below
Ste.-Victoire mountain.
Outdoor pool. Comfortable
rooms with private terraces.
Satellite TV. Restaurant. 10
rooms. AE/MC/VI

Hotel des Quatre Dauphins
(F) ◆◆
54 rue Roux Alpheran
Tel: 04 42 38 16 39
Fax: 04 42 38 60 19
Charming small hotel in the
historic center. Restaurants,
museums and sights
nearby. Traditional Provençal
decor. 12 rooms. MC/VI

Villa Gallici (FFF) ◆◆◆◆
avenue de la Violette
Tel: 04 42 23 29 23
Fax: 04 42 96 30 45
Peaceful, elegant establish-
ment in town center.
Parking. Outdoor pool.
Garden. Restaurant. 19
rooms. AE/DI/MC/VI

13200 Arles
Jules César (FFF) ◆◆◆◆
boulevard des Lices, 13631
Tel: 04 90 93 43 20
Fax: 04 90 93 33 47
In the town center with
parking. Air conditioning.
Suitable for visitors with disabilities. Heated outdoor
pool. Terrace. Restaurant.
56 rooms. AE/DI/MC/VI

Hotel Calendal (F) ◆◆
22 place du Dr. Pomme
Tel: 04 90 96 11 89
Fax: 04 90 96 05 84
Located close to sights.
Attractive rooms overlook
the Roman arena or a
delightful garden.
Restaurant. 27 rooms.
AE/DI/MC/VI

13520 Les Baux-de-
Provence
La Benvengudo (F–FF) ◆◆◆
Vallon de l'Arcoulé
Tel: 04 90 54 32 54
Fax: 04 90 54 42 58
Peaceful farmhouse below
the Alpilles. Outdoor pool.
Tennis. Good restaurant. 20
rooms. AE/MC/VI

13001 Marseille
St.-Ferréol's Hotel (FF) ◆◆◆
19 rue Pisançon
Tel: 04 91 33 12 21
Fax: 04 91 54 29 97
Cozy town-center accommodation on pedestrianized street. Elegant rooms with luxurious facilities. 20 rooms. AE/MC/VI

13210 St.-Rémy-de-Provence
Le Mas de Carassins
(F–FF) ◆◆◆
1 chemin Gaulois
Tel: 04 90 92 15 48
Fax: 04 90 92 63 47
Tranquil rural setting below the Alpilles. Large garden and two lounges for relaxation. 10 rooms. MC/VI

GARD
30000 Nîmes
New Hôtel la Baume
(F–FF) ◆◆◆
21 rue Nationale
Tel: 04 66 73 28 42
Fax: 04 66 76 28 45
Modern comforts and traditional hospitality in central location. Air-conditioned rooms. Restaurant. 33 rooms. AE/DI/MC/VI

HÉRAULT
34000 Montpellier
Holiday Inn Métropole
(FF) ◆◆◆◆
3 rue Clos René
Tel: 04 67 58 11 22
Fax: 04 67 92 13 02
Parking, air conditioning, satellite TV and restaurant. 81 rooms. AE/DIMC/VI

VAR
83470 St.-Maximin-la-Ste.-Baume
France (FF) ◆◆◆
1–3 avenue Albert
Tel: 04 94 78 00 14
Fax: 04 94 59 83 80

Former inn located in town center. Good base for touring. Outdoor pool. Renowned restaurant. 26 rooms. AE/DI/MC/VI

83700 St.-Raphaël
Golf de Valescure
(FFF) ◆◆◆
avenue Paul l'Hermité
Tel: 04 94 52 85 00
Fax: 04 94 82 41 88
Close to the sea. Golf, tennis, outdoor pool. Air conditioning. Suitable for visitors with disabilities. 40 rooms. AE/DI/MC/VI

83990 St.-Tropez
La Mandarine (FFF) ◆◆◆◆
route de Tahiti
Tel: 04 94 79 06 66
Fax: 04 94 97 33 67
In the town center. Half board compulsory. Parking, Heated outdoor pool. Air conditioning. Suitable for visitors with disabilities. 43 rooms. AE/MC/VI

83000 Toulon
Holiday Inn Garden Court
(F) ◆◆◆
1 avenue Rageot de la Touche
Tel: 04 94 92 00 21
Fax: 04 94 62 08 15
Located in town center. Spacious air-conditioned rooms. Garden. Outdoor pool. Parking. Restaurant. 81 rooms. AE/DI/MC/VI

VAUCLUSE
84400 Apt
Auberge du Luberon
(F–FF) ◆◆◆
4 place du Faubourg du Ballet
Tel: 04 90 74 12 50
Fax: 04 90 04 79 49
Located in town center. Parking. Restaurant. 15 rooms. AE/DI/MC/VI

84000 Avignon
Mirande (FFF) ◆◆◆◆
4 place del Mirande
Tel: 04 90 85 93 93
Fax: 04 90 86 26 85
Former cardinal's palace in town center. Air conditioning. Elegant 18th-century interiors and a secluded garden. Parking. Restaurant. 20 rooms. AE/DI/MC/VI

84100 Orange
Arène (F–FF) ◆◆◆
place de Langes
Tel: 04 90 34 10 95
Fax: 04 90 34 91 62
Attractive hotel in the historic center. Air-conditioned rooms. Parking. Restaurant. 30 rooms. AE/DI/MC/VI

THE MASSIF CENTRAL

ALLIER
03160 Bourbon-l'Archambault
Grand Hotel du Parc
(F) ◆◆
4 rue du Parc
Tel: 04 70 67 02 55
Fax: 04 70 67 13 95
Elegant rooms and a garden. Parking. Suitable for visitors with disabilities. Stylish restaurant. 52 rooms. AE/DI/MC/VI

03000 Moulins
Le Parc (F) ◆◆
31 avenue Gén. Leclerc
Tel: 04 70 44 12 25
Fax: 04 70 46 79 35
Pleasant hotel near peaceful park. Parking. Restaurant offers classic cuisine and regional dishes. 28 rooms. MC/VI

CANTAL
15000 Aurillac
Grand Hotel de Bordeaux

(FF) ♦♦♦
2 avenue de la République
Tel: 04 71 48 01 84
Fax: 04 71 48 49 93
*Located in the town center.
Bar and spacious lounge.
Satellite TV. Suitable for visitors with disabilities. 35
rooms. AE/DI/MC/VI*

15320 Garabit
Garabit-Hotel (F) ♦♦
Tel: 04 71 23 42 75
Fax: 04 71 23 49 60
*Parking, garden and an
indoor pool. Restaurant. 47
rooms. MC/VI*

15100 St.-Flour
St.-Jacques (F) ♦♦
8 place de la Liberté
Tel: 04 71 60 09 20
Fax: 04 71 60 33 81
*Attractive hotel near historic
center. Satellite TV. Heated
outdoor pool. Terrace. Good
restaurant uses delicious
local produce. 28 rooms.
MC/VI*

PUY-DE-DÔME
63140 Châtelguyon
Régence (F) ♦♦
31 avenue des Étas-Unis
Tel: 04 73 86 02 60
Fax: 04 73 86 12 49
*Comfortable hotel situated
in well-known spa town.
Spacious day rooms with
period furniture. Garden.
Restaurant offers fine cuisine. 27 rooms. MC/VI*

63000 Clermont-Ferrand
Hotel Frantour Arverne
(F–FF) ♦♦♦
16 place Delille
Tel: 04 73 91 92 06
Fax: 04 73 91 60 25
*Town-center location close
to cathedral and transportation facilities. Air-conditioned rooms. Parking.
Restaurant with views to*

*the mountains of the
Auvergne. 57 rooms.
AE/DI/MC/VI*

THE ALPS AND THE RHÔNE VALLEY

DRÔME
26190 Bouvante
Auberge du Pionnier (F) ♦
Col du Pionnier
Tel: 04 75 48 57 12
Fax: 04 75 48 58 26
*Rural location amid forests.
Terrace. Good restaurant. 9
rooms. No credit cards.*

26230 Grignan
Manoir de la Roseraie
(FFF) ♦♦♦♦
route de Valréas
Tel: 04 75 46 58 15
Fax: 04 75 46 91 55
*A beautiful country house
set in a large park. Heated
outdoor pool, tennis.
Suitable for visitors with disabilities. Restaurant offers
specialties of Provence. 15
rooms. AE/DI/MC/VI*

26200 Montélimar
Le Printemps (FF) ♦♦
8 chemin de la Manche
Tel: 04 75 01 32 63
Fax: 04 75 46 03 14
*Peaceful location with
outdoor pool. Terrace.
Restaurant. AE/MC/VI*

26110 Nyons
Auberge du Vieux Village
d'Aubres (FFF) ♦♦♦
Aubres
Tel: 04 75 26 12 89
Fax: 04 75 26 38 10
*Rural location. Heated outdoor pool, sauna and fitness
center. Air conditioning.
Suitable for visitors with disabilities. Restaurant. 23
rooms. AE/DI/MC/VI*

26260 St.-Donat-sur-l'Herbasse
Chartron (FF) ♦♦♦
1 avenue Gambetta
Tel: 04 75 45 11 82
Fax: 04 75 45 01 36
*Former inn located in town
center. Well-equipped
rooms. Parking. Restaurant
offers truffle specialties and
fine wines. 7 rooms.
AE/DI/MC/VI*

HAUTES-ALPES
05000 Gap
Fons-Regina (F) ♦♦
13 avenue de Fontreyne
Tel: 04 92 53 98 99
Fax: 04 92 51 54 51
*Attractive hotel surrounded
by parkland. Well-furnished
rooms. Delightful garden.
Heated outdoor pool. Bar.
Satellite TV. Restaurant. 25
rooms. AE/DI/MC/VI*

05220 Grignan
Auberge du Choucas
(FF) ♦♦♦
17 rue de la Fruitière
Tel: 04 92 24 42 73
Fax: 04 92 24 51 60
*Charming country inn
located in Alpine village. Air-conditioned rooms. Regional
specialties served in excellent restaurant. 8 rooms.
MC/VI*

HAUTE-SAVOIE
74000 Annecy
Au Faisan Doré (F-FF) ♦♦♦
34 avenue d'Albigny
Tel: 04 50 23 02 46
Fax: 04 50 23 11 10
*In town center near major
sights. Parking. Restaurant
features regional dishes and
fish specialties. 40 rooms.
MC/VI*

74400 Chamonix-Mont-Blanc
De l'Arve (F) ♦♦

60 impasse Anémones
Tel: 04 50 53 02 31
Fax: 04 50 53 56 92
Peaceful riverside setting in town center. Parking. Sauna. Excellent restaurant with views of Mont Blanc. 39 rooms. AE/DI/MC/VI

Au Relais des Gaillands
(F) ◆◆
964 route des Gaillands
Tel: 04 50 53 13 58
Fax: 04 50 55 85 06
Chalet-style hotel in rural setting. Local specialties offered in the restaurant. 21 rooms. MC/VI

74500 Évian-les-Bains
Panorama (F) ◆◆
Grande Rive
Tel: 04 50 75 14 50
Fax: 04 50 75 59 12
Popular spa-town location with views over Lac Léman (Lake Geneva). Good restaurant offers fish specialties. 29 rooms. AE/MC/VI

Verniaz (FFF) ◆◆◆◆
route d'Abondance
Tel: 04 50 75 04 90
Fax: 04 50 70 78 92
Charming hotel in attractive park. Leisure facilities. Bar. Heated outdoor pool. Restaurant. 34 rooms. AE/DI/MC/VI

74120 Megève
Les Fermes de Marie
(FF) ◆◆◆
chemin de Riante Colline
Tel: 04 50 93 03 10
Fax: 04 50 93 09 84
Enchanting hotel with rustic character. Indoor and outdoor pools. Sauna. 68 rooms. AE/MC/VI

ISÈRE
38270 Beaurepaire
Fiard-Zorelle (F) ◆◆

avenue des Terreaux
Tel: 04 74 84 62 02
Fax: 04 74 84 71 13
Comfortable setting for an overnight stop or holiday. Parking. Bar. Restaurant. 15 rooms. AE/DI/MC/VI

38000 Grenoble
Grand Hotel (FF) ◆◆◆
5 rue de la République
Tel: 04 76 44 49 36
Fax: 04 76 63 14 06
Cozy hotel, suitable for visitors with disabilities. Air conditioning. Restaurant. 51 rooms. AE/DI/MC/VI

RHÔNE
69470 Cours-la-Ville
Le Pavillon (F) ◆◆
Col du Pavillon
Tel: 04 74 89 83 55
Fax: 04 74 64 70 26
Attractive countryside setting. Good restaurant. Suitable for visitors with disabilities. 21 rooms. VI

69000 Lyon
Hotel Royal (FF-FFF) ◆◆◆◆
20 place Bellecour 69002
Tel: 04 78 37 57 31
Fax: 04 78 37 01 36
Central location with some rooms reserved for non-smokers. Parking. Air conditioning. Restaurant. 80 rooms. AE/DI/MC/VI

La Tour Rose (FFF) ◆◆◆◆
22 rue du Boeuf 69005
Tel: 04 78 37 25 90
Fax: 04 78 42 26 02
Historic building in town center. Sumptuous interior, air-conditioned rooms. Parking. Innovative restaurant. 12 rooms. AE/DI/MC/VI

SAVOIE
73350 Champagny-en-Vanoise
L'Ancolie (FF-FFF) ◆◆

Les Hauts du Crey
Tel: 04 79 55 05 00
Fax: 04 79 55 04 42
Charming village location amid magnificent scenery. Heated outdoor pool. Sauna. Cozy bar. Restaurant. 31 rooms. No credit cards.

73550 Méribel-les-Allues
Orée du Bois (FF–FFF) ◆◆
route du Belvédère
Tel: 04 79 00 50 30
Fax: 04 79 08 57 52
Comfortable setting amid mountain scenery. Outdoor pool. Restaurant. 35 rooms. AE/MC/VI

73530 St.-Sorlin-d'Arves
Beausoleil (F) ◆◆
Tel: 04 79 57 71 42
Fax: 04 79 59 75 25
Chalet-style hotel, ideal location for winter holidays. Cozy bedrooms with excellent views. Restaurant. 23 rooms. MC/VI

BURGUNDY, ALSACE-LORRAINE AND THE NORTH

AISNE
02100 St.-Quentin
Hotel de Canonniers
(F–FF) ◆◆◆
15 rue des Cononniers
Tel: 03 23 62 87 87
Fax: 03 23 62 87 86
Peaceful 18th-century residence in the town center. Parking. Elegant period interiors. 9 rooms. AE/DI/MC/VI

02140 Vervins
Hostellerie la Tour du Roy
(FFF) ◆◆◆
45 rue du Général Leclerc
Tel: 03 23 98 00 11
Fax: 03 23 98 00 72
In the town center. A pool, terrace and parking. Air

conditioning. Satellite TV. Suitable for visitors with disabilities. Gourmet restaurant. 18 rooms. AE/DI/MC/VI

AUBE
10400 Nogent-sur-Seine
Le Beau Rivage (F) ◆
20 rue Villiers aux Choux
Tel: 03 25 39 84 22
Fax: 03 25 39 18 32
In lovely surroundings away from the town center. Terrace. Fine restaurant. 7 rooms. MC/VI

10220 Piney
Le Tadorne (F) ◆◆
3 place de la Halle
Tel: 03 25 46 30 35
Fax: 03 25 46 36 49
A timbered 18th-century building in the town center. Heated outdoor pool. Restaurant offers regional cuisine. 20 rooms. MC/VI

10000 Troyes
Royal Hotel (F) ◆◆◆
22 boulevard Carnot
Tel: 03 25 73 19 99
Fax: 03 25 73 47 85
Handsome building in the town center, close to the sights. Good restaurant. 37 rooms. AE/DI/MC/VI

BAS-RHIN
67170 Brumath
L'Écrevisse (F) ◆◆
4 avenue de Strasbourg
Tel: 03 85 51 11 08
Fax: 03 88 51 89 02
Traditional family hospitality in town center. Outstanding local cuisine and prestigious wine list. Leisure facilities. 36 rooms. AE/DI/MC/VI

67520 Marlenheim
Cerf (FF-FFF) ◆◆◆
30 rue du Général de Gaulle
Tel: 03 88 87 73 73
Fax: 03 88 87 68 08

This former inn is a charming establishment in the town center. Traditional cuisine served in restaurant. 15 rooms. AE/DI/MC/VI

67710 Obersteigen
Hostellerie Belle-Vue (FF) ◆◆◆
16 route de Dabo
Tel: 03 88 87 32 39
Fax: 03 88 87 37 77
Family-run hotel in forest area of the Vosges region. Ideal for relaxing or leisure activities. Restaurant. 38 rooms. AE/MC/VI

67000 Strasbourg
Maison Rouge (FF) ◆◆◆
4 rue des Francs-Bourgeois
Tel: 03 88 32 08 60
Fax: 03 88 22 43 73
Splendid personal service in this elegant, peaceful hotel in the town center close to sights. Luxurious facilities. 142 rooms. AE/DI/MC/VI

CÔTE-D'OR
21200 Beaune
Hotel de la Poste (FF-FFF) ◆◆◆◆
5 boulevard Clemenceau
Tel: 03 80 22 08 11
Fax: 03 80 24 19 71
Handsome building near the old town. Parking. Belle-époque bar. Restaurant offers fine cuisine. 30 rooms. AE/DI/MC/VI

21140 Semur-en-Auxois
Hotel du Lac (F) ◆◆
Pont-et-Massène, 3 km se.
Tel: 03 80 97 11 11
Fax: 03 80 97 29 25
Beautiful lakeside residence in a forest. Restaurant. 20 rooms. DI/MC/VI

21640 Vougeot
Château de Gilly (FF-FFF) ◆◆◆◆

Gilly-lès-Cîteaux
Tel: 03 80 62 89 98
Fax: 03 80 62 82 34
Historic moated residence in the heart of the Burgundy vineyards. Inspired cuisine served in a magnificent vaulted cellar. 48 rooms. AE/DI/MC/VI

HAUTE-MARNE
52290 Eclaron
Hotellerie du Moulin (F) ◆◆
rue du Moulin
Tel: 03 25 04 17 76
Fax: 03 25 55 67 01
Old timbered mill in rural setting. Peaceful accommodation. Restaurant. 5 rooms. MC/VI

52300 Joinville
Poste (F) ◆◆
place de la Grève
Tel: 03 25 94 12 63
Fax: 03 25 94 36 23
Situated in the town center. Parking. Classic and regional dishes offered in restaurant. 10 rooms. AE/DI/MC/VI

HAUT-RHIN
68760 Le Grand Ballon
Du Grand Ballon (F-FF) ◆◆
Tel: 03 89 76 83 35
Fax: 03 89 83 10 63
Comfortable, rustic establishment in the Vosges. Ideal for walking and skiing. Terrace. Good restaurant has regional specialties. 18 rooms. MC/VI

68140 Munster
Aux Deux Sapins ◆◆
49 rue du neuvième Zouaves
Tel: 03 89 77 33 96
Fax: 03 89 77 03 90
Friendly establishment with modern amenities. Parking. Good restaurant offers delicious cuisine. 25 rooms. AE/DI/MC/VI

68370 Orbey
Les Bruyères (F) ♦♦
35 rue Général de
Gaulle
Tel: 03 89 71 20 36
Fax: 03 89 71 35 30
Situated in the town
center, opposite a
splendid park. Parking.
Sauna. Restaurant. 29
rooms. AE/DI/MC/VI

MARNE
51100 Reims
Climat de France (F) ♦♦
rue Bertrand Russell
Tel: 03 26 09 62 73
Fax: 03 26 87 46 08
Comfortable modern hotel
with well-equipped rooms.
Parking. Restaurant. 38
rooms. MC/VI

MEURTHE-ET-MOSELLE
54850 Mereville
Maison Carrée (F) ♦♦
12 rue du Bac
Tel: 03 83 47 09 23
Fax: 03 83 47 50 75
Pleasant rural location
beside the Moselle, close to
Nancy. Heated outdoor pool.
Restaurant offers sumptu-
ous cuisine. 23 rooms.
MC/VI

54000 Nancy
Albert 1er-Astoria (F) ♦♦
3 rue de l'Armée Patton
Tel: 03 83 40 31 24
Fax: 03 83 28 47 78
Located in the historic cen-
ter. Bar. Garden. Parking.
125 rooms. AE/DI/MC/VI

MEUSE
55120 Futeau
Oreé du Boise (F) ♦♦
Tel: 03 29 88 28 41
Fax: 03 29 88 24 52
Peaceful hotel in forest set-
ting. Comfortable rooms.
Seafood specialties served
in restaurant. 7 rooms. AE

55100 Verdun
Orchidées (F) ♦♦
avenue d'Etain
Tel: 03 29 86 46 46
Fax: 03 29 86 10 20
Convenient location outside
the town center. Peaceful
establishment with modern
facilities. Restaurant. 42
rooms. AE/MC/VI

MOSELLE
**57370 Danne-et-Quatre-
Vents**
Notre-Dame-de-Bonne-
Fontaine (F) ♦♦
Tel: 03 87 24 34 33
Fax: 03 87 24 24 64
Restful forest setting. Cozy
bar. Indoor pool and sauna.
Restaurant. 34 rooms.
AE/DI/MC/VI

NORD
59960 Neuville-en-Ferrain
Des Acacias (FF) ♦♦♦
39 rue du Dronckaert
Tel: 03 20 37 89 27
Fax: 03 20 46 38 59
Near main road but a quiet
location. Pleasant terrace.
Parking. Suitable for visitors
with disabilities. Restaurant.
42 rooms. AE/DI/MC/VI

SAÔNE-ET-LOIRE
71400 Autun
De la Tête Noire (F) ♦♦
1–3 rue de l'Arquébuse
Tel: 03 85 86 33 90
Fax: 03 85 86 33 90
Situated in town center
close to historic sights.
Parking. Restaurant. 27
rooms. MC/VI

71250 Cluny
Bourgogne (FFF) ♦♦♦
place de l'Abbaye
Tel: 03 85 59 00 58
Fax: 03 85 59 03 73
Quiet town-center location.
Terrace. Parking. Suitable
for visitors with disabilities.

Good restaurant. 15 rooms.
AE/DI/MC/VI

71700 Tournus
Le Rempart (FF-FFF) ♦♦♦♦
2–4 avenue Gambetta
Tel: 03 85 51 10 56
Fax: 03 85 51 77 22
In the town center. Suitable
for visitors with disabilities.
Parking. Air conditioning.
Good restaurant. 37 rooms.
AE/DI/MC/VI

SOMME
80790 Fort-Mahon-Plage
Hotel de la Terrasse
(F–FF) ♦♦♦
1461 avenue de la Plage
Tel: 03 22 23 37 77
Fax: 03 22 23 36 74
Pleasant accommodation
overlooking the beach.
Parking. Suitable for visitors
with disabilities. Restaurant
with sea view specializes in
fine French cuisine. 56
rooms. AE/DI/MC/VI

VOSGES
88250 la Bresse
Hotel Les Vallées (FF) ♦♦♦
31 rue Paul Claudel
Tel: 03 29 25 41 39
Fax: 03 29 25 64 38
Situated within a national
park. The hotel offers a
range of leisure facilities.
Restaurant. 53 rooms.
AE/DI/MC/VI

YVELINES
78000 Versailles
Sofitel Château de
Versailles (FFF) ♦♦♦♦
2 avenue de Paris
Tel: 01 39 53 30 31
Fax: 01 39 53 87 30
Grand comfort in Versailles.
Parking. Air conditioning.
Satellite TV. Suitable for visi-
tors with disabilities. Good
restaurant. 152 rooms.
AE/DI/MC/VI

RESTAURANTS

If you're simply aching for a Big Mac or some Tex Mex, you can certainly find these in French cities. We feel safe in assuming, however, that if you have chosen to visit France at least one reason is to try some of its glorious food.

France is unrivaled anywhere for the quality and quantity of restaurants at all levels, from awesome gastronomic palaces to friendly little bistros or *fermes-auberges*, where you can try many kinds of regional dishes. Modern French cooking offers an inventiveness in its use of ingredients combined with a light touch.

The listings point you to places that offer reliably good value and service. As a rule, many restaurants close on Sunday, Monday and in August, and those that do remain open are often fully booked.

In Paris you can find a restaurant to suit every taste, from regional cuisine to North African to Asian. Vegetarians still have a rather hard time, especially in rural areas like the Dordogne where specialties are based on meat.

Many restaurants do not make provisions for non-smokers, but you can always eat outside in summer and air conditioning is becoming more prevalent.

Children are welcome in all but very grand or formal establishments, but they will be expected to behave in a civilized manner and eat what is on the menu.

Remember that many restaurants offer excellent *prix-fixe* (set-price) menus. "Last orders" refers to the latest time a meal can be ordered.

AAA DIAMOND RATING

Diamond ratings are assigned on a scale of one to five and range from simple home-style cooking to excellent standards of cuisine.

◆ **one diamond** denotes simple, carefully prepared food based on good-quality fresh ingredients.

◆◆ **two diamonds** denote cooking that displays a high degree of competence. The menu should include imaginative dishes that make use of interesting ingredients, as well as some favorites.

◆◆◆ **three diamonds** denote imaginative menus with dishes that are expertly prepared, and demonstrate well-developed technical skills and a high degree of flair. Most items will be made in the kitchen, such as breads, pastries, pasta and petit fours.

◆◆◆◆ at the **four diamond** level cuisine should be innovative, daring and highly accomplished, and achieve a noteworthy standard of consistent quality and flair in all elements.

◆◆◆◆◆ **five diamonds** is the supreme accolade, awarded to chefs at the very top of their profession. Creativity, skill and attention to detail will produce dishes with exciting flavors in harmonious combinations, in addition to faultless presentation. Expect to find luxury ingredients such as lobster, truffles and foie gras, sometimes in unexpected combinations.

In this guide we have used the following abbreviations for the major credit cards:

AE   American Express
DI   Diners Club
MC   MasterCard
VI   Visa

It is advisable to have an alternative means of payment in rural areas. A service charge of 12.5 to 15 percent is nearly always included in the check.

The following applies for a meal for one, including service (not drinks):

(F)   under 150FF
(FF)   150–300FF
(FFF)   over 300FF

PARIS

1er arrondissement

Chez Pauline (FFF) ◆◆◆
5 rue Villédo, 75001
Tel: 01 42 96 20 70
Classic fare served in a formal setting on two floors of an intimate old bistro. Last orders 10:30 p.m. Closed Saturday in summer and Sunday. AE/MC/VI

Grand Vefour (FFF) ◆◆◆◆
17 rue Beaujolais, 75001
Tel: 01 42 96 56 27
Dazzlingly sumptuous surroundings beneath the Palais Royal arcades. Sophisticated and expensive food. Last orders 10:15 p.m. Closed Saturday, Sunday and August. AE/DI/MC/VI

4ème arrondissement

L'Ambroisie (FFF) ◆◆◆◆
9 place des Vosges, 75004
Tel: 01 42 78 51 45
Books and tapestries adorn a charming former goldsmith's studio under the arcades. Vivid cooking by Bernard Pacaud. Last orders 10:30 p.m. Closed Sunday, Monday, February and August. AE/MC/VI

Benoit (FF) ◆◆
20 rue St.-Martin, 75004
Tel: 01 42 72 25 76
Reputable, classy and pricey bistro, serving tried-and-true traditional dishes like cassoulet and boeuf à la mode. Last orders 10 p.m. Closed August. No credit cards.

Le Monde des Chimères
(FFF) ◆
69 rue St.-Louis-en-l'Ile, 75004
Tel: 01 43 54 45 27
Traditional family fare served with élan in a charming old bistro by a former TV personality. Last orders 10:30 p.m. Closed Sunday and Monday. MC/VI

Le Temps des Cérises
(F–FF) ◆
31 rue de la Cérises, 75004
Tel: 01 43 67 52 08
This popular bistro offers excellent lunches. Closed in the evening. AE/MC/VI

5ème arrondissement

Auberge des Deux Signes
(FF) ◆◆
46 rue Galande, 75005
Tel: 01 43 25 46 56
Amazing medieval hostelry with beams, vaults and views of Notre-Dame. Courteous service and generous helpings. The lunch in the set menu is good value. Last orders 10:30 p.m. Closed Saturday lunch, Sunday and August. AE/DI/MC/VI

Moissonnier (FF) ◆
28 rue Fossés-St.-Bernard, 75005
Tel: 01 43 29 87 65
The place to try that French favorite – snails. Those cooked lightly in garlic butter are the best. Last orders 11 p.m. Closed Sunday evening, Monday and August. No credit cards.

**Moulin à Vent
"Chez Henri"**
(FF–FFF) ◆
20 rue Fossés-St.-Bernard, 75005
Tel: 01 43 54 99 37
A typical Parisian bistro – busy and good value. Last orders 11 p.m. Closed Sunday, Monday and August. No credit cards.

Rôtisserie du Beaujolais
(FF) ◆
19 quai Tournelle, 75005
Tel: 01 43 54 17 47
Right in the heart of the Quartier Latin. The specialty is coq au vin and the lunch menu offers good value. Last orders 10:30 p.m. Closed Monday. No credit cards.

6ème arrondissement

Allard (FF) ◆
41 rue St.-André-les-Arts, 75006
Tel: 01 43 26 48 23
Just off boulevard St.-Germain, this bistro offers traditional French dishes. Last orders 10:30 p.m. Closed Sunday and August. AE/DI/MC/VI

Jacques Cagna
(FF–FFF) ◆◆◆
14 rue Grands Augustins, 75006
Tel: 01 43 26 49 39
Classic but innovative cuisine in an elegant 17th-century town house. Jacques' sister Anny presides up front. Last orders 10:30 p.m. Closed Saturday lunch, Sunday, August, and December 24 to January 2. AE/DI/MC/VI

7ème arrondissement

L'Arpège
(FFF) ◆◆◆◆
84 rue Varenne, 75007
Tel: 01 45 51 47 33
Grand bourgeois style in a refined dining room of plain wood and etched glass. Near the Musée Rodin. Last orders 10:30 p.m. Closed Saturday and Sunday. AE/DI/MC/VI

Jules Verne
(FF–FFF) ◆◆◆◆

2e étage Tour Eiffel, 75007
Tel: 01 45 55 61 44
*Don't let the dazzling city
views distract you from the
flamboyant, confident fare.
Private elevator. The
lunch menu is good value.
Last orders 10:30 p.m.*
AE/DI/MC/VI

8ème arrondissement
Le Boeuf sur le Toit
(FF) ◆◆
34 rue Colisée, 75008
Tel: 01 43 59 83 80
*Art-deco mirrors reflect a
bustling scene near the
Champs-Élysées. Good
seafood. Last orders 2 a.m.*
AE/DI/MC/VI

La Fermette Marbeuf 1900
(FF) ◆◆
5 rue Marbeuf, 75008
Tel: 01 53 23 08 00
Lovely belle-époque *decor
and commendable wines
accompany robust fare like*
andouillettes *and tenderloin
steak. Terrace tables and
pleasant service. Last orders
11:30 p.m.* AE/DI/MC/VI

Lucas Carton
(FFF) ◆◆◆◆◆
9 place de la Madeleine,
75008
Tel: 01 42 65 22 90
*Sleek, dressy diners
converge amid* belle-époque
*grandeur to feast on
imaginative combinations
like lobster with vanilla. Last
orders 10:30 p.m. Closed
Saturday lunch, Sunday and
August.* AE/DI/MC/VI

Taillevent
(FFF) ◆◆◆◆◆
15 rue Lamennais, 75008
Tel: 01 44 95 15 01
*Discreet unobtrusive service
is the standard at this pillar
of Parisian gastronomy. Fine
wines. Last orders 10:30
p.m. Closed Saturday,
Sunday, public holidays, and
late July to late August.*
AE/DI/MC/VI

10ème arrondissement
Brasserie Flo
(FF) ◆◆
7 cour Petites-Ecuries,
75010
Tel: 01 47 70 13 59
*Cheerful Alsatian brasserie
with authentic* fin-de-siècle
decor. Last orders 2 a.m.
AE/DI/MC/VI

11ème arrondissement
Astier (F) ◆
44 rue Jean-Pierre Timbaud,
75011
Tel: 01 43 57 16 35
*No hidden surprises in
Astier's copious, reasonable
menu. Try fantastic cheeses
at this friendly, unpretentious
local spot. Closed Saturday,
Sunday and spring holidays.*
MC/VI

14ème arrondissement
La Coupole
(FF) ◆◆
102 boulevard du
Montparnasse, 75014
Tel: 01 43 20 14 20
*Sensational 1930s decor,
gorgeous seafood and a
bustling atmosphere mark
this ever-popular Montpar-
nasse flagship of the Flo
group of brasseries. Ernest
Hemingway's ghost lurks.
Last orders 2 a.m.*
AE/DI/MC/VI

16ème arrondissement
La Butte Chaillot (FF) ◆
110 bis avenue Kléber,
75116
Tel: 01 47 27 88 88
*Guy Savoy's latest venue is
one of the smartest places
to eat in Paris.* AE/DI/MC/VI

Joel Robuchon (FFF) ◆◆◆◆
59 avenue R.-Poincaré,
75016
Tel: 01 47 27 12 27
*An art-nouveau setting
provides an elegant stage
for one of the world's
greatest living chefs. Book
well ahead for a gastro-
nomic tour de force. Last
orders 10:15 p.m. Closed
Saturday, Sunday, and early
July to early August.*
AE/DI/MC /VI

Lescure (F) ◆
7 rue Mondovi, 75001
Tel: 01 42 60 18 91
*Well-established, popular
bistro specializing in hearty
meat and game dishes. Last
orders 10:15 p.m. Closed
Saturday dinner, Sunday,
August and December.*
MC/VI

17ème arrondissement
Guy Savoy
(FFF) ◆◆◆◆
18 rue Troyon, 75017
Tel: 01 43 80 40 61
*This chef leads a busy life
overseeing three offspring
bistros, but this is the
original establishment. The
cusine on offer can often
create real fireworks. Last
orders 10:30 p.m. Closed
Saturday lunch, Sunday, and
July 13–19.* AE/MC/VI

Michel Rostang
(FFF) ◆◆◆◆
20 rue Rennequin, 75017
Tel: 01 47 63 40 77
*Quiet innovation on
traditional French country
cooking is the style of this
celebrated chef. View the
kitchen from the smaller
dining room. Last orders
10:15 p.m. Closed Saturday
lunch, Sunday, and August
1–16.* AE/DI/MC/VI

NORMANDY

CALVADOS

14000 Caen
La Bourride (FF–FFF) ◆◆◆
15 rue du Vaugueux
Tel: 02 31 93 50 76
Delightful timber-framed restaurant serving innovative Norman cuisine. Excellent cider and calvados. Last orders 9:45 p.m. Closed Sunday evening, Monday (except holidays), most of January, and last two weeks of August. AE/DI/MC/VI

14800 Deauville
Le Spinnaker (FF) ◆◆
52 rue Mirabeau
Tel: 02 31 88 24 40
Wonderful restaurant near the port – fish naturally takes a bow. Good value and pleasant service. Last orders 9:30 p.m. Closed Monday from September to June, Tuesday from November to Easter, November 11–18, and January. AE/MC/VI

14600 Honfleur
L'Assiette Gourmande (FF–FFF) ◆◆◆
quai Passagers
Tel: 02 31 89 24 88
An impressive restaurant in this pleasant seaside town. Typical meals include tartare de Saint-Jacques en vinaigrette de carotte. Last orders 10 p.m. Closed Sunday evening from November 15 to March 1, and Monday (except July and August). AE/DI/MC/VI

14230 Isigny-sur-Mer
Hôtel de France (F–FF) ◆◆
13 rue Émile Demagney
Tel: 02 31 22 00 33
Excellent-value meals served in the restaurant of this friendly small hotel set in a picturesque fishing port. Closed Wednesday evening and Saturday in winter (except public holidays), and mid-November to mid-February. AE/MC/VI

14360 Trouville
Le Clos Juillet (FF) ◆◆◆
22 boulevard 14 juillet
Tel: 02 25 73 31 32
Interesting restaurant whose specialties include gelée de queue de boeuf au foie gras. Last orders 10 p.m. Closed Sunday evening and Monday, August 13–25, and February 8–24. AE

EURE

27210 Beuzeville
Auberge du Cochon d'Or (FF) ◆◆◆
Le Petit Castel, place du Général-de-Gaulle
Tel: 02 32 57 70 46
Typically lavish use of local produce in this restaurant. Last orders 9 p.m. Rooms available. Closed Monday, and mid-December to mid-January. MC/VI

27620 Giverny
Les Jardins de Giverny (F–FF) ◆◆◆
Tel: 02 32 21 60 80
Seasonal produce, excellent wines, and a warm welcome in a fine Norman house and garden. Last orders 9 p.m. Closed Monday, February, November 1–15, and evening except Saturday. AE/MC/VI

27500 Pont-Audemer
Auberge de Vieux Puits (FF) ◆◆
6 rue Notre-Dame-du-Pré
Tel: 02 32 41 01 48
An attractive timber-framed property, formerly a 17th-century tannery. Ambience of copper and polished wood. Closed Monday, and December 20 to February 1. MC/VI

MANCHE

50400 Granville
La Gentilhommière (F) ◆◆
152 rue Couraye
Tel: 02 33 50 17 99
Accomplished classic dishes are served in a traditional old inn. Closed Sunday evening, Monday (except July and August), and March 2–19. MC/VI

ORNE

61000 Alençon
Au Petit Vatel (F) ◆◆◆
72 place Cdt.-Desmeulles
Tel: 02 33 26 23 78
Homemade ice cream makes a delicious afterthought here, but the appetizers are equally mouthwatering. Last orders 9:30 p.m. Closed Sunday evening, Wednesday, July 27 to August 16, and February vacation. AE/DI/MC/VI

SEINE-MARITIME

76200 Dieppe
La Marmite Dieppoise (FF) ◆◆
8 rue St.-Jean
Tel: 02 35 84 24 26
Named after a famous local seafood dish, this restaurant's specialty is a rich combination of fish and cream. Closed Sunday evening, Monday (except public holidays), Thursday evening in winter, and late November to early December. MC/VI

76000 Rouen
Gill (FFF) ◆◆◆◆
9 quai de la Bourse
Tel: 02 35 71 16 14
Some of Rouen's best cooking emanates from this waterfront establishment, including panaché de poissons *and lobster fricassee. Last orders 9:45 p.m. Closed Sunday (except lunch in winter), Monday, mid-April and in August. AE/DI/MC/VI*

BRITTANY

CÔTES D'ARMOR
22100 Dinan
Mère Pourcel (FF) ◆◆
3 place des Merciers
Tel: 02 96 39 03 80
Seasonal fare in a medieval building with beams and oak paneling. Last orders 10 p.m. Closed Sunday evening and Monday (except July and August), and February vacation. AE/DI/MC/VI

22430 Erquy
L'Escurial (F–FFF) ◆◆◆
boulevard de la Mer
Tel: 02 96 72 31 56
Sea views complement assured handling of local produce, especially Erquy's famous scallops. Last orders 9 p.m. Closed Sunday evening and Monday (except July and August), June 7–15, and November 22 to December 6. AE/MC/VI

29600 Morlaix
Marée Bleue (FF) ◆
3 rampe St.-Mélaine
Tel: 02 98 63 24 21
Good regional menu with fair prices in a stone and timber building near the viaduct. Last orders 10 p.m. Closed Sunday evening, Monday (except July and August), October 14–31, and February vacation. MC/VI

22500 Paimpol
La Vieille Tour (FFF) ◆◆
13 rue de l'Église
Tel: 02 96 20 83 18
Seafood accompanied by a Loire wine is a good choice at this friendly restaurant. Last orders 9 p.m. Closed Sunday evening, Monday lunch in July and August, and Wednesday in winter. AE/MC/VI

29930 Pont-Aven
Moulin de Rosmadec (FF) ◆◆◆
Tel: 02 98 06 00 22
One of Pont-Aven's last remaining water mills, carefully converted into a Breton style restaurant. Excellent welcome and service. Last orders 9:30 p.m. Rooms available. Closed Sunday evening (except mid-June to mid-September), Wednesday, February, and November 15–30. MC/VI

29000 Quimper
L'Ambroisie (FF) ◆◆
49 rue Elie Fréron
Tel: 02 98 95 00 02
Modern variations of classic cuisine in an attractive area near the town ramparts. Last orders 9:45 p.m. Closed Monday evening (except July and August), June 22 to July 4, and November 1. AE/MC/VI

35000 Rennes
Palais (FF) ◆◆◆
7 place du Parlement de Bretagne
Tel: 02 99 79 45 01
Great-value set menus at this adventurous restaurant near the law courts, where technique brings out the best in superb ingredients. Last orders 10 p.m. Closed Sunday evening and Monday. AE/DI/MC/VI

29680 Roscoff
Le Temps de Vivre (FF–FFF) ◆◆◆
place Église
Tel: 02 98 61 27 28
Overlooking the sea, this renowned restaurant offers imaginative seafood specialties. Last orders 9:15 p.m. Closed Sunday evening (except July and August), Monday, Tuesday lunch in July and August, October 1–21, and March 1–17. AE/MC/VI

ILLE-ET-VILAINE
35260 Cancale
Maison de Bricourt (FFF) ◆◆◆
1 rue Duguesclin
Tel: 02 99 89 64 76
Top billing for one of France's greatest provincial restaurants. Olivier Roellinger's cuisine is fresh and innovative, including many variations on Cancale's specialty – oysters. Elegant but relaxing surroundings overlooking the sea. Luxury hotel accommodations. Last orders 9:30 p.m. Closed Tuesday and Wednesday evening (except July and August), and mid-December to mid-March. AE/DI/MC/VI

35400 St.-Malo
A la Duchesse Anne (FF–FFF) ◆◆
5 place Guy La Chambre
Tel: 02 99 40 85 33

Popular restaurant by the town walls. Try grilled lobster. Last orders 10 p.m. Closed Sunday evening and Wednesday in winter, December, and January. MC/VI

35400 St.-Servan-sur-Mer
L'Atre (F) ◆
7 esplanade Cdt. Menguy, port Solidor
Tel: 02 99 81 68 39
Terrace tables and a river view add to the attractions of this small restaurant. Good crisp Muscadet. Closed Tuesday evening and Wednesday (except July and August), and mid-December to mid-January. AE/MC/VI

LOIRE-ATLANTIQUE
44500 La Baule
La Marcanderie (FF) ◆◆◆
5 avenue d'Agen
Tel: 02 40 24 03 12
Outside the town center, a sunny dining room accompanies generous, individual cooking and a good selection of Loire wines. Last orders 9:30 p.m. Closed Monday (except July and August), and Sunday evening. AE/MC/VI

44000 Nantes
Auberge du Chateau
(F) ◆◆
5 place Duchesse Anne
Tel: 02 40 74 31 85
Opposite the château, an unpretentious restaurant where the chef's imagination is unrestricted by modest prices. Last orders 9:30 p.m. Closed Sunday, Monday, August 2–24, and late December. MC/VI

La Cigale (F) ◆◆
4 place Graslin
Tel: 02 51 84 94 94

Superb fin-de-siècle brasserie (all mirrors and tiled mosaics), with tables outside to admire one of Nantes' finest squares. Good seafood and cakes served all day. Assured good service. Open daily until 12:30 a.m. MC/VI

MORBIHAN
56100 Lorient
L'Amphitryon
(FF) ◆◆◆
Quartier Keryado, 127 rue du Col.-Müller
Tel: 02 97 83 34 04
Adventure and skill mark the cooking here, tempting the palate with expertly balanced flavors – a good reason to visit Lorient. Closed Saturday lunch, Sunday, and August 25 to September 5. AE/MC/VI

56130 La Roche-Bernard
Auberge Bretonne
(FF–FFF) ◆◆◆◆
2 place Duguesclin
Tel: 02 99 90 60 28
Traditional home-grown and raised produce from the chef's own farm figure on the menu with many dazzling ideas. Rooms available. Last orders 9 p.m. Closed Thursday, Friday lunch, November 16 to December 6, and early January. AE/MC/VI

THE LOIRE VALLEY AND THE ATLANTIC COAST

CHARENTE
16000 Angoulême
La Ruelle (FF) ◆◆◆
6 rue Trois Notre-Dame
Tel: 05 45 95 15 19
A husband-and-wife team

(she cooks) operate this inventive restaurant in a restored old house with beams and stone walls. Good wine list. Last orders 10 p.m. Closed Saturday lunch, Sunday, most of August, and the third week of April. AE/DI/MC/VI

16100 Cognac
Les Pigeons Blancs
(FF) ◆◆◆
110 rue J.-Brisson
Tel: 05 45 82 16 36
This former post house is the present owner's ancestral home. Jacques prepares local produce while the rest of the family help with serving. Rooms available. Last orders 9 p.m. Closed Sunday evening. AE/DI/MC/VI

CHARENTE-MARITIME
17000 Île d'Oléron
Belle Cordière (F–FF) ◆◆
76 rue République
Tel: 05 46 76 12 87
Fresh fish perfectly served. Last orders 10 p.m. Closed Tuesday evening, Wednesday (except school vacations), March 15–30, and November 15 to December 15. AE/MC/VI

14000 La Rochelle
André (F) ◆
5 rue Saint-Jean-du-Perot
Tel: 05 46 41 28 24
Located at the base of ramparts with a terrace overlooking the port, this restaurant specializes in seafood and fruit de mer decor. AE/DI/MC/VI

Richard Coutanceau
(FF–FFF) ◆◆◆◆
plage de la Concurrence
Tel: 05 46 41 48 19
Celebrated seafood

restaurant on the seacoast. The chef-patron is keen, while his wife is an assured hostess. Exotic desserts complete a meal. Last orders 9:30 p.m. Closed Sunday. AE/DI/MC/VI

CHER
18000 Bourges
Le Jardin Gourmand
(F–FF) ◆◆◆
15 bis avenue E. Renan
Tel: 02 48 21 35 91
An elegant town house with a shady garden, offering well-balanced gourmet food. Last orders 9:30 p.m. Closed Sunday evening, Monday, mid-July, and mid-December to mid-January. AE/MC/VI

18300 Sancerre
La Tour (F–FF) ◆◆◆
Nouvelle Place
Tel: 02 48 54 00 81
Rustic dining room in a 14th-century building overlooking vineyards. Mostly fish, but plenty of other dishes too. There is a well-stocked Sancerre cellar. Open daily until 10 p.m. AE/MC/VI

GIRONDE
33120 Arcachon
Le Patio (F) ◆◆
10 boulevard de la Plage
Tel: 05 56 83 02 72
The verdant garden adds to the attractions here, as does its collection of champagnes. Last orders 10 p.m. (11 p.m. in summer). Closed Tuesday in winter, Monday and Tuesday lunch in July and August, late November, and late February. AE/MC/VI

33000 Bordeaux
Pavillon des Boulevards
(FF–FFF) ◆◆◆
120 rue Croix de Seguey

Tel: 05 56 81 51 02
Quality ingredients are served in this house set in attractive gardens. Though not cheap the set menus and wines offer good value. Last orders 9 p.m. Closed Sunday, Saturday lunch, mid-August and early January. AE/DI/MC/VI

La Tupina (FF) ◆◆
6 rue Porte de la Monnaie
Tel: 05 56 91 56 37
Hearty cooking from the southwest characterizes this restaurant where log fires blaze in winter. Last orders 11 p.m. Closed Sunday and public holidays. AE/DI/MC/VI

33330 St.-Emilion
Francis Goullée
(FF) ◆◆
rue Guadet
Tel: 05 57 24 70 49
Modestly priced menus feature southwestern cooking (poultry, game and foie gras). Last orders 9:30 p.m. Closed Sunday evening, Monday from October to March, and November 23 to December 10. MC/VI

INDRE-ET-LOIRE
37400 Amboise
Le Manoir St.-Thomas
(FF) ◆◆◆
place Richelieu
Tel: 02 47 57 22 52
Grand furnishings set the tone for lavish traditional dishes. Good cheeses and Loire wines. Last orders 9:30 p.m. Closed Monday, and mid-January to mid-March. AE/DI/MC/VI

37100 Tours
Charles Barrier
(FF–FFF) ◆◆◆
101 avenue de la Tranchée

Tel: 02 47 54 20 39
Tried-and-true specialties from this famous kitchen. Grand surroundings. One menu at least is affordable. Last orders 10 p.m. Closed Sunday evening. AE/MC/VI

LANDES
40320 Eugénie-les Bains
Les Prés d'Eugénie
(FFF) ◆◆◆
Tel: 05 58 05 06 07
The king of cuisine minceur, Michel Guérard, presides here in a sumptuously tasteful 19th-century convent set in a park, now a luxury hotel. The elegance will make you gasp. Last orders 10:15 p.m. Closed Wednesday (except July 12 to September 4 and public holidays), Thursday lunch, January, February 27, and December 1–17. AE/DI/MC/VI

LOIR-ET-CHER
41000 Blois
Rendez-vous des Pêcheurs
(F) ◆◆
27 rue de Foix
Tel: 02 54 74 67 48
The fish comes fresh each morning from the Loire or the ocean and is enthusiastically converted into a delicious and inexpensive daily menu. Unpretentious but efficient service. Open until 10 p.m. Closed Sunday, Monday lunch, public holidays, most of August, and February vacation. AE/MC/VI

41250 Bracieux
Bernard Robin
(FF–FFF) ◆◆◆◆
1 avenue de Chambord
Tel: 02 56 46 41 22
Excellent cooking in an immaculately kept inn.

Superb wines and cheeses. Last orders 9 p.m. Closed Tuesday evening, Wednesday (except July and August), and December 20 to January 20. AE/MC/VI

LOIRET
45000 Orleans
Les Antiquaires (FF) ◆◆◆
2 rue au Lin
Tel: 02 38 53 52 35
Fine classic cooking using seasonal produce. Good cellar includes half bottles. Last orders 9:30 p.m. Closed Sunday, Monday and August 2–24. AE/DI/MC/VI

MAINE-ET-LOIRE
49100 Angers
Le Toussaint (F) ◆◆◆
7 place Kennedy
Tel: 02 41 87 46 20
Despite the fine château views this attractive place neither overcharges nor underfeeds its customers. Good range of claret. Last orders 9:30 p.m. (10 p.m. in summer). Closed Sunday evening, Monday and February vacation. AE/MC/VI

49590 Fontrevaud-l'Abbaye
La Licorne (F–FF) ◆◆◆
allée Sainte-Catherine
Tel: 02 41 51 72 49
Elegant surroundings (18th-century building with court-yard) complement the cooking that includes ingredients such as oysters. Anjou and Touraine wines. Last orders 9 p.m. Closed Sunday evening, Monday in winter, and December to mid-January. AE/DI/MC/VI

49400 Saumur
Les Délices du Château
(FF) ◆◆◆
cour du château

Tel: 02 41 67 65 60
Country cooking with a light touch and a choice of excellent wines. Admire the château gardens from the terrace. Last orders 10 p.m. Closed Sunday evening in winter, and December. AE/DI/MC/VI

NIÈVRE
58000 Nevers
Les Jardins de la Porte du Croux
(F) ◆◆◆
17 rue Porte du Croux
Tel: 03 86 57 12 71
Enjoy rampart views from the flowery terrace while sampling offbeat specialties like bleakfish or calf's head. Last orders 10 p.m. Closed Sunday evening, Monday in winter, and January. AE/MC/VI

PYRÉNÉES-ATLANTIQUE
64200 Biarritz
Les Platanes
(FF) ◆◆
32 avenue Beausoleil
Tel: 05 59 23 13 68
After scouring local markets for the freshest produce chef Arnaud Daguin assembles menus of great originality. Friendly atmosphere. Last orders 10 p.m. Closed Monday, Tuesday lunch and mid-January. AE/MC/VI

64310 Sare
Arraya (FF) ◆◆
Tel: 05 59 54 20 46
This beautiful old Basque village house is exquisitely furnished and maintained. Pleasant small garden, sophisticated atmosphere, and a good choice of regional dishes. Rooms available. Closed Monday lunch in winter (except public holidays). AE/MC/VI

SARTHE
72000 Le Mans
Hippolyte (F) ◆◆
12 rue H. Lecornué
Tel: 02 43 87 51 00
An early 20th-century style brasserie, always bustling with diners eager to try its good-value cooking. Terrace tables. Open daily until 11:30 p.m. MC/VI

VIENNE
86000 Poitiers
Maxime (F–FF) ◆◆◆
4 rue St.-Nicolas
Tel: 05 49 41 09 55
A husband-and-wife team who offer sophisticated regional cuisine and excellent wines. Last orders 10 p.m. Closed Saturday, Sunday, mid-July and mid-August. AE/MC/VI

THE DORDOGNE

DORDOGNE
24100 Bergerac
Le Cyrano (F–FF) ◆◆
2 boulevard Montaigne
Tel: 05 53 57 02 76
Good value in this spacious stone house. Try Monbazillac with an iced nougat soufflé. Last orders 9 p.m. Closed Saturday lunch, Sunday (except public holidays), and December 20–29. AE/DI/MC/VI

24310 Brantôme
Moulin de l'Abbaye
(FF) ◆◆◆
1 route de Bourdeilles
Tel: 05 53 05 80 22
Brantôme is a celebrated eating place and this old water mill with gardens makes a relaxing setting to enjoy regional specialties. If your budget cannot stretch

try the bistro annex across the river (Le Fil d'Eau). Last orders 10 p.m. Closed Monday lunch. AE/DI/MC/VI

24250 Domme
L'Esplanade (FF) ◆◆
Tel: 05 53 28 31 41
The Dordogne Valley views alone would be worth a pilgrimage to this famous hotel-restaurant, but the food is also good and prices are affordable. Last orders 9 p.m. Closed Monday from February 16 to late June. AE/DI/MC/VI

24620 Les Eyzies-de-Tayac
Cro-Magnon (FF) ◆◆
Tel: 05 53 06 97 06
Welcoming staff make dining here even more enjoyable. Vines, beams and log fires add to the ambience. Hotel rooms available. Last orders 9 p.m. Closed Wednesday lunch. AE/DI/MC/VI

24000 Périgueux
Restaurant L'Oison (FF) ◆◆
31 rue St.-Front
Tel: 05 53 03 53 59
Within the Château des Reynats. The local vegetables complement the seafood, but there are other dishes too and excellent regional wines. Last orders 9:30 p.m. Closed Monday (except evening in summer), and Tuesday lunch in winter. AE/DI/MC/VI

24250 La Roque-Gageac
La Plume d'Oie (FF–FFF) ◆◆
Tel: 05 53 29 57 05
This idyllic riverside village attracts many visitors. Sample the light, fresh cooking. Rooms available. Last orders 9:30 p.m.

Closed Tuesday lunch and Monday (except July and August), January 15 to early March, lunch in July and August (except Sunday), and November 20 to December 20. MC/VI

HAUTE-VIENNE
87000 Limoges
Philippe Redon (FF) ◆◆◆
3 rue d'Aguesseau
Tel: 05 55 34 66 22
First-class local produce combined in classic dishes with precise skill. 1930s decor. Good value. Last orders 9 p.m. Closed Sunday, Monday lunch, early January and early August. AE/DI/MC/VI

LOT
46000 Cahors
Le Balandre (FF) ◆◆
5 avenue Château de Freycinet
Tel: 05 65 30 01 97
Robust southwestern flavors are generously served in this attractive fin-de-siècle dining room in a hotel. Splendid local wines. Last orders 9:30 p.m. Closed Sunday evening and Monday in winter. AE/MC/VI

46200 Lacave
Château de la Treyne (FFF) ◆◆
3 km w. on D43
Tel: 05 65 27 60 60
Set in fine grounds, this magnificent château dominates a bend of the Dordogne. It is now a grand hotel and impressive restaurant, but prices are not outrageous. Excellent service. Last orders 10 p.m. Closed Tuesday lunch and Wednesday lunch (except July and August). AE/DI/MC/VI

46500 Rocamadour
Beau Site Jehan de Valon (F–FF) ◆◆
rue R.-le-Preux
Tel: 05 65 33 63 08
Lamb and duck's liver and excellent ice cream stand out at this established restaurant. Very good service and wine cellar. Last orders 9 p.m (10 p.m. in summer). Closed mid-November to early February. AE/DI/MC/VI

46330 St.-Cirq-Lapopie
Auberge du Sombral "Aux Bonnes Choses" (F–FF) ◆◆
Tel: 05 65 31 26 08
The simple restaurant at this rustic inn provides a good reason to linger in one of the region's prettiest villages. Last orders 9:30 p.m. Closed Tuesday evening and Wednesday (except July to September 15), and mid-November to March 31. MC/VI

LOT-ET-GARONNE
47300 Villeneuve-sur-Lot
La Toque Blanche (FFF) ◆◆◆
Pujols, 4 km sw.
Tel: 05 53 49 00 30
Highly respected chef offering imaginative cooking amid spectacular views. Good set lunch but à la carte comes at a hefty price. Closed Sunday evening, Monday, June 22 to July 6, and November 23–30. AE/DI/MC/VI

TARN
81000 Albi
Moulin de la Mothe (F–FF) ◆◆◆
rue de la Mothe
Tel: 05 63 60 38 15
A lovely waterfront location enhances traditional dishes

prepared with the best local produce. Good-value wines. Last orders 9:30 p.m. Closed Sunday evening, Wednesday (except July and August) and November 1. AE/DI/MC/VI

THE PYRÉNÉES

AUDE
11000 Carcassonne
Château St.-Martin
"Trencavel" (FF) ♦♦♦
Montredon, 4 km ne.
Tel: 04 68 71 09 53
Artful, powerful cooking using regional ingredients and the best local wines. All this in a lovely setting and garden. Last orders 9:30 p.m. Closed Wednesday. AE/DI/MC/VI

HAUTE-GARONNE
31000 Toulouse
Les Jardins de l'Opéra
(FFF) ♦♦♦♦
1 place du Capitole
Tel: 05 61 23 07 76
Decor is a sensation with glass ceilings and opulent flower arrangements. But so is the food in this centrally located restaurant, one of the city's best. Last orders 10 p.m. Closed Sunday, public holidays, January and August. AE/DI/MC/VI

HAUTES-PYRÉNÉES
65400 Argelès-Gazost
Le Viscos (FF) ♦♦
St.-Savin, 3 km s. on D101
Tel: 05 62 97 02 28
Named after a local mountain, this attractively located auberge also has rooms available. Enjoy dining on the terrace beside the river in summer. Last orders 9:30 p.m. Closed Monday (except school

vacations) and December. AE/MC/VI

65000 Tarbes
L'Ambroisie (F) ♦♦
38 rue Larrey
Tel: 05 62 93 09 34
This pretty place near the covered market offers exquisite local produce. An inexpensive but quality set menu. Last orders 9 p.m. Closed Sunday, Monday and public holidays. MC/VI

PYRÉNÉES-ATLANTIQUES
64000 Pau
Le Viking (FF) ♦♦
33 boulevard Tourasse
Tel: 05 59 84 02 91
Scarcely advertised yet people flock to taste this sparkling cuisine with influences of Normandy and the Loire. Last orders 9 p.m. Closed Saturday, Sunday, public holidays, February vacation, and July 14 to August 15. AE/MC/VI

64220 St.-Jean-Pied-de-Port
Pyrénées (FFF) ♦♦♦
19 place Charles de Gaulle
Tel: 05 59 37 01 01
Reliable and ambitious cooking attracts customers from both sides of the border to this attractive hotel-restaurant. Last orders 9 p.m. Closed Monday evening from November to March, Tuesday (except July and August), and late November to late January (except December 23 to January 5). AE/MC/VI

PYRÉNÉES-ORIENTALES
66400 Céret
Les Feuillants
(FF) ♦♦♦
1 boulevard La Fayette
Tel: 04 68 87 37 88

Celebrated but unstuffy Catalan cooking in a fine belle-époque villa. Excellent local wines. A cheaper brasserie and attractive hotel rooms, too. Last orders 10 p.m. Closed Monday (except evening in July and August), and Sunday evening. AE/MC/VI

PROVENCE AND THE CÔTE D'AZUR

ALPES-MARITIMES
06600 Antibes
Les Vieux Murs (FF) ♦♦♦
promenade Amiral de Grasse
Tel: 04 93 34 06 73
True to its name, the old city walls can be seen from the dining room, but the pleasant welcome and food are the main attractions. Last orders 10:30 p.m. (11 p.m. in summer). Closed Monday from October to March. AE/MC/VI

06310 Beaulieu-sur-Mer
Le Maxilien (FFF) ♦♦♦
boulevard Marinoni
Tel: 04 93 01 47 48
Seafood on the terrace is an appealing thought here but there are plenty of other attactions, including the desserts. Last orders 10:30 p.m. Closed Monday, Tuesday lunch and Thursday lunch from June to September, February vacation, and November 1. AE/DI/MC/VI

06400 Cannes
Côté Jardin (FF) ♦♦
12 avenue St.-Louis
Tel: 04 93 38 60 28
In a city full of overblown

restaurants, this unpretentious establishment is a breath of fresh air. Try the garden in summer. Last orders 9:45 p.m. Closed Sunday, Monday (except evening from May to mid-September), and February 1 to early March. AE/MC/VI

06600 Cap-d'Antibes
Bacon (FFF) ◆◆◆◆
boulevard de Bacon
Tel: 04 93 61 50 02
This renowned restaurant in a ritzy enclave of the Côte d'Azur is a good place to try bouillabaisse. Elegant surroundings and wonderful views. Last orders 9 p.m. Closed Monday (except evening in July and August), and November 1 to January 31. AE/DI/MC/VI

06360 Èze
Richard Borfiga
(FF) ◆◆◆
place Général de Gaulle
Tel: 04 93 41 05 23
The more famous establishments in this hill village may steal the limelight but you're just as likely to find a table here with excellent cooking and a fine view. Last orders 10 p.m. Closed Monday, Tuesday lunch and January. AE/DI/MC/VI

06000 Nice
Don Camillo (FF) ◆◆◆
5 rue des Ponchettes
Tel: 04 93 85 67 95
Small and simple with some of the best local dishes in the old town. Raviolis, cheeses and puddings are particularly good. Closed Monday lunch and Sunday. AE/MC/VI

La Toque Blanche (FF) ◆◆
40 rue de la Buffa

Tel: 04 93 88 38 18
Nice has dozens of good restaurants. This is not one of the most famous but fresh fish, a pretty dining room, a charming welcome and fair prices make a good combination. Last orders 9:30 p.m. Closed Sunday (except lunch from September to June) and Monday. MC/VI

BOUCHES-DU-RHÔNE
13100 Aix-en-Provence
Le Clos de la Violette
(FFF) ◆◆◆
10 avenue de la Violette
Tel: 04 42 23 30 71
Provençal flavors permeate the inventive menu of this famous restaurant. Last orders 9:30 p.m. Closed Sunday (except evening in July), Monday lunch and early November. AE/MC/VI

13200 Arles
L'Olivier (FF) ◆◆◆
1 bis rue Réattu
Tel: 04 90 49 64 88
A courtyard and olive-branch motifs provide a relaxing setting to enjoy this chef's southern style. Last orders 9:15 p.m. Closed Sunday and Monday. MC/VI

13520 Les Baux
La Riboto de Taven
(FFF) ◆◆◆
Val d'Enfer
Tel: 04 90 54 34 23
This striking hill village is a mecca for any visitor to Provence. One of several excellent restaurants, La Riboto is a flower-decked manor offering classic but light cuisine. Hotel rooms also available. Last orders 10 p.m. Closed Tuesday evening in winter, Wednesday, and early

January to early March. AE/DI/MC/VI

13260 Cassis
La Presqu'Ile
(FF) ◆◆◆
route de Port-Miou, Les Calanques
Tel: 04 42 01 03 77
A waterside setting with distinctive flavors of Provençal cooking. Expensive wines. Last orders 10 p.m. Closed Sunday evening (except June to August), Monday, and November 1 to February 28. AE/DI/MC/VI

13002 Marseille
Miramar
(FFF) ◆◆◆
12 quai du Port
Tel: 04 91 91 10 40
Skillful preparation of local seafood. Last orders 10 p.m. Closed Sunday and August. AE/DI/MC/VI

HÉRAULT
34000 Montpellier
Le Jardin des Sens
(FFF) ◆◆◆◆
11 avenue St.-Lazare
Tel: 04 67 79 63 38
Highly skilled and ambitious cooking in a modern setting. Local wines. Last orders 10 p.m. Closed mid-January. AE/DI/MC/VI

MONACO
Monte-Carlo
Café de Paris
(FF) ◆◆
place du Casino
Tel: (00 377) 92 16 20 20
Belle-époque brasserie by the Casino, with a sunny terrace. An upbeat range of seafood and herb-flavored meat, but you can always just enjoy a drink if you prefer. Open daily until 4 a.m. AE/DI/MC/VI

RESTAURANTS

PYRÉNÉES-ORIENTALES
66000 Perpignan
La Passerelle (FF) ♦♦
1 cours Palmarole
Tel: 04 68 51 30 65
Minimally adorned fresh fish is the forté of this attractive bistro. Last orders 9:45 p.m. Closed Monday lunch and Sunday. AE/MC/VI

VAR
83600 Fréjus
Les Potiers (F–FF) ♦
135 rue Potiers
Tel: 04 94 51 33 74
Warm service and a menu offering good value. A good place to relax after sightseeing. Last orders 10 p.m. Closed Tuesday and early December. AE/MC/VI

83700 St.-Raphaël
L'Arbousier (FF) ♦♦♦
6 avenue de Valescure
Tel: 04 94 95 25 00
Vivid southern flavors combine miraculously in this pretty restaurant, one of St.-Raphaël's best and most welcoming. Last orders 10 p.m. Closed Sunday evening, Monday, Tuesday, Wednesday in winter, Wednesday lunch in summer, and December 21 to January 5. AE/MC/VI

VAUCLUSE
84000 Avignon
Hiély-Lucullus (FF) ♦♦♦
5 rue République
Tel: 04 90 86 17 07
This gastronomic benchmark has an awesome reputation. The stately dining room glides smoothly along as it has for over 60 years. Last orders 9:45 p.m. Closed Monday, Tuesday lunch (except July to September), June 22 to July 6, and late January. MC/VI

84100 Orange
Le Parvis (F) ♦♦
3 cours Pourtoules
Tel: 04 90 34 82 00
Some find the dining room austere, but there is nothing cold about the welcome here and the food will not disappoint. Good value. Last orders 9:30 p.m. Closed Sunday evening, Monday (except July to August), late January, and November. AE/DI/MC/VI

84110 Vaison-la-Romaine
Le Bateleur (F) ♦
1 place Th. Aubanel
Tel: 04 90 36 28 04
Tasty regional dishes such as almond-stuffed lamb are served in this attractive flower-filled restaurant. Last orders 9 p.m. Closed Sunday evening, Monday, late June, and November 15 to December 15. MC/VI

THE MASSIF CENTRAL

ALLIER
03200 Vichy
L'Alambic (FF) ♦♦
8 rue N. Larbaud
Tel: 04 70 59 12 71
One of the most accomplished restaurants in Vichy, with a set menu and wine list offering good value. Last orders 10 p.m. Closed Monday, Tuesday lunch (except public holidays), August 23 to September 9, and February 21 to March 9. MC/VI

PUY-DE-DÔME
63000 Clermont-Ferrand
Jean-Yves Bath (FF–FFF) ♦♦♦
place Marché-St.-Pierre
Tel: 04 73 31 23 23
Innovative cuisine is the hallmark of this highly respected restaurant. The decor is equally avant-garde. Last orders 10 p.m. Closed Sunday, Monday, public holidays, February vacation and early September. AE/MC/VI

THE ALPS AND THE RHÔNE VALLEY

DRÔME
26400 Crest
Grand Hôtel (F) ♦
60 rue de Hôtel de Ville
Tel: 04 75 25 08 17
Simple family-run establishment located in the center of a small medieval village. Popular and good-value restuarant in a fine 19th-century building, serving a choice of specialties from the region. Closed Monday evening, Wednesday and February vacation. MC/VI

HAUTE-SAVOIE
74940 Annecy
Le Clos des Sens (FF) ♦♦♦
13 rue J. Mermoz
Tel: 04 50 23 07 90
Accolades are piling up for this imaginative restaurant in the old town. Good wine list. Last orders 10 p.m. Closed Sunday evening and Monday (except July to August), and early September. AE/DI/MC/VI

74400 Chamonix-M.-Blanc
Atmosphère (F) ♦♦
123 place Balmat
Tel: 04 50 55 97 97
In this ski resort you might not expect to find such a surprisingly inexpensive set menu – and with views of

Mont Blanc too. Occasional
live music. Open daily until
11 p.m. AE/DI/MC/VI

74500 Évian-les-Bains
La Toque Royale
(FFF) ◆◆◆◆
Casino Royal
Tel: 04 50 26 87 10
*Console yourself with a
meal here if you have had
bad luck at the tables.
Inventive modern cooking
combines with local
specialties, including fresh
fish. Last orders 10:30 p.m.
Closed Sunday and most of
January. AE/DI/MC/VI*

74120 Megève
Michel Gaudin (F) ◆◆
carrefour d'Arly
Tel: 04 50 21 02 18
*One of the offerings at this
popular ski resort. The rustic
ambience may be simple
but the cooking and set
menus are assured. Last
orders 10:30 p.m. Closed
Monday and Tuesday in
winter. MC/VI*

74200 Thonon-les-Bains
Le Prieuré (FF) ◆◆◆
68 Grande rue
Tel: 04 50 71 31 89
*Elegant and pricey food is
served here, but the quality
is impeccable. Last orders
10:30 p.m. Closed Sunday
evening and Monday.
AE/DI/MC/VI*

ISÈRE
38000 Grenoble
A ma Table (FF) ◆◆
92 cours Jean-Jaurès
Tel: 04 76 96 77 04
*Intimate restaurant with a
warm welcome and well-
crafted cooking. Last orders
9:15 p.m. Closed Saturday
lunch, Sunday, Monday and
August. MC/VI*

SAVOIE
73100 Aix-les-Bains
Lille (FF) ◆◆◆
Le Grand Port
Tel: 04 79 63 40 00
*A family-run lakeside
establishment providing
comfortable hospitality and
good fish dishes. Last
orders 9:30 p.m. Closed
Tuesday evening and
Wednesday (except July
and August). AE/DI/MC/VI*

73000 Chambéry
L'Essentiel (FF) ◆◆◆
183 place de la Gare
Tel: 04 79 96 97 27
*Assured cooking in a floral-
decorated dining room.
Local ingredients such as
polenta and lake fish are
skillfully combined. Last
orders 10:30 p.m. Closed
Saturday lunch and Sunday
in July and August, and
Monday (except July and
August). AE/MC/VI*

BURGUNDY, ALSACE-LORRAINE AND THE NORTH

BAS-RHIN
67000 Strasbourg
Buerehiesel (FFF) ◆◆◆◆
4 parc de l'Orangerie
Tel: 03 88 45 56 65
*This farm building
reassembled in Strasbourg
is a great attraction. So, too,
is the food. Last orders
9:30 p.m. Closed Tuesday,
Wednesday, February
vacation, August, and late
December to early January.
AE/DI/MC/VI*

Maison Kammerzell
(FF) ◆◆◆
16 place de la Cathédrale

Tel: 03 88 32 42 14
*A delight for visitors, this
beautiful medieval building
by the cathedral also has
gained a local following for
its competent Alsatian
cooking. Rooms available.
Last orders 11:30 p.m.
Closed February 17 to
March 10. AE/DI/MC/VI*

CÔTE D'OR
21200 Beaune
Le Jardin des Remparts
(FFF) ◆◆◆◆
10 rue Hôtel-Dieu
Tel: 03 80 24 79 41
*A delightful garden adds to
the attractions of this
restaurant in the heart of
historic Beaune. The
seafood is very good and
there is a well-stocked
cellar. Last orders 9:45 p.m.
Closed Sunday and Monday
(except public holidays),
mid-February to mid-March,
and early August. MC/VI*

21000 Dijon
Le Pré au Clercs
(FFF) ◆◆
13 place Libération
Tel: 03 80 38 05 05
*Excellent cuisine from
praiseworthy chef Jean-
Pierre Billoux. Try paillasson
langoustines or terrine de
pigeon à l'ail confit. Last
orders 9:30 p.m. Closed
Sunday evening and
Monday. AE/MC/VI*

DOUBS
25000 Besançon
Mungo Park
(FF) ◆◆◆
11 rue Jean Petit
Tel: 03 81 81 28 01
*Well worth discovering.
Acclaimed as one of the
region's best restaurants, it
is also one of the most
welcoming. Last orders*

RESTAURANTS

9:30 p.m. Closed Sunday, Monday lunch, early August and February vacation. AE/MC/VI

HAUTE-MARNE
52200 Langres
Grand Hôtel de l'Europe
(F) ◆◆
23 rue Diderot
Tel: 03 25 87 10 88
The restaurant in this traditional hotel in the town center offers generous servings of local cuisine. Closed Sunday evening and Monday evening from November to April. MC/VI

HAUT-RHIN
68650 Lapoutroie
Les Alisiers (F–FF) ◆◆
Tel: 03 89 47 52 82
Converted hilltop farmhouse with small cozy rooms, a restaurant offering robust cooking, and panoramic views. Closed Monday evening and Tuesday. MC/VI

JURA
39100 Dole
Les Templiers (FF) ◆◆◆
35 Grande rue
Tel: 03 84 82 78 78
Jura specialties appear on the menu including the local curiosity vin jaune. Elegant Louis XIII decor. Last orders 10 p.m. Closed Sunday evening and early January. AE/DI/MC/VI

MARNE
51460 L'Épine
Aux Armes de Champagne
(FF) ◆◆
place de la Basilique
Tel: 03 26 69 30 30
A welcoming restaurant with an informal atmosphere and a wide selection of delicately

flavored regional dishes, including Pigeonneau roti cocotte. Closed early January to mid-February, and Sunday evening and Monday from November to March. AE/DI/MC/VI

51100 Reims
Boyer "Les Crayères"
(FFF) ◆◆◆
64 boulevard H.-Vasnier
Tel: 03 26 82 80 80
One of the great restaurants of the Champagne region, this pillar of the gastronomic establishment has lost none of its innovative edge and individuality. Both the château-hotel and the restaurant are charming and comfortable though very grand. Last orders 10:30 p.m. Closed Tuesday lunch and Monday. AE/DI/MC/VI

51400 Sept–Saulx
Le Cheval Blanc
(FF) ◆◆
Tel: 03 26 03 90 27
A rustic inn set in a peaceful village, offering a traditional and wholesome menu. Closed mid-January to mid-February. AE/DI/MC/VI

NORD
59800 Lille
A L'Huîtrière (FFF) ◆◆◆◆
3 rue Chats Bossus
Tel: 03 20 55 43 41
This elegant restaurant serves mainly seafood and is set in an old store that once sold fish. Last orders 9:30 p.m. Closed Sunday evening, in the evening on public holidays, and July 20 to August 20. AE/DI/MC/VI

PAS-DE-CALAIS
62200 Boulogne-sur-Mer
La Matelote (FF) ◆◆◆

80 boulevard Ste.-Beuve
Tel: 03 21 30 17 97
A first-class restaurant in a rather plain town. Try salade de homard tiède. Last orders 9:30 p.m. Closed Sunday evening (except July and August), public holidays, and December 24 to January 10. AE/MC/VI

62100 Calais
Le Channel (FF) ◆◆
3 boulevard de la Résistance
Tel: 03 21 34 42 30
Spacious waterfront restaurant offering all types of fish dishes to tempt travelers as their first or last taste of France. Open until 10:30 p.m. Closed Sunday evening (except public holidays), Tuesday, and July 23 to August 6. AE/DI/MC/VI

SAONE-ET-LOIRE
71000 Mâcon
Le Saint-Laurent (F–FF) ◆
1 quai Bouchacourt
Tel: 03 85 39 29 19
Old-town views across the river at night and a bistro setting for spectacular cooking. Last orders 10 p.m. Closed mid-November to mid-December. AE/DI/MC/VI

SOMME
80000 Amiens
La Couronne (F) ◆◆
64 rue St.-Leu
Tel: 03 22 91 88 57
An attractive venue in the St.-Leu quarter offering classic presentations of fresh produce. Set menus are good value. Last orders 9:30 p.m. Closed Saturday, Sunday evening, mid-July to mid-August, and early January. MC/VI ·

INDEX

A

Aber Wrac'h 76, 77
abers 76, 77
Abîme de Bramabiau 207
Abriès 227
Académie Française 24
accommodations 272
Aigoual, Massif de l' 207
Aiguille du Belvédère 218
Aiguille, Mont 214
Aiguilles 227
Aiguilles de Chamonix 216, 217
Ailefroide 219, 227
Ain, Gorges de l' 232
Ain Valley 232
airlines and airports 259, 269
Aix-en-Provence 172
Aix-les-Bains 213, 214, 223
Albâtre, Côte d' 54, 59
Albert 252
Albi 12, 132
Alençon 55
Alise-Sainte-Reine 231, 237
Allassac 132
Allauch 171
Allier, Gorges de l' 201
L'Alpe d'Huez 224, 226
Alps and the Rhône Valley 211-28
Alsace Ecomuseum 247
Alsace-Lorraine see Burgundy, Alsace-Lorraine and the North
Alsace wines 8-9
Ambert 206
Amboise 98, 116
Amiens 232, 233, 244
Ancy-le-Franc, Château d' 233
Andaines, Forêt des 56
Les Andelys 54, 55
Andorra 153, 154
Anet, Château d' 55
Angers 98, 99, 110
Anglet 152
Angoulême 99
Anjony, Château d' 198, 199
Annecy 214, 223
Annecy, Lac d' 213, 214-15
Antibes 172, 179
apartments and villas 272
Apt 184
Aquarium 24
Arago, François 188
Arbois 9, 233
Arc-et-Senans 234
Arc de Triomphe 24
Arc Valley 225, 228
Arcachon 98, 100
Les Arcs 224
Ardèche, Gorges de 202
Ardennes 234
Arènes 188
Argent, Côte d' 99-100
Argentan 55
Argentat 132-3
Argentière 216, 217
Argol 80
Arles 170, 172-3, 190
Arles-sur-Tech 154-5
Armorique, Parc Naturel Régional d' 87, 89
Arques-la-Bataille 55
Arras 234
Arreau 155
Arromanches-les-Bains 56, 64

art and architecture 12-13, 66
art galleries in Paris 25
art nouveau movement 247
Arthurian myth 86
Arvais, Chaîne des 215
Arz, Ile d' 88
Ascain 152
Aspe, Vallée d' 166
Assy, Plateau d' 216
Astérix, Parc 42, 273-4
ateliers (studios) 37
ATM's 277
Aubazine 131
Aubigny-sur-Nère 100
Aubusson 133, 134
Augirein 159
Aulnay 100
Aure Valley 155
Aurignac 155
Aurillac 198-9, 207
Aussois 225, 228
Autimobile Museum 247
Autoroute du Soleil 214
Autun 234
Auvergne 197
Auxerre 231, 234
Avallon 234
Aven Armand 200, 207
Avérole Valley 225
Avignon 170, 173-4
Avioth Basilica 235
Avranches 56
Avrieux 225
Azay-le-Rideau, Château de 100-1

B

Bagnères-de-Bigorre 160
Bagnères-de-Luchon 161
Bagnoles de l'Orne 56, 66
Baker, Josephine 140
Balleroy, Château 56
Ballon d'Alsace 235
Balzac, Honoré de 35, 120
banks 279
Banyuls-sur-Mer 177
Bar le Duc 235
Barcelonnette 216
Bardot, Brigitte 191
Barèges 163
Barenton 66
Barfleur 57, 59
Barnenez Tumulus 79
Barneville-Carteret 57, 66
Barrage de Grandval 202
Barrage de Sarrans 202
Barre des Écrins 219
Le Barroux 194
Basque country 153, 156
Basque cuisine 157
bastides 145
La Bastille 25
Batailley, Château 103
bateaux mouches 46
battlefields and war cemeteries 252
Batz, Ile de 92
Batz-sur-Mer 76
Baugé 101
La Baule 76-7
Les Baux 174
Bayeux 57, 64
Bayeux Tapestry 57
Bayonne 152, 156
Beardsley, Aubrey 185
Beaubourg 25, 38
Le Beaucet 171
Beaufortain 224
Beaugency 101-2
Beaulieu-sur-Dordogne 134
Beaulieu-sur-Mer 174
Beaulieu-en-Rouergue 131

Beaumes-de-Venise 194
Beaumont-Hamel 252
Beaune 232, 235
Beauport Abbey 93
Beauregard, Château de 102
bed and breakfast, guesthouses 272
Belfort 235, 236
Belle-Ile 77
Belleville 25
Belvédère du Cirque 227
Bennecourt 62
La Bérarde 219
Bercy 26
Bergerac 134, 140
Les Bergeries 218
Bergues 236
Berlioz, Hector 190
Besançon 236-7
Bessans 225
Besse-en-Chandesse 199, 206
Bétharram, Grottes de 156-7, 162
Bethmale Valley 159
Beynac-et-Cazenac 134, 135
Béziers 174
Biarritz 102, 152, 154, 156
Bibliothèque Humaniste 251
Bibliothèque Nationale 26
bicycle rental 266
Bigorre 157
Binic 93
Biot 174-5
Biron, Château de 134
Blanc, Lac 218
Blanc, Mont 4, 212, 214, 217
Blassac 201
Blériot, Louis 248
Blois 102-3, 118
bocage 57
Bois de Boulogne 26-7
Bois de Vincennes 26-7
Bonaguil, Château de 131, 135
Bonnard, Pierre 190, 216
Bonneval 225, 228
Bordeaux 10, 98, 103, 104
Bort, Lac de 199
Bort-les-Orgues 199
Boscodon, Forêt de 227
Boudin, Eugene 63
boulevard St. Michel 27
Boulogne-sur-Mer 236, 237
Boumois, Château de 103
La Bourboule 199, 205
Bourdeilles 135
Bourdouze, Lac de 199
Bourg-en-Bresse 237
Bourg-St.-Maurice 224
Bourges 103-4
Bourget, Lac du 217
La Bourse 27
Bouziès 143
Bracieux 125
Brantôme 136
Braque, Georges 72, 216
Brèche de Roland 157
Brélévenez 87
Bresse 237
Brest 74, 77
Breton corsairs 92
Briançon 213, 217
Bricquebec 59
Brinon-sur-Sauldre 125
Brioude 201
Brissac, Château de 104
Brittany 73-94
Brou 237
Burgess, Anthony 179
Burgundy 9, 232

Burgundy, Alsace-Lorraine and the North 229-56
bus services 259, 269-70
Bussy-Rabutin, Château de 237

C

Cabinet des Médailles et Antiques 26
Cabourg 53, 58
Cadouin 136
Caen 53, 54, 58
café life 279
cafés in Paris 28
Cagots 168
Cahors 136, 203
Calais 238, 239
Calanque d'En Vau 177
Calanque de Port-Miou 177
Calanque de Port-Pin 177
Les Calanques 177
Camaret 80
Camargue 175
Camargue, Parc Naturel Régional de la 175
Cambrai 238
camping 272
Canal d'Orléans 115
canals 243
Cancale 78
Candes 104
Cannes 175
Cannes Film Festival 174
Cany, Château de 58
Le Cap d'Agde 187
Cap d'Antibes 176
Cap Blanc-Nez 248
Cap de Carteret 56
Cap d'Erquy 84
Cap Ferrat 176, 178
Cap Fréhel 84, 85
Cap Gris-Nez 248
La Capelière 175
car rental 262, 263, 268
Carantec 78-9
Carcassonne 157
Carennac 137
Carjac 143
Carnac 78, 79
Carnac-Plage 79
Carol Valley 158
Carpentras 177
Cartier, Jacques 82, 145
Cascade de l'Estrech 180
Cascades du Hérisson 232
Casse Déserte 227
Cassel 238
Cassis 176, 177
Castell 168
Castelnaud 131, 137
Castillon 179
Castillon en Couserans 159
Castres 157
catacombs and sewers of Paris 27
Catalans 154
Catharism 131, 168
Cathédrale d'Images 174
Caudebec-en-Caux 53, 58-9
Causse Méjean 200
Causse Noir 200
Causse Sauveterre 200
causses (upland plateaux) 197, 200
Cauterets 158, 162
Cavalry Academy 123
Le Caylar 200
Cerdagne 158
Cère, Vallée de la 200
Céret 158
Cerisy-le-Forêt 56
Cézanne, Paul 172
Chablis 231, 238

ACKNOWLEDGEMENTS

All photographs are held in the Association's own library (AA PHOTO LIBRARY) and were taken by the following photographers:

M ADELMAN 16; A BAKER 81, 85, 183, 184/5, 191, 192; P BENNETT 151, 156, 167; S DAY 75, 86, 92/3; J EDMANSON 12/3, 95, 102, 105, 106/7, 109, 122, 124/5; P ENTICKNAP 24, 30, 39, 40; P KENWARD 10, 119, 132/3, 135, 141, 147; J MILLAR 154/5; R MOORE 14, 64, 67, 71, 111, 114, 126; R MOSS 249; D NOBLE 48/9; T OLIVER 195, 197, 198, 200, 207, 236, 244, 250; K PATERSON 26/7, 29, 32/3, 41; B REIGER 36; K REYNOLDS 153, 158/9, 163; C SAWYER 51, 54, 55, 57, 58, 60/1, 63, 68; M SHORT 1, 113, 229, 233, 234, 235, 241, 242/3, 254/5; B SMITH 99, 101, 129, 136, 137, 144, 148, 164, 214/5, 239, 253, 283; T SOUTER 6, 13, 15, 22/3, 34, 43, 257; R STRANGE 8/9, 9, 12, 77, 78, 88, 90, 169, 173, 174, 176, 187, 189, 202/3, 211, 213, 216, 218/9, 221, 225, 226/7; R VICTOR 73; W VOYSEY 17, 44/5, 47

CONTRIBUTORS

Copy editors: Janet Tabinski, Barbara Vesey, Brigitte Lee, Jack Messenger
Researcher: Elizabeth Morriss
Indexer: Marie Lorimer